# *Karen Brown's*
# Italy
## *Charming Bed & Breakfasts*

Written by

**NICOLE FRANCHINI & CLARE BROWN**

Illustrations by Elisabetta Franchini & Barbara Maclurcan Tapp

Cover Painting by Jann Pollard

Karen Brown's Guides, San Mateo, California

# Karen Brown Titles

*Austria: Charming Inns & Itineraries*

*California: Charming Inns & Itineraries*

*England: Charming Bed & Breakfasts*

*England, Wales & Scotland: Charming Hotels & Itineraries*

*France: Charming Bed & Breakfasts*

*France: Charming Inns & Itineraries*

*Germany: Charming Inns & Itineraries*

*Ireland: Charming Inns & Itineraries*

*Italy: Charming Bed & Breakfasts*

*Italy: Charming Inns & Itineraries*

*Mexico: Charming Inns & Itineraries*

*Mid-Atlantic: Charming Inns & Itineraries*

*New England: Charming Inns & Itineraries*

*Pacific Northwest: Charming Inns & Itineraries*

*Portugal: Charming Inns & Itineraries*

*Spain: Charming Inns & Itineraries*

*Switzerland: Charming Inns & Itineraries*

*To Chiara and John and their continued happiness*

*Cover: Villa Schuler, Taormina, Sicily*

*Editors: Anthony Brown, Karen Brown, June Eveleigh Brown, Clare Brown, Iris Sandilands, Lorena Aburto Ramirez, Debbie Tokumoto, Yvonne Sartain.*

*Illustrations: Elisabetta Franchini.*

*Cover painting: Jann Pollard.*

*Technical support & graphics: Michael Fiegel, Gary Meisner.*

*Maps: Michael Fiegel.*

*Copyright © 2005 by Karen Brown's Guides.*

*This book or parts thereof may not be reproduced in any form without obtaining written permission from the publisher: Karen Brown's Guides, P.O. Box 70, San Mateo, CA 94401, USA, email: karen@karenbrown.com.*

*Distributed by Fodor's Travel Publications, Inc., 1745 Broadway, New York, NY 10019, USA., tel: 212-751-2600, fax: 212-940-7352.*

*Distributed in Canada by Random House Canada Ltd., 2775 Matheson Boulevard, East, Mississauga, Ontario, Canada L4W 4P7, tel: 888-523-9292, fax: 888-562-9924.*

*Distributed in the United Kingdom, Ireland and Europe by Random House UK, 20 Vauxhall Bridge Road, London, SW1V 2SA, England, tel: 44 20 7840 8400, fax: 44 20 7233 8791.*

*Distributed in Australia by Random House Australia, 20 Alfred Street, Milsons Point, Sydney NSW 2061, Australia, tel: 61 2 9954 9966, fax: 61 2 9954 4562.*

*Distributed in New Zealand by Random House New Zealand, 18 Poland Road, Glenfield, Auckland 10, New Zealand, tel: 64 9 444 7197, fax: 64 9 444 7524.*

*Distributed in South Africa by Random House South Africa, Endulani, East Wing, 5A Jubilee Road, Parktown 2193, South Africa, tel: 27 11 484 3538, fax: 27 11 484 6180.*

A catalog record for this book is available from the British Library.

ISSN 1532-8775

# Contents

**INTRODUCTION**

| | |
|---|---|
| General Information on Agritourism | 1–3 |
| About Bed & Breakfasts | 4–15 |
| About Itineraries | 16–17 |
| About Italy | 18–28 |
| Regions of Italy | 29–40 |

**ITINERARIES**

| | |
|---|---|
| Italian Highlights by Train & Boat–or Car | 41–70 |
| Romantic Tuscany | 71–88 |
| The Haunting Beauty of Umbria | 89–98 |
| Mountain & Lake Adventures | 99–114 |
| Rome to Milan via the Italian Riviera | 115–126 |
| Highlights of Southern Italy | 127–138 |
| Exploring the Wonders of Sicily | 139–150 |

| | |
|---|---|
| HOTEL DESCRIPTIONS | 151–415 |
| INDEX | 416–431 |

MAPS

| | |
|---|---|
| Places to Stay & Itineraries | Color Section at Back of Book |

*We are proud to present*
*for our 2005 cover painting*
*Villa Schuler*
*Taormina, Sicily*

# Introduction

BED AND BREAKFAST ITALIAN-STYLE—*agriturismo*, as the bed and breakfast activity is called in Italy, has made great strides over the past decade or so. The bed and breakfast concept is relatively new to Italy, which followed suit after France and England originated the trend. Accommodations vary from simple farmhouses to noble country villas, all promising unique and memorable stays. "*Agritourism*" travel offers visitors to Italy the unique opportunity to observe daily life "up close" as a guest in someone's home. It is a superb way to interact directly with Italians, experiencing their way of life as a participant rather than just an observer. It offers a more intimate contact with the country's traditional ways of life than can ever be experienced during hotel stays. It is the alternative vacation for curious visitors who wish to explore the back roads of this fascinating country and depart with a more in-depth understanding of Italians and their lifestyles than they could possibly get from city stays and sightseeing alone. The individual who will benefit most from agritourism will have an open, inquiring mind and a certain amount of flexibility. In return, agritourism rewards the traveler with a feeling of being "at home" while abroad. The warm welcome and the value you'll receive will tempt you back to the agritourism track year after year.

HISTORY: *Agriturismo*, defined as agricultural tourism, was launched in 1965 as part of the Italian government's national agricultural department's plan to make it possible for farmers to supplement their declining income in two ways: through offering accommodation to tourists and through direct sales of their produce.

After World War II, during reconstruction and the subsequent industrial boom, Italians abandoned the countryside in droves in search of employment in urban centers, reducing the rural population from eight to three million people. Consequently, farmhouses, villas, and castles all across the country were neglected and went to ruin. This phenomenon also disrupted the centuries-old tradition of passing customs and property from one generation to the next.

The agritourism concept—with its government funding, proclaimed tax breaks, and an increasing need to escape congested cities—has lured proprietors back to their land and ancestral homes, providing them with the incentive to restore and preserve these historical buildings (with many treasures among them) without spoiling the natural landscape. An additional consequence is an improved distribution of tourism between Italy's overcrowded cities and the countryside, which serves to raise awareness of the many marvelous historical and cultural attractions, from art and architecture to scenery and cuisine, that await tourists off the beaten track.

Each of Italy's 20 regions participates in agritourism, with over 12,000 properties offering accommodation and a full 60% of participants concentrated in Tuscany and Trentino-Alto Adige. This edition of *Italy: Charming Bed & Breakfasts* includes selections from 17 of Italy's regions. Unfortunately, this type of accommodation is still very scarce in Italy's southernmost regions such as Calabria, Basilicata, and Campania. We are happy to offer a new selection of bed and breakfasts in Sardinia and Sicily, where the activity is gradually taking hold, although mostly in more spartan accommodation.

In practical terms, agritourism was developed to stimulate the local economy in rural areas by encouraging the creation of accommodations (rooms, apartments, and campgrounds) in places where they had never before been available. In a more long-term and idealistic sense, it was hoped that the promotion and development of tourism in rural Italy would also bring about greater environmental awareness as well as rescue traditional folklore and customs, such as regional cuisine and handicrafts, from oblivion.

For Italians, agritourism facilitates an exchange of views between farmers and urbanites who come in search of a peaceful vacation surrounded by natural beauty. In fact, agritourism and the rich culture of the farmer represent for many an affirmation and validation of their heritage. Lamentably, some Italians still have a misconception of agritourism because it was originally organized as an exchange of very basic room and board for work in the fields. A wave of positive press in recent years and higher quality standards however, have helped enormously to change this outdated image.

Controversy also surrounds the fact that there are few established regulations governing this type of activity, and they differ greatly from one region to another. Consequently, few clearly defined quality standards exist and those participants with limited economic resources resent wealthier proprietors, whom they accuse of running accommodations resembling hotels more than farm stays. Moreover, it does not simplify matters that agritourism is organized in typical Italian fashion, with responsibility divided among three associations, each with its own regulations, politics, and guidelines. Each association produces a directory and may be contacted by writing to:

AGRITURIST, Corso Vittorio Emanuele 101, Rome 00168, Italy
Email: agritur@confagricoltura.it

TERRANOSTRA, Via 14 Maggio 43, Rome 00187, Italy
Email: terranostra@coldiretti.it

TURISMO VERDE, Via E. Franceschini 89, Rome 00155, Italy
Email: info@turismoverde.it

# About Bed & Breakfasts

Our goal in this guide is to recommend outstanding places to stay. All of the bed and breakfasts featured have been visited and selected solely on their merits. Our judgments are made on charm, setting, cleanliness, and, above all, warmth of welcome. However (no matter how careful we are), sometimes we misjudge an establishment's merits, or the ownership changes, or unfortunately sometimes standards are not maintained. If you find a recommended place is not as we have indicated, please let us know, and accept our sincere apologies. The rates given are those quoted to us by the bed and breakfast: please use these figures as a guideline only and be certain to ask at the time of booking what the rates are and what they include.

Please visit the Karen Brown website (*www.karenbrown.com*) in conjunction with this book. It provides comments and discoveries from you, our readers, information on our latest finds, post-press updates, the opportunity to purchase goods and services that we recommend (airline tickets, rail tickets, car rental, travel insurance), and one-stop shopping for our guides and associated maps. Most of our favorite places to stay participate in our website where you can find color photos and direct links to their own websites and email.

## ACCOMMODATION

The most important thing to remember as you consider an agritourism vacation is that you will be staying in the private homes of families who are obligated to run their bed and breakfasts without hiring additional personnel aside from family and farmhands. Do not forget that, in most cases, the primary responsibility of your hosts is the running of their farm, so, with a few exceptions, do not expect the service of a hotel. **Rooms may not necessarily always be cleaned daily** (sometimes linens are changed every three to seven days). Nevertheless, do anticipate a comfortable and enjoyable stay, because the proprietors will do everything possible to assure it. Cost will vary according to the level of service offered. (For the traveler's convenience, some city hotels have been included that are similar to a bed and breakfast in style, but go by the name *Albergo*, *Pensione*, or Hotel.)

ROOMS: Agritourism accommodations should not be thought of strictly in terms of the British or American definitions of bed and breakfasts, as in Italy they vary greatly according to each proprietor's interpretation of the concept. The bed and breakfasts in this guide have been described in terms of the criteria used in their selection—warmth of hospitality, historic character, charm of the home, scenery, proximity to sites of touristic interest, and quality of cuisine. Obviously, all of these attributes are not always found in each one. Most of them have an average of six rooms situated either within the family's home or in a separate guesthouse. Unless otherwise indicated in the bottom description details, all bedrooms have private bathrooms. Furthermore, we have tried to include only those with en-suite bathrooms. Having another bed or two added to a room at an extra charge for families with small children is usually not a problem. According to laws of the European Community, all new or renovated establishments must now offer facilities for the handicapped. It is best to enquire about the individual bed and breakfast's facilities when making reservations to see if they have accommodation that is suitable for you.

APARTMENTS: Since more and more travelers are learning that it is much more advantageous to stay for longer periods in one place (distances are so short between towns within a specific region), apartment-type accommodations with fully equipped kitchenettes are flourishing. And, in fact, jumping around from one place to another for one or two nights defeats the purpose of a more intimate contact with host families. Apartment accommodation is offered either within the farmhouse along with other units for two to six persons, or as a full house rental for six to ten persons. They are rented by the week from Saturday to Saturday throughout the country, the exception being during the low season. No meals are included unless the bed and breakfast also has a restaurant or makes special arrangements for breakfast. Rates include use of all facilities (unless otherwise indicated), linens, and utilities. There is usually an extra charge for heating and once-a-week cleaning. Average apartments for four persons run $800 weekly, a rate hotels cannot beat.

## AFFILIATIONS

ABITARE LA STORIA is an association of hotels and bed and breakfasts that includes some of the finest places to stay in Italy. Many of their properties are featured either in this guide or our companion guide *Italy Charming Inns & Itineraries*. Their standards of quality, welcome and charm match perfectly with our own selection criteria. Properties that belong to this group have Abitare La Storia noted on their description page.

# CREDIT CARDS

Whether or not an establishment accepts credit cards is indicated in the list of icons at the bottom of each description by the symbol ▆⃗. We have also specified in the accommodation description which cards are accepted as follows: AX–American Express, MC–MasterCard, VS–Visa, or simply, all major.

# FOOD

A highlight of the agritourism experience is without a doubt the food. Most travelers would agree that a bad meal is hard to find in Italy, a country world-famous for its culinary skills. In the countryside you'll be sampling the traditional regional recipes from which Italian cuisine originates. Since, whenever possible, all of the ingredients come directly from the farms where you'll be staying and are for the most part organically grown, you'll discover the flavorful difference freshness can make. A peek into the farm kitchen is likely to reveal pasta being rolled and cut the old-fashioned way—by hand. Many country cooks prefer to prepare food using traditional methods, and not rely on machines to speed up the process. Guests are usually welcomed into the kitchen for a look around and actual cooking lessons are becoming very popular.

MEALS OFFERED: Bed and breakfasts often serve only a continental breakfast of coffee, tea, fresh breads, and jams. However, many prepare a buffet breakfast plus other meals and offer (sometimes require) half- or full-board plans. Half board means that breakfast and dinner are both included in the daily per-person room rate. Full board includes the room and all three meals and is less common, since most guests are out and about during the day, or prefer one lighter meal. Dinner is a hearty three-course meal, often shared at a common table with the host family, and normally does not include wine and other beverages. Menus might be set daily, according to the availability of fresh produce, or a limited choice may be given. Some farms have a full-fledged restaurant serving non-guests as well. Travelers who are not guests at a particular bed and breakfast may take advantage of this opportunity to sample other fare (it is advisable to reserve in advance). When a listing offers dinner by arrangement we indicate this with the icon ♨. If a property has a restaurant, we use the icon ❗.

## ENGLISH

English and other languages spoken at each bed and breakfast are indicated as follows: fluent, good, some, very little, and none. We would like to note, however, that this is just an indication, as the person who speaks English may or may not be there during your stay. In any case, it is helpful (not to mention rewarding) to have a few basic Italian phrases on hand. A phrase book or dictionary is indispensable. And when all else fails, the art of communicating with gestures is still very much alive in Italy!

## FINDING YOUR BED AND BREAKFAST

At the back of the book is a key map of the whole of Italy plus maps showing each recommended bed and breakfast's location. The pertinent regional map number is given at the right on the *top line* of each bed and breakfast's description. Directions to help you find your destination are given after each bed and breakfast description. However, they are only guidelines, as it would be impossible to find the space to give more details, and to know from which direction the traveler is arriving. The beauty of many of these lodgings is that they are off the beaten track, but that characteristic may also make them very tricky to find. If you get lost, a common occurrence, first keep your sense of humor, then call the proprietors and/or ask locals at bars or gas stations for directions. It is important to know that addresses in the countryside often have no specific street name. *A common address consists of the farm name, sometimes a localita' (an unincorporated area, or vicinity, frequently not found on a map and outside the actual town named), and the town name followed by the province abbreviated in parentheses. (The bed and breakfast is not necessarily **in** that town, but it serves as a post office reference.)* The *localita'* can also be the name of the road where the bed and breakfast is located, to make things more confusing. We state the *localita'* in the third line of the bed and breakfast details and many times that name is the map reference name as well. Ask to be faxed a detailed map from the B&B upon confirmation.

Detailed maps for the area in which you will be traveling are essential and we recommend purchasing them in advance of your trip, both to aid in the planning of your journey and to avoid spending vacation time searching for the appropriate maps. We like the regional Michelin maps (1 cm = 4 km).

| REGION | Michelin Map # | REGION | Michelin Map # |
|---|---|---|---|
| Abruzzo | 563 | Lombardy | 561 |
| Aosta Valley | 561 | Marches | 563 |
| Apulia | 564 | Molise | 564 |
| Basilicata | 564 | Piedmont | 561 |
| Calabria | 564 | Sardinia | 566 |
| Campania | 564 | Sicily | 565 |
| Emilia-Romagna | 562 | Trentino-Alto Adige | 562 |
| Friuli-Venezia Giulia | 562 | Tuscany | 563 |
| Lazio | 563 | Umbria | 563 |
| Liguria | 561 | Veneto | 562 |

If you are traveling to several regions consider the *Michelin Tourist and Motoring Atlas of Italy,* a book of maps with a scale of 1:300,000 (1 cm = 3 km). We sell the Michelin atlas, regional maps, and green guides (sightseeing guides) in our online store at *www.karenbrown.com.* Another fine choice is the Touring Club Italiano map set, in an easy-to-read three-volume format divided into North, Central, and South. Even the smallest town or, better, *localita'* is listed in the extensive index.

## ICONS

We have introduced these icons in the guidebooks and more on our website, *www.karenbrown.com*. ❄ Air conditioning in rooms, ☕ Breakfast included in room rate, 🧒 Children welcome (age given on website), ♨ Cooking classes offered, 💳 Credit cards accepted, ☎ Direct-dial telephone in room, 🍴 Dinner served upon request, 🐕 Dogs by special request, 🛗 Elevator, 🤸 Exercise room, 🚭 Some non-smoking rooms, **P** Parking available, 🍽 Restaurant, 🛎 Room Service, ❀ Spa, 🏊 Swimming pool, 🎾 Tennis, 📺 TV in bedrooms, 💒 Wedding facilities, ♿ Wheelchair accessible, 🏖 Beach nearby, 🏛 Archealogical site nearby, ⛳ Golf course nearby, 🥾 Hiking trails nearby, 🐎 Horseback riding nearby, ⛷ Skiing nearby, 🚣 Water sports nearby.

Icons allow us to provide additional information about our recommended properties. When using our website to supplement the guides, positioning the cursor over an icon will in many cases give you further details. For easy reference an icon key can be found on the last page of the book.

## LENGTH OF STAY

Agritourism is most advantageous for those who have more than the standard one week to travel. Bed and breakfast accommodations take longer to reach, for one thing, and *often they are neither set up nor staffed for one-night stays*, which increase costs and defeat the purpose of this type of travel. There are numerous exceptions, however, especially in bed and breakfasts near cities, where overnight guests are accepted. It is noted in the description where a minimum stay is required.

*Introduction–About Bed & Breakfasts*

# RATES

Room rates vary according to size, location, season, and level of service. Rates range from $80 to $300 for two people with breakfast (indicated as B&B in the following descriptions) and from $75 to $150 per person for room with half board (dinner also included). *Approximate prices for two persons in a room for 2005 are indicated in euros and are by no means fixed. Rates include tax and must be confirmed at the time of reservation.* If breakfast is included this is indicated with the ☕ icon. Because of its cost advantages, agritourism is an ideal choice for families. Children under eight are offered a discount and hosts will almost always add an extra bed for a small charge. There are some wonderful benefits to traveling in Italy in the low season (November to March with the exception of holidays). The considerable reduction in bed and breakfast rates combined with irresistibly low air fares makes for a super-economical vacation. And then, there's the ultimate advantage of not having to fight for space with crowds of other tourists. Italy is all yours!

# RESERVATIONS

Whether you plan to stay in several bed and breakfasts or decide to remain for an extended period in just one, *advance reservations are preferred.* Not only do many of the bed and breakfasts have only a few bedrooms available, but also they are often in private homes that are not prepared to take walk-in traffic. It is important to understand that once reservations for accommodation are confirmed, whether verbally by phone or in writing, you are under contract. This means that the proprietor is obligated to provide the accommodation that was promised and that you are obligated to pay for it. If you cannot, you are liable for a portion of the accommodation charges plus your deposit. As a courtesy to your hosts, in the case of cancellation, please advise them as soon as possible. Although some proprietors do not strictly enforce a cancellation policy, many, particularly the smaller properties in our book, simply cannot afford not to do so. Similarly, many airline tickets cannot be changed or refunded without penalty. We recommend insurance to cover these types of additional expenses arising from cancellation due to unforeseen circumstances.

When making your reservations, be sure to identify yourself as a "Karen Brown traveler." The hosts appreciate your visit, value their inclusion in our guide, and frequently tell us they take special care of our readers. We hear over and over again that the people who use our guides are such wonderful and appreciative guests!

There are several ways to make a reservation:

*Email*: This is our preferred way of making a reservation. All hotels/bed and breakfasts featured on the Karen Brown Website that also have email addresses have those addresses listed on their web pages (this information is constantly kept updated and correct). You can often link directly to a property from its page on our website. (Always spell out the month as the Italians reverse the American month/day numbering system.)

*Fax*: If you have access to a fax machine, this is a very quick way to reach a bed and breakfast. If the place to stay has a fax, we have included the number in the description. Following is a reservation request form in Italian with an English translation. (See comment above about spelling out the month.)

*Reservation Service*: If you want to pay for the convenience of having the reservations made for you, pre-payments made, vouchers issued, and cars rented, any of the bed and breakfasts in this guide can be booked through **Hidden Treasures of Italy**, a booking service run by the author of this guide, Nicole Franchini. Further information can be found at the back this book.

*Telephone*: You can call the bed and breakfast directly, which is very efficient since you get an immediate response. The level of English spoken is given in each bed and breakfast description. To telephone Italy from the United States, dial 011 (the international code), then 39 (Italy's code), then the city area code (including the "0" unless it is a cellular phone number), and then the telephone number. Italy is six hours ahead of New York.

**BED & BEAKFAST or HOTEL NAME & ADDRESS**—clearly printed or typed

Vi richiediamo la seguente prenotazione:
*We would like to request the following reservation:*

Numero delle camere o appartamenti _____ con bagno o doccia privata a _____ posti letto
*Number of rooms or apartments with private bath or shower for how many persons*

Numero di adulti _____ Numero di bambini _____ Età _____
*Number of adults        Number of children and ages*

Numero delle camere o appartamenti _____senza bagno o doccia privata a_____ posti letto
*Number of rooms or apartments without private bath or shower for how many persons*

Numero di adulti _____ Numero di bambini _____ Età _____
*Number of adults        Number of children and ages*

Data di arrivo _____ Data di partenza _____ Totale notti_____
*Date of arrival          Date of departure          Number of nights*

Tipo di servizio richesto:
*Type of meal plan requested:*

_____ Pernottamento con prima colazione (*B&B*)

_____ Mezza Pensione (*Half Board—breakfast and dinner included*)

_____ Pensione Completa (*Full Board—all three meals included*)

Costo giornaliero:  B&B (two persons) _____
*Daily rate*        MP (Half Board—per person) _____

PC (Full Board—per person) _____

Sono previsti sconti per bambini e quanto? _____
*Is there a discount for children and what is it?*

E' necessaria una caparra e quanto? _____
*Is a deposit necessary and for how much?*

Ringraziando anticipatamente per la gentile conferma, porgo cordiali saluti,
*Thanking you in advance for your confirmation, cordial greetings,*

**YOUR NAME, ADDRESS, TELEPHONE & FAX NUMBER**—clearly printed or typed

# REGIONAL FARM NAMES

The following names for farms, seen throughout this guide, vary from area to area.

*azienda agricola*—a general term meaning farm, not necessarily offering hospitality

*borgo*—a small stone-walled village, usually of medieval origins

*casale, casolare*—variations of farmhouse, deriving from "casa"

*cascina and ca'*—farmhouse in Piedmont, Lombardy, and Veneto

*fattoria*—typically a farm in Tuscany or Umbria

*hof and maso*—terms meaning house and farm in the northern mountain areas

*locanda*—historically a restaurant with rooms for travelers passing through on horseback

*masseria*—fortified farms in Apulia, Sicily

*podere*—land surrounding a farmhouse

*poggio*—literally describes the farm's position on a flat hilltop

*stazzo*—typical stone farmhouse in Sardinia

*tenuta*—estate

*torre*—tower

*trattoria*—a simple, family-run restaurant in cities and the countryside

*villa and castello*—usually former home of nobility and more elaborate in services

# WHEN TO VISIT

Since agritourism accommodation is usually in permanent residences, many remain open all year, but most are open only from Easter through November. If you are traveling outside this time, however, it is worth a phone call to find out if the bed and breakfast will accommodate you anyway (at very affordable rates). The best time for agritourism is without a doubt during the spring and fall months, when nature is in its glory. You can enjoy the flowers blossoming in May, the *vendemmia*, or grape harvest, at the end of September, the fall foliage in late October, or olive-oil production and truffle hunts in November and December. Southern Italy can be mild and pleasant in the winter, which might be perfect for travelers who like to feel they are the only tourists around. The vast majority of Italians vacation at the same time, during the month of August, Easter weekend, and Christmas, so these time periods are best avoided, if possible.

# WHAT TO SEE AND DO

Bed and breakfast proprietors take pride in their farms and great pleasure in answering questions about their agricultural activity. They will often take time to explain and demonstrate procedures such as wine making, olive pressing, or cheese production. They are the best source for, and are happy to suggest, restaurants and local itineraries including historic sites, picturesque villages, and cultural activities. Your hosts feel responsible for entertaining their guests and many have added swimming pools or tennis courts if they are not already available in the vicinity. Other activities such as archery, fishing, hiking, and biking are sometimes offered. Horseback riding has made an enormous comeback and farms frequently have their own stables and organize lessons and/or excursions into the countryside. In most circumstances, a charge is made for these extra activities.

# About Itineraries

In the itinerary section of this guide you'll be able to find an itinerary, or portion of an itinerary, that can be easily tailored to fit your exact time frame and suit your own particular interests. If your time is limited, you can certainly follow just a segment of an itinerary. In the itineraries we have not specified the number of nights at each destination, since to do so seemed much too confining. Some travelers like to see as much as possible in a short period of time. For others, just the thought of packing and unpacking each night makes them shudder in horror and they would never stop for less than three or four nights at any destination. A third type of tourist doesn't like to travel at all—the destination is the focus and he uses this guide to find the perfect place from which he never wanders except for daytime excursions. So, use this guide as a reference to plan your personalized trip.

Our advice is not to rush. Part of the joy of traveling is to settle in at a hotel that you like and use it as a hub from which to take side trips to explore the countryside. When you dash too quickly from place to place, you never have the opportunity to get to know the owners of the hotels and to become friends with other guests. Look at the maps in the back of this guide to find the places to stay in the areas where you want to travel. Read about each hotel in the hotel description section of this book and decide which sound most suited to your taste and budget, then choose a base for each area you want to visit.

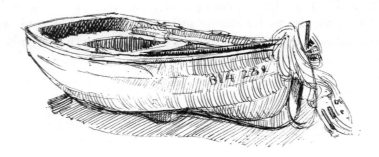

# MAPS

Each of our driving itineraries is preceded by a map showing the route, and each place to stay is referenced to a map at the back of the book. These are drawn by an artist and are not intended to replace commercial maps. We use the *Michelin Tourist and Motoring Atlas of Italy,* a book of maps with a scale of 1:300,000 (1 cm = 3 km). We also find the regional Michelin maps very useful. To outline your visit to Italy you might want to consider the one-page map of Italy, Michelin map 735. Italy hotel maps in this book can be cross-referenced with those in our companion guide, *Italy: Charming Inns & Itineraries.* We sell Michelin maps in our website store at *www.karenbrown.com.* Another fine choice is The Touring Club Italiano map set, in an easy-to-read three-volume format divided into North, Central, and South. Even the smallest town or, better, *localita* is listed in the extensive index.

# SIGHTSEEING

Ideas on what to see and do are suggested throughout the seven itineraries. However, we just touch upon some of the sightseeing highlights. There is a wealth of wonders to see in Italy, plus, of course, many local festivals and events. Before you leave, check with the tourist office for further information targeted at exactly where you plan to travel. And, once on the road, make it a habit to always make your first stop the local tourist office to pick up maps, schedules of special events, and sightseeing information. Even more important, before you drive out of your way to see a particular museum or place of interest, check when it is open. As a general guideline, most museums are closed on Mondays except for the Vatican museums, which are closed on Sundays (except for the last Sunday of the month). The most important museums now have continuous hours and either have a full- or half-day schedule but do not close for a few hours and then reopen. Smaller museums are usually open until 2 pm. Outdoor museums usually open at 9 am and close about an hour before sunset. Most monuments and museums close on national holidays. NOTE: To save waiting in line for hours to buy entrance tickets, buy tickets for major museums in advance from travel agencies, hotels, or tobacco shops.

# *About Italy*

The following pointers are given in alphabetical order, not in order of importance.

## AIRFARE

Karen Brown's Guides have long recommended Auto Europe for their excellent car rental services. Their air travel division, Destination Europe, an airline broker working with major American and European carriers, offers deeply discounted coach- and business-class fares to over 200 European gateway cities. It also gives Karen Brown travelers an additional 5% discount off its already highly competitive prices (cannot be combined with any other offers or promotions). You can make reservations online via our website, *www.karenbrown.com*, (click on *Discount Airfares* on our home page) or by phone at (800) 223-5555. When phoning, be sure to use the Karen Brown ID number 99006187 to secure your discount.

## BANKS–CURRENCY

Normal banking hours are Monday through Friday from 8:30 am to 1:30 pm and 3 to 4 pm, with some city banks now opening on Saturday mornings. Cash machines accepting U.S. bank cash cards and credit cards are now widely distributed throughout Italy. An increasingly popular and convenient way to obtain foreign currency is simply to use your bankcard at an ATM machine. You pay a fixed fee for this but, depending on the amount you withdraw, it is usually less than the percentage-based fee charged to exchange currency or travelers' checks. *Cambio* signs outside and inside a bank indicate that it will exchange traveler's checks or give you cash from certain credit cards. Also privately run exchange offices are available in cities with more convenient hours and comparable rates. The euro (€) is now the official currency of most European Union countries, including Italy, and has completely replaced European national currencies. Visit our website (*www.karenbrown.com*) for an easy-to-use online currency converter.

## CAR RENTAL

An International Driver's Permit is not necessary for renting a car as a tourist: a foreign driver's license is valid for driving throughout Italy. Readers frequently ask our advice on car rental companies. We always use Auto Europe—a car rental broker that works with the major car rental companies to find the lowest possible price. They also offer motor homes and chauffeur services. Auto Europe's toll-free phone service, from every European country, connects you to their U.S.-based, 24-hour reservation center (ask for the Europe Phone Numbers Card to be mailed to you). Auto Europe offers our readers a 5% discount (cannot be combined with any other offers or promotions) and, occasionally, free upgrades. Be sure to use the Karen Brown ID number 99006187 to receive your discount and any special offers. You can make your own reservations online via our website, *www.karenbrown.com* (select *Auto Europe* from the home page), or by phone (800-223-5555).

# DRIVING

A car is a must for this type of travel—most bed and breakfasts are inaccessible by any other means of transportation. A car gives the traveler a great deal of independence (public transportation is frequently on strike in Italy), while providing the ideal means to explore the countryside thoroughly. It is best to reserve a vehicle and pre-pay by credit card before your departure to ensure the best rates possible.

Italy is not quite the "vehicular-free-for-all" you may have heard about, at least not outside big cities (particularly Rome, Florence, and Milan). When visiting Rome, it's advisable to do so at the beginning or end of your trip, before you pick up or after you drop off your car, and, by all means, avoid driving within the city. Italians have a different relationship with the basic rules of the road: common maneuvers include running stop lights and stop signs, triple-parking, driving at 100 mph on the highways, passing on the right, and backing up at missed highway exits. But once out of the city, you will find it relatively easy to reach your destination. Road directions are quite good in Italy and people are very willing to help.

DISTANCES: Distances are indicated in kilometers (one kilometer equals 0.621 miles), calculated roughly into miles by cutting the kilometer distance in half. Distances between towns are also indicated in orange alongside the roads on the Touring Club Italiano maps. Italy is a compact country and distances are relatively short, yet you will be amazed at how dramatically the scenery can change in an hour's drive.

GASOLINE: Gas prices in Italy are the highest in Europe, and Americans often suspect a mistake when their first fill-up comes to between $55 and $100 (most of it in taxes). Most stations now accept Visa credit cards, and the ERG stations accept American Express. Besides the AGIP stations on the autostrade, which are almost always open, gas stations observe the same hours as merchants, closing in the afternoon from 12:30 to 4 and in the evening at 7:30. Be careful not to get caught running on empty in the afternoon! Many stations have a self-service pump that operates on off-hours (€10 or €20 accepted).

MAPS: An above-average map of Italy is absolutely essential for this type of travel. The Touring Club Italiano maps, in an easy-to-read three-volume format divided into North, Central, and South, are a superior selection. Even the smallest town or, better, *localita'* is indicated in the extensive index. Another fine choice is the Michelin series of maps. We use the Michelin 400 series maps (six regional maps) and the *Michelin Tourist and Motoring Atlas of Italy* (a book of maps). We sell these and regional Michelin green guides (sightseeing guides) in our website store at *www.karenbrown.com*.

ROADS: Names of roads in Italy are as follows:

*Autostrada*: a large, fast (and most direct) two- or three-lane tollway, marked by green signs bearing an "A" followed by the autostrada number. As you enter you receive a ticket from an automatic machine by pushing a red button. Payment is made at your exit point. If you lose your card, you will have to pay the equivalent amount of the distance from the beginning of the autostrada to your exit. Speed limit: 130 kph.

*Superstrada*: a one- or two-lane freeway between secondary cities marked by blue signs and given a number. Speed limit: 110 kph.

*Strada Statale*: a small one-lane road marked with S.S. followed by the road number. Speed limit: 90 kph.

*Raccordo* or *Tangenziale*: a ring road around main cities, connecting to an autostrada and city centers.

ROAD SIGNS: Yellow signs are for tourists and indicate sites of interest, hotels, and restaurants. Black-and-yellow signs indicate private companies and industries.

TOLLS: Tolls on Italian autostrade are quite steep, ranging from $15 to $28 for a three-hour stretch, but offering the fastest and most direct way to travel between cities. Fortunately for the agritourist, tollways are rarely necessary. However, if it suits your needs, a *Viacard*, or magnetic reusable card for tolls, is available in all tollway gas stations for €20–€50, or even more convenient, a MasterCard or Visa card can be used in specified lanes (the lines for these automatic machines are notably shorter).

# HOLIDAYS

It is very important to know Italian holidays because most museums, shops, and offices are closed. National holidays are listed below:

New Year's Day (January 1)
Epiphany (January 6)
Easter (and the following Monday)
Liberation Day (April 25)
Labor Day (May 1)

Assumption Day (August 15)
All Saints' Day (November 1)
Christmas (December 25)
Santo Stefano (December 26)

In addition to the national holidays, each town also has its own special holiday to honor its patron saint. Some of the major ones are listed below:

Bologna—St. Petronio (October 4)
Florence—St. John the Baptist (June 24)
Milan—St. Ambrose (December 7)

Palermo—Santa Rosalia (July 15)
Rome—St. Peter (June 29)
Venice—St. Mark (April 25)

The Vatican Museums have their own schedule and are closed on Sundays (rather than on Mondays as in the case with all other National museums), with the exception of the last Sunday of each month when admission is free of charge.

# INFORMATION

Italian Government Travel Offices (ENIT) can offer general information on various regions and their cultural attractions. They cannot offer specific information on restaurants and accommodations. If you have access to the Internet, visit the Italian Tourist Board's websites: *www.italiantourism.com* or *www.enit.it.* Offices are located in:

*Chicago*: Italian Government Travel Office, 500 N. Michigan Ave., Suite 2240, Chicago, IL 60611 USA; tel: (312) 644-0996, fax: (312) 644-3019. (Mail, fax, or phone only.)

*Los Angeles*: Italian Government Travel Office, 12400 Wilshire Blvd., Suite 550, Los Angeles, CA 90025, USA; tel: (310) 820-1898, fax: (310) 820-6357.

*New York*: Italian Government Travel Office, 630 5th Ave., Suite 1565, New York, NY 10111, USA; tel: (212) 245-4822, fax: (212) 586-9249.

*Toronto*: Italian Government Travel Office, 175 Bloor Street East, Suite 907, Toronto, Ontario M4W 3R8, Canada; tel: (416) 925-4882, fax: (416) 925-4799.

*London*: Italian State Tourist Office, 1 Princes Street, London WIB 2AY, England; tel: (020) 7408-1254, fax: (020) 7493-6695.

*Sydney:* Italian Government Travel Office, Level 26, 46 Market Street, Sydney NSW 2000, Australia; tel: (61292) 621.666, fax: (61292) 621.677.

*Rome*: ENTE Nazionale Italiano per il Turismo (Italian Government Travel Office), Via Marghera, 2/6, Rome 00185, Italy, tel: (06) 49711, fax: (06) 4463379.

# REGIONS

To assist you in planning your trip *Places to Stay* are grouped alphabetically by region from Abruzzo to Veneto. For reference, the 20 regions of Italy from north to south, with their capital cities in parentheses, are as follows:

*NORTH*—Aosta Valley (Aosta), Liguria (Genova), Piedmont (Torino), Friuli Venezia Giulia (Trieste), Trentino-Alto Adige (Trento & Bolzano), Lombardy (Milan), Veneto (Venice), and Emilia-Romagna (Bologna).

*CENTRAL*—Tuscany (Florence), Umbria (Perugia), Marches (Ancona), Lazio (Rome), Abruzzo (L'Aquila), and Molise (Campobasso).

*SOUTH*—Campania (Naples), Apulia (Bari), Calabria (Cantazaro), Basilicata (Potenza), Sicily (Palermo), and Sardinia (Cagliari).

# SAFETY

If certain precautions are taken, most unfortunate incidents can be avoided. It is extremely helpful to keep copies of passports, tickets, and contents of your wallet in your room in case you need them. Pickpocketing most commonly occurs in cities on buses, train stations, crowded streets, or from passing motorbikes. WARNING: At tollway gas stations and snack bars, **always** lock your car and beware of gypsies and vendors who try to sell you stolen merchandise. This practice is most prevalent south of Rome. In general, **never** leave valuables or even luggage in the car. Also, **never** set down luggage even for a minute in train stations.

# SHOPPING

Italy is a shopper's paradise. Not only are the stores brimming with tempting merchandise, but the displays are works of art, from the tiniest fruit market to the most chic boutique. Each region seems to specialize in something: in Venice hand-blown glass and handmade lace are popular; Milan is famous for its clothing and silk; Florence is a center for leather goods and gold jewelry; Rome is a fashion hub, where you can stroll the pedestrian shopping streets and browse in some of the world's most elegant shops boasting the latest designer creations. Religious items are also plentiful in Rome, particularly near St. Peter's Cathedral. Naples and the surrounding area (Capri, Ravello, and Positano) offer delightful coral jewelry and also a wonderful selection of ceramics. You will be enticed by the variety of products sold at the farms such as wines, virgin olive oil, jams and honeys, cheese, and salami, along with local artisans' handicrafts. NOTE: For reasons of financial control and the tax evasion problems in Italy, the law states that clients **must** leave commercial establishments with an official receipt in hand, in order to avoid fines.

For purchases over €155 an immediate cash refund of the tax amount is offered by the Italian government to non-residents of the EU. Goods must be purchased at an affiliated retail outlet with the "tax-free for tourists" sign. Ask for the store receipt **plus** the tax-free shopping receipt. At the airport go first to the customs office where they will examine the items purchased and stamp both receipts, and then to the "tax-free cash refund" point after passport control.

U.S. customs allows U.S. residents to bring in $400-worth of foreign goods duty-free, after which a straight 10% of the amount above $400 is levied. Two bottles of liquor are allowed. The import of fresh cheese or meat is strictly restricted unless it is vacuum-packed.

# TELEPHONES

The Italian phone company (TELECOM) has been an object of ridicule, a source of frustration, and a subject of heated conversation since its inception. More modern systems are gradually being installed, and most areas have touch-tone phones now. Telephone numbers can have from four to eight digits, so don't be afraid of missing numbers. Cellular phones have saved the day (Italians wouldn't be caught dead without one) and are recognized by three-digit area codes beginning with 3. We have added cellphone numbers for the majority of properties in the guide. Cellphones offer the B&B owner great flexibility and give guests the advantage of always finding someone "home."

It is now very easy to rent cellular phones for your stay in Italy either through Auto-Europe car rental or directly at airports.

All calls to Italy need to include the "0" in the area code, whether calling from abroad, within Italy, or even within the same city, *cellphone numbers drop the "0" in all cases.*

Dial 113 for emergencies of all kinds—24-hour service nationwide.

Dial 116 for Automobile Club for urgent breakdown assistance on the road.

Dial 118 for Ambulance service.

Remember that no warning is given when the time you've paid for in a public phone is about to expire (the line just goes dead), so put in plenty of change or a phone card. There are several types of phones (in various stages of modernization) in Italy:

*Regular rotary phones* in bars, restaurants, and many bed and breakfasts, which you can use *a scatti,* meaning you can pay the proprietor after the call is completed.

*Bright-orange pay phones*, as above with attached apparatus permitting insertion of a *scheda telefonica,* reusable magnetic cards worth €5–€25, or coins.

To call the United States from Italy, matters have been eased by the ongoing installation of the Country Direct System, whereby you can reach an American operator by dialing either 172-1011 for AT&T or 172-1022 for MCI. Be patient and wait the one to two minutes before a recording or U.S. operator comes through. Either a collect call or a credit-card call can then be placed. If you discover this system doesn't work from some smaller towns, dial 170 to place a collect call, or, in some cities, try dialing direct (from a *scatti* phone), using the international code 001 + area code + number.

## TIPPING

*Hotels*: Service charges are normally included in four- and five-star hotels only. It is customary to leave a token tip for staff.

*Restaurants*: If a service charge is included, it will be indicated on the bill, otherwise 10–15% is standard tipping procedure.

*Taxis*: 10%.

## TRAIN TRAVEL

Although a car is an absolute necessity to reach most bed and breakfasts, it is often convenient and time-saving to leave the car and take a train for day trips into the city. NOTE: Your ticket must be stamped with the time and date **before** you board the train; otherwise, you will be issued a €20 fine. Tickets are stamped at small (and not very obvious) yellow machines near the exits to the tracks. Unstamped tickets may be reimbursed with a 30% penalty. In order to avoid long lines at the station it is strongly advised that you purchase your ticket (including seat reservation) in advance through a local travel agency when you arrive in Italy or contact CIT train reservation service to book tickets from the States (tel: 800-248-8687). The IC and ES trains to major cities are the most efficient. If you plan to travel by train throughout Europe, you can research schedules and fares and purchase tickets and passes online. (Note that many special fares and passes are available only if purchased in the United States.) For information and the best possible fares, and to book tickets online, visit our website, *www.karenbrown.com*.

# TRANSFERS INTO CITIES

Travelers from abroad normally arrive by plane in Milan, Rome, or Venice (sometimes Florence) and pick up their rental car at the airport. However, if your first destination is the city and you plan on picking up your car after your stay, approximate transfer rates are as follows:

## MILAN

| | |
|---|---|
| From Malpensa to city by taxi (70 min) | €80 |
| From Malpensa to Cadorna station by train (every 30 min) | €12 |
| From Malpensa to central station by bus (every 20 min) | €16 |
| From Linate to city by taxi (20 min) | €40 |
| From Linate to city by bus (every 20 min) | €6 |

## ROME

| | |
|---|---|
| From Da Vinci to city by train (every 30 min) | €12 |
| From Da Vinci to city by taxi (45 min) | €60–80 |

## VENICE

| | |
|---|---|
| From airport to city by waterbus (1 hour) | €12 |
| From airport to city by private waterbus | €80 |
| From station to city by waterbus (15 min) | €8 |
| From station to city by private waterbus | €75 |

## FLORENCE

| | |
|---|---|
| From airport to city by taxi (30 min) | €40 |

We wish you the best in your travels to Italy and always welcome your comments and suggestions. *Buon Viaggio!*

*Regions of Italy*

29

**ABRUZZO:** Although it is one of the smallest regions of Italy, rugged Abruzzo boasts the highest peaks of the Apennine range, the Gran Sasso. In fact, most of the territory is made up of majestic mountains spilling down to the coast of the Adriatic Sea. Unsuitable for agriculture, the region's economy depends on pastoral activity and specialty artisans (goldsmiths, wood and stone carvers, wrought-iron craftsmen) and  tourism. Abruzzo is the ancestral land of many Americans who return to Italy in search of their roots. The region's four major national parks and nature reserves are ideal for hiking, free climbing, alpine, cross-country, and downhill skiing. Our favorite medieval villages to explore include Sulmona, Scanno, Penne Atri, Tagliacozzo, Saepinum and the historic capital town of L'Aquila with its Fontana delle 99 Cannelle, a fountain built in 1272 with 99 spouts. In Sulmona you find Ceramics of Castelli, a tradition since the Middle Ages. *Gastronomic specialties:* A large variety of pastas come from this region. Inland you find lamb dishes and a special variety of pecorino cheeses, while the coast offers seafood delights including stuffed squid. Highly prized wines come from Montepulciano d'Abruzzo.

**AOSTA VALLEY:** In the uppermost corner of northwest Italy is Valle d'Aosta, a region made up entirely of mountains, with its Alps bordering France and Switzerland. The capital city, Aosta, derives its name from Ottaviano Augusto who founded the city in 25 AD. It is one of two Italian regions that have been run as completely autonomous administrations since 1946, with its own constitution and laws. Besides  having preserved Patois, its original dialect, both French and Italian are also spoken fluently. This region has many ski resorts including: Cervinia, Courmayeur, and Mont Blanc on the French-Swiss border. You will also find 130 medieval castles in Aosta, with the Fenis and Issogne being the most famous. The Gran Paradiso National Park, with its Alpine refuges, is a haven for nature and wildlife lovers, hikers, and climbers. *Gastronomic specialties:* Fontina cheese (excellent in fondues) and many prestigious wines (including Pinot Gris) come from the Aosta Valley.

**APULIA**: Apulia is a delightful surprise with unique scenery barely resembling that which you see in the rest of Italy. Over the centuries it was invaded by Greeks, Arabs, Normans, Swedes, Aragonesi, Spaniards, and Saraceni, all of whom left their mark on the land. There are many castles in Apulia including: Castel del Monte, di Trani, d'Otranto, and di Copertino. Octagonal-shaped Castel del Monte is the most impressive of  the buildings commissioned by Frederick II. This region is also home to Gargano Peninsula National Park, which is heavily forested and has scenic beaches. Our favorite towns to explore are Vieste and Monte San'Angelo. You must also visit the whitewashed towns of Ostini, Alberobello, and Locorotondo, the touristic heart of the region and home to the trulli (whimsical-looking, cone-shaped houses). Located on the "heel" of the boot, and not to be forgotten, are the beautiful baroque cathedral cities of Lecce, San Matteo, Santa Chiara, and Santa Croce. *Gastronomic specialties:* Olive oil and wine (which are strong and full-flavored), various cheeses from sheep's milk; local ear-shaped pasta (called orecchiette), seafood dishes with mussels; fava beans and chicory are all found in the region.

**BASILICATA**: Basilicata, located at the "instep" of the boot, is another of Italy's smaller regions that is not often visited by tourists. It reaches the shores of the Gulf of Taranto as well as a small stretch of the Tyrrhenian Sea on the western coast. Matera is no doubt the most interesting city in this region. Its ancient neighorhood, Sassi, has been preserved as an outdoor museum with cave-like dwellings built into the  tufo rock where many citizens of this impoverished and forgotten region lived along with their livestock. While in Matera you must also visit its Romanesque cathedral and its several 9th-century churches with Byzantine frescoes. Another highlight of Basilicata is picturesque Maratea—a medieval village tucked in the hills above a beautiful coast that is enhanced by pretty beaches and hidden coves. The archaeological ruins of Eraclea and Metapontum are also part of this region.

**CALABRIA:** One of the most mountainous regions of Italy, Calabria, at the "toe" of the boot, is a peninsula flanked by two seas, the Ionian and the Tyrrhenian. Agriculture remains its mainstay even though the mountains are arid and the terrain subject to landslides. The rugged highlands of Aspromonte and the wooded Sila areas in the center are sparsely inhabited. Our favorite cities include: Catanzaro, Cosenza, Reggio di Calabria (ferryboats to Sicily) and Crotone. Damage from four major earthquakes and the effects of bombing in World War II have left these cities with few historic monuments. The National Museum of Magna Graecia in Reggio di Calabria (colonized by the Greeks in 750 B.C.) contains the most important art collection in southern Italy. When exploring this region, take the coastal road from Maratea going south towards Sicily which is far more scenic than the autostrada. There are gorgeous cliffs at Capo Vaticano, near Tropea, on the road from Vibo Valentia. One long beach with clear blue water runs along the Gulf coast from Reggio di Calabria all the way up to Taranto (500 km).

**CAMPANIA:** The Campania region, hugging the Tyrrhenian coast, is squeezed between its four neighbors: Lazio, Molise, Apulia, and Basilicata. With the country's third-major city, Naples, as its capital, Campania boasts one of the most famous coastlines in the world: the Amalfi Coast. The restored historic center of Naples (with its Piazza del Plebiscito, Palazzo Reale, Galleria Umberto, San Francesco di Paola, San Gennaro, Piazza Mercato, and Piazza Garibaldi) is definitely the highlight of this region. Nearby Naples, the archaeological sites of Pompeii, Paestum, Herculaneum, Capua, and Velia are also a must-see. Santa Maria di Castellabate and Acciaroli are two favorite towns on the Cilento coast south of the Amalfi Coast. This coastal area offers lovely, quiet, seaside resorts. Campania also boasts many gorgeous islands. After seeing the famed Capri, try lesser-known islands with more local flavor such as Ischia (specializing in thermal spas) and Procida. *Gastronomic specialties:* Campania is home of fresh Buffalo mozzarella from Paestum, pizza from Naples, and spaghetti with clams.

**EMILIA-ROMAGNA**: Emilia Romagna covers a large stretch of territory from the Adriatic Sea to almost the opposite side of the country. The bordering regions to the north are Veneto, Lombardy, Piedmont, and Liguria; and to the south, Tuscany and Marches. Italy's main autostrada runs right through Emilia-Romagna, dividing the flat plains to the north from the lush fertile hills to the south. There is a  wealth of precious works of art in this region from the magnificent Byzantine mosaics in Ravenna, wonderful Romanesque churches in Modena and Parma, to Renaissance art and architecture in Ferrara and Bologna. From the beaches of Rimini where international youth swarm in the summer months, dancing until dawn, to some of the most important opera and music festivals of international fame in Modena, Bologna, and Parma, this region has it all. *Gastronomic specialties:* Emilia–Romagna produces Italy's best and most famous food, starting with Parmesan cheese, Parma ham, balsamic vinegar, endless varieties of salami, tortellini and many other pastas.

**FRIULI VENEZIA GIULIA**: In the far northeastern corner of Italy, is the Friuli Venezia Giulia region. Half of its territory is made up of mountains, with the remaining area flatland bordering the Adriatic Sea. Its capital city, at the region's most easterly point, is Trieste, located on the Slovenian border and home to many shipyards. The highlighs of this  region include the medieval villages of Portogruaro, Summaga, Sesto Al Reghena, and Aquileia (the Roman colony founded in 181 B.C. whose artifacts are displayed in the Museo Archeologico). Also Cividale del Friuli, another city of ancient Roman origins (founded by none other than Caesar himself), boasts an interesting museum located in the Palladio-designed Palazzo Pretorio. If you like art, Giambattista Tiepolo, Venice's favorite 18th-century painter, is well represented in Udine, within the cathedral and Museo Diocesano. *Gastronomic specialties*: This region is home to some of the sweetest of prosciutto hams made in the town of San Daniele dei Friuli. Fine DOC regional wines including Pinot Bianco, Riesling, Riva Rossa, Carso Terreno, and Refosco come from this region (wine estates are concentrated around the hillsides of Gorizia).

**LAZIO**: It is only in the past decade or so that foreigners have begun to explore and appreciate the many historic, artistic, and natural wonders of the Lazio region, home to the nation's capital city Rome. Highlights of this region include the fascinating world of the Etruscans with more than 30 sites, a comprehensive archaeology museum in Tarquinia, and well-preserved tombs in the area of Tarquinia and Cerveteri. Lazio is
home to many famous gardens including the Tivoli and the extraordinary gardens and fountains of Villa d'Este. In addition, one of Italy's best-preserved Renaissance gardens, the Villa Lante, is also in Lazio. This region also boasts picturesque lakes. Lakes to the north of Rome include Bracciano, Bolsena, and Vico; and to the south are lakes Nemi and Albano. Rieti, backed by the Terminillo mountains and the scenic Sabine mountain area, is perfect for those seeking spots off the beaten path. Our favorite seaside attractions are the charming fishing villages on the islands of Ponza and Ventotene, plus the coast from Circeo to Gaeta. *Gastronomic specialties:* Top-rated olive oil, which rivals that of Tuscany and Puglia, is made in Riete.

**LIGURIA**: Liguria is best known for its Riviera tourism. The Ponente coast, including the flower capital of Italy, San Remo, is a highlight of this region. The gardens of Ventimiglia and the villages of Alassio, Albenga, Cervo, Dolceacqua, and Taggia are also worth visiting. Of course one must also visit the Levante coast which has stolen the spotlight with such gems as Portofino, Camogli, San Fruttuoso abbey,
Santa Margherita, and the very popular stretch of hill towns above the sea called Cinque Terre. We also love "Poet's Gulf," just south of the Cinque Terre where you find the charming fishing villages of Tellaro, San Terenzo, and Fiascherino. The hilly and mountainous inland areas, which give the region its verdant reputation, have yet-to-be-discovered villages (such as Uscio), and offer quiet havens from the more popular coastal destinations. A mountain excursion can be taken to Santo Stefano d'Aveto, an hour and a half's drive from the coast. *Gastronomic specialties*: Focaccia pizza using its famed olive oil, delectable pesto sauces, and many seafood specialties are common here.

**LOMBARDY**: The Lombardy region's capital, Milan, does not steal the limelight from the rest of its territory, which encompasses the beloved lake regions. Still, a shopping expedition down the famed Via Monte Napoleone and a peek at Leonardo da Vinci's "Last Supper," plus the Duomo and La Scala are all a must. Regional highlights include the historic small city of Vigevano near Milan with its magnificent arcaded  piazza and baroque cathedral. Our favorite Lombard cities include the beautifully austere Bergamo with its ancient stone center on the upper half of the city; Pavia with its monumental Certosa abbey and surrounding Pavese wine country; Cremona, the capital of violins and homeland of Monteverdi; and Mantova with its three interconnecting lakes. Tourists have always been highly attracted to the romantic northern lakes in Italy. Como sits at the top of the list, then Maggiore; Garda, the largest, with its fairy-tale medieval town; Sirmione; then minor lakes, Orta, Varese, Lugano, Iseo, all dotted with charming villages. The Franciacorta wine area, stretching between Brescia (Lombardy's second-biggest city), and Lake Iseo, is in this region and produces Italy's best sparkling wines.

**MARCHES**: The Marches, stretching along the Adriatic coast, runs close behind Tuscany and Umbria in the way of scenic beauty, history, art, and cultural offerings. It is a prosperous region offering seaside resorts, the Sibillini mountain peaks, bucolic countryside, and Renaissance towns. Urbino, Ascoli Piceno, and Loreto are the most outstanding of the Renaissance towns in the region. Other highlights  include the towns of Pesaro (on the sea and the birthplace of Rossini) and Macerata (a medieval city with summer music festivals). The scenically situated Renaissance town of Recanati is also wonderful. The Monte Conero coast south of Ancona is decidedly the most beautiful seaside area of the region, with intimate, rocky beaches and coves best reached by boat. This is a regional park with cliffs swooping down to the sea. Our favorite village here is the charming Sirolo, a walled town perched above the coast. Torre di Palma is another enchanting ancient village by the sea with delightful outdoor dining. The fascinating pink stalactite caves of Grotte di Frasassi are also worth seeing.

**MOLISE**: Molise, another of Italy's forgotten, mostly mountainous regions, is relatively isolated and sparsely populated. Until recently there were very few roads here, with just three main arteries cutting across the entire region. Isernia and Campobasso, the two main cities of Molise, are its highlights. Isernia has been severely damaged over the years by earthquakes and bombing and little remains of its history. It  does have, however, a museum with relics of the Paleolithic civilization recently discovered here, the most ancient finding in all of Europe to date. There are remote mountaintop villages in the area surrounding Isernia including Capracotta, Agnone, Pietrabbondante, and Scapoli, where the zampogna bagpipes, a local tradition among shepherds, are demonstrated in the yearly fair. The quaint villages of Larino, Ferrazzano, and Garanello surrounding Campobasso are lovely. The Tremiti islands of Molise and can be reached by ferryboat from Termoli or Vasto.

**PIEDMONT**: Piedmont is at the foothills of the Alps, which make up almost half of the region—the rest being divided between hillside and plains. Piedmont has a colorful past and today boasts one of Italy's strongest economies. Turin, the capital city of Italy until 1860 (now the  home of Fiat industries) maintains an impressive historic center (Piazza San Carlo), and has the world's most important collection of Egyptian art. The Langhe and Monferrato wine country is certainly the favorite area as far as tourism is concerned; this countryside south and east of Turin is characterized by medieval villages, ancient fortified castles, and hills lined with kilometer after kilometer of vineyards and fruit orchards. Other towns of interest include Alba, La Morra, Cherasco, Barolo, and Monforte. *Gastronomic specialties*: Risotto is common in Piedmont (the region along with Lombardy being Europe's rice capital). The region also boasts prized white truffles, and some of the country's finest wines: Barbaresco, Barbera, Barolo, and Dolcetto.

**SARDINIA**: Until recently, Sardinia was Italy's forgotten island, the farthest from the mainland with a rocky, arid interior covered with grazing sheep. Its Caribbean-blue waters, hidden coves, and isolated white beaches have attracted the sailing and yachting set who all converge in the summer months on the northern Emerald Coast. The rest of the year the island is a haven for explorers discovering it's fascinating ancient history,  dating back to 300 B.C. Over 7,000 ancient nuraghes (stone structures built for defense as far back as the 9$^{th}$ century B.C. up to the Roman period) are scattered about the entire island in various states of preservation. A vast variety of traditional festivals occur throughout the year where Sardinians, mostly dressed in traditional costumes, express their identity. These festivals are the best way to really come to understand their unique culture. The region also includes the picturesque islands of Sant'Antioco, San Pietro, La Maddalena, Caprera, and Asinara. *Gastronomic specialties:* A wide variety of good wines are made in Sardinia, especially sweet wines (Vernaccia). Recipes that are based either on lamb and wild boar or seafood specialties, including octopus, are popular.

**SICILY**: The culture, traditions, and history of Sicily are intensely rich. Its fertile terrain is just as varied with rugged mountains (including Europe's highest volcano, Mount Etna), flatland lined with endless citrus groves, spectacular coastlines, and 16 unique islands. The classic tour takes you to Palermo, Segesta's temple and amphitheatre, medieval Erice, the Greek ruins at seaside Selinunte, the Valley of the Temples in  Agrigento, the Roman villa and mosaics at Piazza Armerina, Syracuse, and the resort town of Taormina. Other areas worth visiting are the town of Cefalù on the northern coast, the ceramic center at Santo Stefano, Marsala and the Egadi Isles on the western coast, and the Madonie Mountains with their intact heritage. *Gastronomic specialties:* Fresh pastas made with a variety of Mediterranean vegetables; seafood combinations with sardines, tuna, and a range of local fish; rich desserts with ricotta and marzipan; and sweet wines including Moscato and Marsala, are all indicitive of this region.

**TRENTINO-ALTO ADIGE**: Trentino-Alto Adige combines two regions that have distinctly different flavors and traditions. Trentino is the southern tip of this far northern mountainous region, bordering Veneto's portion of the Dolomites on one side and Lombardy on the other. Whereas Trentino is Italian in tradition, the upper section of Alto Adige touching Austria is Tyrolian in flavor (more German is spoken than Italian). The town of Trento is a highlight, featuring a 13<sup>th</sup>-century cathedral, Palazzo Pretorio, medieval tower, art museum Diocesano Tridentino, and Buonconsiglio Castle. The scenic Fassa and Fiemme valleys, a cross-country skiers' paradise where the ancient Ladin language is still in use, are also of interest. The Brenta Dolomites, where skiers gather at the Madonna di Campiglio resort, is in this region. Visit Alto Adige's capital city, Bolzano, with its Gothic cathedral and archaeological museum displaying the 5,300-year-old mummy, Otzi, discovered under the glaciers in 1991. We also love the beautiful Val Gardena valley extending to Cortina in neighboring Veneto, featuring the Siusi Alps with fairy-tale-like scenery and the centuries-old tradition of woodcarving.

**TUSCANY**: Tuscany has become synonymous with Italy. Travelers flock to its famous cities and well-preserved countryside not only to view the breathtaking art found here, but also to be swept away by the magic of its enchanting landscapes. Florence is a highlight with its rich display of Renaissance masterpieces all concentrated within the historical center of 3 square kilometers. One must also visit the Piazza del Campo in Siena, one of Italy's most stunning squares, hosting the world-famous Palio horse races in July and August. The charming medieval hill towns of Montepulciano, Montalcino, and San Gimignano are home to some of the region's finest wines. The small historic cities of Lucca, Pisa, Arezzo, and Cortona, each with its own individual architectural characteristics, are also well worth visiting. Tuscany is also home to the famous Chianti area, with its endless vineyards and monumental castles. Maremma, in the southern, lesser-known reaches of the region touching the sea, is rich in Etruscan history and dotted with numerous stone villages to explore.

**UMBRIA**: Enchanting Umbria, bordering Tuscany, is located in the lush heart of Italy. A circular road in the center of the region touches the well-known cities of Perugia, Assisi, Spello, Spoleto, Todi, and Deruta. The two most spectacular towns outside of the loop are Gubbio and Orvieto. Highlights include the town of Perugia, a modern-day town with the stunning Palazzo Dei Priori where the majority of the finest Umbrian paintings are exhibited in the Galleria Nazionale dell'Umbria.

Assisi is another highlight with its many beautiful churches, including the mystic Basilica di San Francesco. The northern reaches of Umbria offer remote countryside and unspoiled landscapes. Umbria is home to world-famous ceramic centers, first and foremost, Deruta, and then Gubbio, producing hand-painted pieces for the past 600 years. Umbria also boasts the famous Orvieto Classico wine: varieties can be tasted at enotecas in Orvieto with its monumental cathedral and astounding façade.

**VENETO**: Wealthy Veneto boasts a handful of stunning artistic cities; the most beautiful slice of the Dolomites surrounding the popular resort, Cortina; the 18 villas of Andrea Palladio in and around Vicenza; and the eastern half of scenic Lake Garda. Venice with its 120 inlets, 100 canals, and 400 bridges is the highlight of this region. Venice's neighboring islands of Burano with its colorfully painted houses; Murano, the glass

center; and Torcello, are all of interest. Farther south you find Chioggia and its wondrous fish market; Cappella Scrovegni with Giotto's frescoed masterpiece and the 13th-century university (with graduates such as Dante and Galileo). Verona, a magical well-preserved city, is also part of this region. Verona is famous for its still-standing 1st-century amphitheatre, its summer opera festival, the Piazza Erbe with its open market, the Renaissance square, and the Piazza dei Signori. The houses of both Romeo and Juliet in Verona are a pilgrimage point where lovers sign a book of confessions, enhancing the fairy-tale aura. Top wines from Valpolicella, Soave, and Barbarano, and grappa from Bassano del Grappa are produced in Veneto.

*Colosseum, Rome*

# Italian Highlights
## by Train & Boat–or Car

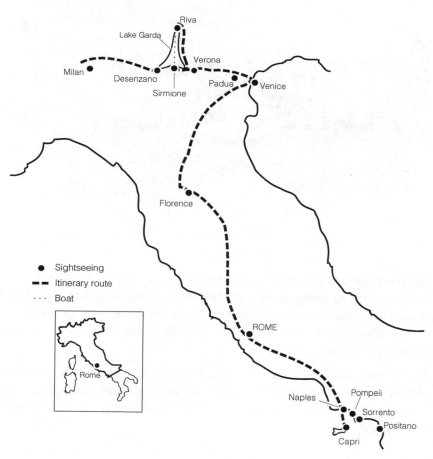

Riva
Lake Garda
Verona
Milan
Desenzano
Padua
Venice
Sirmione

Florence

- ● Sightseeing
- ● ● ● Itinerary route
- · · · Boat

Rome

ROME

Naples
Pompeii
Sorrento
Positano
Capri

# Italian Highlights by Train & Boat–or Car

*Island of Burano, near Venice*

This itinerary provides you with a glimpse of some of the highlights of Italy and will tempt you to return to delve more deeply into the wonders that Italy has to offer. This itinerary is woven around towns that are conveniently linked by public transportation. Although this itinerary shows how to travel by train and boat, if you prefer to drive, you can easily trace the same route in your car.

Approximate train and boat times have been included as a reference to show you how the pieces of this itinerary tie together. Schedules are constantly changing, so these must be verified. Also, many boats and some trains are seasonal, so check schedules before making your plans.

Remember to travel lightly—when burdened by heavy suitcases, the charm of public transportation quickly diminishes!

**Recommended Pacing:** To follow this itinerary in its entirety you need a minimum of three weeks—and this is really rushing it. We recommend two nights in Milan to see its major sights and enjoy shopping in its multitude of gorgeous boutiques, three nights in Sirmione to give you time to take boat trips on Lake Garda, two nights in Verona to wander its quaint streets and superb Roman amphitheater, three nights in Venice to enjoy its rich beauty, three nights in Florence to visit its many museums, three nights in Rome (an absolute minimum for its many sights to see and shopping), three nights in Naples to give time give time to visit its fabulous museums plus side trips to Pompeii and the Amalfi Drive, and three nights in Capri to just relax and play on this romantic island. If your time is limited, this itinerary lends itself well to segmentation, so if you can't include all of the suggested stops, choose just a portion of the itinerary and "finish up" on what you have missed on your next trip to Italy.

## ORIGINATING CITY          MILAN

This highlight tour begins in **Milan**, a most convenient city since it is the hub of airline flights and trains. While it is a sprawling industrial city at its heart is a truly charming old section.

While in Milan you must not miss visiting the **Duomo**, the third-largest cathedral in the world. There is no denying the beauty of the interior but best of all is the exterior, so take an elevator or the stairs to the roof where you can admire the view and examine at close hand the statues that adorn this lacework fantasy.

Facing the Duomo is one of the world's most beautiful arcades, the forerunner of the modern shopping mall, but with far more style. Even if you are not a shopper, be sure to just browse and have a cup of tea in the **Galleria Vittorio Emanuele.** In this Victorian-era fantasy creation, there are two main intersecting wings, both completely domed with intricately patterned glass. Along the pedestrian-only arcades are boutiques and beautiful little restaurants with outside tables for people watching.

*Duomo, Milan*

After more than two decades of controversial restoration, Leonardo da Vinci's famous mural, **The Last Supper**, is once again on view in the church of **Santa Maria delle Grazie**. The mural, which covers an entire wall of the church, has been a problem for many years mainly because Leonardo experimented with painting onto drywall rather than employing the more usual fresco technique of applying paint to wet plaster. In an effort to prevent further damage, air filters, special lights, and dust-absorbing carpets have been installed, and the small groups of visitors are limited to a stay of 15 minutes. It is vital that you make an appointment in advance: from the USA call 011-39 (Europe, 00-39) 0289-421146; from within Italy, (199) 19 91 00. The unilingual Italian-speaking reservationists will make you an appointment and give you a confirmation number. Arrive at the church about 15 minutes before your appointment, confirmation number in hand, and pay cash for your ticket.

Milan's other great claim to fame is **La Scala**, one of the world's most renowned opera houses. In addition to wonderful opera, other types of performances are given here. If it is opera season, try your best to go to a performance; if not, try to get tickets for whatever is playing. It is such fun to watch the lights go down and the curtains go up in this magnificent theater with row upon row of balconies rising like layers on a wedding cake. Tickets are sold in the ticket office located around the left-hand side of the theater.

## DESTINATION I                    SIRMIONE

Sirmione is located on Lake Garda. The station where you need to disembark is in the town of Desenzano, which is on the main rail route between Milan and Venice. There are many trains each day between Milan and Venice, but not all stop in Desenzano. One we suggest runs as follows:

| | |
|---|---|
| 1:10 pm | depart Milan Central Station by train |
| 2:21 pm | arrive Desenzano |

When the train arrives in the ancient port of **Desenzano**, you can take a taxi to the pier where hydrofoils, steamers, and buses leave regularly for Sirmione. However, although it is more expensive, we suggest you splurge and take a taxi directly to Sirmione (about 10 kilometers away). This is definitely the most convenient means of transportation since you are taken directly to your hotel.

**Sirmione** is a walled medieval village fabulously located on a tiny peninsula jutting out into **Lake Garda**. This peninsula seems more like an island because it is connected to the mainland by just a thread of land. To enter the ancient town, you first cross over a moat, and then enter through massive medieval gates. Unless you are one of the lucky ones with a hotel confirmed for the night, you cannot take your automobile inside the town walls, since only pedestrians are allowed through the entrance. But if you have hotel reservations, stop near the entrance at the information office where you are given a pass to enter in taxi.

It is an easy walk to the dock in the center of town where you can study the posted schedule to decide which boat you want to take for your day's excursion. You can glide around the lake all day and have a snack on board, or get off in some small jewel of a town and enjoy lunch at a lakefront café. There is a choice of transportation: either the romantic ferry boats or the faster hydrofoils.

There are some **Roman ruins** on the very tip of the Sirmione peninsula which can be reached either on foot, or, if you prefer, by a miniature motorized train that shuttles back and forth between the ruins and the village.

## DESTINATION II          VERONA

There are trains almost every hour that cover the half-hour journey between Desenzano and Verona. But if it is a beautiful day, it is much more romantic to incorporate sightseeing into your transportation and take a boat and bus instead of the train. If this appeals to you, the following gives an idea of how this can be done.

| | |
|---|---|
| 10:20 am | depart Sirmione by ferry |
| 2:20 pm | arrive Riva |

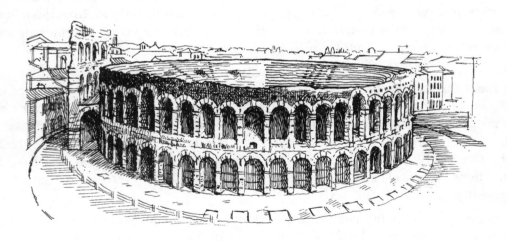

*Amphitheater, Verona*

You can have lunch on board the ferry or else you can wait until you reach the medieval town of **Riva**, located on the northern shore of Lake Garda. The interesting ancient core of Riva is small, so it doesn't take long to stroll through the old city.

After lunch and a walk through the old part of town, leave Riva by bus for Verona (buses run every 15 minutes in summer), tracing a scenic route along the eastern shore of the lake.

When you arrive in **Verona** you are in for a treat. This is a town that is all too frequently bypassed by the tourist, but what a prize it is. This medieval gem is the perfect city to explore on foot. Buy a detailed map and be on your way.

Definitely not to be missed is the **Roman amphitheater**, one of the largest in Italy. This dramatic arena, dating from the 1$^{st}$ century, has perfect acoustics and hosts operatic performances in summer. As you continue to wander through Verona's enchanting streets, you discover many delights, including the **Piazza delle Erbe** (Square of Herbs), which is the old Roman forum where chariot races used to take place. Follow your map to nearby 21 Via Cappello to find the 13$^{th}$-century **Casa di Giulietta** and the balcony where Juliet rendezvoused with Romeo. Another colorful square, the **Piazza dei Signori**, features a stature of Dante in its center and 12$^{th}$- and 13$^{th}$-century buildings. The **Castelvecchio** (Old Castle) built by Congrande II of the Della Scala family in the 14$^{th}$ century, houses an art museum with paintings, sculptures, jewelry, and armaments. The 14$^{th}$-century **Ponte Scaligero** (Scaliger Bridge) links the Castelvecchio with the opposite side of the river. The **Cathedral**, dating from the 12$^{th}$ century, is well worth a visit to see its fine red marble columns and richly adorned interior. Just across the river from the heart of the old city, visit the old **Roman theater** where performances are still held in summer.

*St. Mark's Square, Venice*

When you are ready to leave Verona, there is frequent train service to **Venice** so the following departure time is just a suggestion. NOTE: As you approach Venice, be sure not to get off the train at the Venice Mestre station, but instead wait for the next stop, the Santa Lucia station (about ten minutes further).

| | |
|---|---|
| 2:33 pm | depart Verona Porto Nuova station by train |
| 3:55 pm | arrive Venice, Santa Lucia station |

As you come out of the front door of the train station, you find that the station is directly on the **Grand Canal**. It is a few short steps down to where you can board a boat to take you to your hotel. The **vaporetti** are the most popular means of transportation and are a very inexpensive means of getting about the city. They are like boat buses that constantly shuttle back and forth from the train station to St. Mark's Square. If you have a lot of luggage you might want to consider a watertaxi. The **motoscafi** (watertaxis) cost about €50 but deliver you right to the door of your hotel, provided there is a motorboat dock (noted in the hotel description). The third choice of transportation is the **gondola**, but these are much slower and very expensive, so save your gondola ride for a romantic interlude rather than a train connection.

**Venice** has many hotels in every price range. In our description we give the closest boat stop to each hotel so that you know where to disembark if you come by canal from the train station. For a few of the hotels, you need to change boats at the San Marco boat stop.

Venice has so many sights—marvelous restaurants, beautiful boutiques, and fascinating little alleyways to explore—that you could happily stay for weeks.

Of course, you must savor the incomparable ambiance of **Piazza San Marco** (St. Mark's Square). Late afternoon is especially romantic as music wafts across the enormous square, courtesy of the tiny orchestras entertaining visitors as they enjoy an aperitif. A colonnaded walkway encloses the square on three sides, forming a protected path for window-shoppers at the beautiful boutiques and fancy cafés. The fourth side of the square is dominated by the **Basilica di San Marco** (St. Mark's Cathedral), richly endowed with gold and mosaics. The church dates back to the 12th century when it was built to house the remains of St. Mark. Next to the church rises the 99-meter-tall **campanile** (bell tower) where in the 15th century priests were suspended in a cage to repent their sins. If you are in the plaza on the hour, watch the two Moors strike the hour with their huge bronze hammers as they have for 500 years. To the right of the basilica is the **Palazzo Ducale** (Doge's Palace), a sumptuous fantasy of pink and white marble— open now as a museum. The Palazzo Ducale faces on to the **Piazzetta**, a wide square opening onto the Grand Canal. The square's nickname used to be the *Piazzetta Il Broglio* (Intrigue) because in days of yore, only nobles were allowed in the square between 10 am and noon, at which time the area buzzed with plots of intrigue. Adorning the center of the square are two granite columns, one topped by the Lion of St. Mark and the other by a statue of St. Theodore.

There is no better way to get into the mood of Venice than to join the crowd at St. Mark's pier as they climb aboard one of the ferries that ply the city's waterways. It is a real bargain to board the vaporetto and enjoy the many wonderful palaces bordering the Grand Canal. In addition to exploring the canals that lace Venice, you can take ferries to the outlying islands. Go either on your own or on a tour to the three islands: **Murano** (famous for its hand-blown glass), **Burano** (famous for its colorfully painted fishermen's cottages and lace making), and **Torcello** (once an important city but now just a small village with only its lovely large church to remind you of its past glories).

*Glass Blowing, Island of Murano*

Another all-day outing by boat is to take the **Il Burchiello,** named for a famous 17th-century Venetian boat. From March to November, this boat departs Tuesdays, Thursdays, and Saturdays at 8:45 am from the Pontile Giardinetti pier near St. Mark's Square and travels the network of rivers and canals linking Venice and Padua. (The schedule might change, so verify dates and times.) This little boat, with an English-speaking guide on board, stops at several of the exquisite palaces en route. Lunch is served and there is time for sightseeing in **Padua** before returning to Venice by bus. Reservation office: Siamic Express, Via Trieste 42, 35121 Padua, Italy, tel: (049) 66 09 44, fax: (049) 66 28 30.

A favorite pastime in Venice is wandering—just anywhere—exploring the maze of twisting canals and crisscrossing back and forth over some of the 400 whimsical bridges. One of the most famous, the **Rialto Bridge**, arching high over the canal, is

*Italian Highlights by Train & Boat—or Car*

especially colorful because it is lined by shops. Also much-photographed is the **Bridge of Sighs**, so named because this was the bridge prisoners passed over before their execution.

Although all of Venice is virtually an open-air museum, it also has many indoor museums. Two excellent ones are both easy to find near the Accademia boat stop. The **Galleria dell'Accademia** abounds with $14^{th}$- to $18^{th}$-century Venetian paintings. Within walking distance of the Galleria dell'Accademia is the **Peggy Guggenheim Museum**, featuring 20th-century art. The paintings and statues were the gift of the now-deceased wealthy American heiress, Peggy Guggenheim. The lovely museum was her canal-front home.

## DESTINATION IV                    FLORENCE

There are several direct trains each day from Venice to Florence: however, in summer, space is at a real premium, so be sure to reserve a seat in advance. Some of the express trains must have prior seat reservations and require a supplemental fee. NOTE: During the busy season, if you want to dine on the train, it is necessary to make advance reservations when you buy your ticket.

11:45 am     depart Venice, Santa Lucia station (reservations obligatory)
 2:42 pm     arrive Florence

When you arrive in **Florence** take a taxi to your hotel.

Be generous with your time and do not rush Florence—there is too much to see. You must, of course, pay a visit to Michelangelo's fabulous **David** in the **Galleria dell'Accademia** located just off the **Piazza San Marco**.

*Ponte Vecchio, Florence*

During your explorations of Florence, you will cross many times through the **Piazza della Signoria**, located in the heart of the old city. Facing this characterful medieval square is the 13th-century **Palazzo Vecchio**, a stern stone structure topped by a crenellated gallery and dominated by a tall bell tower. It was here that the *signoria* (Florence's powerful aristocratic ruling administrators) met for two months each year while attending to government business. During this period they were forbidden to leave the palace (except for funerals) so that there could not be a hint of suspicion of intrigue or bribery. Of course, you cannot miss one of Florence's landmarks, the **Ponte Vecchio**. Spanning the Arno in the heart of Florence, this colorful bridge is lined with quaint shops just as it has been since the 14th century.

Don't miss the fantastic museums and cathedrals—the world will probably never again see a city that has produced such artistic genius. Florence's Duomo is one of the largest in the world. The cathedral's incredible dome (over 100 meters high) was designed by Brunelleschi. Climb the 464 steps to the top of the dome for a superb view of Florence. The **Baptistry** has beautiful mosaics and its bronze doors by Ghiberti were said by Michelangelo to be worthy of serving as the gates to paradise. The main door shows scenes from the life of John the Baptist, the north door shows the life of Jesus, and the east door shows stories from the prophets of the Old Testament. The **Uffizi Museum** (housed in a 16<sup>th</sup>-century palace) is undoubtedly one of the finest museums in the world. You can make advance reservations at the Uffizi Museum but you must prepay for the tickets by postal wire in euros (tel: 055 29 48 83) or call Hidden Treasures (888) 419-6700. Also, do not miss the **Pitti Palace** with its fabulous art collection, including paintings by Titian and Raphael. NOTE: In addition to regular hours, museums stay open during June, July, August, and September until 11 pm. Be sure to buy a guidebook and city map at one of the many magazine stalls and study what you want to see. We just touch on the many highlights. Florence is best appreciated by wandering the historic ancient streets: poke into small boutiques;

*Palazzo Vecchio, Piazza della Signoria, Florence*

stop in churches that catch your eye—they all abound with masterpieces; sit and enjoy a cappuccino in one of the little sidewalk cafés and people watch; stroll through the piazzas and watch the artists at their craft—many of them incredibly clever—as they paint portraits and do sculptures for a small fee. End your day by finding the perfect small restaurant for delicious pasta made by mama in the back kitchen.

There is an excellent train service from Florence to Rome. It is probably best to take one of the midday trains—this allows you to enjoy lunch as you soak in the beauty of the Tuscany hills flowing by your window. Remember that you need both seat and dining reservations.

 12:01 pm depart Florence via train
  1:55 pm arrive Rome, Termini station

As the train pulls into Rome, you feel overwhelmed by its size and confusion of traffic, but once you settle into your hotel, you realize that Rome is really not as cumbersome as it looks. The ancient part of the city is manageable on foot—a fabulous city for walking with its maze of streets and captivating boutiques just begging to be explored.

According to legend, Rome was founded in 753 B.C. by **Romulus**, who, along with his twin brother, **Remus** (whom he later conveniently "did in"), were suckled by a "she wolf." Although a far less colorful story, historians concur that it was the Etruscans who first settled here and gave the city its name. By the time Christ was born, Rome controlled the entire Italian peninsula plus many areas around the Mediterranean.

Rome is bursting with a wealth of fantastic museums, ancient monuments, spectacular cathedrals, gourmet restaurants, beautiful boutiques, colorful piazzas, whimsical fountains, inspiring statues, theater, and opera—the city itself is virtually a museum. You cannot possibly savor it all. Either before you leave home or once you arrive in Italy, purchase a comprehensive guidebook and decide what is top priority for your special interests. There are many stalls along the streets as well as bookstores throughout Rome where guidebooks are available and every hotel has brochures that tell about sightseeing tours. If there are several in your party, a private guide might be money well spent since he will custom-tailor your sightseeing—with a private guide you squeeze much more sightseeing into a short period of time.

To even begin to do justice to Rome's many wonders, this entire book would need to be devoted to its sightseeing possibilities. However, we cannot resist mentioning a few places you must see.

You must see the **Vatican City** which includes in its complex **St. Peter's Basilica**, the largest church in the world. The original construction was begun in the 4$^{th}$ century by Emperor Constantine over the site of St. Peter's tomb. In 1447 Pope Nicolas V began plans for the new cathedral, which took over 100 years to build. It is no wonder the complex is so utterly breathtaking— all of Italy's greatest Renaissance artists were called upon to add their talents—Bramante, Michelangelo, Raphael, and Sangallo, to name just a few.

The Vatican is a miniature nation tucked within the city of Rome. It is ruled by the Pope, has its own flags, issues its own postage stamps, has its own anthem, mints its own coins, and even has its own police force—the Swiss Guard who still wear the uniform designed by Michelangelo.

Fronting the cathedral is the **Piazza San Pietro**, a breathtaking square designed by Bernini. It is so large that it can hold 400,000 people (making the square a favorite place for the Pope to address large audiences).

*Vatican–Swiss Guard*

*St. Peter's Basilica, Rome*

A double semicircle of columns encloses the square, so perfectly designed that the columns fade into each other, giving the illusion that there is a single row. In the center of the square is a towering ancient Egyptian obelisk—adorned, of course, by a Christian cross. As you stand at a distance, the **Piazza San Pietro** forms a visual frame for the cathedral.

To fully appreciate all the Vatican City has to offer, you could easily spend two days, one in St. Peter's Basilica and one day in the **Vatican museums**. The Basilica is like a museum. Not only is the structure magnificent, but the vast collection of works of art inside are almost unbelievable: imagine gazing at such masterpieces as the **Pietà** (the ethereal sculpture of Mary holding Jesus in her arms after the crucifixion, carved by Michelangelo when he was only 25) and the **Baldaccchino**, the bronze canopy over the papal altar created by another master, Bernini. Also, be aware when you gaze up at the double-columned dome, that this too was designed by Michelangelo.

The **Sistine Chapel** alone is well worth a trip to Rome. Savor the breathtaking beauty of its ceiling painted by Michelangelo. In addition to St. Peter's Basilica and the Vatican museums, the gardens and the rest of the Vatican can be visited, but only on guided tours. If you are interested, inquire at the Ufficio Informazioni Pellegrini et Turisti in St. Peter's Square. NOTE: The Vatican museums are closed on Sundays, except for the last Sunday of the month when they are open free of charge.

Vatican City, as spectacular as it is, is just one small part of what Rome has to offer. You must see the gigantic **Colosseum**, the entertainment center for the citizens of ancient Rome. Here 50,000 people gathered to be entertained by flamboyant spectacles that included gladiatorial contests, races, games, and contests where Christian martyrs fought against wild beasts.

Another landmark is the **Forum**. It is difficult to make out much of this site because it is mostly in ruins, but at one time this was the heart of Rome. Once filled with elegant palaces, government buildings, and shops, it teemed with people from throughout the known world.

My favorite building in Rome is the **Pantheon**. It is difficult to imagine that this perfectly preserved jewel of a temple dates back to 27 B.C. Step beyond the heavy bronze doors which open into a relatively small, beautifully proportioned room lit only by light streaming in from an opening in the top of the dome.

No trip to Rome would be complete without a stroll down the **Via Veneto**, lined by fancy hotels and luxury boutiques. There are also many outdoor restaurants where a cup of coffee costs almost as much as a meal in a simple trattoria. However, along with your coffee, you are paying the price for the fun of people-watching along one of Rome's most elite avenues.

While walking the back streets of Rome, you find many picturesque squares, usually enhanced by a fountain adorned with magnificent sculptures. Especially popular is the **Trevi Fountain** into which tourists go to throw a coin—assuring that they will return to Rome.

Rome has many festivals including the **Festa de Noantri** (Our Festival), which starts on the third Sunday in July. It takes place in **Trastevere**, which is transformed into the venue of a village fair with stalls, open-air taverns, band music, and theatrical shows throughout the neighborhood. The event is wrapped up with fireworks over the River Tiber.

The **Spanish Steps** are definitely a landmark of Rome. Topped by the twin spires of the Church of the Trinity of the Mountains, the wide avenue of steps leads down to the Piazza di Spagna (Spanish Square). This large square is highlighted by the Fountain of Baraccia (Fountain of the Boat), a masterpiece by Bernini. The steps are usually crowded both with tourists who come to capture the moment on film and vendors who lay out their wares to sell.

*Spanish Steps, Rome*

Leading from the Piazza di Spagna, the Via Condotti is an avenue lined by shops and boutiques selling the finest of merchandise. Branching off the Via Condotti are the narrow lanes of Old Rome, again featuring exquisite small boutiques.

When you are ready to relax, walk to the **Villa Borghese**, a splendid large park in the center of Rome that originated in the 17<sup>th</sup> century as the private gardens of the Borghese family. Stroll through the park watching the children at play. If you are not saturated with sightseeing, there are many museums to see in the park. One of the loveliest is the **Museo di Villa Giulia**, a museum in a pretty villa that features artifacts from the Etruscan era.

## DESTINATION VI                NAPLES

You could spend endless weeks discovering the museum that is Rome, but if you have time to add a few more highlights, venture farther south to visit Naples, using it as a hub from which to take side trips to Pompeii, Capri, Sorrento, and the Amalfi Drive. If you want a special treat, instead of visiting romantic Capri as a day excursion, end your holiday there.

There is frequent train service from Rome to Naples. A suggestion for your departure is given below:

    10:45 am    depart Rome, Termini station
    12:30 pm    arrive Naples, Main station

When you arrive in Naples, take a taxi from the train station to your hotel. If you are arriving by car, be sure to buy a detailed city map in advance and mark with a highlight pen the route to your hotel. In addition, ask for exact directions when making your hotel reservation because Naples is a confusing city in which to find your way by car. However, once you get settled in your hotel, you will discover Naples an excellent city to explore on foot.

Naples, a fascinating city whose history dates back 25 centuries, reflects its rich heritage in its architecture and culture. It seems everyone at one time claimed Naples as "theirs," including the Greeks, the Romans, the French, and the Spanish. Until the unification of Italy, Naples was an important European capital, and is still today a vibrant, exciting city with a stunning setting on the edge of the sea. For many years Naples had the reputation of being a dirty city that was plagued by petty crime. Most tourists came to see its fabulous Museo Archeologico Nazionale and then move quickly on. However, recently a great effort has been made to freshen up the entire city plus deal with the crime issue. Today a great transformation has taken place and Naples is indeed well worth a visit. It is a wonderful city filled with intriguing small squares, an unbelievable assortment of churches, a colorful waterfront, palaces, fortresses and world class museums. Plus Naples makes an excellent base from which to take side trips.

Below are some suggestions on what to see and do in and around Naples:

## SIGHTSEEING IN NAPLES

If you enjoy walking, you can visit almost all of the sights listed on foot. Or, at least walk one way and return to your hotel by taxi.

**Museo Archeologico Nazionale**: The Museo Archeologico Nazionale is considered one of the finest museums in the world, and rightly so. It has an incredible collection of jewels of antiquity, including unbelievably well-preserved statues, intricate mosaics, and delicate frescoes. There are endless marvels to see. You are bound to be awestruck as you stroll through the corridors lined with the dazzling Farnese collection of ancient sculptures. You could spend endless hours gazing in wonder at the huge statues and deftly carved marble busts that line the well-lit hallways. If you include a visit to Pompeii (which you *must*) you will find that the originals of the most outstanding mosaics and sculptures have been transferred to the Museo Archeologico Nazionale for safekeeping. The mosaics alone are worth a trip to Naples.

Within the museum there is an "off limits" section that is called the *secret cabinet* which is a series of rooms that display a collection of quite risqué paintings, sculptures and mosaics discovered under the ash at Pompeii (only a limited number of people are allowed in at a time and you need a special ticket that can be bought when you arrive at the museum).

Arrive at the Museo Archeologico Nazionale when it opens in the morning in order to be among the first visitors. As the day progresses, busloads of tourists descend. After looking at your map, if you decide walking round trip to is too strenuous, we suggest taking a taxi to the museum then strolling back to your hotel since the return will be downhill. NOTE: Museum closed on Tuesdays.

**Capodimonte Hill**: Perched on Capodimonte Hill, which rises above the city, is a splendid park with over 4,000 varieties of centuries-old trees. Within these grounds is the Palazzo Capodimonte, built in 1738 as a hunting lodge for the King Charles III. Housed within the palace is the Museo e Gallerie Nazionale di Capodimonte featuring a breathtaking art collection of the wealthy Bourbon kings, including works by such masters as Bellini, Michelangelo, Titian, and Botticelli.

You can walk to Capodimonte from the Museo Archeologico, but it is a steep, uphill climb so you might well want to take a taxi, or save the excursion for a separate day. (NOTE: Museum closed on Mondays.)

**Spaccanapoli District**: For savoring the delights and charm of Naples, our favorite tour is in the Spaccanapoli District. Here, on the site of the old Greek-Roman city, you find tiny plazas, little boutiques, outdoor restaurants, coffee shops, markets, and a seemingly endless number of churches. Make your way to the pretty **Piazza Gesù Nuovo**, where you will find the tourist office facing the square. Pop in here and ask for their map that outlines a walk exploring the Spaccanapoli District. If for any reason, the office is closed, the route is easy to find on your own. Basically what you do is follow streets in a rectangular pattern, returning where you began in Piazza Gesù Nuovo. Leaving the square, head east on Via Benedetto Croce that soon changes its name to Via San Biagio dei Librai. Continue on until you come to Via Duomo where you turn left and go a couple of streets to until you see on your right the **Cathedral** (**Duomo di San Gennaro**). Next, retrace your steps on Via Duomo for a half a block and turn right, heading west on Via Tribunali. When the road dead-ends at Via San Sebastiano, turn left, go one block, turn right and you are back where you began. You will see many churches along your way, including two that are on the Piazza Gesù Nuovo (The **Church of Guesù Nuovo** and the **Cloister of Santa Chiara**). Most of the churches are open only during services, but the fun of this walk is not so much sightseeing as savoring the flavor of this colorful, ancient part of the city. Make this a leisurely stroll, looking into the little shops, sitting in the small square, maybe a cappuccino at a small café or a pizza, which originated in Naples.

**The Piazza Plebiscito and Place to Visit Nearby**: The Piazza Plebiscito is a large, bustling square located just at the lower part of one of Naples's principal boulevards, Via Toledo. This is a major square, so it is not surprising there are many monuments and museums nearby. Listed below are some of the recommended places to visit.

**Palazzo Reale**: Dominating the east side of the Piazza Plebiscito is the large, impressive Palazzo Reale, an outstanding palace that was built for the Spanish Viceroys in 1600, in honor of King Philip II's arrival in Naples. Accenting the façade are niches with statues of the kings of Naples. This is an massive complex, and it might take a while to find your way to the ticket office. Once you have your tickets, you climb an imposing double staircase that sweeps to the floor above where the royal quarters have been opened as a museum. You might want to rent a cassette which gives commentary on what you will be seeing. It is fun to wander through the endless rooms in this noble residence, including the queen's private chapel, the throne room, a quaint 18<sup>th</sup>-century theater, and an assortment of sumptuously adorned apartments. NOTE: Closed on Wednesdays.

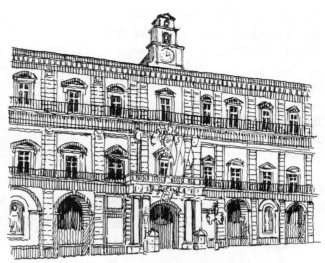

*Palazzo Real, Naples*

**Theatre San Carlo**: Just around the corner from the Piazza Plebiscito, in a wing of the Palazzo Reale that faces the Piazza Trieste e Trento, you find the dazzling Theatre San Carlos. Commissioned by Charles of Bourbon in 1737, this jewel is reminiscent of La Scala Theatre in Milan. It looks like an ornate wedding cake with 186 private, gilt adorned boxes that rise in six tiers that face an imposing stage. Sometimes there are tours of the theater so you might want to drop by to check the schedule before visiting the museum in the Palazzo Reale.

**The Umberto Gallery**: Just to the north of Piazza Plebiscito, facing a second small square, the Piazza Trieste e Trento, is the Belle-Epoque-style Umberto Gallery, a shopping arcade dating to 1887 which is made of four wings radiating like a cross from its core (if you have been to Milan, the Umberto Gallery is similar to the Galleria there). Wander in to admire the handsome mosaic floor and the ornate, glass-domed ceiling which soars over 50 meters.

**Castel Nuovo**: Just to the east of the Palazzo Reale, the Castel Nuovo rises on a bluff above the Porto Beverello, the dock from which the ferries leave for Capri and Sorrento. The Castel Nuovo (New Castle) certainly isn't very new—it dates back to the 13th century. The building is definitely dramatic, a rectangular stone building punctuated huge round stone towers. In the 15th century a splendid white marble Triumphal Arch was added, a true masterpiece whose beauty contrasts pleasantly with the stern, fortress like castle. A deep moat, originally filled with sea water, embraces the fortress. Within the museum you can visit the Museo Civico that contains 14th-century frescoes. It is also possible to visit the Palatine Chapel and the Baron's Hall.

*Castel Nuovo, Naples*

**Castel dell'Ovo**: Leaving the Piazza Plebiscito, head down to the waterfront and turn right, following the Via Nazario Sauro as it traces the waterfront. As it rounds a bend, the name of the boulevard changes to Via Partenope, which is fronted by deluxe hotels that face onto Santa Lucia Harbor. Built on a rocky peninsula that juts into the sea and forms one side of the harbor, is the Castel dell'Ovo, built by the Norman King William I in the

12<sup>th</sup> century. The name means Castle of the Egg, which supposedly originated from a legend that a magic egg was buried in the castle, and if ever broken, bad luck would descend upon Naples.

## SIDE EXCURSIONS FROM NAPLES

Naples makes a convenient hub from which to make side trip to some of Italy's jewels, including Sorrento, the Amalfi Drive, Capri and the archaeological sites of Herculaneum and Pompeii, all accessible by either organized tour or "do it yourself" by public transportation.

**Pompeii & Herculaneum**: Near Naples are two exciting archaeological wonders: Herculaneum and Pompeii. Both are fascinating, but if you don't have time to visit both, don't miss Pompeii. You can choose between joining a guided tour or taking a train to the site. A company called **Circumvesuviana** has narrow-gauge trains leaving Naples' Central Station about every half hour, arriving at the Pompeii Villa dei Misteri station (located across from the entrance to the site) about 40 minutes later. At the entrance to Pompeii, we suggest either buying a map explaining what to see or hiring a certified guide.

An aura of mystery lingers in the air as you wander the streets of Pompeii. All visitors are touched by this ancient city of an estimated 25,000 inhabitants, which in one day became frozen for all time. Probably there is nowhere else in the world where you can so vividly step back in time. Much of what you see today has been reproduced, but the reality is pure. Plaster was poured into molds formed by the lava that demolished the buildings and buried so many families that fateful day. Thus it became possible for latter-day archaeologists to reconstruct houses and make reproductions of people and pets. Walk through the town along the sunken streets crossed by high stepping-stones, strategically placed so that pedestrians did not get their feet wet on rainy days. Be sure not to miss some of the reconstructed villas that allow you a glimpse into the daily life of long ago. The **Casa del Fauno**, a fine example of how the wealthy lived, has two inner courtyards and several dining rooms. The **Casa del Poeta Tragico**, a more modest home, has a sign in mosaic saying "Cave Canem" (beware of the dog). At the **Villa di Giulia Felice** you see the example of an entrepreneur—in addition to using it as a private villa, the owner rented out rooms, had shops on the ground floor, and operated an adjacent bathhouse. If traveling with children, you might want to go alone into the **Lupanare** (Pompeii's brothel) where there are erotic paintings on the walls. At the **Terme Stabiane** you see a sophisticated underground water-heating system.

There are many more places to visit than those listed above. As you explore Pompeii, there is no need to watch the time. There is a narrow-gauge train departing from the Pompeii Villa dei Misteri station about every 20 minutes for the half-hour scenic journey to Sorrento.

**Sorrento**: Sorrento is a picturesque city that sits on the top of a bluff overlooking the sea. Below is a colorful harbor with ferries constantly gliding in and out, en route to such picturesque destinations as Capri, Positano and Amalfi. The historic center is charming, richly reflecting its ancient Greek and Roman legacy. Pretty boutiques and outdoor cafes becken as you stroll the narrow streets and explore intimate plazas. The same **Circumvesuviana** trains that depart Naples's Central Station for Pompeii, continue on to Sorrento. The total time is a little over an hour. Another option for visiting Sorrento, is to take one of the hydrofoils that ply between the two towns.

**Amalfi Coast**: The strip of coast that runs south from Sorrento to Salerno is world famous for its beauty. A two lane road hugs the steep, winding coastline, capturing breathtaking views as the bluffs fold around the brilliant blue Mediterranean. Enchanting villages dot the coast, further enhancing its idyllic beauty. One of the most accessible of these villages is **Positano**, a postcard-perfect fishing hamlet snuggled in a cove that is wrapped by an exceeding steep hill. Colorfully painted houses, trendy boutiques, cute restaurants, and cascades of brilliant bougainvillea add to the appeal of this jewel. From Naples you can take a ferry to Sorrento and then on to Positano, or take the train to Sorrento and a bus from there (the buses leave from the train station).

**Capri**: Several shipping companies have ferries that leave frequently from Naples to the romantic island of Capri, leaving from Molo Beverello, the dock below Castel Nuovo. By choosing an early morning departure, it is easy to visit Capri and return in time for dinner in Naples. However, if time permits, we would suggest spending a few days in this beautiful small island. For sightseeing in Capri, see the following destination.

## DESTINATION VII                    CAPRI

When it is time to leave Naples, there is excellent service by either hydrofoil (aliscafo) or ferry (traghetto) to Capri. The following schedule is a suggestion:

    12:15 pm    depart Naples (Molo Beverello dock)
     1:05 pm    arrive Capri

Your hydrofoil arrives at the **Marina Grande**, a small harbor filled with colorful boats and edged by brightly painted shops. When the boat docks, you find hotel porters on the pier along with carrier services that go to all of the hotels. They relieve you of your luggage and take it directly to the hotel of your choice, freeing you to take either a minibus or the funicular to the main town of Capri, which is located on a flat saddle of land high above the sea. There are many charming places to stay on Capri.

Capri has many wonders. The most famous is its submerged cave, the **Blue Grotto**, which can be accessed by boat when the seas are calm. Large boats begin leaving the harbor every day at 9 am for the short ride to the entrance to the grotto, where you are transferred into tiny rowboats. The earlier you go the better since the seas are calmer in the morning. The excursion is an adventure in itself. As you approach the tiny cave opening, it seems impossible that there is adequate room for a boat to enter, but suddenly the sea surges forward and in you squeeze. Like magic, you see it—the mysterious, stunning blue light reflecting from some hidden source that illuminates the grotto. The cost isn't great, but be aware of the system: You pay for a ticket for the motorboat that takes you to the cave, and then you pay again, on site, to the oarsman who skillfully maneuvers his little rowboat through the hole and into the grotto. It is appropriate to tip

*Marina Grande, Capri*

your boatman—he will do his best to make your short ride memorable and quite probably serenade you within the cave.

Capri is a superb island for walking. As you stroll the trails, all your senses are treated by the fragrant flowers, the gorgeous vistas of the brilliant blue waters, and the sound of birds luring you ever onward. There are many spectacular walks. Follow the trail winding down the cliffs to the small harbor **Marina Piccola**, located on the opposite side of the island from the ferry dock. At the Marina Piccola there are lovely views of the shimmering aqua waters as you make your way to the small beach where you can enjoy a swim before your return. Instead of walking back up the hill, take the little bus that delivers you quickly back to the main square.

Another absolutely spectacular walk—although a long one of at least 45 minutes each way—is to Emperor Tiberius's Palace, **Villa Jovis**, perched high among the trees on the cliffs on the western tip of the island. This is the grandest of the palaces left by Tiberius. Although it is mostly in ruins, you can easily appreciate its former magnificence as you climb about exploring the ruins of the terraced rooms. From the palace there are stunning panoramic vistas: you have an overview of the whole island and can watch the ferries shuttling back and forth to the mainland. A much shorter walk, but one equally as beautiful, is to the **Cannone Belvedere**. This path guides you near delightful private villas hidden behind high walls (you get glimpses through the gates) and on to a promontory overlooking the sea.

Another excursion is to **Anacapri**, the only other town on the island, to visit the **Villa San Michel**, a lovely villa overlooking the sea that was the home of the Swedish scientist Axel Munthe. His residence is now open as a museum. Anacapri is a bit too far to walk easily but buses leave regularly from the main square in town.

During the day, Capri is swarming with tourists on package tours who descend like a swarm of locusts from the constant stream of hydrofoils and ferries. You might surmise that in the evening the activity subsides, but it isn't so. The tour groups leave at dusk but then a new group of people emerges from the secreted villas and fancy hotels. Guests in chic clothes and fancy jewelry stroll the streets—both to see and be seen.

When the real world calls and you must leave Capri, there is frequent ferry or hydrofoil service back to Naples. From Naples, you can take a train to Rome or a plane to your next destination.

# Romantic Tuscany

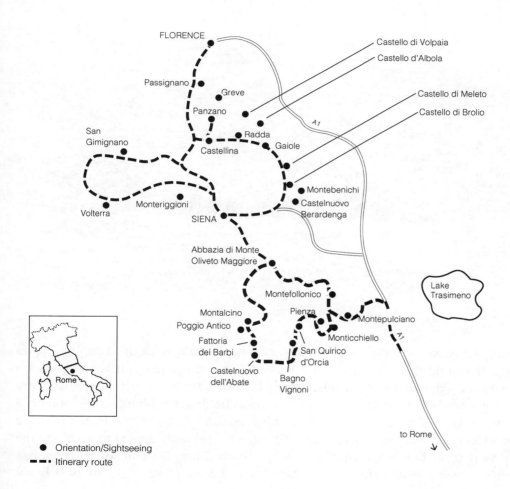

FLORENCE

Castello di Volpaia
Castello d'Albola

Passignano
Greve
Panzano
Castello di Meleto
Castello di Brolio

A1

San Gimignano
Radda
Castellina
Gaiole

Volterra
Monteriggioni
SIENA
Montebenichi
Castelnuovo Berardenga

Abbazia di Monte Oliveto Maggiore

Lake Trasimeno

Montefollonico
Montalcino
Pienza
Poggio Antico
Montepulciano
Fattoria dei Barbi
Monticchiello
San Quirico d'Orcia
A1
Castelnuovo dell'Abate
Bagno Vignoni

Rome

to Rome

● Orientation/Sightseeing
■ ■ ■ Itinerary route

# Romantic Tuscany

*Monteriggioni*

Nothing can surpass the exquisite beauty of the countryside of Tuscany—it is breathtaking. If you meander into the hill towns any time of the year, all your senses are rewarded with the splendors that this enchanting area of Italy has to offer. Almost every hillock is crowned with a picture-perfect walled town; fields are brilliant with vibrant red poppies; vineyards in all their glory and promise lace the fields; olive trees dress the hillsides in a frock of dusky gray-green; pine forests unexpectedly appear to highlight the landscape. As if these attributes were not enough, tucked into the colorful villages is a treasure-trove of some of the finest small hotels and B&Bs in Italy. If this is still not sufficient to tempt you away from the normal tourist route, remember that the food and wines are unsurpassed.

If you are planning to include Florence on your trip to Italy, slip away into the countryside and treat yourself to Tuscany. You will be well rewarded with a wealth of memories that will linger long after you return home. The following itinerary suggests two stops—one in Chianti Classico wine region and the other in Southern Tuscany.

A convenient place to begin your journey is in **Florence**, Tuscany's jewel. Magnificent art is not confined to the city limits of Florence and you will see impressive cathedrals and museums hosting spellbinding works of art throughout Tuscany. See the *Italian Highlights by Train & Boat—or Car* itinerary for sightseeing suggestions for Florence.

**Pacing:** To explore the hill towns of Tuscany you need at least a week (in addition to the time you allocate to Florence). We recommend a minimum of four nights in the heart of Tuscany's Classico Wine Region, which stretches from Florence south to Siena. This will give the minimum time needed to enjoy the tranquil beauty of the hill towns and to sample the delicious Chianti wines. The second suggested stop is southern Tuscany where we suggest three nights to explore the stunning small towns that dot the hillsides, visit breathtaking monasteries, and taste more of Italy's superb wines: Vino Nobile, grown near Montepulciano, and Brunello, grown near Montacino.

Tuscany is laced with narrow roads that twist through the picturesque countryside. Take a detailed map so that if you get lost, you can find your way home, but part of the joy of Tuscany is to be unstructured. Enjoy the freedom to discover your own perfect village, your own charming restaurant, and your own favorite wine. Although in your wanderings you are sure to find some very special places that we have missed, we share below some of the towns we find irresistible and vineyards that are especially fun to visit.

CHIANTI CLASSICO WINE REGION

This idyllic area lives up to every dream of Tuscany—hills crowned by picture-perfect villages, medieval walled towns, straight rows of towering cypresses, romantic villas, ancient stone farmhouses, vast fields of brilliant poppies, forests of pine trees, vineyards stretching to the horizon. Instead of moving about, packing and unpacking, choose a place to stay anywhere within the area and use it us your hub for exploring this utterly beguiling region of Italy. Below we give suggestions for towns to visit and some of our favorite wineries.

SUGGESTED SIGHTSEEING: TOWNS TO VISIT

**Monteriggioni:** If you are looking for a town that is truly storybook-perfect, none can surpass the tiny, magical hamlet of Monteriggioni. It is such a gem that it is hard to believe it is real and not a creation by Disney! You can spot it from afar, nestled on the top of a small hill, with 14 towers punctuating the perfectly preserved enclosing walls.

*Monteriggioni*

No cars are allowed here, so you have to park in the designated area below the walls before walking up to the town, which is composed almost entirely of a main square with small streets radiating from it. On the square you find a Romanesque church, restaurants, boutiques, and shops selling olive oil, cheeses, and wine. It takes only a few minutes to stroll from one end of the town to the other but I assure you, you will be enchanted. As a bonus, Monteriggioni produces its own fine wine, Castello di Monteriggioni.

**Passignano in Chianti:** Passignano in Chianti is rarely on a tourist route, but we can't help mentioning this tiny hamlet that exudes such a tranquil beauty. For sightseeing, there really isn't much to see except the **Badia a Passignano Abbey**, founded by Benedictine monks in the 11th century. The abbey is set in a pocket of lush landscape and dominates the village, which is no more than a cluster of houses and a restaurant. However, as you drive into the valley, approaching from the west, the abbey with its towering ring of cypresses has such an idyllic setting that it is one of our favorites—a photographer's delight. The abbey can be visited on Sundays at 3 pm; tours leave from the church (please check to verify the abbey is open the Sunday you want to visit). Fine wines, produced by the abbey's vineyards, can be purchased at the Osteria, tel: (055) 80 71 278.

**Radda:** Located in the very heart of the Chianti wine region, Radda makes a good base of operations. However, not only is the town very conveniently located for sightseeing, it is also extremely quaint and some of its walls are still intact. It was in Radda in 1924 that 33 producers gathered to create a consortium to protect a very special blend of wine that was known as **Chianti Classico**. Only vintners who maintain the standards of the consortium are allowed to proudly display its symbol of the black rooster.

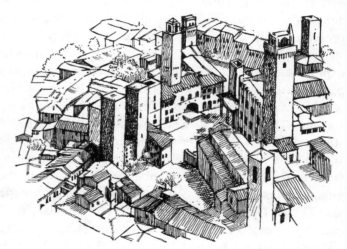
*San Gimignano*

**San Gimignano:** During your exploration of Tuscany, one town you must not miss is San Gimignano. What is so dramatic about San Gimignano is that at one time the walls of the town were punctuated by 72 towers. During the Middle Ages it was a status symbol for noble families to build their own personal towers for their protection—the higher the tower, the greater the image of wealth and importance. It is amazing that 14 of the original towers are still standing. They make a striking silhouette, soaring like skyscrapers, and on a clear day you can see them on the horizon from far away. San Gimignano is truly a jewel—plan to spend at least a day here. There are many shops and marvelous restaurants tucked along the maze of streets. On Fridays there are walking tours with English-speaking guides that leave from the Porta San Giovanni at 11 am (best check with the tourist office to be sure the time and day haven't changed). One of our favorite restaurants in San Gimignano is the delightful **Ristorante Dorando,** which has great food served in cozy rooms with coved ceilings that create the ambiance of an old wine cellar. Located on Vicolo del Oro 2, a small side street just off Piazza Duomo, tel: (0577) 94 18 62. Another favorite, **Ristorante Il Pino**, offers mouthwatering homemade pastas—some of the best we have ever eaten. Located on Via Collolese, 8–10, just down the street from L'Antico Pozzo, tel: (0577) 94 04 15.

**Siena:** This is an entrancing walled hill town that deserves many hours to savor its rich delights—you should allow yourself at least one full day here. The ramparts are perfectly preserved with a series of massive gates guarding a meticulously maintained medieval stronghold. Drive as close as you can to the main square, park your car, and set out to explore on foot. You cannot drive into the center of the city, but there are designated parking areas (marked by "P") near each of the gates. One of the most convenient is the parking at the Porta Romana. Once you leave your car, strike off for the giant **Piazza del Campo**. This central piazza is immense and, instead of being square, is fan-shaped and slopes downward like a bowl. Eleven streets surrounding the square converge into it like spokes of a massive wheel. Like the Spanish Steps in Rome, the Piazza del Campo is a favorite for tourists who linger here just enjoying the medieval ambiance. It is in this gigantic piazza that the colorful **Palio delle Contrade** (dating back to the 11$^{th}$ century) takes place twice a year, on July 2 and August 16. The horse race is only a part of a colorful spectacle of medieval costumes, impressive banners, and parades, and the festivities extend beyond the actual date of the races. Monopolizing one side of the Piazza del Campo is the 13th-century Gothic **Palazzo Pubblico** (Town Hall) whose graceful arches are embellished with Siena's coat of arms. The Palazzo Pubblico is open as a museum where you can stroll through the governor's living quarters.

Although Siena looks like a large city, it is easily negotiable on foot and most of the museums are in one small area. After visiting the Piazza del Campo, most of the other major places of interest are just a few minutes' walk away, clustered about the Piazza del Duomo. There are excellent tourist signs that will guide you along the maze of narrow streets to all the museums.

You absolutely must not miss Siena's 12th-century **Duomo**, facing the Piazza del Duomo. This is one of Italy's most astounding cathedrals. Not only is its exterior breathtaking, but once you enter, you will be overwhelmed by its dramatic black-and-white, zebra-striped marble columns. Don't miss the intricately carved, 13th-century panels depicting the life of Christ on the octagonal pulpit. Also, be sure to see the **Piccolomini Library**. You need to buy a ticket to enter, but it is well worth it. This relatively small room is totally frescoed with gorgeous murals in still-vibrant colors portraying the life of Pope Pius II. The cathedral also has 59 fabulous inlaid-marble mosaic panels on the floor depicting religious scenes. However, some of the most precious of these are covered to protect them and are on display only from the end of August to the first of October.

After visiting the Duomo, the following museums are just steps away. One of our favorites is the **Ospedale di Santa Maria della Scala**, located across from the entrance to the Duomo. At first glance, it is difficult to truly appreciate its wealth of things to see. The museum goes on and on—it is enormous. Just when you think you have finished, a discreet sign will lead you ever downwards to a lower level and a stunning array of artifacts. The building, dating back to the 800s, was originally constructed as a hospital. Be sure not to miss the former infirmary with its lushly colored frescoes by the master Domenico di Bartolo depicting scenes of patients being treated by their doctors. Another nearby museum is the **Baptistry**, a small museum that, as its name implies, houses the baptismal font for the Duomo. In addition to its beautifully frescoed walls and vaulted ceiling, of prime interest is the 15th-century baptismal font, which is adorned by religious scenes cast in bronze by some of Italy's most famous Renaissance masters, including one panel by Donatello. The **Museo dell'Opera Metropolitana** is worth a visit if for no other reason that to see the sublime *Maestá* by Duccio, painted in 1311. The central scene of the Virgin Mary is truly awesome. For art lovers, the **Museo Civico** must not be missed. Here you will see stunning masterpieces by Ambrogio Lorenzetti, Spinello

Aretino, and Simone Martini. It is overwhelming to ponder how Italy could have produced so many geniuses.

NOTE: There is a comprehensive ticket valid for three days that allows you entrance into many of Siena's prime sightseeing attractions—this is a bargain compared to buying individual tickets. When you buy your ticket for the first museum ask about it and which museums it includes.

**Volterra:** Just a short drive from San Gimignano, Volterra is a delightful, non-touristy town enclosed by still-intact, 12th-century walls. Like so many of the cities founded by the Etruscans, Volterra is built upon the flat top of a steep hill. As you drive toward the city, the landscape becomes increasingly barren, since the soil is not conducive to growing grapes or olive trees. Instead, alabaster is king here and objects made of alabaster are sold in all of the shops. Not to be missed is the alabaster museum called **Museo Etrusco Guaracci**, which has a fabulous collection of works of art, including sculptures and beautiful vases, displayed with great taste in a series of interlinking rooms that show the art to perfection. There is an adjacent shop selling many alabaster items. The whole town is a jewel whose charm is best experienced by strolling through the narrow cobbled streets. Its main square, **Piazza dei Priori**, the heart of the town, is surrounded by fine examples of beautifully preserved medieval buildings and with its towers, splendid town hall (the oldest in Tuscany), and Romanesque church, it is considered by some to be one of the finest squares in Tuscany. Stroll to visit one of the main gates, the **Porta all'Arco**, the origins of which date back to the 7th century B.C. During World War II, the loyal citizens of Volterra buried the stones of the gate to keep the Nazis from blowing it up.

**Suggested Sightseeing: Wineries**

The production of wine plays an enormous role throughout Tuscany, and between Florence and Siena (where **Chianti Classico** is produced) you are constantly reminded of this as you pass through vast rolling hills splendidly adorned with neatly tended vineyards. The Chianti Classico area covers over 172,000 acres, with Siena and Florence being the two "capitals" of the region. Included in the area are the towns of Castellina, Gaiole, Greve, Radda, and some of Barberino Val d'Elsa, Castelnuovo Berardenga, Poggibonsi, San Casciano Val di Pesa, and Tavarnelle Val di Pesa. Even if you are not a wine connoisseur, it would be a pity not to make at least one winery stop both for the fun of observing the production process and for an understanding of the industry that is so central to the soul and character of Tuscany. Many of the wineries also have gift shops and sell marvelous olive oils and cheeses in addition to wine.

As you meander through the countryside you see signs with Chianti Classico's black rooster symbol and you can buy directly from the producer where you see *Vendita Diretta*. In some cases there are also tours of the winery (these are sometimes free, but sometimes there is a charge). A *Cantina* sign means that the winery has a shop where wine is sold and can usually be sampled. One of the delights of touring the back roads of Tuscany is just to stop on whim. When you spot a *Vendita Diretta*, drive in, introduce yourself, and sample some wines. You might well discover one that will become one of your favorites.

Some of our favorite wineries to visit are listed below:

**Castello di Brolio:** If you visit only one winery, Castello di Brolio should be it since this is not only one of the oldest wineries the world, but also where Chianti wine was "born." Although the production of wine in Tuscany dates back to Etruscan times, the enormously wealthy Ricasoli family, owners of the Castello di Brolio since 1167, are responsible for the special blending of grapes we now consider "Chianti Classico." At one time the enormously powerful Ricasoli family owned most of the land and castles lying between Florence and Siena. The remote family castle, Castello di Brolio, had largely been abandoned when Bettino Ricasoli decided to move into it (so the story goes) after becoming jealous at a winter ball in Florence when his young bride danced a bit too closely to one of her young admirers. Thinking it best to take his wife away from temptation, he rebuilt the huge, remote, crenellated castle, replanted the vineyards, and experimented with the blending of grapes, coming up with the original formula that forms the basis of what is known today as Chianti Classico. The fortified castle tops a high, forested hill. You leave your car in the designated parking area and climb for about 20 minutes up a path or on the road through a parklike forest to the castle gates. Open daily from 9 am to noon and 3 pm to sunset. The castle is located about 10 kilometers south of Gaiole. Tel: (0577) 74 90 66.

*Castello d'Albola, wine tasting*

**Castello d'Albola:** The Castello d'Albola, a spectacular property just a short drive north of Radda on a gentle hill laced with grapes, is owned by the Zonin family, who have restored the entire medieval complex beautifully. This is an intimate, extremely pretty place to taste wines and take a tour. What we particularly like about the Castello d'Albola is that it is in such a beautiful setting and offers delightfully informal, friendly, free tours. Drive up the hill to the castle, leave your car in the parking area, and walk into an inner castle courtyard, off which you find the wine tasting room and cantina. Before or after wine tasting, your hostess leads you on a short, professional tour showing you how fine wines are produced. The owner has other enormous estates as well as the Castello d'Albola and is one of the largest producers of wine in the world. Tours start at noon, 3 pm, and 5 pm daily. The cantina is open for complimentary wine tasting Monday through Friday from 10:30 am to 6:30 pm. Tel: (0577) 73 80 19, *www.albola.it*.

**Castello di Volpaia:** The 12<sup>th</sup>-century Castello di Volpaia, located on a narrow lane about 7 kilometers north of Radda, is one of our favorite places for wine tasting. Plan to spend a day on this outing, with ample time to meander through the countryside en route, tour the winery, taste the superb wines, and enjoy a wonderful lunch at the winery's excellent restaurant, La Bottega. Although the winery is called *Castello* it really isn't located inside a castle at all, but rather in various medieval stone houses in a picture-perfect village wrapped by vineyards where you find a small church, a cluster of houses, La Bottega Ristorante, and the wine tasting room. You need to preplan this wine tour and also make reservations for lunch since both are very popular and usually booked far in advance. There is a fee for the tour based on the number of people in the group. Tel: (0577) 73 80 66, *www.volpaia.com*.

**Castello di Meleto:** Another favorite destination for wine tasting is the beautiful Castello di Meleto, which has an idyllic setting in the gentle hills near the town of Gaiole. Just across from the dramatic castle you find a pretty wine tasting room and gift shop where fine wines and olive oils produced on the estate can be purchased. On request, tastings of olive oil and aromatic vinegars can be arranged. What makes this a very special experience is that there is an added bonus: not only can you sample wines, but you can also visit the beautiful interior of the castle. In addition to splendidly frescoed rooms, the castle has one exceptionally intriguing feature—a whimsical private theater complete with its original stage settings. Call ahead, tel: (0577) 73 80 66, to find out the time and cost of the guided tours of the cellars and castle. The Castelo is also a recommended place to stay.

SOUTHERN TUSCANY

The area of Tuscany that lies south/southeast of Siena is famous for its superb wines. A great bonus is that these vineyards are in one of Italy's most picturesque regions, filled with quaint villages and amazing abbeys, thus making your adventures even more enchanting. Whereas Chianti Classico wine is renowned in the area between Florence and Siena, the vineyards farther south also produce some of the mostly highly regarded wines in the world, the most famous of these being **Vino Nobile**, grown near Montepulciano, and **Brunello**, grown near Montacino. There are many wineries open to the public where wine can be tasted and purchased. Many wine tastings are free, although some wineries charge a minimal fee. As you drive through the countryside look for signs reading *Cantina* (wine shop) or *Vendita Diretta* (direct sales).

## LOOP VISITING WINERIES, ABBEYS, AND QUAINT VILLAGES

We suggest a loop that covers some of our favorite wineries, medieval towns, and picturesque abbeys. It would be impossible to squeeze everything in this itinerary into one day unless you rush madly from place to place. Therefore, if your time is limited, don't stop at each place suggested but just choose a few of the sightseeing suggestions below that most appeal to you. But better yet, take several days and follow the itinerary in its entirety, covering a small section each day at a leisurely pace.

This loop begins in **Montepulciano**, a rare jewel of a walled hill town that not only oozes charm in its narrow, cobbled streets but is also center stage for the delicious Vino Nobile di Montepulciano. This wealthy town was home to many aristocrats who built magnificent palaces here. The heart of the city is the **Piazza Grande** where you find the dramatic 13th-century **Palazzo Comunale** accented by a stone tower. Also facing the square is the picturesque **Palazzo Contucci**, fronted by a charming Renaissance well decorated with the Medici coat of arms and highlighted by two stone lions. Leading off the Pizza Grande are small streets that crisscross the town, connected by staircases.

A masterpiece you absolutely must not miss when visiting Montepulciano is the **Temple of San Biagio**, a stunning church located on the west edge of town. You can walk from town, but it is a long way down the hill and then back up again, so you might want to drive, especially in hot weather. Made of creamy travertine, the church's façade is extremely picturesque and its elegant interior is equally lovely—nothing cluttered or dark but rather light and airy, with fine marble pastel-colored walls.

Within Montepulciano there are many boutiques, restaurants, and cantinas selling wine. Our favorite wine shop here is an extremely special one, the very old **Cantina del Redi**, located just down the street from the Piazza Grande with its entrance next to the Palazzo Ricco. Once you enter, an ancient staircase leads ever deeper into the hillside, passing rooms filled with huge wooden casks of wine. When you finally reach the lowest level, you wind your way through more casks until you arrive at the cantina where you can sample and purchase wine. When finished, you discover that you have descended quite a way down the hillside and the main entrance to the winery faces onto a lower terrace.

Another of our favorite wineries, **Dei**, is just a few kilometers outside Montepulciano's city walls. What is especially fun about this winery is that it is family-owned and managed by the lovely daughter, Maria Caterina Dei, who still lives in the beautiful family villa on the property. Maria Caterina is passionate about wine and with great professionalism can explain about the production of the Dei wines, which have won many awards. Before taking over the family's vineyards, the multitalented Maria Caterina trained in music and the theater, and sometimes she entertains the guests during wine tours. There is a fee for tours, depending upon what is requested. Lunches and wine tasting can be prearranged. Call in advance for tours: Dei, Villa Martiena, Montepulciano, tel: (0578) 71 68 78.

Leaving Montepulciano, take the S146 west toward Pienza. After driving about 3 kilometers, take a small road on the left marked to **Monticchiello**. You soon arrive at a sweet, tiny, charming walled town whose allure is its unpretentious, non-touristy ambiance. Park your car in the designated area outside the main gate. As you enter through the gate, you will see on your left **La Porta**, a charming restaurant with an outside terrace sitting on the town walls—a great place to stop for lunch. As you stroll through Monticchiello (it won't take you long), take a look inside the 13th-century church where you will see a beautiful altarpiece by Pietro Lorenzetti.

*Il Chostro di Pienza, Pienza*

From Monticchiello, continue on the back road to **Pienza**. This is one of our favorite walled hill towns in Tuscany, a real gem that mustn't be missed. The town is perched on the top of a hill and is pedestrian-only so you need to park your car outside the walls. It is no wonder that the town is so perfect even though so tiny: it was here in the 15th century that Pope Pius II hired a famous architect, Bernardo Rossellino, to totally redesign the town where he was born, making it into a masterpiece. You will find many restaurants if you are inclined to dine.

Leaving Pienza, take S146 west to **San Quirico d'Orcia**, a very attractive small medieval town with a lovely Romanesque church. If you stop to see the town, you must not miss its lovely garden, called **Horti Leonini**. An entrance about a block from the main square leads into a tranquil Renaissance garden, originally designed as a beautiful resting place for the pilgrims who stopped here on the road to Rome. This cool oasis with clipped box hedges and shade trees makes an interesting stop. If you are hungry, the **Osteria del Leone** makes a good choice for lunch.

From San Quirico d'Orcia, head south on S2 for about 6 kilometers and watch for a small road to the right leading to **Bagno Vignoni**. This is a most unusual, very small town, known for the curative value of its hot sulphur springs. In the center of town, you find what would have been the town square made into a huge sulphur bath built by the Medicis. The pool is surrounded by picturesque medieval buildings that complete the interesting scene.

Leaving Bagno Vignoni, don't continue on the S2, but take S323 directly south for 12 kilometers and then turn right following signs to Montalcino. In a few minutes you come to **Castelnuovo dell'Abate** where, just a few minutes outside town, you will find the superb Romanesque **Abbey Sant'Antimo**, whose origins date back to the 9th century when it was founded as a Benedictine monastery. The abbey—a simple, pastel-pinkish stone church serenely set amongst fields of olive trees—makes a beautiful picture. Try to arrive at 11 am or 2:45 pm when the Benedictine monks, clad in long, pure-white robes, gather at the altar to chant their prayers in Latin. This is a haunting, beautiful experience. The singing lasts only a short time, and the times might vary from the ones we mention above, so to confirm the schedule call tel: (0577) 83 56 59.

Leaving Castelnuovo dell'Abate, drive north on the road for Montalcino. In a few minutes you will see a sign to the **Fattoria dei Barbi**. Turn right and follow a small road up the hill to the Barbi winery, an excellent winery to visit. It is extremely pretty with many gardens and a charming cantina where you can sample the vineyard's fine wines and purchase wine and other gift items. Its restaurant serves wonderful meals made with only the freshest products, accompanied, of course, by their own wines. Free tours of the winery are given hourly from 10 am to noon and 3 pm to 5 pm. tel: (0577) 84 82 77, *www.fattoriadeibarbi.it.*

After your visit to the Fattoria dei Barbi, continue north for 5 kilometers to **Montalcino**, which is world-famous, along with Montepulciano, for its superb wine, Brunello di Montalcino. There are many places in town where wine can be tasted and purchased. In addition to wine, the town is famous for its fine honey, which can be purchased in many of the shops. Montalcino is fun for wandering—it is not large and you can in no time at all cover the area within the walls by foot. On the east edge of town is an imposing 14th-century fortress.

From Montalcino, head south on the road to Grosetto for a little over 3 kilometers to another of our favorite wineries, **Poggio Antico**. Excellent tours are offered and, of course, you can also sample the superb wines. These tours are very popular so you should reserve in advance at tel: (0577) 84 80 44. For dining, the winery's **Ristorante Poggio Antico** serves outstanding Tuscany cuisine. Reservations for the restaurant are also highly recommended—tel: (0577) 84 92 00, email: rist.poggio.antico@libero.it.

After visiting Poggio Antico, retrace your way north to Montalcino and continue on for 9 kilometers to where the road intersects with the S2. Turn left here, going north toward Siena. In 10 kilometers, turn right on S451 and continue for another 10 kilometers to the **Abbazia di Monte Oliveto Maggiore**. Founded in the early 14th century by wealthy merchants from Siena as a Benedictine retreat, this fascinating abbey is well worth a detour. Be prepared to walk since you must park your car and follow a long path through the forest to the abbey's entrance, which is through a gatehouse crowned by a beautiful della Robbia terracotta. Once through the gate, you continue through the woodlands to the huge brick complex. After visiting the church, it seems you could wander forever through the various hallways. Before you get too distracted, however, ask directions to the cloister because you don't want to miss this marvel. Here you find 36 frescoes depicting scenes of the life of St. Benedict, some painted by Luca Signorelli, others by Antonio Bazzi.

In the region around the abbey you will come across an entirely different type of landscape, called the *crete*. Here, tucked among the green rolling hills, you unexpectedly come across bleak, canyon-like craters, caused by erosion. These are especially out of character as the surrounding scenery is so soft and gentle.

From Abbazia di Monte Oliveto Maggiore, weave your way through the small back roads to Montepulciano. Follow signs to San Giovanni d'Asso, then Montisi, then Madongino, then **Montefollonico**. Take time to stop in Montefollonico because this is another "sleeper"—a quaint, small, medieval walled town that is fun to explore. For the gourmet, there is a superb restaurant on the edge of town called **La Chiusa.**

From Montefollonico, go south on S327. When you come to the S146, turn left to complete your loop back to Montepulciano.

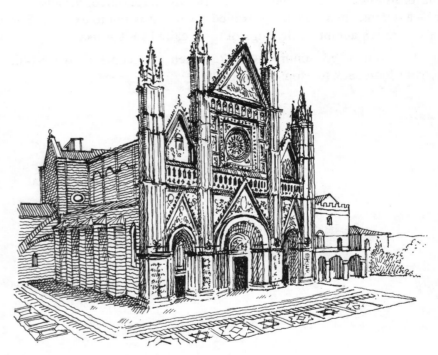

*Duomo, Orvieto*

# The Haunting Beauty of Umbria

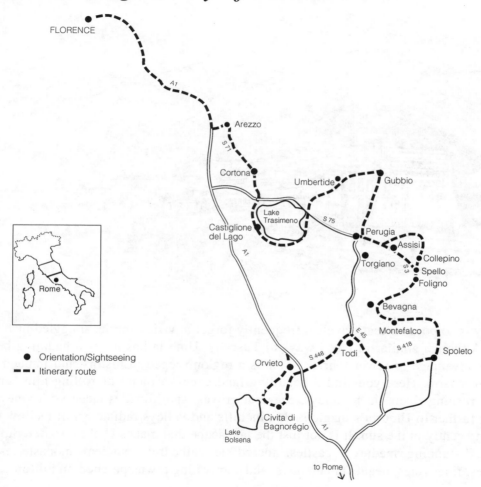

FLORENCE

A1

Arezzo

S 71

Cortona

Umbertide

Gubbio

Lake
Trasimeno

S 75

Castiglione
del Lago

Perugia

Assisi

A1

Torgiano

Collepino
S 3
Spello

Foligno

Bevagna

Montefalco

E 45

● Orientation/Sightseeing

- - - Itinerary route

Orvieto

S 448

Todi

S 418

Spoleto

Civita di
Bagnorégio

A1

Lake
Bolsena

to Rome
↓

Rome

# The Haunting Beauty of Umbria

*Assisi*

Tuscany is so popular that travelers frequently forget to visit Umbria, snuggled just "next door." Although similar in many ways to Tuscany, Umbria has its own haunting beauty and the advantage of fewer tourists. This is a region seeped in history and imbued with romantic charm. Here you find a beguiling landscape—a blend of rolling hills, craggy forests, rushing rivers, lush valleys, chestnut groves, and hillsides laced with vineyards. Adding further to Umbria's magic is that its hills and valleys radiate a soft mellow light, gleaming gently in the sun. It is not just the landscape that makes Umbria so delightful. It also has stunning medieval castles, incredible cathedrals, ancient monasteries, art treasures, fine wines, beautiful ceramics, and captivating towns perched on hilltops.

**Pacing:** You can conveniently follow this itinerary either before or after a tour of Tuscany. If you already have visited Tuscany on a previous trip to Italy, this itinerary stands alone. After the finishing the itinerary, you can loop back to Florence by heading north on the A1, or head south on the A1 to Rome. Whichever way you choose, in order to capture its beauty and many sightseeing possibilities, you need at least five nights in the Umbria region: We suggest three nights in the eastern part of Umbria. Choose a place to stay and in use it as a hub from which to journey out each day to explore a different sightseeing target. Next, loop south and choose a place to stay for two nights in the western part of Umbria, somewhere near Orvieto.

## EASTERN UMBRIA

NOTE: This itinerary of Eastern Umbria is much too long for one day. Use it only as a framework for how the most interesting towns can be looped together. Once you choose which town you are going to use as the hub for your explorations, tailor the itinerary to visit the places mentioned in the itinerary that most appeal to you.

As you depart from Florence you are bound to run into a lot of traffic, but there are many signs to the expressway. Follow signs that lead to the A1 and take it south toward Rome.

**Arezzo:** About 65 kilometers after leaving Florence you come to a turnoff to **Arezzo,** located about 10 kilometers east of the highway. Arezzo is still in Tuscany, but since it is so close to Umbria and "on the way," now is the time for a visit. Arezzo has a rich history dating back to the Etruscan era, but is not as quaint as some of its smaller neighbors. It is well known as one of the largest gold centers in Europe and has many shops selling gold jewelry. Arezzo is also famous for its **Antique Fair** that is held in the Piazza Grande on the first Saturday and Sunday of every month. Here you find many unusual items such as antique coins, jewelry, furniture, stained glass remnants, paintings, light fixtures, handmade linens, pottery, trunks, etc. The fair is considered one of the most important ones in Italy and so popular that people come from far and near to browse the rich collection of antiques. Arezzo was the birthplace of Guido Monaco who around the year 1000 A.D. devised musical notes and scales. One of Arrezo's famous inhabitants was the powerful 14<sup>th</sup>-century poet Pietro Aretino who took great glee in writing scandalous poetry about the rich and famous. Aretino's greatest skill was gentle blackmail, extorting great sums from princes and popes who paid him not to expose their indiscretions in poetry.

**Cortona**: From Arezzo follow S71 south to Cortona, a gem of a walled town terraced up a steep hillside covered with olive trees and vineyards. Like Arezzo, Cortona is still in Tuscany, but fits more conveniently into the itinerary for Umbria since it is on the route. Stop to enjoy the atmosphere of this medieval town: its narrow, twisting, cobbled streets, jumble of small squares, lovely boutiques, excellent restaurants, and colorful buildings are delightful. The heart of the town is the **Piazza della Repubblica**, the main square, which has many narrow streets feeding into it. If you are up for walking, climb the twisting streets to the old fortress standing guard over the town.

**Lake Trasimeno**: Leaving Cortona, continue driving south on S71 toward Lake Trasimeno. In about 11 kilometers you come to a four-lane expressway. Do not get on the highway, but instead continue south on S71, which traces the west shore of Lake Trasimeno, Italy's fourth largest lake, which is fed by underground channels linked to the Tiber river basin. Fascinatingly, the early Romans built these underground waterways many centuries ago. Follow the road south for 9 kilometers to **Castiglione del Lago**, the most interesting town on the lake. Built on a high rocky promontory that juts out into the water, the old walled city with its battlements and towers has lots of character. Artifacts and tombs nearby indicate it was originally an Etruscan settlement, but what you see today dates from the Middle Ages. In the 1500s it was the dukedom of the Corgna. In the church of Santa Maria Maddalena you can see a 16<sup>th</sup>-century panel with paintings of the Madonna and Child by Eusebio da San Giorgio. Also visit the Palazzo del Capitano del Popolo, the Palazzo della Cornna, and the Leone fortress.

**Umbertide**: Continue the loop around the lake then take the road toward Magione, which is is just before the junction with the expressway heading to Perugia. In a few minutes, you see the four-lane expressway, but do not get on it. Instead, continue over the highway and follow the back roads through the countryside to Umbertide. Stop for a

*The Haunting Beauty of Umbria*

short visit to this small, 10<sup>th</sup> century town that hugs the banks of the Tevere River. In addition to the castle, you might want to visit the Church of Santa Maria della Reggia, which is an intriguing octagonal, three-tired building topped by a cupola. Another church, the Holy Cross, is famous for its lovely painting by Signorelli, called *Deposition from the Cross*.

**Gubbio:** Leaving Umbertide, take the road that passes over the highway E45 and continue on to Gubbio. This splendidly preserved, medieval walled town is perched high on the slopes of Monte Ingino. The setting is superb and the view from the plaza that sits like a shelf overlooking the countryside is breathtaking. The narrow, cobbled streets and walkways lacing the hillside are delightful to explore. The town is filled with architectural masterpieces, one of these, the Basilica, dominates the town. There is much to see including the Cathedral, the Consuls Palace, the Piazza Pensile, the Pretorio Palace, and the Santa Maria Nuova church where you can see Ottaviano Nelli's *Madonna del Belvedere*. Outside the city walls, nestled below the town, there are the remains of a Roman theater—another reminder of how important the city was in its prime.

**Perugia:** From Gubbio head south on S298 in the direction of Perugia. There is a turnoff to Perugia, which is surrounded by many modern commercial buildings. If time is short, bypass Perugia (which is not as pristine as many of Umbria's other jewels) and continue on to the junction of S75 and continue east following signs to Assisi. However, if you want to "see it all," Pergugia has many delights. Perugia is a large medieval city surrounded by ramparts. An important Umbrian city since Etruscan days, the old town has at its heart the **Piazza IV Novembre**, a beautiful square with an appealing fountain, the **Fontana Maggiore**, built in the late 13<sup>th</sup> century. Although Perugia is rich in history and has a delightful medieval core, it is surrounded by modern commercial development and is not one of our one of our favorites since it does not exude the romantic appeal and the intimacy of some of the other hill towns in Umbria.

**Assisi:** Coming from either Perugia or Gubbio, take S75 east following signs for Assisi, one of our favorite targets in Umbria. Built up the steep slopes of Mount Subasio, this magical city is a tribute to St. Francis. Although he was born into a family of wealth,

*St. Francis of Assisi*

after several visions in which Christ appeared to him, St. Francis left his privileged life. He was obviously a person with a deeply poetic soul and his tender teachings of reverence for the beauties of nature and kindness to all animals and birds still appeal to us today. To remember your visit, you might want to buy a statue of St. Francis to bring home. You will find statues in all sizes and price ranges in the many shops.

Even if it were not for the lingering memory of the gentle St. Francis, Assisi would be a "must see" for it is one of the most spectacular hill towns in Umbria. Perhaps there are a few too many souvenir shops, but this is a small price to pay for the privilege of experiencing such a very special place. The town walls begin on the valley floor and completely enclose the city as it climbs the steep hillside to the enormous castle at its summit. Assisi with its maze of tiny streets is a marvelous town for walking (you must wear sturdy shoes) and it is great fun as you come across intriguing little lanes opening into small squares. When you stop to rest, there are breathtaking vistas of the lovely Umbrian fields stretching out below. Along with many other historic buildings, Assisi's most famous monument, **St. Francis' Basilica,** was severely damaged by an earthquake in September 1997. However, almost all of the repairs have now been completed and the town looks remarkably "back to normal." The basilica, which also houses a monastery, faces onto a large square bound by columns forming vaulted covered walkways. In addition to the monastery, there are two basilicas—upper and lower. Both are adorned with excellent frescoes that were unfortunately damaged by the earthquake. Also while in Assisi, visit **Santa Chiara** (St.

Clara's Church). Clara, a close friend of St. Francis, founded the Order of St. Clares. Go into the church to view the lovely frescoes of Santa Clara and her sisters. Part of the enjoyment of Assisi is just to stroll through its narrow, cobbled streets—the whole town is like a living museum. If you have time, hike up to the **Rocca Medioevale**, an enormous 14th-century fortress perched on the hillside overlooking the city. From here you have a magnificent bird's-eye view of Assisi and beyond to the enchanting Umbrian countryside sweeping out to the distant hills.

**Collepino:** From Assisi you can continue on the S75 in the direction of Foligno. However, if you feel adventuresome and enjoy getting off the beaten path, there is a narrow twisting, very scenic back road that leads through the hills making a loop from Assisi that ends up back on the S75 in Spello, about 5 kilometers before Foligno. The driving is difficult, but you can enjoy the beauty of the rugged forested mountains, an area of Umbria seldom seen by tourists. The road begins at the upper part of Assisi. Follow signs in the direction of Gualdo Tadino, but before you get there, take the road marked to Armenzano where you continue on following signs to Spello. After going through Armenzano, the road passes the adorable secluded hamlet of Collepino, which oozes charm with its winding cobbled streets and stone houses. It is so tiny that you quickly see it all. After Collepino, it is 7 kilometers on to Spello, where the road joins the S75, which you take going south.

**Bevagna:** Five kilometers south of Spello you come to **Foligno** where we suggest leaving the S75 and taking instead the back roads that to enjoy the lovely villages and scenery. From Foligno S316 toward Bevagna, which you reach after about 8 kilometers. Bevagna is an enticing, intimate, charming walled village, founded by the Romans. In addition to just enjoying the allure of the town, there is much to see including a stunning 19th-century opera house, the beautiful San Michele church, well-preserved mosaics in the old Roman baths, and a paper press making paper just as it has been for centuries. If it is mealtime, there is a wonderful place for lunch, L'Orto degli Angeli.

**Montefalco:** From Bevagna, take the road marked to Montefalco (located 7 kilometers from Bevagna). Montefalco is a walled town that crowns a hill with sweeping views of the Umbrian countryside. The town is a maze of small, narrow streets. For sightseeing, the main attraction is **San Francisco**, a church now converted into a museum that displays some of the finest work of Benozzo Gozzoli, including the fresco *Life of St. Francis*. Also, a delicious wine, *Sagrantino*, is produced here.

**Spoleto:** From Montefalco, loop back to the main road, S75, and continue south following signs to Spoleto. Not only is medieval Spoleto dramatically perched atop a hill, but it also has an almost unbelievable bridge dating from Roman times. This **Ponte delle Torri**, spanning the deep ravine between Spoleto and the adjoining mountain, was built over an aqueduct existing in the 14th century. This incredible engineering wonder is 230 meters long and soars 81 meters high. It is supported by a series of ten Gothic arches and has a fort at the far end as well as a balcony in the center. The 12th-century **Cathedral** in Spoleto is also so lovely that it alone would make a stop in this charming town worth a detour. The exterior of this very old cathedral, with its beautiful rose window and intricate mosaics, is truly charming. Although a great sightseeing destination at any time of the year, Spoleto is very popular in late June and early July when it hosts the world-famous Spoleto Festival, featuring great music, dance, and theater. During the festival season rooms are usually more expensive and almost impossible to secure so should be booked far in advance.

**Torgiano**: Torgiano, in the center of a rich wine region, has a lovely small wine museum. You would never dream that such a tiny town could boast such a gem, but it is not a coincidence: the Lungarotti family owns the vineyards for many kilometers in every direction. Signor Lungarotti furnished the museum with artifacts pertaining to every aspect of wine production from the earliest days, creating an interesting and beautifully displayed collection worthy of a detour by anyone interested in wines. In the center of town, the Lungarotti family owns, **Le Tre Vaselle**, a charming choice for lunch.

## WESTERN UMBRIA

From Spoleto, a scenic route connecting the eastern part of Umbria to the western part of Umbria is to take the S418, which twists west from Spoleto for 25 kilometers through beautiful hills to the E45. Turn north on E45 for about 21 kilometers and turn west on S448, following signs to the A1 and Orvieto.

**Todi**: The picture-perfect village of Todi makes a great midway stop between Spoleto and Orvieto. It is located near the junction of E45 and S448 and is well signposted. This adorable small town crowning a hilltop like icing on a cake is one of our favorites. No, there isn't much to see—it is the town itself that is so picturesque. It is just fun to wander the twisting cobblestone streets, enjoy the medieval ambiance, and stop to enjoy a cappuccino in one of the sidewalk cafés. As you stroll through the small village, watch for the Cathedral, the People's Square, the intimate San Ilario Church, and the Roman/Etruscan Museum.

When you come to the A1, don't get onto the freeway, but instead follow signs to Orvieto. NOTE: When deciding on a town in the area to use as a hub for sightings, don't limit your choice to those in Umbria. You will also find a rich selection of places to stay very nearby in Tuscany and Lazio.

**Orvieto:** Originally founded by the Etruscans, Orvieto later became a prosperous Roman city, famous for its production of ceramics. Orvieto is spread across the top of a hill that drops down on every side in steep volcanic cliffs to the Umbrian plain 200 meters below—you wonder how the town could ever have been built! Drive as far as you can up to the town, park your car, and proceed on foot. Have a good map handy because you pass so many churches and squares that it is difficult to orient yourself—Orvieto is a maze of tiny piazzas and narrow twisting streets. Continue on to Orvieto's center where a glorious **Duomo** dominates the immense piazza. You may think you have seen sufficient stunning cathedrals to last a lifetime, but just wait—Orvieto's is truly special, one of the finest examples of Romanesque-Gothic architecture in Italy. It is brilliantly embellished with intricate mosaic designs and accented by lacy slender spires stretching gracefully into the sky. Within the Duomo, you absolutely must not miss the **Chapel of San Brizio;** here you find frescos by Fra Angelico and Luca Signorelli. Also of interest in Orvieto is **St. Patrick's Well**, hewn out of solid volcanic rock. Pope Clement VII took refuge in Orvieto in 1527 and to ensure the town's water supply in case of siege, he ordered the digging of this 62-meter-deep well. It is unique for the 70 windows that illuminate it and the two spiral staircases that wind up and down without meeting. Other sights to see include the Papal Palace, the Town Hall, and the archaeological museum.

**Civita di Bagnorégio:** Although **Civita di Bagnorégio** is not in Umbria, it's located just southwest of Orvieto, so it conveniently ties in with this itinerary. If you are a photographer and love picturesque walled villages, few can surpass the setting of this small town. Take the N71, which twists west from Orvieto toward **Lake Bolsena**. Stay on N71 for about 20 kilometers and then turn left heading to Bagnorégio. Go into town and follow signs to Civita, which crowns the top of a steep, circular-shaped, rocky outcrop. There is no road into the village—the only access is by walking over a long, narrow suspension bridge that joins the two sides of a deep ravine. Once you arrive, you will find a few shops, some Etruscan artifacts, a church, and a restaurant. However, the main focus is the town itself with its narrow arcaded alleyways and a dramatic 180-degree view of the desolate, rocky canyons that stretch out around the town with a haunting beauty.

# Mountain & Lake Adventures

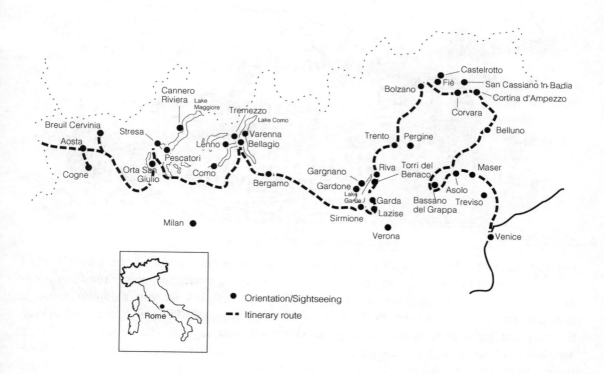

Orientation/Sightseeing

Itinerary route

Castelrotto

Fiè

San Cassiano In Badia

Bolzano

Cortina d'Ampezzo

Corvara

Belluno

Cannero Riviera

Lake Maggiore

Tremezzo

Lake Como

Varenna

Bellagio

Trento

Pergine

Breuil Cervinia

Stresa

Lenno

Maser

Aosta

Pescatori

Riva

Torri del Benaco

Gargnano

Cogne

Orta San Giulio

Como

Gardone

Lake Garda

Garda

Asolo

Treviso

Bergamo

Sirmione

Lazise

Bassano del Grappa

Milan

Verona

Venice

Rome

# Mountain & Lake Adventures

*Santa Maria Rezzónico, Lake Como*

For the traveler who wants to combine the magic of seeing some of the world's most splendid mountains with the joy of visiting Italy's scenic northern lakes, this itinerary is ideal. Contrasts will heighten the impact of visual delights as you meander through dramatic mountains and then on to some of the most romantic lakes in the world. Along the way are giant mountains piercing the sky with their jagged granite peaks and lush meadows splashed with wildflowers. Continuing on you arrive at lazy blue lakes whose steep shorelines are decorated with villages wrapped in misty cloaks of siennas and ochres. This itinerary can stand alone. However, it is also perfect for the traveler arriving in or departing from neighboring countries. All too often the tourist thinks he has finished Italy when his tour ends in Venice, and he rushes north into Austria or Switzerland. What a waste—a very picturesque region still remains. Please linger to enjoy the mountains and lakes that truly are some of Italy's greatest natural treasures.

**Recommended Pacing:** To do this itinerary "well" you need three weeks. This may seem to be dawdling a bit, but less time than indicated would not allow you to enjoy your destinations. Remember that three nights really means only two full days with travel in between. Allow at least three nights in **Venice**—more would be preferable, especially if you want to explore some of the small islands such as Murano (famous for its hand-blown glass) and Burano (well-known for its colorful cottages and hand-made lace). Your next stop, **Asolo**, needs two nights. Not only is the town delightful, but also you will want to visit some of the Palladian mansions in the area. Your next suggested stop, the **Dolomites**, needs another three nights. The scenery is spectacular and you will want time to explore some of the exquisite mountain back roads and take hikes. From the Dolomites your next destination is spectacular **Lake Garda**. Again, you need three nights. You must have time to take advantage of the romantic boat trips around the lake and also a side trip to nearby Verona. Your next stop is another exquisite highlight, **Lake Como**. Here you need three nights to enjoy the boat excursions around the lake. From Lake Como, it is on to **Lake Maggiore**, another lovely destination. Here you need three nights to enjoy both boat trips around the lake and visits to the romantic islands in the lake. After Lake Maggiore it is on to **Lake Orta**, a much smaller lake with great personality. Because it is not so large, two nights should suffice here. From Lake Orta you leave the Lake District and are in the splendid **Aosta Valley** in the **Alps**, which trace the border with France and Switzerland. Here you need another two nights in order to have sufficient time to take walks and enjoy the awesome parks. You might not have the luxury of time to spend three weeks on this *"Mountain & Lake Adventures."* If not, tailor this itinerary for your own schedule. Perhaps visit just one of the lakes instead of all four, or save the lakes for another trip and leisurely enjoy just Venice and the Dolomites. Whatever your choice, you are in for a special treat in this incredibly beautiful region of Italy.

**VENICE**: This itinerary begins in **Venice**, one of the most romantic cities in the world. Venice's many narrow waterways are crisscrossed by storybook bridges and shadowed by majestic palaces whose soft hues reflect warmly in the shimmering water. Black gondolas quietly glide through the narrow canals as the gondolier in his red-and-white-striped shirt softly serenades his passengers with an operatic selection.

Venice is not a traditional city with streets and automobile traffic, but rather an archipelago of 117 islands glued together by 400 bridges.

There is a wealth of things to do and see in Venice. See our chapter *Italian Highlights by Train & Boat–or Car* for sightseeing suggestions.

When it is time to leave Venice for Asolo, you need to take a boat to your car since all the "streets" in Venice are canals. If you are renting a car, take the boat to **Piazzale Roma** where most of the car rental companies are located. Also in the Piazzale Roma there are overnight car parks for storing your car if you drive into Venice. The choice of conveyance to the Piazzale Roma, Venice's hub of transportation, will depend upon your budget and your inclination. The **vaporetti** are the most reasonable: similar to river buses. They leave regularly from St. Mark's Square, stopping along the way to pick up passengers. It is approximately a half-hour ride to the Piazzale Roma. The **motoscafi** are motorboats that duck through the back canals and usually take about 15 minutes to the Piazzale Roma. The motoscafi are like private cabs and are much more expensive than the "bus," but can be very convenient, especially if your hotel has a private motorboat landing. The most romantic mode of transportation is by private **gondola**: however, these are very expensive and usually take about an hour to reach the Piazzale Roma.

Once you have retrieved your car from the parking garage, head north from Venice toward **Treviso**, about an hour's drive. If time allows, stop here. Stroll through this picturesque city spider-webbed with canals and surrounded by 15th-century ramparts—perhaps have a cup of coffee or a bite of lunch. Treviso is famous for its arcaded streets, churches lavishly decorated with frescoes, and painted houses. You might want to climb the ramparts for a view of the Alps beckoning you on.

**ASOLO**: From Treviso it is approximately another hour north to Asolo. However, just a few kilometers before you reach Asolo you see signs for the town of **Maser** where the **Villa di Maser** (sometimes called by the name of **Villa Bararo**) is located. This is a splendid villa designed by **Palladio** and fabulously decorated with frescoes by Paolo Veronese. It also has a very interesting museum of old carriages and antique cars. This elegant villa has erratic days and hours when it is open to the public—usually in late afternoons on Tuesdays, Saturdays, and Sundays. However, it is only about 1½ kilometers out of your way, so it is well worth a detour to investigate.

Your prize tonight is **Asolo,** a gem of a medieval village snuggled on the side of a hill with exquisite views of the countryside. The town is so romantic that it is no wonder Robert Browning was captivated by it and chose Asolo as his home. As you drive toward Asolo, the terrain does not seem to hold much promise—just modern towns and industry. Then a side road winds up a lovely hillside and into the intimate little town. Although definitely a tourist destination, Asolo maintains the atmosphere of a *real* town with colorful fruit stands, candy shops, and the neighborhood grocer for those lucky few who live here. In addition, there are boutiques with exquisite merchandise for the tourist. Of course, a castle adorns the hill above the village—mostly in ruins but setting the proper stage. Naturally, there is a wonderful cathedral dominating the square, just as it should. You will find all this plus vineyards and olive trees on the hillsides and the scent of roses in the air.

There are a couple of towns that are worth seeing while you are in the Asolo area. If brandy holds a special interest for you, visit **Bassano del Grappa**, an old town famous for its production of grappa (or brandy). The town is also a pottery center. However, Bassano del Grappa is rather large and, in our estimation, much less interesting than **Marostica**, a tiny town just a few kilometers farther on. If you are in this area in September, check your calendar and consider a stop in Marostica. Here, during the first part of September (in alternate years) the central square is transformed into a giant chessboard and local citizens become the human chess pieces. Even if it isn't the year of the chess game, you will enjoy this picturesque little medieval town encircled by ramparts, its pretty central square enclosed by colorful buildings and castle walls. There is also a second castle guarding the town from the top of the hill.

**THE DOLOMITES**: From Asolo, you head north to one of the most stunning regions of Italy, the **Dolomites**— breath-taking mountains. It is important to have a very detailed map of the region because this is a confusing area for driving. Adding to the confusion of finding your way is the fact that most of the towns have two names: one Italian and one German. Before World War I this section of Italy belonged to the Austrian Empire, and most of the towns have retained their original names along with their new ones. The food is a mixture of Italian and German—strudel is the favorite dessert and ravioli stuffed with meat, vegetables, and cream cheese is called either ravioletti or schulpfkrapfeln.

There are various routes for driving north into the Dolomites. The major highway heads north through **Feltre** and **Belluno** and then goes on to Cortina d'Ampezzo. However, if the day is nice and your spirit of adventure high, there is really nothing more fun than taking the back roads through the mountains. Journey through tiny hamlets and gorgeous mountain valleys far from the normal tourist path—always keeping a map accessible so that you don't wind up hopelessly lost.

You might want to travel casually and stop in a village that captures your heart as you drive through the picturesque Dolomite valleys. A good base for exploring the region is **Corvara**, a small village ringed by breathtaking mountains. Another excellent choice is **Cortina d'Ampezzo**, a tourist center that is larger due to its excellent skiing facilities. Its location is truly breathtaking—the town spreads across a sunny meadow ringed by gigantic granite peaks. Although the true allure of Cortina is its beauty, there are a few other attractions—the lovely frescoes in the Romanesque **Church of SS Filippo e Giacomo**; the **stadium** where the 1956 Olympic ice-skating competition was held; and the **Museo Ciasa de Ra Regoles** with its geological display and contemporary art exhibition.

This is a mountain lovers' area where the roads are slow and winding. The scenery is beautiful, with green valleys dominated by the stark mountain walls, but the driving is hard, with lots of hairpin bends. Many routes are spectacular. The 48 and 241 from Cortina to Bolzano form the stupendous **Great Dolomite Road** (*Grande Strada delle Dolomiti*). Another lovely route runs through the **Alpe di Siusi,** high Alpine meadowlands beneath towering mountains. (From the Verona-Brennero autostrada exit at Bolzano Nord and follow a route through Völs [Fiè allo Sciliar], Siusi, and Castelrotto.) It continues on into the **Val Gardena** (Grödner Tal) to **Ortisei** (Sankt Ulrich) and up to the **Sella Pass**. We enjoyed a sensational 50-kilometer drive over four mountain passes that ring the **Gruppo Sella** mountain group—from Corvara we took the Gardena Pass, the Sella Pass, the Podoi Pass, and the Campolongo Pass, which returned us to Corvara.

The only relaxing (albeit strenuous) way to truly appreciate the Dolomites is to get out of your car and walk the well-marked trails that feather out into the hills. Cable cars and ski lifts run in summer and are excellent ways to assist the walker to higher altitudes. At gift shops or tourist offices you can purchase detailed hiking maps that show every little path.

**LAKE GARDA**: Your next stop is Lake Garda. From the mountains, drive to Bolzano where you join the expressway (E7), heading south toward Trento (Trent). **Trent** is best known as the town where the Catholic Council met in the 16th century to establish important articles of faith that emphasized the authority of the Catholic Church.

Leave the freeway at Trent and head west on 45 toward the small, but lovely, green **Lake Toblino,** which is enhanced by a superb castle on its north shore where you can stop for lunch. From Toblino head south on the pretty country road, lined with fruit trees and vineyards, heading directly south toward Lake Garda, Italy's largest lake. When you come to Arco, the road splits. Take the road to the left and continue south to Lake Garda and then follow the 249 as it curves along the eastern shore of the lake.

Lake Garda abounds with romance. Don't rush. Take time to explore the lake by boat. Get off at colorful small hamlets that capture your fancy, it is hard to choose since each seems impossibly tempting. Have lunch, then hop back on a later boat to continue along your way. The boat schedules are posted at each dock, and if you ask the attendant, he can usually give you a printed timetable.

There are many alluring villages you should not miss, each a gem. One of the most picturesque towns is **Sirmione,** accessible by a picturesque drawbridge. This walled medieval village at the south end of Lake Garda is positioned on a miniature peninsula that juts into the lake. During the summer Sirmione is absolutely bursting with tourists, but you can easily understand why: this is another one of Italy's "stage-set" villages, almost too perfect to be real.

At the north end of the lake is the larger town of **Riva.** Although much of the town is of new construction, it has at its medieval core the **Piazza III Novembre** and 13th-century **Tower of Apponale.** A good place to eat lunch is on the terrace of the **Hotel Sole,** located directly across from the boat dock.

Along the western shore of the lake our favorite villages are **Gargnano** and its tiny adjacent neighbor, **Villa di Gargnano.** Both are medieval jewels hugging the waterfront with colorful fishing boats tucked into little harbors—truly adorable towns.

Also on the western shore of Lake Garda is **Gardone Riviera.** From here it is just a short drive to a **Vittoriale,** once the home of Gabriele d'Annunzio, the celebrated Italian poet. (For those who are fascinated by stories of romance, **Gabriele d'Annunzio** is also famous for his love affair with Eleanora Duse.)

The east side of Lake Garda also abounds with unbelievably quaint towns, each so perfect that you want to get out your camera or sketchbook to capture the beauty. Our favorites are the medieval walled towns of **Garda**, **Lazise**, and **Torri del Benaco**—each a gem. You mustn't miss them. Of the three, Torri del Benaco is our favorite.

It will be easier to leave the Lake Garda knowing that beautiful Lake Como awaits your arrival.

On your way from Lake Garda to Lake Como, stop at **Bergamo**, about an hour's drive west on the A4. As you approach Bergamo, the congested city doesn't appear to be worth a stop—but it is. The shell of the city is deceiving because it hides a lovely kernel, the **Cita Alta**, or high city. The lower part of Bergamo is modern and a bit dreary, but the old medieval city snuggled on the top of the hill holds such treasures as the **Piazza Vecchia**, the **Colleoni Chapel**, and the **Church of St. Mary Major**. Should you want to time your stop in Bergamo with lunch, there are several excellent restaurants. One suggestion would be the **Agnello**

**d'Oro**, a cozy, charming, 17<sup>th</sup>-century inn in the Cita Alta. From Bergamo it is a short drive on to **Lake Como**.

**LAKE COMO**: Lake Como is spectacular. The lower half of the lake is divided into two legs, the western branch called Lake Como and the eastern branch called **Lake Lecco**, enclosed by soaring cliffs that give a fjord-like beauty to the area. On the tip of land where the two lower sections of the lake join, is a one of the lake's most delightful towns, **Bellagio**, a medieval jewel that exudes great charm. The town traces the shore of the lake and has a medieval walled entrance into the picture perfect central square from which narrow lanes lined with colorful boutiques and restaurants lead up hill. Views of mountains, painted medieval buildings, flowers everywhere, promenades around the lake, and paths into the hills enhance your stay here. A particularly appealing walk follows a path that climbs up the wooded hill behind Bellagio and drops down into a tiny village, Pescallo, that nestles in a small cove on the other side of the peninsula.

*Bellagio, Lake Como*

*Mountain & Lake Adventures*

In addition to Bellagio there is a rich selection of gems on the lake—picturesque, softly hued little hamlets, tucked into intimate coves around the shore. Most of these villages are accessible by boat. You can settle onto a steamer equipped with bar and restaurant and from your armchair lazily enjoy the constantly changing but always intriguing shoreline as the boat maneuvers in and out of the colorful little harbors, past elegant private villas, by enchanting villages. It is great fun to hop aboard one of the ferries and get off at one of the towns for lunch. There are also some swift hydrofoils that will whisk you about the lake and car ferries that transverse the lake, making it convenient to travel from one side to the other without going all around the lake.

Another bonus of Lake Como (besides the quaint towns to explore) is that it has exceptional villas to visit, many accessible by ferry. One of these on the western shore near **Tremezzo** is the **Villa Carlotta**, a fairy-tale-like 18<sup>th</sup>-century palace—worthy of the Prussian Princess Carlotta for whom it was named. Built by the Marquis Clerici, the villa with its surrounding formal gardens filled with rare plants and trees is outstanding. From the terrace you have an enchanting view over the lake to Bellagio. You reach the villa by a short drive from the ferry landing at Tremezzo along the beautiful tree-lined Via del Paradiso, *www.villacarlotta.it*. The interior of the villa with its prominent art collection and statues is open every day from 9 am to 6 pm from April to September. It is also open in March and October from 9 am to 11:30 pm in the morning and in the afternoon from 2 pm to 4:30 pm.

Our favorite villa to visit because of its extraordinary beauty and romantic setting is **Villa del Balbianello** at **Lenno**, located on the west side of Lake Como. Built in 1700 by Cardinal Durini, this picture-post-card perfect villa is so beautiful it looks like a painting (and many artists have captured it on canvas). It is perched on the tip of a tiny peninsula with terraced gardens down to the lake. Have plenty of film in your camera because as the ferry approaches the town of Lenno you will see the villa to your left and won't be able to stop taking photos. When your ferry arrives into Lenno, ask for directions to Sala Comacina, where you take a special motorboat to the landing where a flight of steps leads up to the gardens that are open to the public from the beginning of April until the end of

October on Tuesday, Thursday, Friday, Saturday, and Sunday from 10 am to 12:30 pm and again in the afternoon from 3:30 pm to 6 pm.

**Como**, located at the southern tip of Lake Como, is one of the larger towns on the lake. It is a pretty walled town with excellent shopping—including a colorful market every Saturday. Como is easily accessible from Milan and has many ferry departures from its dock.

**Varenna** is another small lakeside town accessible by ferry that is exceptionally attractive. Located about midway up the east side of the lake, it nestles on a promontory with great views. The heart of the town has a quaint, tiny square lined by medieval buildings. From Varenna sightseeing visits are possible to the both **Villa Cipressi** and the 13th-century **Castello di Vezio**. Varenna is a main hub for ferries, including car ferries that shuttle back and forth from Varenna to Bellagio and **Menaggio**, enabling you to quickly cross the lake without having to drive around it.

*Cannero Riviera–Lake Maggiore*

**LAKE MAGGIORE**: From Lake Como, the next stop is Lake Maggiore. Take advantage of the expressways to make your drive as easy as possible because there is usually heavy traffic in this part of Italy. It is best to head directly south in the direction of Milan to pick up the freeway.

Keep on the bypass that skirts the north side of Milan and take the freeway northwest to Lake Maggiore. Like Lake Garda and Lake Como, Maggiore offers ferries to many of its quaint towns and adds a special treat, the **Borromean Islands**, a small archipelago of three small islands, **Isola Bella**, **Isola Madre**, and **Isola dei Pescatori**. These enchanting islands can be reached by ferry from Stresa, Baveno, or Pallanza, but the most convenient of these departure points is **Stresa.** There are private taxi-boats available, but the most reasonable transportation is by public ferry.

Our two favorites of the Borromean Islands are Isola Bella and Isola dei Pescatori. You can easily visit them both in one day. If you enjoy gardens, be sure not to miss Isola Bella (Beautiful Island). Allow enough time to see its sumptuous palace, which is bound by formal gardens that terrace down to the lake. Fountains and sculptures make the gardens even more alluring. Afterwards, head to Isola dei Pescatori (Fisherman's Island) for lunch. Isola dei Pescatori is an enchanting island with twisting, narrow, alley-like streets and colorful fishermen's cottages. As the name implies, this is still an active fishing village. During the tourist season the island teems with people and the streets are lined with souvenir shops, but it is hard to dull the charm of this quaint town.

Another sightseeing excursion on Lake Maggiore is to the park at **Villa Taranto**. Its gardens, created in the 20th century by a Scottish captain, Neil McEacharn, are splendid with over 2000 species of plants, including huge water lilies, giant rhododendrons, and colorful azaleas. Adding to the botanical masterpiece, are fountains, waterfalls, beautiful trees and sculptures.

*Isola Bella, Lake Maggiore*

**LAKE ORTA**: Lake Orta, situated just west of Lake Maggiore, is one of our favorite lakes. Because it is so close to Lake Maggiore, it can be visited as a day trip from there. However, because it so appealing, we feel it deserves a stopover on its own. One doesn't hear much about Lake Orta, although it abounds with a charm and is filled with of Romanesque and Baroque treasures. It is probably less known because it is so small and doesn't have many quaint towns tucked along its shoreline. However, it does have one outstanding village, Orta San Giulio. It is picture perfect with a tiny square facing the water, narrow cobbled streets, noble mansions, a wonderful, very old, town hall, many boutiques, fragrant gardens, painted houses, and picturesque churches.

Adding to the perfection, just across from the town, you see **Isola San Giulio** shimmering in the water. You can take a boat out to this tiny island where you can walk the narrow street that circles the island and visit the Romanesque style church with 15th and 16th-century frescoes.

**THE ALPS**: After visiting Lake Orta, drive south to the main freeway and head west on A4 toward Turin heading for the Italian Alps. Before Turin, when the freeway branches, take A5 heading northwest toward Aosta and beyond to the French border. As you head into the mountains, many small roads lead off to narrow, valleys accented by gorgeous meadows, blanketed in summer with wildflowers. Most of these roads dead end when they are stopped by impregnable mountain ranges. In the winter, this is a paradise for downhill or cross-country skiing. One of the most famous ski areas is **Breuil-Cervinia**, almost at the Swiss border, just over the mountain from the Swiss resort, Zermatt. In summer the mountains beckon one to explore the beautiful paths that lead off in every direction.

*Cogne-Valnontey*

Our favorite place for walking or hiking is in the **Grand Paradis National Park**, just south of **Cogne**. To reach the park, from the A5, take the road south to Cogne. From here you can walk through a glorious meadow that stretches to the foot of the Grand Paradis, a majestic mountain that soars over 4,000 meters into the sky. If you drive a few kilometers beyond Cogne to where the road ends, you find Valnontey, a stunning hamlet of rustic, centuries-old, stone houses enhanced by pots of geraniums. As you stroll through the tiny village, it seems you have stepped back many centuries—it is so perfect, so untouched.

When it is time to continue your journey, the A5 continues on through the Mont Blanc tunnel and into France.

# Rome to Milan via the Italian Riviera

- Orientation/Sightseeing
- - - Itinerary route

MILAN

Pavia Carthusian Monastery

A7

Genoa

A12

Camogli

Portofino

Sestri Levante

Levanto

Colonnata

Monterosso al Mare

Carrara

Cinque Terre

La Spezia

Lucca

Portovenere

Pisa

Livorno

FLORENCE

Elba

Orbetello Peninsula

Orbetello

Porto San Stefano

Porto Ercole

Tarquinia

Civitavecchia

ROME

Rome

# Rome to Milan via the Italian Riviera

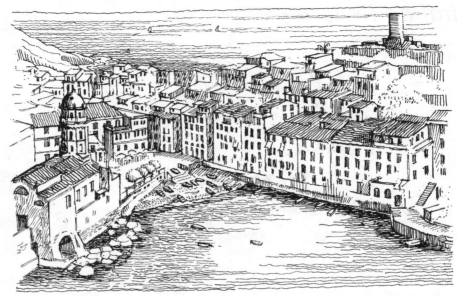

*Vernazza, Cinque Terre*

This itinerary traces the western coast of Italy as far as Genoa before heading north for the final stretch to Milan. To break the journey, the first stop is Orbetello, a picturesque peninsula-like island joined to the coast by three spits of land. The next destination is Cinque Terre—a string of five tiny fishing villages along the coast that have not yet fallen prey to a great influx of tourists. As you follow the highway up the coast, it becomes a masterpiece of engineering—bridging deep ravines and tunneling in and out of the cliffs, which rise steeply from the sea. Along the way you pass picturesque small towns snuggled into small coves. Then it's on to Portofino—one of Italy's most treasured jewels—before the final destination of Milan.

**Recommended Pacing:** This itinerary can be run quickly if it is being used as simply as a means of transportation between Rome and Milan (or visa versa), but it is much more fun to savor the small towns along the way. You need a minimum of three nights in Rome—you could spend a week and still only touch on what this fabulous "living museum" has to offer. Once on your way between Rome and Milan, there are outstanding places to stay and things to see along the coast. However, if your time is strictly limited, choose just one of the three stopovers we recommend (Porto Ercole, Cinque Terre or Portofino) and plan to stay for three nights. Ideally, if you have the luxury to meander along the way, then plan to spend at least two nights in all three. Every suggested stopover is lovely in its own way and will give you a glimpse of the beauty of Italy's small, delightful, coastal towns.

This itinerary begins in **Rome**, a perfect introduction to Italy. The joy of Rome is that every place you walk you are immersed in history. The whole of the city is a virtual museum—buildings over 2,000 years old, ancient fountains designed by the world's greatest masters, the Vatican, Renaissance paintings that have never been surpassed in beauty. Buy a guidebook at one of the many bookstores or magazine stands to plan what you most want to see and do. Also buy a detailed city map and mark each day's excursion. Most places are within walking distance—if not, consider taking the subway, which stretches to most of the major points of interest.

For sightseeing suggestions in Rome, see the *Italian Highlights by Train & Boat—or Car* itinerary.

From Rome follow the well-marked signs for the expressway heading west toward the Leonardo da Vinci airport. About 5 kilometers before you arrive at the airport, head north on A12 in the direction of **Civitavecchia**.

About 13 kilometers beyond the Civitavecchia Nord exit, turn right (east) on S1 BIS in the direction of Viterbo. Continue a bit more than 3 kilometers and turn left toward **Tarquinia**, an Etruscan city that historians date back to the 12th-century B.C. Even if it is not quite that old, archaeologists have established that people were living here as early as

600 years before Christ. Before you reach Tarquinia, you will see on your right an open-air **museum**—an open field dotted with Etruscan tombs. The site is not well-marked, but your clue will be tour buses lining the road. Park your car, buy a ticket at the gate, and explore the fascinating tombs. There are over a thousand tombs stretching over 5 kilometers, but only a small, select group is open to the public. You can wander at leisure. Each tomb has a sign describing what drawings are found within. You will find a rich treasure trove of paintings depicting the life of the ancient Etruscans, including scenes of hunting, dining, fishing, drinking, and frolicking. All of the burial sites are underground. To access a tomb, you have to climb down a narrow flight of steps and when you reach the bottom, everything is semi-dark. However, when you push a button, the tomb is magically illuminated behind a glass window. Each tomb is individually decorated with paintings that offer a poignant glimpse of life over a thousand years ago. There is no way you can visit all the burial chambers, but one of the most popular is the **Tomb of the Leopards** where there is a well-preserved banquet scene.

After viewing the tombs, ask the attendant at the gate for directions to the **Museo Nazionale Tarquiniese** which is located in the center of town in the 15th-century **Vitelleschi Palace**. Even if you do not have time to savor all of the beautiful Etruscan vases and handsome carved stone sarcophagi, you must make at least a brief stop to view the astonishing winged horses dramatically displayed in a large room on an upper floor. You will be spellbound by these superb horses on an ornate relief that adorned the altar of the Queen's temple.

After your brush with Etruscan civilization, continue north for approximately 50 kilometers to Scalo/Orbetello where you turn west. The road crosses 6 kilometers of lagoons on a narrow spit of land (going through the town of Orbetello) before reaching the large, bulbous peninsula dominated by Monte Argentario. Turn left when you reach the peninsula (which looks like an island) and continue through the town of **Porto Ercole** (see *Hotel Descriptions* for accommodations), following signs for the picturesque old fishing village of **Porto Santo Stefano**.

Return to S1 and head north on the highway as it follows the coast. About 35 kilometers before you come to the large city of Livorno (which you want to avoid at all costs), the road divides. One split goes to Livorno and the other becomes the A12, which heads inland and bypasses the city. The next large town after Livorno is **Pisa**. Take the *Pisa Nord* exit which takes you directly to the city walls and the historic part of the old town. Your target is the **Piazza del Duomo**, a huge square studded by fabulous buildings, including Pisa's landmark, its **Leaning Tower**. However, it is not only the Leaning Tower that makes the Piazza del Duomo such a winner, it is studded with many other magnificent buildings, which are all outstanding architectural jewels and happily are open to the public as museums. You can buy one ticket allowing entrance to all. Climb to the top of the Leaning Tower (which is once again open for visitors after being strengthened by massive cables). Also, don't miss the breathtaking **Duomo** or the **Baptistery**. Since we first visited Pisa many years ago, an awesome transformation has taken place. The buildings have been scrubbed cleaned and returned to their original splendor, making Pisa a joy to visit.

*Rome to Milan via the Italian Riviera*

119

About 25 kilometers northeast of Pisa is the extremely picturesque city of **Lucca.** Lucca too is an ancient, perfectly preserved city. Completely surrounding the town is an enormous wall—a wall so wide that it even supports pretty, small parks and a path that runs along the top that is a favorite for joggers. Lucca is truly a jewel. Take time to wander through her maze of narrow streets, admiring imposing mansions and colorful squares.

Leaving Lucca, return to the expressway A12 and head north to Genoa. Along the way you see what appears to be a glacier shimmering white in the mountains that rise in the distance to the right of the highway. This is not snow at all, but rather your introduction to the renowned white Italian marble. Detour to visit some of the marble quarries. Exit the highway at Carrara and take the winding drive up into the hills to the ancient village of **Colonnata**—famous through the ages for its marvelous white marble. As you wander this tiny town you're following the footsteps of Michelangelo, who used to come to here to choose huge blocks of marble from which to carve his masterpieces.

Take the small road from Carrara west to join the A12 and continue north for an entirely different kind of experience—exploring the lovely, remote coast called **Cinque Terre**.

This area is quickly becoming linked with civilization, so do not tarry if you love the thrill of discovering old fishing villages hardly touched by time. En route you come to an exit to **La Spezia**, a large seaport and navy town. If you want to take a detour, go to La Spezia and from there take the short drive to the tip of the peninsula south of town to visit the old fishing village of **Portovenere** which clings to the steep rocks rising from the sea. This was one of Lord Byron's haunts when he lived across the bay at **San Terenzo**. After Portovenere, return to the A12 and continue north.

Along the Cinque Terre there used to be five completely isolated fishing villages dotted along the coast between La Spezia to the south and Levanto to the north. First only a footpath connected these hamlets, then a train was installed, and now civilization is encroaching, with a road under construction, which will open them up to greater commercialism. Three of these little villages, (**Riomaggiore Monterosso** and **Manarola**) are already accessible by road. Still completely cut off from car traffic are the colorful fishing hamlets of **Vernazza** and **Corniglia**.

If you want to spend the night in one of the villages along the Cinque Terre, **Monterosso al Mare** offers the best selection of accommodations. To reach Monterosso al Mare, exit the A12 at Carrodano and follow signs to Levanto. From Levanto take the road up the hill at the south end of town, signposted Monterosso al Mare. A massive rock formation jutting into the sea divides Monterosso into two distinct sections that are connected by a train tunnel. You can walk between the two parts of town, but you cannot drive. So if you leave your car in the public parking area, which is located in the "north" village, you will need to take a taxi to hotels located in the "south" village.

You do not need a car to enjoy the Cinque Terre: this is a region that lures those who love to hike and be out of doors. You can explore the villages by train,

*Rome to Milan via the Italian Riviera*

boat, or walking: the most fun is to combine all three. If you have the time, plan to spend several days here. If the weather is pleasant, hike the trail that traces the rocky coast and links the villages, stopping for lunch along the way (one of our favorite restaurants is the Pensione Cecio in Corniglia). After lunch, hop aboard one of the frequent trains (each of the towns has a train station and the schedules are clearly posted) or take one of the ferries (which only operate in the summer season) to return "home." Let your mood and the weather dictate your explorations. Although this is a remote coast, be prepared that you will not be alone: the path along the Cinque Terre is popular and always busy—filled with the holidaymakers who have come to enjoy the natural beauty.

If you have time to see only one of the scenic towns, **Vernazza**, which clings perilously to a rocky headland above a tiny harbor, is the most picturesque. This colorful jewel has brightly painted fishermen's houses, quaint restaurants, a harbor with small boats bobbing in the clear, turquoise water, and a maze of twisting narrow steps that lead up to the promontory overlooking the village.

Leaving Cinque Terre, continue north beside the coast. Stop in **Sestri Levante**, one of the most picturesque coastal villages en route. Continue along the small coastal road that goes through Chiàvari and on to San Margherita where you take the small road south for the short drive to the picture-book village of **Portofino**. This last section of the road, especially in summer, is jammed with traffic, but the prize at the end is worth the trials endured to reach it. Portofino is by no means undiscovered, but is well deserving of its accolades—it is one of the most picturesque tiny harbors in the world.

Portofino is a national treasure—it truly is a jewel. Its tiny harbor is filled with glamorous yachts, small ferries, and colorful fishing boats. Enveloping the harbor are narrow fishermen's cottages, poetically painted in warm tones of sienna, ochre, and pink and all sporting green shutters. Bright flowerboxes accent the windows and the laundry flaps gaily in the breeze.

Vivid reflections of these quaint little houses shimmer in the emerald water. In the center of town is a small square, lined with restaurants, which faces the harbor. Forming a backdrop to the town are steep, heavily forested hills, which complete this idyllic scene.

*Portofino*

When it is time to leave Portofino, return to the A12 highway and continue west for about 30 kilometers to Genoa. As go through the city, watch for the A7 going north to Milan. An interesting detour on the last leg of your journey is the **Pavia Carthusian Monastery** (*Certosa di Pavia*). Probably the simplest way to find it is to watch for the turnoff to Pavia (96 kilometers north of Genoa): take the road east to Pavia and from there go north about 10 kilometers to the monastery. Lavishly built in the 15th century, this splendid monastery is claimed by some to be one of the finest buildings in Italy. (Check carefully the days and hours open—the monastery is usually closed on Mondays and for several hours midday.) The outside of the building is lavishly designed with colorful marble and intricate designs. Inside, the small cloisters are especially charming with 122 arches framed by beautiful terracotta moldings. It also has a baroque fountain and several small gardens. Next to the monastery you find the **Palace of the Dukes of Milan**, which is now a museum. After your tour of the monastery it is approximately 26 kilometers farther north to **Milan**.

The outskirts of Milan are not very inviting—you find frustrating traffic and modern commercial buildings. However, the heart of Milan has much to offer. Take time to see Leonardo da Vinci's famous mural, **The Last Supper**, in the church of **Santa Maria delle Grazie**. It is vital that you make an appointment in advance: from the USA call 011-39 (Europe, 00-39) 0289-421146; from within Italy, (199) 19 91 00. The unilingual Italian-speaking reservationists will make you an appointment and give you a confirmation number. Arrive at the church about 15 minutes before your appointment, confirmation number in hand, and pay cash for your ticket.

If you enjoy shopping (and Milan has some of the finest shops in Italy), pay a visit to the splendid **Galleria Vittorio Emanuele**, one of the prettiest shopping arcades in the world. Even if you are not a shopper, you should take time to browse. Located between Milan's other two sightseeing stars, the Duomo and La Scala, the Galleria Vittorio Emanuele is the forerunner of the modern shopping mall, but with much more pizzazz. In this Victorian-era fantasy there are two main, intersecting wings, both completely domed with intricately patterned glass. Along the pedestrian-only arcades you find many boutiques and colorful restaurants with outside tables.

After a stroll through the arcade, you emerge into an imposing square dominated by the truly spectacular **Duomo**, the third-largest cathedral in the world. Not only is the size impressive, but this sensational cathedral has a multicolored marble façade enhanced by over 100 slender spires piercing the sky. This spectacular cathedral faces onto an enormous square lined with cafés, office buildings, and shops. Stop to have a snack at one of the outdoor restaurants—you could sit for hours just watching the people go by.

*La Scala, Milan*

Another site not to be missed is Milan's opera house. Every opera buff knows about **La Scala**. Even if you have not been an opera enthusiast in the past, if you are going to be in Milan during the opera season (which usually runs from December to May), write ahead and try to get tickets. The theater is stunning and an experience not to be missed. When it is not opera season, there is usually some other performance or concert featured. If you haven't purchased seats in advance, you can try to buy them on the day of the performance (the ticket office is located down a flight of stairs to the left of the opera house).

# *Highlights of Southern Italy*

127

# Highlights of Southern Italy

*Amalfi Coast*

Memories of childhood history lessons vaguely call forth such names as Pompeii, Herculaneum, and Paestum, yet, all too frequently, the urge to visit these jewels is lost in the misconception that southern Italy is a rather lack luster destination. What a mistake! Southern Italy has fascinating archaeological sites, appealing medieval towns, white sand beaches and the dazzling Amalfi Coast with its picture perfect villages. Travelers who venture south from Rome are thrilled when they wander through the fabulous Greek site of Paestum with its splendidly-preserved temples rivaling those found in Greece or discover the mysterious town of Alberobello with its twisting streets lined by cute, whitewashed, beehive-like Trulli houses.

**Recommended Pacing:** Spend a minimum of three nights in Rome. Then, choose one town along the **Amalfi Coast** and stay for a minimum of five nights so that you will have time to make an excursion to Capri. Your next stop, Maratea, does not have much sightseeing but is a perfect place to relax for a couple of nights. The final destination is near the "heel" of Italy. Choose one place to use as your home base in Apulia and plan to spend at least three nights so that you will have time to explore this remote, beautiful part of Italy.

This itinerary makes a circle of the south in order to suit the travel needs of a wide selection of tourists. Follow the entire route or select the portion best for you since this itinerary is particularly suitable for the traveler who wants to take only a segment. For instance, the journey from Rome to Brindisi is a favorite one for the lucky tourists on their way to Greece, while the west coast is a popular drive for the tourist who wants to visit Sicily and then return to Rome by air or ferry. Most popular of all is the segment from Rome to the Amalfi Drive. This itinerary allows you to custom-tailor your journey and gives you tantalizing sightseeing along the way.

**Rome** is a most convenient starting point to begin a tour of southern Italy, since its airport is the destination of planes from all over the world. In Rome you can immerse yourself in a wealth of history, art, architecture, museums, and monuments—and build a foundation for the sights that will be encountered on your journey southward. For sightseeing suggestions in Rome, refer to the chapter *Italian Highlights by Train & Boat—or Car*.

If you arrive into Rome by plane, do not reserve your rental car until the day of your departure. Just take a taxi to your hotel or board the train from the airport that whisks you to the center of the city. When it is time to leave Rome bear in mind that the city has a monumental traffic problem. To guide you, look for strategically placed signs indicating that there is an expressway ahead. It might be quite a distance, but be patient as these signs lead you to the outskirts of Rome to the highway that makes a ring around the city with various spokes going off to different destinations. Follow the ring and take the exit for the A2, the expressway heading south toward Naples. Continue south for approximately 128 kilometers to the exit for **Cassino** where you leave the expressway. Actually, you can spot your destination from several kilometers away—the **Abbey of**

**Monte Cassino** crowns the top of a large mountain to the left of the highway as you drive south. The road that winds up to the summit of the mountain to the Abbey is clearly marked about midway through Cassino. This abbey, founded by St. Benedict in 529 A.D., is extremely interesting both religiously and historically. For war historians it brings back many battle memories—this is where the Germans staunchly held out against the Allied forces for almost a year in World War II. When the mountain was finally conquered in May 1944, it opened the way for the Allies to finally move into Rome. As you read your history books, it seems strange that one fort could hold out for so long, but when you see the abbey you understand: it is an enormous building on the crest of a precipitous mountain. In the siege the abbey was almost destroyed, but it has been rebuilt according to the original plans.

NOTE: For those of you who for sentimental or historical reasons are especially interested in World War II, there is another destination you might well want to visit in this day's journey. **Anzio** is a town on the coast about 56 kilometers south of Rome and could easily be included as a stop before Cassino. It was at Anzio that the British and Americans forces landed in January 1944. The emotional reminder of this terrible battle is a few kilometers south at **Nettuno** where 8,000 white crosses and stars of David range—row after row across the green lawn. There is a circular drive around the beautifully manicured, parklike grounds where you also find a memorial chapel and small war museum. For those who lost family or friends during the invasion, there is an information office to the right as you drive in where you can stop to find out exactly where your loved ones are buried—you will need help because the park is huge.

From Cassino return to the expressway and continue south for about 60 kilometers until you see the sign for **Pompeii**. Unless you have absolutely NO interest in archaeology, you must see the city of your childhood history books. This is where time was frozen in 79 A.D. for the 25,000 people who were smothered by ashes from the eruption of **Mount Vesuvius**. If you are a dedicated student of archaeology, you must also visit the **Museo Archeologico Nazionale** (National Archaeological Museum) in **Naples**, which houses many of the artifacts from Pompeii.

*Highlights of Southern Italy*

Time slips back 2,000 years and you feel the pulse of how people lived in ancient times as you wander the streets of Pompeii and visit the temples, lovely homes, wine shops, bakeries, and public baths. Many of the private homes have been reconstructed so you can marvel at the pretty inner courtyards, sumptuous dining rooms in Pompeii-red with intricate paintings on the walls, fountains, servants' quarters, bathrooms, and gardens. At the entrance to Pompeii there are souvenir stands where you can purchase a guidebook to the city, or, if you prefer, you can hire a private guide at the entrance. There is a nice terrace restaurant by the entrance and also a café inside.

Much of what you see today has been reproduced, but the reality is pure. Plaster was poured into molds formed by the lava that demolished the buildings and buried so many families that fateful day. Thus it became possible for latter-day archaeologists to reconstruct houses and make reproductions of people and pets. Walk through the town along the sunken streets crossed by high stepping-stones, strategically placed so that pedestrians did not get their feet wet on rainy days. Be sure not to miss some of the reconstructed villas that allow you a glimpse into the daily life of long ago. The **Casa del Fauno**, a fine example of how the wealthy lived, has two inner courtyards and several dining rooms. The **Casa del Poeta Tragico**, a more modest home, has a sign in mosaic saying *Cave Canem* (beware of the dog). At the **Villa di Giulia Felice** you see the example of an entrepreneur—in addition to using it as a private villa, the owner rented out rooms, had shops on the ground floor, and operated an adjacent bathhouse. If traveling with children, you might want to go alone into the **Lupanare** (Pompeii's brothel) where there are erotic paintings on the walls. At the **Terme Stabiane** you see a sophisticated underground water-heating system.

If you have time, visit the nearby ruins of **Herculaneum** which was also buried in the ashes of Vesuvius.

Leaving Pompeii, head to the coast in the direction of Sorrento where the **Amalfi Drive** begins, tracing one of the most beautiful stretches of shoreline in the world. Be sure to make the journey in daylight because you want to savor every magnificent vista as well as safely negotiate this extremely twisty and precipitous road.

*Positano*

It is hard to recommend our favorite town along the Amalfi Drive since each has its own personality: **Sorrento**, is an old fishing town perched on a rocky bluff overlooking the sea. It makes an especially convenient place to stay if you want to make a side trip to Capri by ferry or hydrofoil. **Ravello** is a tiny village tucked high in the hills above the coast with absolutely dazzling views down to the sea. **Positano** is an especially romantic coastal town with a picturesque medley of whitewashed houses terracing down an ever-so-steep embankment to a pebble beach dotted with brightly painted fishing boats. **Amalfi** is a small harbor town nestled in a narrow ravine.

*Highlights of Southern Italy*

From whatever hub you choose as your hotel base, venture out to do some exploring. The traffic during the tourist season is staggering, with buses, trucks, and cars all jockeying for position on the narrow twisting roads. Prepare for much shouting, waving of hands, honking, and general bedlam as long buses inch around the hairpin curves. The best advice is to relax and consider the colorful scene part of the sightseeing. Also, begin your excursions as early in the day as possible to try to avoid the major traffic.

If you are not overnighting in **Ravello**, you must plan to take the narrow winding road up to this romantic clifftop town. When you arrive, leave your car in one of the designated parking areas, pick up a map at the tourist office, then walk along the well-marked path to the **Villa Rufolo** and the **Villa Cimbrone**—both have beautiful gardens that are open to the public and enchanting views of the Bay of Salerno.

If you are not overnighting in **Positano**, by all means make this a day's excursion. The town is a photographer's dream—houses painted a dazzling white step down the impossibly steep hillside to a pebble beach lapped by brilliant blue water. To reach the small plaza dominated by a church topped by a colorful mosaic-tiled dome you have to climb one of the town's many staircases. Today Positano attracts artists and tourists from around the world, but in the 16th and 17th centuries it was an important seaport with tall-masted ships bringing in wares from around the world. When steamships came into vogue in the 19th century, Positano's prosperity declined and three-quarters of its population emigrated to the United States.

If you have not been able to include an interlude on **Capri** during your Italian holiday, it is easy to arrange an excursion to this enchanted island as a side trip from the Amalfi Coast. Steamers and hydrofoils depart regularly from Sorrento, Amalfi, and Positano. Ask at the tourist bureau or your hotel for the schedule.

We also highly recommend spending a day in **Naples**, which, although not on the Amalfi Coast, is conveniently close. Since it is quite difficult to drive into Naples without getting lost, we suggest the following options: Train from Sorrento, boat from Sorrento, or boat from Positano. Naples, the third largest city in Italy, is well-worth a side trip; it has many places of interest plus one of the worlds finest archaeological museums, the **Museo Archeologico Nazionale,** where most of the original artifacts from Pompeii are displayed. For more in depth suggestions for what to see and do in Naples, read the itinerary *Italian Highlights by Train & Boat—or Car.*

While exploring the Amalfi Coast, be sure to include the **Emerald Grotto**, located between the towns of Amalfi and Positano. After parking, buy a ticket and descend by elevator down the steep cliff to a small rocky terrace. Upon entering the water-filled cave, you're rowed about the grotto in a small boat. Your guide explains how the effect of shimmering green water is created by a secret tunnel allowing sunlight to filter from deep below the surface. The cave is filled with colorful stalactites and stalagmites which further enhance the mysterious mood. There is also a nativity scene below the water which mysteriously appears and then drifts again from view.

When it is time to leave the Amalfi area, take the coastal road south as it twists and turns along the dramatic cliffs toward Salerno. At Salerno, join the expressway A3 for about 19 kilometers until the turnoff for **Paestum** which is located on a side road about a half-hour drive from the freeway. Magically, when you enter the gates of the ancient city, you enter a peaceful environment of a lovely country meadow dotted with some of the world's best-preserved Greek temples. As you walk along the remains of streets crisscrossing the city, your senses are thrilled by the sound of birds singing and the scent of roses.

From Paestum return to the A3 and continue south until you come to the Lagonegro Nord-Maratea exit. Do not be tempted by some of the short cuts you see on the map that lead to the coast, but stay on the main road 585. In about 25 kilometers the road comes to the sea where you turn north at Castrocucco, following signs to **Maratea**. Plan on spending several days in the Maratea area.

Not well known to foreigners, this lovely section of coast, known as the **Gulf of Policastro**, is a popular resort area for Italians. The loveliest section of the road is between Maratea and Sapri where the road traces the sea along a high corniche, providing lovely vistas of small coves and rocky promontories. This is not an area for intensive sightseeing, but provides a quiet interlude for several days of relaxation.

*Maratea, Gulf of Policastro*

From the Gulf of Policastro, take road 585 back to the A3 and continue south for about 75 kilometers, turning east at Frascineto-Castrovillari toward the instep of Italy's boot. After about 25 kilometers you near the coast. Here you turn left on 106 to **Taranto**. Stop to see this ancient port, which is connected by a bridge to the modern city. Even if you are not interested in ancient history, it is fun to see the Italian naval ships—giant gray monsters—sitting in the protected harbor.

From Taranto take 172 north and continue on for about 45 kilometers following signs to Alberobello. You are now in the province of **Apulia**, not a well-known destination, but all the more fun to visit because it is off the beaten path. Choose a hotel in the area as your hub, venture out to explore the fascinating sights that follow:

**Trulli District**: Trulli houses (whose origins date back to at least the 13<sup>th</sup> century) are some of the strangest structures in Italy—circular stone buildings, usually in small clusters, standing crisply white with conical slate roofs and whimsical, twisted chimneys. Outside ladders frequently lead to upper stories. Often several of these houses are joined together to form a larger complex. What a strange and fascinating sight—these beehive-like little houses intertwined with cobbled streets form a jumble of a small village that looks as though it should be inhabited by elves instead of *real* people. The heart of the trulli region is **Alberobello** where there are so many trulli houses (more than 1,000 along the narrow streets) that the trulli district of town has been declared a national monument.

Trulli houses are not confined just to the town of Alberobello though this is where you find them composing an entire village. In fact, the trulli houses you see outside Alberobello are sometimes more interesting than those in the town itself. As you drive along the small roads, you spot gorgeous villas cleverly converted from trulli houses, now obviously the homes of wealthy Italians. Others are now farmhouses with goats

*Trulli Houses, Alberobello*

munching their lunch in the front yard. Occasionally you spot a charming old trulli home nestled cozily in the center of a vineyard. But most fun of all are the trulli homes of the free spirits: their homes, instead of displaying the typical white exteriors, have been painted a brilliant yellow, pink, or bright green with contrasting shutters.

**Grotte di Castellana**: As you are exploring the countryside near Alberobello, take the short drive north to see the Castellana Caves—the largest in Italy. In a two-hour tour you see many rooms of richly colored stalagmites and stalactites.

**Coastal Villages**: Be sure to include in your sightseeing some of the characterful towns along the coast. They look entirely different from the colorful fishing villages in the north of Italy. These are Moorish-looking, with stark-white houses lining narrow, alley-like streets. The Adriatic looks an even deeper blue as it laps against the white buildings, many of which rise from the sea with small windows perched over the water. Besides **Monopoli** other coastal towns to see are **Polignano a Mare** and **Trani**.

**Castel del Monte**: On the same day that you explore the coastal villages, include a visit to the 13th-century Castel del Monte. Built by Emperor Frederick II of Swab, it is somewhat of a mystery, having none of the fortifications usually associated with a medieval castle. Nevertheless, it is dramatic—a huge stone structure crowning the top of a hill with eight circular towers, which stretch 24 meters into the sky. There are stunning views in every direction.

**Matera**: Plan one full day to visit Matera, an intriguing town of stark beauty (so extraordinary UNESCO has listed it as a World Heritage site). As you approach Matera, you can't help but wonder what is so special—it looks like quite an ordinary, modern city. But, continue on, following signs for "Sassi." Upon arrival, park your car and go to the central plaza in the heart of the old city. From the plaza, steps lead down to a secreted town beneath, hugging the walls of a steep canyon laced by narrow alley-like lanes and ancient houses. These dwellings, called **Sassi**, have facades fronting cave-like homes. The scene is haunting with a jumble of monotone houses and churches clinging to, and blending with, the hillside. There is not a hint of color to liven the scene. Some scholars think that this site, which began thousands of years ago as cave homes, might well be the oldest inhabited place in Italy. The city had been almost totally abandoned by the mid-1900s, but it is being rediscovered and, as a result, art galleries, restaurants, shops, and a few places to spend the night are reappearing. Mel Gibson is responsible for some of the most recent interest in the town, since he filmed here for his movie, *The Passion of the Christ*. The only way to explore this ancient part of Matera is on foot (the tourist office provides maps with various suggested routes).

When it is time to leave Apulia, you can breeze back to Rome by an expressway. Or, if your next destination is Greece, it is just a short drive to **Brindisi** where you can board the ferry for Corfu, Igoumenitsa, or Patras. Best of all, if you can extend your holiday in Sicily (see *Exploring the Wonders of Sicily* itinerary).

*Castel del Monte*

# Exploring the Wonders of Sicily

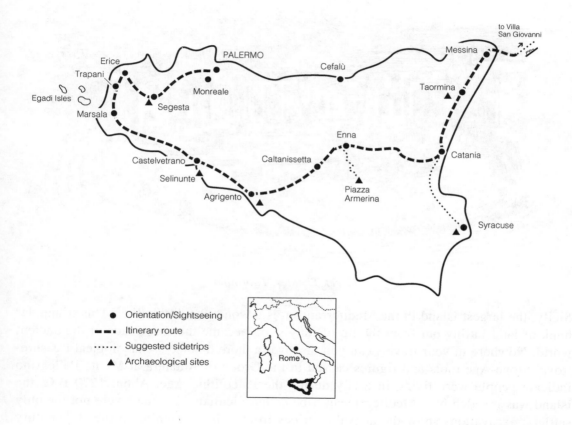

- ● Orientation/Sightseeing
- ▪▪▪ Itinerary route
- ····· Suggested sidetrips
- ▲ Archaeological sites

Egadi Isles

Trapani
Erice
Marsala
Monreale
Segesta
PALERMO
Cefalù
Messina
to Villa San Giovanni
Taormina
Catania
Enna
Caltanissetta
Castelvetrano
Selinunte
Agrigento
Piazza Armerina
Syracuse

Rome

# Exploring the Wonders of Sicily

*Greek Theater, Taormina*

Sicily, the largest island in the Mediterranean, is a wondrous destination. This triangular hunk of land jutting out from the tip of Italy's toe became the crossroads of the ancient world. Nowhere in your travels can you discover a more diverse archaeological treasure-trove. Stone-Age tools and figures carved in the Grotta di Addaura at Monte Pellegrino indicate people were living in Sicily during the Paleolithic Age. About 1270 B.C. the island was invaded by a Mediterranean tribe called Siculians, but they were not the only settlers: excavations show the arrival of tribes from Asia. Beginning in the 10th century

B.C., pioneering Phoenicians took a fancy to this fertile land, followed later by their descendants, the Carthaginians. However, the true dawn of Sicily's reign of glory began with the colonization by the Greeks whose enormous influence permeates Sicily today. However, the rich fabric of Sicily's heritage does not end with the Greek influence: later the Romans invaded, then the Normans, then the Spanish, and on and on. This resulting melting pot of cultures makes Sicily an absolute MUST for those who delight in the romance of archaeology. The true magic of Sicily is that most of the ruins are so natural in their setting. Frequently you discover you are alone—the only tourist walking through a field of wildflowers to gaze in awe at an exquisite temple.

**Recommended Pacing:** We recommend a minimum of a week to follow this itinerary. If you are passionate about archaeology, you could stay in Sicily for a month or more to delve in depth with its many glorious sites. Plan to spend two nights in Taormina (one of Sicily's most attractive cities) two nights in Agrigento to see the incredible temples in the *Valle dei Templi*, and then three nights in northwest Sicily (Palermo or another hub) to visit Palermo, Segesta, Monreale, and Erice.

The greatest age of glory for Sicily began when the Greeks founded their first colony here about 770 B.C. Apparently these early Greeks left their native country for economic and political reasons, but many were also undoubtedly motivated by pure curiosity—the desire to discover what awaited across the sea. Like the immigrants who came to America, the early settlers wanted a fresh start in a new land and an opportunity to establish a better life for themselves. And they did. Prospering enormously from the richness of the fertile soil, the early Greeks became extremely wealthy. As the *nouveaux riche* tend to do, they flaunted their success, building great cities, elaborate houses, theaters, spas, and stadiums—all bigger and better than those they left at home. Syracuse, the mightiest city in Sicily, eventually became more powerful than Athens. The temples they built surpassed in size and splendor those left in their native land. Not losing their passion for sports, every four years the new colonialists sent their finest athletes back to Greece where they dominated the Olympic games.

Twice an hour ferries cross the narrow channel from **Villa San Giovanni** to **Messina**, Sicily. After buying your ticket, go to the indicated lane and wait with all the trucks, campers, and other cars for the signal to drive onto the boat. When on board, you may leave your car and go upstairs to the lounge area where you can buy snacks while traversing the short channel. In 35 minutes the large ferry draws up to the pier in Messina and you drive off to begin your adventures.

If you prefer to fly to Sicily, just reverse this itinerary. Start in Palermo and finish in Taormina. Alternatively, you can take a ferry from Naples to Palermo (a ten-hour journey).

Picture-perfect **Taormina** with the dramatic peak of **Mont Etna** as a backdrop, hugs the crest of a small peninsula that juts out to the sea. Steep cliffs drop to the unbelievably blue sea. Quaint streets wind through the colorful town where you can browse in the many smart boutiques, sip a cappuccino at a small café, or simply enjoy the incredible view. The scent of oranges is in the air and brilliantly colored bougainvilleas lace the medieval buildings.

However, it is not just the natural beauty of its spectacular setting that makes Taormina so popular. As in all of Sicily, your leisure pleasure is enhanced with fabulous sights to see. The prime archaeological target for your sightseeing is the **Greek Theater** From the center of town an easy walk up Via Teatro Greco takes you to a magnificent theater dug into the sloping hillside above the town. Built by the Greeks in the 3rd century B.C., the open-air amphitheater has only a token few of its original columns remaining, making the effect even more romantic. As you gaze beyond the rows of seats to the stage below and out to the vivid blue sea beyond, you will think there is no prettier picture in all of Italy.

After visiting the Greek Theater, most of the remainder of your sightseeing can be done informally while strolling through town. First pick up a map and general information at the tourist office in the **Palazzo Corvaia**, a 15th-century palace located on the Piazza Vittorio Emanuele. From the Palazzo Corvaia, continue through town and stop at the 17th-century **St. Giuseppe Church** in Piazza Nove Aprile. As you walk on, be sure to

*Exploring the Wonders of Sicily*

step inside the 13<sup>th</sup>-century **Cathedral** in the Piazza del Duomo to enjoy the paintings. Farther on you come to the 12<sup>th</sup>-century **Torre dell'Orologio**, the portal that leads into the oldest and most colorful part of Taormina, **Borgo Medieval**.

Leaving Taormina, follow the A18 south toward Catania. When you reach Catania, take the A19 west in the direction of Palermo, then when the highway splits (not long after passing Enna), instead of continuing north to Palermo, head southwest in the direction of Caltanissetta and Agrigento. After Caltanissetta, the expressway ends and you are on a two-lane road for the final leg of your journey to Agrigento.

Along the route from Taormina to Agrigento, we recommend two excursions. It would make your day too long to include them both, but if you get an early start, you will have enough time to squeeze in one of them.

*Suggested Excursion I*: If you are a Greek history buff, take this 128-kilometer detour to see one of the wealthiest, most powerful cities of the ancient Greek Empire (rivaling only Athens in importance). When you reach Catania, don't turn west toward Palermo, but continue south, following signs to **Syracuse**, founded in 734 B.C. by the Corinthians. In the **Archaeological Park** at the edge of town are two theaters—a 6<sup>th</sup>-century B.C. **Greek Theater** (one of the most magnificently preserved in the world) and the ruins of a 2<sup>nd</sup>-century A.D. **Roman Amphitheater** (one of the largest arenas the Romans ever built). From the Archaeological Park, skip the sprawling modern city and cross the Ponte Nuovo that spans Syracuse's harbor to **Ortygia**, the island where the Greeks first founded Syracuse. Visit the two main squares, the beautiful **Piazza del Duomo** where the cathedral (built upon the ancient temple of Minerva) is located and the **Piazza Archimede** enhanced by a baroque fountain. After sightseeing in Syracuse, return to Catania and take A19 west in the direction of Palermo.

*Suggested Excursion II*: If you are a Roman history buff, take this 74-kilometer round-trip excursion to visit the Villa of Casale. En route from Taormina to Agrigento on the A19, turn south at Enna to **Piazza Armerina**. Continue southwest beyond Piazza Armerina for 5 kilometers to your sightseeing target, the **Villa of Casale**, rivaling in splendor the home built by Tiberius on the island of Capri. The foundations of this sumptuous Roman villa were hidden under a blanket of mud for 700 years—not discovered by archaeologists until 1950. The fact that this ostentatious villa was built when the Roman Empire was on the verge of financial ruin is all the more fascinating. You cannot help wondering if the obviously vast expense of its construction was indicative of the flamboyant spending style that led to the collapse of the Roman Empire.

Built in the 3$^{rd}$ century A.D., this mansion surely must have belonged to someone of enormous importance—perhaps Emperor Maximilian. The ruins are beautifully displayed

in a covered museum with walkways guiding you from one opulent room to the next, each overlooking courtyards. But don't start until you have studied a mockup as you enter showing an artist's rendering of what the huge villa looked like in its prime—a look at this will increase your appreciation of the incredible grandeur of what you will be seeing. In all, the home covers an area almost three times the size of a football field. The outstanding feature is the 3,500 square meters of mosaics that decorated the floors of this splendid villa. Following the home's foundations are 40 mosaic floors of extraordinary quality. These beautifully preserved ancient Roman mosaics are considered the finest in the world. Slip back almost 1,700 years and imagine what life must have been like: the scenes show hunting expeditions, wild animals, mythical sea creatures, chariot races, cupids fishing, slaves working, girls cavorting. Once you have visited this Roman showplace, return north to Enna, then turn west following the route to Agrigento.

**Agrigento** is a congested, not very pretty city. We recommend you stay instead outside the heart of the city near the archeological zone. Follow the signs for the **Valle dei**

*Exploring the Wonders of Sicily*

**Templi**. The name is misleading: the archeological site is actually on a plateau to the west of town — not in a valley at all.

Plan to spend two nights in Agrigento so that you can spend one entire day leisurely seeing the ruins. A wide pedestrian road connects the temples — start at one end and savor the haunting beauty of each. Most of these Doric temples are in ruins, with only enough columns remaining to give you an idea of what they used to be in their glory. The best preserved is the **Temple of Concord** which dates back to 440 B.C. See them all: the **Temple of Juno**, the **Temple of Hercules**, the **Temple of Dioscuri**, the **Temple of Jupiter**, and the **Temple of Castor and Pollux**. The setting is beautiful with the sea in the distance and wildflowers in the surrounding fields. It is a thrill to stroll from one temple to the other, marveling at their grandeur and trying to envision what these incredible structures dedicated to Greek gods looked like 2,000 years ago.

To complement your sightseeing at the temples, walk to the **Archaeological Museum**. The museum has a mock-up of the Temple of Jupiter, plus many vases and artifacts from the site.

From Agrigento, continue west on 115 toward Castelvetrano. About 10 kilometers before you arrive in Castelvetrano, turn left onto the 115 dir toward the coast, signposted to Selinunte. For such major ruins, there is little commercialism. You might well miss the main east entrance on the 115 dir—as you drive toward the coast, look for a parking area to the right of the road (if you go under the railroad tracks, you have gone too far).

Park your car in the designated area, buy your ticket, and walk through the tunnel into the enormous field where the remains of the temples of Selinunte lie scattered amongst the wildflowers. In its prime, **Selinunte** was one of the finest cities in Sicily. It met disaster in 407 B.C. when the Carthaginians (it is thought under the command of Hannibal) razed the city, slaughtered 16,000 people, and took thousands into slavery. The giant temples, however, were probably destroyed by earthquake, not by the sword. Here, spread along a huge plateau overlooking the ocean, are the impressive remains of some of the most gigantic temples built by the Greeks. It is staggering to imagine how more than 2,500 years ago they had the skill and technology to lift and piece together these huge blocks of stone weighing over 100 tons each (slaves undoubtedly helped). Of the original seven temples, only one has been reconstructed, but the massive columns lying on the ground indicate the scope and grandeur of what used to be.

From Selinunte, return to the 115, taking the coastal route to Erice. En route, stop for lunch at one of the restaurants along the seafront promenade in **Mazara del Vallo**, an ancient city that was at one time a colony of Selinunte. Browse through the historic center of town to see the beautiful **Piazza della Repubblica** and the **Cathedral**.

The next large town after Mazara del Vallo is **Marsala**, a city well known throughout the world for its excellent wine. Ironically, it was not an Italian, but an Englishman, named John Woodhouse, who experimented by lacing the native wine with an extra bit of alcohol. Based on Woodhouse's formula, Marsala quickly became one of the staples of the British Navy and a special favorite of Lord Nelson. Along the road between Selinunte and Marsala are various wineries that are open to the public. One of the most popular is the **Florio Winery**—one of the three original companies to produce Marsala.

*Exploring the Wonders of Sicily*

*Erice, Sicily*

From Marsala, the road heads north to Trapani. Bypass Trapani and head northeast to **Erice**. Positioned over 750 meters above the coast (about 10 kilometers from Trapani), Erice is a delightful medieval walled town, cooled by breezes from the sea. Park your car and walk through the **Porta Trapani** and up the cobbled street. Erice is best discovered by exploring on foot. Narrow cobbled streets and steep stairways form a maze throughout the town, which is so small that you cannot get lost for long. Just wander, discovering tiny churches, picturesque squares, characterful stone houses, arcaded passageways, and shops selling the locally produced handmade carpets with colorful geometric designs. Walk to the **Castello Normanno**, built upon the ruins of the Temple of Venus. From the tower you have a splendid view looking over the town of Trapani and out to the sea.

If you like to get off the beaten path, from Erice drive down to Trapani and take a hydrofoil to the **Egadi Isles**, all less than an hour away. Just a short distance off shore, **Favignana**, the largest of the three islands, was once a great center for tuna. The major cannery was owned by Ignazio Florio (the same Florio who founded the Florio Winery). **Levanzo**, the smallest of the islands, has a very small population due to its lack of fresh water. The island farthest from Trapani, **Maréttimo**, is basically a fishermen's island.

Wind down the hill from Erice and turn left on the A29 going east in the direction of Palermo. Thirty kilometers after getting on the freeway, take the Segesta exit and follow signs for the **Segesta** archaeological site, located close the highway. Although you have seen many ruins by this stage of your holiday in Sicily, don't miss this one—it is special. First drive to the designated parking area and walk up the hillside to visit what most experts believe to be the world's finest example of a **Doric temple**. The temple with 36 columns looks much as it must have in 400 B.C. There is no roof—there never was because this isolated temple to some unknown god was never completed. One of the most superb aspects of this temple is its setting—there is nothing to jar the senses. The temple stands alone in a field of wildflowers with great natural beauty all around. Enjoy the romance of this gem at your leisure, then drive down the hill and park your car by the information center where there is a nice restaurant. Eat lunch here and then walk the marked path to see the **Greek Theater**. It is about a kilometer away, but a lovely walk through untouched fields. There are so few signs, you'll wonder if you are going the right way and be tempted to verify your destination with a fellow tourist you pass en route. Again, the location is what makes this theater so special. What an eye the Greeks had for beauty: the stage is set in such a way that the spectators look out across the mountains to the sea. The theater is mostly in ruins, but sit on one of the ancient benches, enjoy the beautiful surroundings, and imagine dramas that took place over 2,000 years ago.

Continue to **Palermo**. Palermo is a commercial, traffic-congested city, but there are some very interesting places to see both within the city and on its outskirts.

The most dramatic sightseeing excursion (just 8 kilometers south of Palermo) is to visit **Monreale**, an awesome cathedral built by William II in 1174. It seems that William II was visited in a dream by an angel who told him of a secret treasure, and with his new-found wealth he built Monreale, one of the world's greatest medieval monuments. From the outside, the cathedral doesn't look special, but just wait: the interior is stunning. When you step inside you find 130 panels of shimmering mosaic, illustrating stories from both the Old and the New Testaments. The bronze doors of the cathedral are spectacular, designed by Bonanno Pisano in the 12th century. This is a cathedral not to be missed.

Another sight near Palermo is **Monte Pellegrino**, a 600-meter mountain rising on the west edge of the city. There are several caves in the mountain. The **Grotta di Addaura** is a three-chamber cave with carvings dating to the Paleolithic Age. Another cave has been transformed into a chapel, the **Sanctuary of Santa Rosalia**, commemorating Santa Rosalia, the niece of King William II, who became a hermit—living and dying in this cave. You need to obtain permission from the National Archaeological Museum in Palermo if you want to visit these caves.

Another recommended side trip from Palermo is to visit the ancient fishing village of **Cefalù** built on a rocky peninsula about an hour's drive east from Palermo. Not only is this a very colorful fishing village, complete with brightly-hued boats and twisting narrow streets, but there is also a splendid Norman **Cathedral** built by King Roger II in the 12th century in fulfillment of a promise he made to God for sparing his life during a storm at sea.

From Palermo you can take one of the many flights to Rome, board a ferry to Naples, or complete your circle of Sicily by driving to Messina for the short ferry ride back to the mainland.

*Taormina, Greek Theater*

# *Places to Stay*

A pleasant, budget choice for touring the Veneto region is found just outside Padua at Casa Ciriani, a lovely pale-yellow rectangular-shaped home. Silvana and her mother, Mariantonia, thoroughly enjoy the international cultural exchange that their bed and breakfast business brings. Within the large family home, where Silvana grew up, are four simply decorated, homey guestrooms; which have been left pretty much as they were, complete with family photos, drawings, and other personal artifacts. Although the house is of newer construction, it has the feeling of an older home. All bedrooms except one (with a small terrace and a bathroom just outside the door) have an en suite bathroom. A bedroom with king bed, plus a twin bedroom combination with one bathroom, serves families well. Downstairs, guests have plenty of common space including a living room, large yard, and outside terrace overlooking the garden and grounds, where a breakfast of breads, cereals, fruit, cakes, and yogurt is served during summer. During the winter, two fireplaces create a cozy, intimate atmosphere. Casa Ciriani organizes wine tours, hill walks, spa visits, Italian language and cooking lessons. Frequent trains for Venice leave from town (5 km) and take 50 minutes. *Directions:* From the north, exit from A4 at Padova Ovest and follow signs for Abano (10 km); coming from Bologna on A13, exit at Terme Euganee. Silvana can send a map.

*CASA CIRIANI*
*Host: Silvana Ciriani*
*Via Guazzi 1*
*Abano Terme (PD) 35031, Italy*
*Tel & fax: (049) 715272, Cellphone: (368) 3779226*
*4 rooms, Double: €67–€80*
*Minimum nights required: 2*
*Open: all year*
*Other languages: good English*
*Region: Veneto, Michelin Map: 562*
*karenbrown.com/italy/ciriani.html*

In the heart of the wine valley of Piedmont, just above the town of Alba, lies the stately, cream-colored villa belonging to Giuliana Pionzo, her doctor husband Giuseppe, and sons Andrea and Fabrizio—Cascina Reine's warm and gracious hosts. Accommodation is offered within the ivy-covered main house, each room finely decorated with antiques, paintings, and the family's personal objects. A suite consisting of a bedroom, sitting room with two extra beds, bath, kitchenette, and large terrace is ideal for a family of four. Other equally charming rooms and apartments (one with facilities for the handicapped) are on the ground and first floors of the adjoining wing, one with its own private terrace. A full breakfast is served either outside under big umbrellas overlooking the vineyards and woods or inside in the pristine dining room with vaulted ceilings. A swimming pool is set in the best possible position taking in views over the city, soft hillsides, river valley, and distant Alps. Alba boasts some of the finest restaurants in Italy and is also famous for its regional wines and prized truffle festival. The Giacosas have a piece of land dedicated to experimentation (with Torino University) of the cultivation of truffles. *Directions:* From Alba's center follow signs for Barbaresco and Mango. Halfway up the hill on a large curve, watch for a small yellow sign indicating a gravel road on the left and then the wrought-iron gates of the property at the end of the road.

*CASCINA REINE (VILLA LA MERIDIANA)*
*Host: Giacosa family*
*Localita: Altavilla 9*
*Alba (CN) 12051, Italy*
*Tel & fax: (0173) 440112, Cellphone: (338) 4606527*
*5 rooms, Double: €85, 4 apartments: €85 daily*
*Minimum nights required: 2*
*Open: all year*
*Other languages: good English*
*Region: Piedmont, Michelin Map: 561*
*karenbrown.com/italy/cascinareine.html*

On the island's west coast you find the ancient port town of Alghero, Sardinia's lobster and coral capital. With origins dating back as far as 1100, the walled seaside village still preserves evidence of a strong Spanish influence. The road bordering the coast takes you past the archaeological site of Palmavera with its typical Nuraghi construction from the Bronze Age; the bay of Porto Conte with its nature park; and the Capo Caccia scenic point with the fascinating Nettuno cave. In the near vicinity is the Porticciolo agritourism farm, named after the ancient watchtower on the coast. The flat property made up of cultivated fields surrounds the family's simple white rectangular house and new restaurant. Like most farms in Sardinia, buildings are all of recent construction as the agritourism activity is in its beginning stages. Just behind the building that houses the restaurant are six separate guesthouses for four persons each with a bedroom, bathroom, loft bed, and living area with kitchenette, nicely appointed with wood furnishings and wrought-iron beds. The enormous glassed-in dining room with fireplace where fish and meats are grilled is where Maria and her entire family work together presenting delectable Sardinian specialties topped off with the island's myrtle-berry cordial. *Directions:* From Alghero (16 km) take the S.S.127 to Fertilla, go past Porto Conte bay, and turn right for S.M. La Palma. Turn left at the first road to Porticciolo.

*PORTICCIOLO*
*Host: Maria Angius family*
*Localita: Porticciolo*
*Alghero (SS) 07041, Italy*
*Tel & fax: (079) 918000, Cellphone: (347) 5231024*
*6 apartments: €620–€785 weekly*
*Open: May to Oct, Credit cards: all major*
*Other languages: very little English*
*Region: Sardinia, Michelin Map: 566*
*karenbrown.com/italy/porticciolo.html*

Seven kilometers from historic Bergamo and within easy reach of beautiful Lakes Como, Iseo, and Garda is the home of the region's agritourist former president, Gianantonio Ardizzone. On the property, next to the recently constructed residence where he and his family live, is a sprawling 15th-century farmhouse and barn quad complex of the type known in Lombardy as a cascina. Installed within the cascina are five guest apartments, each including one or two bedrooms, bathroom, and kitchen (though breakfast is served). The apartments are furnished modestly but comfortably, with a decidedly rustic ambiance. The cascina is nestled in pretty surroundings, looking onto the small town of Nese and backing onto the green hills where well-tended riding horses are kept. Gianantonio delights in showing guests his hobbies—a collection of antique farm tools, fruit orchard, and ostrich breeding—and wife Lalla takes care of guests' daily requests including dinner with prior confirmation. The Grumello offers self-catering, conveniently located accommodation and outstanding value. Your hosts are exceptionally helpful and sincerely warm. *Directions:* Exit from the A4 autostrada at Bergamo and follow signs for Alzano Lombardo, Valle Seriana. Exit at Alzano after 6 km and follow hospital signs; go straight on for Nese and turn left on Via Grumello after 300 meters.

*CASCINA GRUMELLO*
*Host: Gianantonio Ardizzone family*
*Localita: Fraz. Nese*
*Alzano Lombardo (BG) 24022, Italy*
*Tel: (035) 510060, Cellphone: (340) 2487185*
*Fax: (035) 738703*
*5 apartments: €60 double B&B*
*Open: all year, Credit cards: VS*
*Other languages: some English*
*Region: Lombardy, Michelin Map: 561*
*karenbrown.com/italy/grumello.html*

One of the most attractive features of Florence is that its surrounding countryside hugs the city limits, giving the possibility of staying in the tranquil foothills of Chianti. In the nearby village of Antella warm hosts Azelio and Luisa have completely restored their part of an enormous estate divided into three 14th-century villas. The downstairs area includes a large living/dining room, main kitchen, and separate kitchenette for guests' use during the day. The vaulted antique cantina below displays an enviable collection of reserve wines. Up a steep flight of stairs are the four well-appointed guestrooms, all with superb views over countryside all the way to Brunelleschi's cupola. Three regular doubles are individually decorated with country antiques and one has a hydrojet bathtub. The real treat is the large junior suite with its high wood-beamed mansard ceilings, sitting area, and canopy bed. Originally the outdoor loggia, it retains its columns and seven windows looking out to both sides of the property. A country breakfast is served either in the small breakfast room or in the garden. Do not miss a chance to sample one of Luisa's delectable Tuscan meals or, better yet, cooking lessons. *Directions:* Leave the A1 at Firenze Sud. After the toll, turn first right for Siena and after about 1.5 km turn left for Antella. In Antella the Via Montisoni starts from the square with the church on your left.

*VILLA IL COLLE*
*Hosts: Azelio & Luisa Pierattoni*
*Via Montisoni 45*
*Antella–Florence (FI) 50011, Italy*
*Tel & fax: (055) 621822, Cellphone: (347) 8778178*
*4 rooms, Double: €110–€160*
*Minimum nights required: 2*
*Open: all year, Credit cards: MC, VS*
*Other languages: good English*
*Region: Tuscany, Michelin Map: 563*
*karenbrown.com/italy/colle.html*

Borgo Argenina has all the elements of a "bestseller" bed and breakfast: the perfect location in the heart of Chianti surrounded by vineyards, very comfortable accommodation in an ancient stone farmhouse, glorious countryside views, and, above all, Elena, the Borgo Argenina's gregarious hostess. She left behind a successful fashion business in Milan and bought an entire abandoned village, restoring two of the stone houses for herself and the bed and breakfast. She chose the best artisans in the area and literally worked with them to create the house of her dreams. Everything from painting stenciled borders in rooms through restoring furniture to sewing quilted bedspreads was executed exclusively by Elena herself. The downstairs living rooms and breakfast room are beautifully done in rich cream and soft yellows that complement perfectly the brick-vaulted ceilings and terra-cotta floors. Elena is up at dawn baking cakes for breakfast accompanied by classical music. Every little detail has been attended to in the pink-and-blue bedrooms adorned with white eyelet curtains, patchwork quilts, and dried flower arrangements. Three bedrooms have kitchen facilities and across the way is a very comfortable three-bedroom, independent house. *Directions:* Follow S.S.408 from Siena for Montevarchi and after 15 km turn off to the right at Monti. Just before Monti and S. Marcellina there is a sign on the right for Argenina.

*BORGO ARGENINA*
*Host: Elena Nappa*
*Localita: Argenina-Monti*
*Argenina–Gaiole in Chianti (SI) 53013, Italy*
*Tel: (0577) 747117, Fax: (0577) 747228*
*7 rooms, Double: €150–€200*
*3 houses: €200–€ 400 daily, Minimum nights: 3*
*Open: all year, Credit cards: all major*
*Other languages: good English, French*
*Region: Tuscany, Michelin Map: 563*
*karenbrown.com/italy/argenina.html*

The delightful Malvarina farm with its charming, country-style accommodations, excellent local cuisine, warm and congenial host family, and ideal location has been a long-time favorite of our readers. Just outside town, yet immersed in lush green vegetation at the foot of the Subasio Mountains, the property is comprised of the 15th-century stone farmhouse where the family lives and four independent cottages (converted barn and stalls) divided into bedrooms and suites with en suite bathrooms, plus three apartments with kitchenettes for two to four persons. Casa Angelo has several bedrooms plus a sweet breakfast room with a corner fireplace and cupboards filled with colorful Deruta ceramics. Great care has obviously been taken in the decor of rooms, using Mamma's family's heirloom furniture. The old wine cellar has been cleverly converted into a cool and spacious taverna dining room with long wooden tables for dining en famille if not out on the veranda terrace. Cooking classes are very popular here. A collection of antique farm tools and brass pots cover walls near the enormous fireplace. Horses are available for three- to seven-day trekking trips into the scenic national park just beyond the house, led by gregarious host, Claudio. A welcome feature is a swimming pool. *Directions:* Exit at Rivotorto from the Perugia-Spello route 75. Turn right then left on Via Massera (Radio Subasio sign) and follow the road up to Malvarina.

*MALVARINA*
*Host: Claudio Fabrizi family*
*Localita: Malvarina 32*
*Assisi (PG) 06080, Italy*
*Tel & fax: (075) 8064280*
*10 rooms, Double: €93–€165, 3 apartments: €98 daily*
*Minimum nights required: 3*
*Open: all year, Credit cards: MC, VS*
*Other languages: some English*
*Region: Umbria, Michelin Map: 563*
*karenbrown.com/italy/malvarina.html*

Fabrizio and Bianca, the Milanese hosts originally from this part of Umbria, restored their inherited La Fornace farmhouse, situated in the very desirable location just 2km from Assisi, with their guests' comfort foremost in mind. With careful attention to detail, six comfortable apartments and two guestrooms were fashioned within the three stone houses. Each apartment has one or two bedrooms, bathroom, fully equipped kitchenette, and eating area. Interesting decorating touches such as parts of antique iron gates hung over beds, terra-cotta and white ceramic tiles in the immaculate bathrooms, and antique armoires give the accommodations a polished country flavor. Le Pannocchie includes a corner fireplace, while Papaveri looks out over the flat cornfields up to magnificent Assisi and the Subasio Mountains beyond. Anna and Franco look after guests when the owners are away. A small dining room has been created on the ground floor, next to the 18th-century wood oven, for morning breakfast. At guests' request guided tours are arranged to Umbria's top sights. Besides a lovely swimming pool for guests, a small gym, bikes, ping-pong, and games for children are on hand. *Directions:* From Perugia-Spoleto highway 75, exit at Ospedalicchio on route 147, turn left for Tordibetto after the bridge, then right for Assisi and follow signs for La Fornace.

*PODERE LA FORNACE*
*Hosts: Bianca & Fabrizio Feliciani*
*Via Ombrosa 3*
*Assisi, Tordibetto di (PG) 06081, Italy*
*Tel: (075) 8019537, Fax: (075) 8019630*
*2 rooms, Double: €80, 6 apartments: €55– €170 daily*
*Minimum nights required: 3*
*Closed: Jan & Feb, Credit cards: all major*
*Other languages: good English*
*Region: Umbria, Michelin Map: 563*
*karenbrown.com/italy/lafornace.html*

After many years of traveling to Italy at any opportunity, Jennie and Alan left England to move to Tuscany and fell in love immediately with Villa Mimosa, a rustic, 18th-century home with a shady front courtyard facing the village street and the church. They have created three sweet bedrooms and one attic mansard suite for four persons, each with a different theme and with lovely mountain views. A cozy sitting room and a library with grand piano are reserved upstairs for guests and decorated with the Pratts' own antiques imported from England. Jennie and Alan delight in sharing their passion for this part of the country known as Lunigiana (very near the Cinque Terre coastal area and one hour from both Parma and Lucca) and give their guests lots of personal attention, while making them feel right at home. Guests are treated to breakfast on the terrace overlooking the pretty garden and swimming pool with the Apennine Mountains as a backdrop and delight in Jennie's creative cuisine straight off the Aga, based on fresh garden vegetables and local recipes. Tea and homemade cakes are served in the shady garden. *Directions:* Leave the A15 autostrada (Parma-La Spezia) at Pontremoli from the north or Aulla from the south and head north alongside the autostrada S562 to Villafranca, then Bagnone. Enter town through the gateway, then over the bridge. Turn left for Corlaga, and the villa is on the right 50 meters before the church.

*VILLA MIMOSA*
*Hosts: Jennie & Alan Pratt*
*Localita: Corlaga*
*Bagnone (MS) 54021, Italy*
*Tel & fax: (0187) 427022, Cellphone: (335) 6264657*
*4 rooms, Double: €77–€105*
*Dinner served on request*
*Open: all year*
*Other languages: fluent English*
*Region: Tuscany, Michelin Map: 563*
*karenbrown.com/italy/mimosa.html*

Bagno Vignoni is a charming little village whose unique piazza is actually an ancient stone pool with thermal water. In medieval times the large bath was divided for men and women who came to soak in the rejuvenating waters, hoping to cure such ailments as arthritis and rheumatism. Today, tourists come to view this remarkable place and take advantage of these same curative properties in the nearby falls or modern pool facilities. With the success of their wine bar (enoteca) here, it was only natural that the young Marinis should open a bed and breakfast for travelers. The stone building dates to the 1300s and was thoughtfully restored after having been abandoned for more than 30 years. The eight double bedrooms and large living room with loft and grand piano are very cozy and purposely old-fashioned in feeling. The beamed guestrooms and pretty new bathrooms each have their own theme and corresponding soft pastel color schemes and are romantically appointed with lace curtains and pillows, antique beds and armoires, and painted stencil borders. Breakfast is served across the way in the historic enoteca, which was once part of the Capuchin friars' monastery. With its informal and warm hospitality, it is no wonder that the bar is a favorite place for artists and writers. *Directions:* Bagno Vignoni is 5 km south of San Quirico. Park in the town lot and walk the short distance to the locanda.

*LA LOCANDA DEL LOGGIATO*
*Hosts: Sabrina & Barbara Marini*
*Piazza del Moretto 30*
*Bagno Vignoni (SI) 53023, Italy*
*Tel: (0577) 888925, Cellphone: (335) 430427*
*Fax: (0577) 888370*
*8 rooms, Double: €130–€150*
*Open: all year, Credit cards: MC, VS*
*Other languages: some English, French*
*Region: Tuscany, Michelin Map: 563*
*karenbrown.com/italy/loggiato.html*

In the heart of the Veneto region, south of Vicenza, you find the Castello winery and estate, a handsome 15th-century villa watching proudly over the sweet town of Barbarano Vicentino and the home of the Marinoni family for the past century. Signora Elda, along with her two young children, Lorenzo and Maddalena, carries on the tradition. The large walled courtyard with manicured Renaissance garden is bordered by the family's home, the guesthouse (originally the farmer's quarters), and converted barn, where concerts and banquets are organized. A lovely courtyard overlooks the family's expansive vineyards from which top-quality (D.O.C.G.) red wines are produced. The independent two-story guesthouse overlooking the garden can be rented out as one house or divided into three apartments. Each apartment has one or two bedrooms, bathroom, and kitchenette with sitting area, and is decorated simply but pleasantly with the family's furnishings. This is an excellent, economical base from which to visit the beautiful Veneto region. It's an easy drive to Padua and Venice where you may opt to leave your car and take the train. *Directions:* Exit from the A4 at Vicenza Est towards Noventa Vicentino, then Barbarano Vicentino. From the center of town, follow signs to Il Castello (20 km total).

*IL CASTELLO*
*Host: Elda Marinoni family*
*Via Castello 6*
*Barbarano Vicentino (VI) 36021, Italy*
*Tel: (0444) 886055, Fax: (0444) 777140*
*3 apartments: €26.50–€29.50 daily (per person)*
*Minimum nights required: 7*
*Open: all year*
*Other languages: good English*
*Region: Veneto, Michelin Map: 562*
*karenbrown.com/italy/ilcastello.html*

The area around the city of Alba is true wine country, where vineyards cover every possible inch of land. Giovanna, an independent producer of wine, admirably manages her grandparents' farm and bed and breakfast single-handedly and has taken on the ultimate challenge of producing Barbaresco, Barbera, and Dolcetto wines right on the premises. Giovanna loves welcoming travelers who are looking for a home away from home, wholesome foods, and the simple pleasures of country life. The mustard-colored house backed by striped hillsides has a separate guest entrance. A large informal living room filled with books and local wine itineraries includes a corner kitchen where guests sit at a table for a self-service breakfast. Upstairs are the three country-style bedrooms. The pink room has twin beds and a vineyard view while the green and blue rooms have queen beds. They each have new, immaculate bathrooms, and are decorated with grandmother's lace curtains, old photographs, brass beds, and patchwork quilts. Four similarly appointed apartments are situated on two floors in a wing off the main house. Also organized are truffle hunts, and participation in the wine harvest activities. *Directions:* From Alba (6 km) drive towards Barbaresco. Before town, at the sign for Tre Stelle, look for the B&B on the left. From Asti follow signs for Alba-Barbaresco–Treiso. After Barbaresco, on the road for Alba, watch for Tre Stelle and the B&B on the right.

*CASCINA DELLE ROSE*
*Host: Giovanna Rizzolio*
*Localita: Tre Stelle, Barbaresco (CN) 12050, Italy*
*Tel: (0173) 638292, Fax: (0173) 638322*
*3 rooms, Double: €85–€100*
*4 apartments: €530–€990 weekly, €85–€160 daily*
*Minimum nights required: 2, 4 in apartments*
*Open: all year, Credit cards: all major*
*Other languages: good English, French, German*
*Region: Piedmont, Michelin Map: 561*
*karenbrown.com/italy/dellerose.html*

La Casa Sola is just that—an ancient villa standing alone atop a hill on a gorgeous 400-acre vineyard estate in the heart of Chianti. The gracious proprietors and hosts, the Gambaro family, produce prestigious Chianti Classico Riserva, Supertuscan-Montarsiccio, and extra-virgin olive oil of the highest quality. There are six large guest apartments on two floors of a rose-covered stone farmhouse down the road from the main villa. All the apartments consist of a living room, kitchen, bedrooms, and baths, with private entrances and garden (with flowers to match the color scheme of each apartment!). The apartments (numbers 3 and 5 being the loveliest) are furnished stylishly with selected country antiques, and details such as botanical prints hung with bows, eyelet curtains, fresh flowers, and a bottle of wine are welcome touches. Number 5, for up to eight people, is the most spacious, with four bedrooms, a fireplace, and magnificent views over the Barberino Valley and cypress woods. Il Capanno in the converted barn is a delightful "nest" for honeymooners. An inviting swimming pool overlooks the valley surrounding the main villa. Wine-cellar visits with wine tasting are organized once a week and marked hiking trails lead guests through picture-perfect landscapes. *Directions:* Leave the Florence-Siena superstrada at San Donato in Poggio. 1.5 km after San Donato at the church, turn right for Cortine/Casa Sola, and drive for 2.5 km.

*FATTORIA CASA SOLA*
*Host: Count Gambaro family*
*Localita: Cortine, Barberino Val d'Elsa (FI) 50021, Italy*
*Tel: (055) 8075028, Fax: (055) 8059194*
*6 apartments: €540–€2,150 weekly (Jul & Aug),*
*€70–€84 daily (2 people)*
*Heating and cleaning extra, Minimum nights required: 2*
*Open: all year, Credit cards: all major*
*Other languages: good English, French, Spanish*
*Region: Tuscany, Michelin Map: 563*
*karenbrown.com/italy/fattoriacasasola.html*

Strategically positioned midway between Siena and Florence sits the square stone farmhouse with cupola (actually one of the bedrooms!) dating to 1700 owned by Gianni and Cristina, a couple who have dedicated their lives to the equestrian arts. The Paretaio appeals particularly to visitors with a passion for horseback riding, for the de Marchis offer everything from basic riding lessons to dressage training, and day outings through the gorgeous surrounding countryside. In fact, the Paretaio is recognized as one of the top riding "ranches" in Tuscany, with more than 30 horses. On the ground floor is a rustic living room with country antiques, comfy sofas, and piano enhanced by a vaulted brick ceiling and worn terra-cotta floors, off which are two bedrooms. Upstairs, the main gathering area is the dining room, which features a massive fireplace and a seemingly endless wooden table. This room gives access to more bedrooms, each decorated with touches such as dried flowers, white lace curtains, and, of course, equestrian prints. A vast collection of over 300 pieces with an equestrian theme is displayed about the home. Il Paretaio also organizes courses in Italian and is an excellent base for touring the heart of Tuscany. The swimming pool gives splendid views over olive groves and vineyards. *Directions:* Head south from Barberino on route 2 and after 2 km take the second right-hand turnoff for San Filippo. Continue on 1.5 km of dirt road to the house.

*IL PARETAIO*
*Hosts: Cristina & Giovanni de Marchi*
*Localita: San Filippo*
*Barberino Val d'Elsa (FI) 50021, Italy*
*Tel: (055) 8059218, Fax: (055) 8059231*
*8 rooms, Double: €70–€120,*
*2 apartments: €400–€1,250 weekly*
*Per person half board: €67–€75*
*Open: all year, Other languages: good English, French*
*Region: Tuscany, Michelin Map: 563*
*karenbrown.com/italy/ilparetaio.html*

The Mulino dell'Argenna, a 16th-century grain mill miraculously transformed into an elegant bed and breakfast, sits among woods along a small river. Cordial hosts Liliana and Pierpaolo took on the challenging project of restoring the stone mill. Pierpaolo provided the know-how, having worked on the restoration of homes for many years, while Liliana added style in her careful selection of antiques, rich fabrics, and soft color schemes in rooms. Five romantic bedrooms accessed from the exterior of the mill have smart travertine bathrooms and many hotel amenities, with special touches such as embroidered linen sheets. The charm of the home comes not only from its decor, but also from its being built on different levels with terraces, balconies, and archways leading to private corners. Behind the house is an enchanting apartment, Il Mulinetto, a miniature version of the mill, with a one-bedroom loft, kitchenette, and terrace. Breakfast is served in bedrooms, out on private patios, or in the intimate dining room. Divine four-course gourmet dinners are accompanied by a very selective list of wines. Close to the house is a large swimming pool with Jacuzzi. This property lends itself well for a full-house rental by the week for family reunions. *Directions:* Exit at S. Donato from the Florence-Siena highway and after S. Donato town follow signs for Castellina. Turn left at the second road after the La Ripa sign at km 9.5. (Located near the main road.)

*RELAIS MULINO DELL'ARGENNA*
*Hosts: Liliana Cajelli & Pierpaolo Porcù*
*Localita: S. Silvestro 17*
*Barberino Val d'Elsa (FI) 50021, Italy*
*Tel: (055) 8072354, Fax: (055) 8072310*
*5 rooms, Double: €114–€145*
*1 apartment: €1,291–€1,808 weekly*
*Minimum nights required: 3*
*Closed: Nov to Mar, Other languages: very little English*
*Region: Tuscany, Michelin Map: 563*
*karenbrown.com/italy/dellargenna.html*

When the Caccettas and three other families purchased the 250-acre property more than 20 years ago, they were true pioneers in agritourism. After many years of restoring both the land and historic 16th-century hunting lodge, today they have a self-sufficient organic farm producing top-quality Chianti, white and rosé wines, grappa, and virgin olive oil, and the first in Europe to be awarded certification (Uni En Iso) as an "organic agricultural park" for quality level and comprehensive agritouristic activity. Spacious guestrooms are divided between the main house, with two suites and three bedrooms, and an adjacent house. All are decorated with care and attention to detail using lovely family antiques, which blend in perfectly with the overall refined ambiance. The very cozy common rooms include a living room with fireplace and stone walls, card room, small bar area, and dining rooms where breakfast and dinner are served. During the warmer months a buffet breakfast and dinner are served outside under the pergola overlooking deep woods. A set four-course dinner consists of traditional Tuscan recipes using primarily fresh vegetables and herbs. A swimming pool, grass tennis courts, many hiking trails, and horseback riding at a nearby stables are all available. *Directions:* From the Siena-Florence highway, exit at San Donato, drive to Tavarnelle then Barberino, and turn right at Via XXV Aprile the La Spinosa sign. Take the dirt road to the very end.

*LA SPINOSA*
*Hosts: Caccetta, Presezzi, Ossola & Videsott families*
*Via Le Masse 8, Barberino Val d'Elsa (FI) 50021, Italy*
*Tel: (055) 8075413, Fax: (055) 8066214*
*9 rooms, Double: €150–€180*
*Per person half board: €115–€130*
*Minimum nights required: 2*
*Open: Mar to Nov, Credit cards: MC, VS*
*Other languages: good English*
*Region: Tuscany, Michelin Map: 563*
*karenbrown.com/italy/laspinosa.html*

The Bad Dreikirchen is situated up in the Dolomite foothills with an enchanting view over a lush green valley and distant snowcapped mountain peaks. The young and energetic Wodenegg family works diligently at making guests feel at home in their lovely residence and at running the busy restaurant, which serves typical local meals to non-guest patrons as well as guests since it shares the site of a unique historical monument—Le Tre Chiese, three curious, attached, miniature medieval churches. This unique inn is accessible only by taxi or Jeep, or on foot. An exhilarating half-hour hike takes you up to the typical mountain-style chalet with long wood balconies in front. The most charming rooms are those in the older section, entirely wood-paneled, with fluffy comforters and old-fashioned washbasins. The rambling house has several common areas for guests as well as a swimming pool. This is truly an incredible spot, near the Siusi Alps and Val Gardena where some of the best climbing in Europe can be found. *Directions:* Exit from the Bolzano-Brennero autostrada A22 at Chiusa, cross the river, and take S.S.12 south to Ponte Gardena. Take the road on the right up to Barbian and call the hotel from the village for a pickup by Jeep (€12).

*BAD DREIKIRCHEN*
*Hosts: Annette & Matthias Wodenegg family*
*San Giacomo 6*
*Barbian (BZ) 39040, Italy*
*Tel: (0471) 650055, Fax: (0471) 650044*
*30 rooms, Double: €68–€104*
*Per person half board: €95–€131*
*Open: May 4 to Oct 26, Credit cards: MC, VS*
*Other languages: good English*
*Region: Trentino-Alto Adige, Michelin Map: 562*
*karenbrown.com/italy/baddreikirchen.html*

Just 2 kilometers outside Barolo in the area where the famous wine is produced sits the long, rectangular, antique-pink-colored farmhouse of Raffaella Pittatore, passed down to her from her grandparents. After years of working for a major tour-operator company and living in many parts of the world, she came back home with her young son to impart her hospitality experience to her own guests. She is a natural hostess, friendly and accommodating, with a joie de vivre that is truly refreshing. One year after opening, four bedrooms in the attached former barn were added to those already existing on the first floor. These are simply furnished with the family's country furniture and each has its own bathroom. One also has a kitchenette. Downstairs you find an informal living room and breakfast room with original brick ceilings and floors. Guests can use the kitchen or barbecue, if desired, and breakfast is served out on the front patio in fine weather. Although there are no particular views, the crossroads location is convenient for touring this beautiful Piedmont wine country, the price economical, and the hospitality exceptional. Raffaella has put together many interesting local itineraries including quaint villages, castles, wine museums, and vineyards. *Directions:* From Alba (10 km) follow signs for Barolo and at the turnoff stay to the left. The entrance to the bed and breakfast is on the right-hand side of the road just at this fork.

*IL GIOCO DELL'OCA*  €80
*Host: Raffaella Pittatore*
*Via Crosia 46*
*Barolo (CN) 12060, Italy*
*Tel & fax: (0173) 56206, Cellphone: (338) 5999426*
*6 rooms, Double: €60–€70*
*1 apartment*
*Open: Mar to Dec, Credit cards: MC, VS*
*Other languages: very little English*
*Region: Piedmont, Michelin Map: 561*
*karenbrown.com/italy/ilgioco.html*

*[handwritten: double €75, 4 beds? €110]*

The expansive Pomurlo farm, home to the congenial Minghelli family, covers 370 acres of hills, woods, and open fields and is an excellent base for touring Umbria. A winding dirt road leads to the typical stone house, which contains a restaurant featuring organically grown, farm-fresh specialties. An antique cupboard and old farm implements on the walls enhance the rustic setting. A nearby converted stall houses two adorable independent rooms looking out over the lake. Other guestrooms and apartments are found in two large hilltop homes commanding a breathtaking view of the entire valley with its grazing herds of longhorn cattle. The main house, a 12th-century tower fortress where the inn's personable hostess Daniela resides, accommodates guests in three additional suites of rooms. Breakfast fixings are provided in rooms. The acquisition of the neighboring property has resulted in a center (Le Casette) offering more service— two stone farmhouses containing several other rooms and a restaurant around a large swimming pool. Comfortable and cheerful, all rooms are decorated with wrought-iron beds, colorful bedspreads, and typical regional country antiques. Activities such as tennis, soccer, and mountain biking are available. *Directions:* The farm is conveniently located near the Rome-Florence autostrada. Take the Orvieto exit from the A1 and follow signs for Todi, not for Baschi. On route S.S.448 turn right at the sign for Pomurlo.

*POMURLO VECCHIO*
*Hosts: Lazzaro Minghelli & family*
*Localita: Lago di Corbara,*
*Baschi (TR) 05023, Italy*
*Tel: (0744) 950190 or 957645, Fax: (0744) 950500*
*30 rooms, Double: €32.50–€37.50*
*Minimum nights required: 3, 7 July & Aug*
*Open: all year, Credit cards: MC, VS*
*Other languages: some English, French*
*Region: Umbria, Michelin Map: 563*
*karenbrown.com/italy/pomurlovecchio.html*

Only 30 kilometers from Milan, the Cascina Caremma is the pure definition of agritourism: a 100-acre working farm using strictly organic methods; offering accommodation and meals using produce from the farm, and organizing lessons in organic production and the agri-ecosystem. It is also part of the Ticino River Park reserve, which can be explored by bike, horse, or foot only. This typical northern Italian cascina is a quad formation with large inner courtyard lined with multi-colored houses, stalls, and barns. Over the years the very involved hosts have vastly improved the comfort level and charming decor of the accommodations, which are situated in two colorful side-by-side houses. Cheerful, air-conditioned rooms have country furnishings and beamed ceilings and are accented with matching floral curtains and bedspreads. The delightful downstairs dining rooms maintain their true country flavor with antiques, fireplace, and ancient wood-burning oven. On weekends people from the city come to enjoy the excellent, wholesome meals. A new well-being center offers an indoor pool, steam bath, sauna, and yoga classes. Within reach are Malpensa airport and the lake region. *Directions:* Exit the A7 (Genova-Milano) at Binasco and head towards Casorate Primo, Besate. In the small town of Besate look for a sign for the cascina and follow this country road for 2 km to the farm.

*CASCINA CAREMMA*
*Host: Gabriele Corti family*
*Strada per il Ticino*
*Besate (MI) 20080, Italy*
*Tel & fax: (02) 9050020, Cellphone: (348) 3049848*
*14 rooms, Double: €100–€120*
*Per person half board: €55, Dinner Thur to Sun only*
*Closed: Aug, Credit cards: all major*
*Other languages: good English*
*Region: Lombardy, Michelin Map: 561*
*karenbrown.com/italy/cascinacaremma.html*

The Locanda, a pale-yellow and brick house dating from 1830, sits on the border between Tuscany and Umbria and is an excellent base from which to explore this rich countryside. The villa's dining room features a vaulted ceiling in toast-colored brick, an enormous fireplace, French windows opening out to the flower garden, and antiques including a cupboard adorned with the family's blue-and-white china. The upstairs quarters are reserved primarily for guests, and contain five comfortable rooms all off one hallway and an inviting sitting room and library. The cozy bedrooms have mansard ceilings, armoires, lovely linens, and washbasins. Additional guestrooms are located on the ground floor of the converted barn between the house and a small garden, where a swimming pool has been added. These are more spacious, private, and modern in decor. Cordial hostess Palmira assists with local itineraries. Excellent regional fare including divine vegetarian dishes with local produce is prepared by Chef, Walter Redaelli. Siena is only 45 kilometers away, and the quaint medieval and Renaissance villages of Pienza, Montepulciano, and Montalcino are close by. *Directions:* Exit from the Rome-Florence autostrada at Val di Chiana. Head toward Bettolle, then bear right toward Siena. Follow signs for La Bandita.

*LOCANDA LA BANDITA*
*Host: Palmira Fiorini*
*Via Bandita 72*
*Bettolle (SI) 53040, Italy*
*Tel & fax: (0577) 624649, Cellphone: (335) 6945920*
*8 rooms, Double: €85–€105*
*No dinner Tue*
*Open: Mar to Dec, Credit cards: all major*
*Other languages: good English*
*Region: Tuscany, Michelin Map: 563*
*karenbrown.com/italy/locandalabandita.html*

The vast Torre Burchio property is immersed in 1,500 acres of wooded wildlife preserve where wild boar, deer, hare, and pheasant abound. Seemingly far away from "civilization," this Italian version of a ranch offers a relaxing holiday in close touch with nature, while still being in reach of Umbria's top sights. The reception, restaurant, and six guest bedrooms are within the main 18th-century farmhouse, which maintains the ambiance of the original hunting lodge with hunting trophies on the walls, large open fireplace, cozy living room, and library. The upstairs breakfast room, from which the bedrooms lead, is lined with colorful Deruta ceramics. An additional ten bedrooms are found in a single-story house just across from the lodge, while the very comfortable apartments with kitchenettes are in a beautifully restored 230-year-old stone house with inner courtyard 4 kilometers down the road. The rooms and apartments are very nicely appointed with antiques, pretty fabrics, paintings, and large bathrooms, and have telephones and televisions. Guests gather in the busy restaurant in the evening for a hearty meal based on organic products from the farm. Many activities such as cooking classes, horseback-riding weeks, and sports are available. *Directions:* 20 km from either Perugia or Assisi. From the center of Bettona, follow signs for 5 Cerri-Torre Burchio and follow the dirt road through the woods for 5 km to the main house/reception.

*TORRE BURCHIO*
*Host: Alvaro Sfascia*
*Bettona (PG) 06084, Italy*
*Tel: (075) 9885017, Fax: (075) 987150*
*16 rooms, Double: €77–€104,*
*13 apartments: €672–€878 weekly*
*Minimum nights required: 3, 7 in high season*
*Closed: Jan, Credit cards: all major*
*Other languages: good English*
*Region: Umbria, Michelin Map: 563*
*karenbrown.com/italy/burchio.html*

Luisa and Sergio left their fashion business in Parma and settled in this peaceful and varied landscape 3 kilometers from the coast after the stone farmhouse was extensively restored. The stylish, impeccable home clearly reflects the personalities of the warm and reserved hosts who themselves tastefully designed both the exterior and interiors. Each of the four corner bedrooms upstairs has its own large private terrace and beautiful floral-tiled bathroom and all offer beds made with linen sheets and splendid views over fruit orchards and olive groves to the sea. While the hosts occupy the cupola, guests have a separate entrance to the upstairs rooms, giving utmost privacy to all. Common areas include the living room and open kitchen with large arched window and doors looking out to the surrounding garden. An ample fresh country breakfast with cakes all prepared by Luisa is served here. A separate cottage next to the main house offers a double room and beamed living room with stone fireplace and kitchen, and a second apartment is available within another cottage. Day trips include Elba Island, Volterra and San Gimignano, Lucca, Siena, private beaches, Etruscan itineraries, visits to the wine estates of Bolgheri, and biking in the nearby nature park. *Directions:* Exit from Aurelia on route 1 at Bibbona and turn left. Pass through La California and turn left for Bibbona. Podere Le Mezzelune is before town, well marked to the left. Pisa airport is 40 km away.

*PODERE LE MEZZELUNE*
*Hosts: Luisa & Sergio Chiesa*
*Via Mezzelune 126, Bibbona (LI) 57020, Italy*
*Tel: (0586) 670266, Fax: (0586) 671814*
*4 rooms, Double: €166–€176*
*2 apartments: €166– €176 daily*
*Minimum nights required: 3*
*Open: all year, Credit cards: MC, VS*
*Other languages: French*
*Region: Tuscany, Michelin Map: 563*
*karenbrown.com/italy/mezzelune.html*

This guide includes some small urban hotels for the convenience of travelers who would like to do some metropolitan sightseeing. For some reason, the city of Bologna is often bypassed by visitors, despite its rich past, beautiful historic center, arcaded streets, and elegant shops. Cristina, Serena, and Mauro Orsi, the owners of the splendid, four-star Hotel Corona d'Oro, mentioned in another of our guides, Italy: Charming Inns & Itineraries, own two other centrally located, smaller hotels: the Orologio and the Commercianti. Just steps away from Bologna's main piazza and Basilica you find the nicely renovated Orologio, so-called because it looks onto city hall with its clock tower. The reception desk on the ground floor leads upstairs to a large sitting and dining room where a buffet breakfast is served. From this level there is an elevator up to the guestrooms with their lovely antiques, fabric walls, and white and gray marble bathrooms. The elegantly decorated rooms have all amenities and most have views of the square. Bicycles are available free of charge to our readers to visit the city's historical center and main monuments. The owners also organize personalized cooking classes, tickets for special events, and private tours of Bologna and surrounding cities. *Directions:* Located in the heart of the old city. Private garage facilities are available upon reservation (restricted traffic in historical center).

*HOTEL OROLOGIO*
*Manager: Cristina Orsi*
*Via IV Novembre 10*
*Bologna 40123, Italy*
*Tel: (051) 745 7411, Fax: (051) 745 7422*
*34 rooms, Double: €179–€320*
*mini-flat from €270– €454*
*Open: all year, Credit cards: all major*
*Other languages: good English*
*Region: Emilia-Romagna, Michelin Map: 562*
*karenbrown.com/italy/hotelorologio.html*

Bolsena is a quaint, ancient village 18 kilometers from Orvieto right on picturesque Lake Bolsena with its small ports and two islands. Marco Zammarano, with his long hotelier experience in Rome, took over the family's 60-acre hillside farm property just above town and opened lovely bed and breakfast accommodation offering utter tranquillity. The main stone farmhouse holds eleven beamed bedrooms each with en suite bathroom, satellite TV, and fridge, simply but comfortably appointed with a mix of wicker furniture and country antiques. All but two have gorgeous views over the manicured garden and swimming pool out to the lake. Four bedrooms are found farther up the wooded road in another house with its own swimming pool and there is a third residence with an additional twelve rooms. Two apartments are available within yet another separate building. A restaurant for guests only has an ample outside terrace enjoying sunsets over the lake and takes advantage of ingredients fresh from the farm. Here you have the convenience of being near town and many interesting Etruscan sights, while the lake itself offers many activities including a fascinating boat ride to the small, historic island of Bisentina. *Directions:* Exit the A1 autostrada at Orvieto and follow signs for Bolsena. Just before town at the Trattoria Castagneta, turn right up to La Riserva. Shuttle service is available from the Rome airport or Orvieto train station.

*LA RISERVA MONTEBELLO*
*Host: Marco Zammarano*
*Strada Orvietana km 3*
*Bolsena (VT) 01023, Italy*
*Tel & fax: (0761) 798965, Cellphone: (335) 5310801*
*27 rooms, Double: €102–€112*
*Per person half board: €65–€81*
*Closed: Jan, Credit cards: all major*
*Other languages: good English*
*Region: Lazio, Michelin Map: 563*
*karenbrown.com/italy/lariservamontebello.html*

The prestigious Monsignor della Casa property extending over 600 acres is a true country resort with all the trimmings in the beautiful area north of Florence called Mugello. This is the land from which such masters as Giotto, Cimabue, and Fra Angelico came and was the actual home of 15th-century writer and Vatican secretary, della Casa, whose portrait hangs in Washington's National Gallery. The Marzi family meticulously restored a cluster of six stone farmhouses on the vast estate next to their own stately villa. The refined bi-level apartments exude pure Tuscan charm and can accommodate from two to six guests. Two individual villas, each with private swimming pool, can take a group of eight to sixteen. The finest linens and fabrics were chosen to accent exposed stone walls, brick floors, and wood-beamed ceilings. Spend your days touring or in any of a variety of activities for every age and interest-biking, hiking, or horseback riding in the nearby woods, golf, swimming in one of two pools, tennis, volleyball, and children's playground. An elegantly rustic restaurant and wine bar serves guests in the evening with cordial host Alessio making sure nothing is overlooked. The "wellness center" offers sauna, steam bath, Jacuzzi, and other services. Indulge! *Directions:* From Borgo San Lorenzo follow signs for Faenza. Just after the turnoff for Scarperia turn right for Mucciano, coming first to the resort (3 km total). 27 km from Florence.

*MONSIGNOR DELLA CASA*
*Host: Marzi family*
*Via di Mucciano 16, Borgo San Lorenzo (FI) 50032, Italy*
*Tel: (055) 840821, Fax: (055) 8408240*
*21 apartments: €415–€2,625 weekly, €145–€545 daily*
*2 villas: €1,590–€4,600 weekly, Breakfast not included*
*Minimum nights required: 2, 7 in high season*
*Open: all year, Credit cards: AX, MC, VS*
*Other languages: good English*
*Region: Tuscany, Michelin Map: 563*
*karenbrown.com/italy/monsignor.html*

The town of Brisighella is a gem and comes to life during the first weekend of July with its annual Medieval Festival when games of the period are re-enacted, and medieval music, literature, and dance are produced. Locals attire themselves in appropriate costume and torches illuminate the village's narrow streets nightly for the occasion. Just out of town sits the sweet farmhouse of Ettore (a former architect) and Adriana, with its 25 acres of organically cultivated vineyards and orchards. Guests can learn about the production of the hosts' excellent Sangiovese and Chardonnay wines. The renovated barn next to their small brick house holds two guestrooms and a rustic dining area with exposed beams and a large fireplace where guests gather for typical Romagna-style meals. A third bedroom is within their own home and the ex-barn provides two cozy apartments for two to five people. Breakfast is served out on the covered terrace overlooking a quiet valley lined with vineyards. Rooms are decorated with simple country furnishings. The atmosphere is casual and the value excellent. "Must sees" are the mosaics in Ravenna, Bologna's historical center, and the international ceramic museum in Faenza. La Torre golf club is 8 kilometers away. *Directions:* Take the Faenza exit from the A14 between Bologna and Rimini, follow signs for Brisighella or Florence. At town turn left for Terme/Modigliana. Il Palazzo is on the left after the Hotel Terme.

*IL PALAZZO*
*Host: Ettore Matarese family*
*Via Baccagnano 11, Brisighella (RA) 48013, Italy*
*Tel & fax: (0546) 80338*
*3 rooms, Double: €62–€68*
*2 apartments: €100–€130 daily*
*Minimum nights required: 3*
*Open: Mar to Oct, Credit cards: all major*
*Other languages: good English*
*Region: Emilia-Romagna, Michelin Map: 562*
*karenbrown.com/italy/ilpalazzo.html*

Tall cypress trees protect the cluster of ancient stone farmhouses making up the idyllic Iesolana property, situated atop 300 acres of cascading vineyards, olive groves, and sunflowers, with 360 degrees of breathtaking Tuscan views. After years of meticulous restoration of the three ochre-stained houses, eight high-level apartments are offered, most with private terraces. Apartments have from one to four bedrooms and are elegantly appointed with rustic furnishings, country fabrics, and modern kitchens and baths that harmonize beautifully with the cool stone floors and original wood-beamed ceilings. Among the many services available are individual telephones, satellite TV, barbecue facilities, swimming pool, and mountain bikes for leisurely rides. The impeccable landscape is studded with terra-cotta pots overflowing with brightly colored geraniums. The fabulously restored barn now hosts a stylish wine bar for tastings of Iesolana's own wines, oils, and honey. Breakfast and dinners of regional cuisine are also served in the comfortable restaurant with outdoor seating as an option. A state-of-the-art meeting room is available for groups. Centrally located for day trips to Siena, Florence, and Rome, this is the perfect spot for relaxing and exploring. *Directions:* Leave the A1 at Valdarno for Montevarchi, Bucine (8 km). From town follow signs up to Iesolana, passing over a stone bridge (2 km) to the end of the road.

*BORGO IESOLANA*
*Host: Giovanni Toscano*
*Localita: Iesolana, Bucine (AR) 52021, Italy*
*Tel: (055) 992988, Fax: (055) 992879*
*8 apartments: €490–€2,100 weekly, €130–€380 daily\**
*\*Breakfast not included: €10*
*Minimum nights required: 2, 7 in high season*
*Open: all year, Credit cards: all major*
*Other languages: good English*
*Region: Tuscany, Michelin Map: 563*
*karenbrown.com/italy/iesolana.html*

The Ripolina farm property is a vast 500-acre farm comprised of several different brick farmhouses. Self-catering apartments (two for up to ten people) and individual guest bedrooms are divided among five farmhouses dotting the soft hills of the property. Two very charmingly authentic apartments are found within the Pieve di Piana, a cluster of houses grouped around an ancient church with bell tower dating to the 9th century. The richly historic Pieve sits on a hill and enjoys panoramic views of vineyards and fields of grain and sunflowers extending as far as the eye can see. Hostess and owner Laura Cresti resides in the house called S. Ferdinando where there are two apartments with two bedrooms with a separate entrance. Five rooms are next door in the Ripoli house, each being individually appointed with appropriate country local antiques. Walls are painted in warm earth colors and the upstairs loggia, a typical open porch with four large arched windows, has been enclosed and transformed into the breakfast room. A full country breakfast buffet includes fresh coffee cakes, fruit, cereals, yogurt, and cheeses. This is strikingly beautiful countryside chock-full of hilltowns to explore. A beautiful swimming pool and bicycles are available for guests. *Directions:* From Siena (25 km) take the S.S.2 to Buonconvento and turn right in town following signs for Bibbiano. After crossing the river, turn right at La Ripolina and drive up to the main house.

*LA RIPOLINA*
*Host: Laura Cresti*
*Pieve di Piana*
*Buonconvento (SI) 53022, Italy*
*Tel & fax: (0577) 282280, Cellphone: (335) 5739284*
*7 rooms, Double: €75–€90*
*7 apartments: €35–€55 daily (per person)*
*Open: all year, Credit cards: MC, VS*
*Other languages: good English, French*
*Region: Tuscany, Michelin Map: 563*
*karenbrown.com/italy/laripolina.html*

With only a handful of hotels in Sicily meeting the charming, historic ambience category, the agriturismo route is definitely growing, many appearing in just the past 3 years. On the northwest corner of the island around Trapani, an ideal touring base for the island, a group of owners have transformed their ancient, ancestral baglio farm properties into accommodation for guests. Typically, the stone-walled structure with large, inner courtyard housed everything from the family residence, farmer's quarters, oil and wine press, to barns and stalls. The Baglio Fontana farm dates from the late 1700s and has been restored with care by the original Fontana family from Trapani. On the outskirts of a rather unappealing town, the huge, front doors of this fortress farm open to a stone courtyard. The courtyard leads to a large, rustic, beamed dining room with fireplace, and an ancient oil stone press, where dishes from typical, local recipes using all local farm products are served to guests. The austere, main villa has 6 guestrooms. Additional loft bedrooms and ground floor apartments are located in another section. The farm still produces wine, honey, and olive oil. Comfortable rooms, all with air conditioning, have new wood furnishings, bathrooms, and smart plaid fabrics. A cozy living room in the main villa, decorated with family antiques and paintings, is where guests gather after dinner to chat. An inviting pool is found in the large garden.

❋ ⚓ 🛏 ⚓ [CREDIT] ☎ 🐾 👭 P ⁕ ⚓ ♿

*BAGLIO FONTANA       New*
*Host: Di Vita family*
*Via Palermo, Buseto Palizzolo, Sicily (TP) 91012, Italy*
*Tel: (0923) 855000, Cellphone:(360) 870713*
*Fax: (0923) 24383*
*11 rooms, Double: €70–€100*
*Minimum nights required: 2*
*Open: all year, Credit cards: all major*
*Other languages: good English*
*Region: Sicily, Michelin Map: 565*
*karenbrown.com/italy/bagliofontana.html*

We recommend the Piccolo Golf hotel in order to offer the less-adventurous traveler a more classic accommodation than the rather spartan agritourism choices of the region. It is also a more reasonable alternative to the expensive hotels for which the Emerald Coast is so famous. Beautifully positioned, the peach-colored stone hotel immersed in Mediterranean vegetation overlooks the Pevero Golf Club to one side and the bay of Cala di Volpe to the other. This is a more secluded and peaceful area of the Emerald Coast, with small, hidden coves and rocky beaches, between the more famous towns of Porto Cervo and Porto Rotondo. The large reception and bar area have wicker furnishings and lead out to the surrounding garden and swimming pool. To the right of the entrance is a simple veranda dining room where regional meals are served. Bedrooms are practical and basic, with light-blue bedspreads and trimmings accenting cream-colored walls. Rooms have either garden or sea views (slightly higher rate), with the top-floor rooms catching glimpses of the turquoise-blue sea, which is very reminiscent of the Caribbean. This is a perfect location for viewing the coast or exploring the more rugged interior landscapes of the island—the "real" Sardinia. *Directions:* 30 km from Olbia airport. Drive towards Palau and turn off right for Porto Cervo then right again for Capricciolo. Cala di Volpe is 4 km before town and the hotel is opposite the luxurious Hotel Cala di Volpe.

*IL PICCOLO GOLF*
*Host: Mario Azzena*
*Localita: Cala di Volpe*
*Cala di Volpe, Porto Cervo (SS) 07020, Italy*
*Tel: (0789) 96520, Fax: (0789) 96565*
*17 rooms, Double: €73–€207*
*Minimum nights required: 15*
*Open: all year, Credit cards: AX, VS*
*Other languages: some English*
*Region: Sardinia, Michelin Map: 566*
*karenbrown.com/italy/piccolo.html*

British expatriate Jane Ridd settled in the wild west of Sardinia many years ago and with her husband took over the family cheese farm. The 150-acre property consists of cork woods, vineyards, and pastures where livestock, mostly sheep, roam. Over the years, Jane has gained fame, and Michelin mention, for her completely homemade local Gallura cuisine using primarily the farm's own products. Below the dining room local women can be seen working away in an enormous kitchen creating gnocchi and a variety of pastas of all shapes, and filling ravioli with a selection of ricotta and cheeses made right on the farm. Two rustic dining rooms, one open-air for summer months, accommodate many culinary enthusiasts who gather here. Completely immersed in the trees, the four guestrooms are in an attached section of the restaurant almost carved out of the enormous granite rock that backs the property. Their decor is very basic and practical, with white walls, double beds (one is a quadruple), armoires, and new bathrooms. Besides interesting nature hikes and the nearby sea, one can explore inland local towns and follow fascinating archaeological itineraries (there are over 6,000 examples of the prehistoric round stone structures of the Bronze-Age Nuraghi civilization on the island). *Directions:* From Olbia (20 km away) head for Tempio-Calangianus, turn right at the top of Monte Pino and continue to Priatu. 2 km after the village, turn left at the sign.

*LI LICCI*
*Host: Jane Elizabeth Ridd*
*Localita: Valentino-Priatu*
*Calangianus (SS) 07023, Italy*
*Tel: (079) 665114, Fax: (079) 665029*
*4 rooms, Double: €90–€115*
*Minimum nights required: 2*
*Open: all year*
*Other languages: fluent English*
*Region: Sardinia, Michelin Map: 566*
*karenbrown.com/italy/lilicci.html*

After living in South Africa for 20 years, the Tosi family returned to their homeland in search of a piece of land that in some way resembled their beloved Africa. The gorgeous Montebelli property, situated in Maremma, the wild west of Italy, fit the bill with its 300-plus acres of mountain, hills, and plain, all close to the sea—the one essential element, according to Lorenzo, which brings people "allegria". Lorenzo, his simpatica wife, Carla, and son, Alessandro, now divide their time and energy between their guests and production of wines and olive oil. At the foot of the hills is the main guesthouse where most of the rooms are situated. Others, each with separate entrance, are in two one-story wings connecting to an outdoor dining area. The best rooms are in the main house, decorated tastefully with antiques and including all the amenities of a regular hotel. The half-board requirement allows guests to sample the marvelous cuisine of the area within the characteristic dining room featuring the stone wheel from the original press. This is unexplored territory, full of historical treasures and Etruscan remains. Scenic walks on marked trails (a must for the views!), a swimming pool, tennis courts, horse riding, and summer concerts are available right on the property. *Directions:* From the north, exit at Gavorrano Scalo from Aurelia S.S.1, following signs for Caldana. Just before Caldana, turn at the Montebelli sign and take the dirt road to the end.

*MONTEBELLI*
*Hosts: Carla & Lorenzo Tosi*
*Localita: Molinetto, Caldana (GR) 58020, Italy*
*Tel: (0566) 887100, Fax: (0566) 81439*
*21 rooms, Double: €210–€250\**
*\*Includes breakfast & dinner*
*Minimum nights required: 2*
*Closed: Jan 11 to Feb 13, Credit cards: MC, VS*
*Other languages: good English*
*Region: Tuscany, Michelin Map: 563*
*karenbrown.com/italy/montebelli.html*

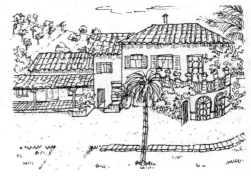

The quaint medieval village of Calvi is just on the border between Lazio and Umbria and conveniently located at 15 kilometers from the autostrada and 80 kilometers from Rome. Louise, from Sweden, divides her time between Rome and the countryside where the farm's activities include production of wine and olive oil, and horse breeding on the 150-acre property. The fascinating family residence in town is a historic 15th-century palazzo filled with period furniture, paintings, and frescoed ceilings. Hospitality is offered in the ochre-colored farmhouse within four comfortable apartments, each with private garden area. Accommodations on the first and second floors are a combination of one or two bedrooms, living room with fireplace, fully equipped kitchen, bathroom, and outdoor barbecue. The house has been restored with new bathrooms and tiled floors, while maintaining original beamed ceilings and a country flavor in antique furnishings. Besides wandering around the many surrounding villages, you can visit Rome, Viterbo, and Orvieto, within one hour by car, or relax by the swimming pool. A children's playground and an exercise course are available. *Directions:* Leave the Rome-Florence autostrada A1 at Magliano Sabina. After Magliano turn left for Calvi. Just before Calvi you see signs for San Martino on the right.

*CASALE SAN MARTINO*
*Host: Louise Calza Bini*
*Colle San Martino*
*Calvi dell'Umbria (TR) 05032, Italy*
*Tel: (328) 1659514, Fax: (0744) 710644*
*4 apartments: €60–€150 daily*
*Minimum nights required: 2, 7 in Jul & Aug*
*Open: all year*
*Other languages: English, French, German, Spanish*
*Region: Umbria, Michelin Map: 563*
*karenbrown.com/italy/casalesanmartino.html*

The Villa Bellaria, situated right in the picturesque village of Campagnatico with its stone streets and houses and magnificent views over the Ombrone Valley and up to Mount Amiata, retains the authentic flavor of a noble country home from centuries past. Credit goes to gracious hostess Luisa who oversees the 900-plus-acre property, once belonging to such powerful families as the Aldobrandeschi and Medici. It was partially destroyed during World War II and completely restored by the Querci della Rovere family. Talented Luisa runs not only the hospitality activity but the entire farm as well, while her husband produces Morellino wine from another property. With its large surrounding balustraded park with cypress-lined trails and swimming pool, one forgets that it is all part of the actual town (with its many conveniences). The spacious bedrooms with family antiques and two of the apartments are situated within the main villa while the other newer but characteristic ones are spread out on three floors in the transformed olive-press building. They have either one or two bedrooms, bathroom, and sitting room with kitchenette and are appointed with the family's country furniture. This is a lovely base for exploring the area. *Directions:* From Siena (55 km) or Grosseto (20 km) exit from highway 223 at Campagnatico and continue for 4 km to the town. The villa is the second right in town—drive up to a green gate.

*VILLA BELLARIA*
*Host: Luisa Querci della Rovere*
*Campagnatico (GR) 58042, Italy*
*Tel: (0564) 996626, Fax: (0564) 996626*
*4 rooms, Double: €60–€80*
*10 apartments: €500–€1000 weekly*
*Minimum nights required: 2*
*Open: all year, Credit cards: all major*
*Other languages: good English*
*Region: Tuscany, Michelin Map: 563*
*karenbrown.com/italy/bellaria.html*

The vast Masseria Pernice property sits on the hills south of Palermo, in the Alcamo wine area of Sicily. The vast 300-acre estate has always been in the noble Sallier de la Tour family from Palermo. Gracious host, Prince Filiberto—combining his passion for the countryside, wine and olive oil making, horses, and entertaining—opened the farm home to guests just recently. Although, from the road, the rust-colored, 300-year-old house and surrounding working farm seem rather basic, the well-appointed interiors have obviously been given prime attention. One bedroom and three comfortable apartments have been reserved for guests, each with independent access from the cobblestone main courtyard, covered with magenta-colored bougainvillea vines. The spacious "Papare", with exposed beams, has a bedroom and sofabed and a living area, while the largest apartment comes complete with a kitchen. "Fiori" sleeps five persons in two bedrooms, one being a loft with three beds. "Piume" is a double bedroom, and "Caccia" has a kitchenette and sitting room. Perfect for a full house rental, as well. Accessible day trips include Palermo, Monreale, Segesta, Selinunte, Erice, Cefalu, and the cantinas of the wine roads in the area with visits arranged by your host. *Directions:* From Monreale (50 km), take the highway straight south towards Camporeale and follow signs to Pernice.

*MASSERIA PERNICE*     *New*
*Host: Prince Filiberto Pernice family*
*Via Atrio Principe 8*
*Camporeale, Sicily (PA) 90043, Italy*
*Tel: (0924) 36797*
*1 room, Double: €180*
*3 apartments €75–€320 daily*
*Open: all year, Credit cards: all major*
*Other languages: fluent English, French*
*Region: Sicily, Michelin Map: 565*
*karenbrown.com/italy/pernice.html*

For those who have a passion for horseback riding, or with an urge to learn, Tenuta La Mandria provides the opportunity to do either while on holiday. Host and horseman Davide Felice Aondio's horse farm has been in existence for over 35 years and has been a model for riding resorts. Situated near the foothills of the Alps and between the cities of Turin and Milan, the vast, flat property borders a 15,000-acre national park, offering spectacular scenery and endless possibilities for horseback excursions. The complex is made up of horse stables, indoor/outdoor ring, haylofts, guestrooms, dining room, and the private homes of the proprietor and his son Marco's family. The whole forms a square with riding rings in the center. As a national equestrian training center, it offers lessons of every kind for all ages. Six very basic bedrooms with bath are reserved for guests and good local fare is served in the rustic dining room. Golf, swimming, and tennis facilities are available nearby. Two side trips that must not be missed are first, to lovely Lake Maggiore, and then to the intriguing medieval town of Ricetto where the houses and streets are made of smooth stones. *Directions:* Take the Carisio exit from the Milan-Turin autostrada. Head toward Biella, but at the town of Candelo turn right for Mottalciata. La Mandria is on the right.

*TENUTA LA MANDRIA*
*Host: Marco Aondio family*
*Candelo (BI) 13062, Italy*
*Tel: (015) 2536078, Fax: (015) 2530743*
*6 rooms, Double: €82*
*Per person half board: €67*
*Open: all year*
*Other languages: good English*
*Region: Piedmont, Michelin Map: 561*
*karenbrown.com/italy/lamandria.html*

Poetically named after a classic Italian tale by Cesare Pavese, a native of this area, the Luna e i Falo (meaning "the moon and the fire") farmhouse was lovingly restored by congenial hosts Ester and Franco Carnero. The ritual described in the story is still performed in August every year when local farmers burn old grapevines under the full moon in hopes of a good crop. On that night, the bonfires dotting hills surrounding the farm create quite a spectacle. The Carneros' brick home has arched windows and arcaded front and side terraces, with three double or triple rooms and one apartment for four persons within the villa, which they have made available to visitors. For a country home, the spacious living/dining area is elaborately furnished with Renaissance period pieces. The bedrooms enjoy a combination of old and new decor and sweeping views of the countryside, known for its wineries. The emphasis at the Luna e i Falo is on the cuisine: the proprietors previously owned a top-rated restaurant in Turin and continue to practice their culinary skills, producing delicacies from ancient recipes to guests' delight. Regardless of the language barrier, they have a way of making guests feel right at home. *Directions:* From Asti follow the signs for Canelli and, before town, take a right up the hill to Castello Gancia. The farmhouse is on the right after Aie.

*doubles €50 per person*
*½ board ?*

*LA LUNA E I FALO'*
*Hosts: Ester & Franco Carnero*
*Localita: Aie 37*
*Canelli (AT) 14053, Italy*
*Tel & fax: (0141) 831643, Cellphone: (328) 7191567*
*3 rooms, Double: €110–€170\**
*\*Includes breakfast & dinner*
*Minimum nights required: 2*
*Open: Mar to Nov, Other languages: French*
*Region: Piedmont, Michelin Map: 561*
*karenbrown.com/italy/laluna.html*

The Canonica a Cerreto property is truly a marvel to behold, with an extraordinary combination of features. Perfectly located in lower Chianti and equidistant to most of Tuscany's highlights, it offers not only very comfortable accommodation in a fascinating historic dwelling but also seemingly endless vistas of gorgeous countryside, and welcoming and gracious hosts. Iron gates open up to an entrance lined with gorgeous terra-cotta pots in the form of lions, overflowing with geraniums and oleander plants giving accents of color to the façade of the ancient stone church and attached canonica, the summer residence of the Vescovo of the Duomo of Siena. Within the walls is a complex including the family's residence, three guest apartments in the monks' former rooms, quarters for the farmhands, and a cantina. Signora Lorenzi proudly shows guests her museum-caliber art collection and magnificent home where large period paintings adorn frescoed walls and elegant antique pieces are displayed. The apartments, in an elegant country style, are tastefully appointed with antiques and include a bedroom, bathroom, and living area with kitchenette. The largest apartment has two bedrooms, each with its own bathroom. A lovely, secluded swimming pool has superb countryside views. *Directions:* From Siena follow the S.S.408 towards Gaiole and just after Pianella, take the first left (Canonica a Cerreto is marked on most maps).

*CANONICA A CERRETO*
*Host: Egidio Lorenzi family*
*Canonica a Cerreto*
*Castelnuovo Berardenga (SI) 53010, Italy*
*Tel & fax: (0577) 363261*
*3 apartments: €730–€1,250 weekly*
*Minimum nights required: 7*
*Open: Apr to Oct, Credit cards: all major*
*Other languages: good English*
*Region: Tuscany, Michelin Map: 563*
*karenbrown.com/italy/canonica.html*

The turreted medieval village of Capalbio, perched on a hilltop, has the double advantage of being close to one of the prettiest seaside spots—Argentario—plus having the beautiful countryside and villages of Maremma to explore. Monica and husband Filippo run an efficient little bed and breakfast operation, having left a long career in the restaurant business. Breakfast, composed of fresh homemade cakes, breads, and jams, is served in the stone-walled dining room or out on the patio. Ten rooms in a row, each with independent entrance from the garden, are situated next door to the main house; while five new bedrooms have been added in the adjacent converted barn. Rooms are nicely decorated in a classic style, and have such amenities as television, telephone, hairdryer, and air conditioning. This comes in handy on hot summer evenings, although there is always a cool breeze passing through (hence the Etruscan name "Iced Woods") and the swimming pool surrounded by a manicured lawn is wonderfully refreshing. The farm property extends over 30 acres of olive groves and fields of grain and oats. Not to be missed is an unforgettable meal at Tullio's famed restaurant in town and the absolutely delightful sculpture park of Niki de St. Phalle 4 km away. *Directions:* From Rome on the coastal highway 1, exit before Capalbio at Pescia Fiorentina. At Pescia stay left for 3 km. Ghiaccio is 1 km after the fork for Manciano.

*GHIACCIO BOSCO*
*Hosts: Monica Olivi & Filippo Rinaldi*
*Strada della Sgrilla 4*
*Capalbio (GR) 58011, Italy*
*Tel & fax: (0564) 896539, Cellphone: (339) 5662578*
*15 rooms, Double: €75–€105*
*Open: all year*
*Other languages: some English*
*Region: Tuscany, Michelin Map: 563*
*karenbrown.com/italy/ghiaccio.html*

The Villa Krupp, built in 1900, is a delightful, small, family-run hotel, whose claim to local fame can be found in its guest book, boasting such illustrious names as Lenin and Gorky. The warm Coppola family, who turned the property into a hotel in the '60s, offer charming accommodation in 12 bedrooms within a somewhat modern and boxy white building alongside their own residence. The Krupp is dramatically situated in one of the most beautiful corners of Capri's Augusto Park, atop a steep, sheer cliff dropping to the sparkling turquoise sea beneath. The site overlooks the Faraglioni rock formation and Marina Piccola, one of Capri's two ports. A set of stairs leads up to the best vantage point from which to admire this spectacular and privileged panorama away from crowds of tourists. The renovated light-filled guestrooms, featuring individual balconies, are decorated with scattered antiques and pastel-colored ceramic tiles and some have air conditioning. Breakfast is served either out on the front terrace overflowing with potted flowers or in the luminous veranda bar/dining room. Mother-daughter team Valentina and Donatella do an excellent job of caring for their guests, many of whom are regulars. Reserve well in advance. *Directions:* Take the cable car up to Capri center (la piazzetta). Walk to Via Emanuele, past the Quisisana hotel, down to Viale Matteotti. The hotel is to the right up a ramp, as indicated (ten minutes from the main square).

❄ ☕ 🛵 CREDIT ☎ 👤

*VILLA KRUPP*
*Hosts: Valentina & Donatella Coppola*
*Viale Matteotti 12*
*Capri (NA) 80073, Italy*
*Tel: (081) 8370362 or 8377473, Fax: (081) 8376489*
*12 rooms, Double: €120–€150*
*Minimum nights required: 3*
*Open: Mar 20 to Oct 31, Credit cards: MC, VS*
*Other languages: some English, French, German*
*Region: Campania, Michelin Map: 564*
*karenbrown.com/italy/krupp.html*

La Minerva, a full-fledged hotel with many amenities, is located in a quiet section of Capri, slightly off the beaten track, yet still quite central, permitting easy access to the more bustling areas of town—a walkers' paradise with no motorized transportation allowed. Glass entrance doors look straight through the capacious reception/sitting area across glossy blue-and-white tiled floors out to a view of the sea through another set of glass doors at the opposite end of the room. The captivating sea views through umbrella pine trees will strike you every time you come and go, as well as from most bedrooms. Rooms, all below this level, are reached by elevator, as is a small breakfast area, although most guests prefer breakfast served in rooms on their private balconies. The hotel's royal-blue-and-white tile theme follows through in the luminous guestrooms (standard or larger superior doubles), which are accented by an occasional antique piece. Deluxe doubles have Jacuzzi bathtubs and larger terraces with sea view. A rooftop solarium is an unusual bonus. *Directions:* Stop at the tourist office as you get off the hydrofoil for a detailed map indicating Via Occhio Marino. The cable car or a taxi takes you from the port to the piazza at the center of town. From there it's a ten-minute walk to the hotel. Prearrange to have your luggage picked up at the port, otherwise, pack light!

*LA MINERVA*
*Host: Luigi Esposito*
*Via Occhio Marino 8*
*Capri (NA) 80073, Italy*
*Tel: (081) 8377067, Fax: (081) 8375221*
*18 rooms, Double: €150–€270*
*Closed: Jan & Feb, Credit cards: all major*
*Other languages: good English*
*Region: Campania, Michelin Map: 564*
*karenbrown.com/italy/laminerva.html*

Capri has long had a reputation as an exclusive island, with prices only the elite were able to afford. However, the cost of tourism across Italy has soared, bringing other destinations more in line with Capri in terms of expense and making it relatively more affordable than it once was. Besides the many hotels, there are just a few true bed and breakfasts and Villa Vuotto is one of the best. Antonino Vuotto and his wife, a local couple both with hotel experience, opened up their centrally located, prim white home in the town of Capri, making four bedrooms down one hall available to guests. The very pleasant and airy rooms are extremely clean and neat, with typical tiled floors, and private baths and balconies in each. All have a full or partial view of the sea. Breakfast is not served because there are no common rooms for guests but the Villa Vuotto's convenient location makes it easy to get to any of Capri's fine restaurants for breakfast, lunch, and dinner. It would be impossible to find another accommodation with such an absolutely incredible price/quality rapport. A marvelous value! *Directions:* Take the cable car up to Capri. Go through the main town square to Via Emanuele, past the Quisisana Hotel, and continue to the end of the street. Turn left onto Via Certosa, then left again on Cerio. The Villa is on the corner of Campo di Teste and is marked with its original name, Villa Margherita.

*VILLA VUOTTO*
*Host: Antonino Vuotto family*
*Via Campo di Teste 2*
*Capri (NA) 80073, Italy*
*Tel & fax: (081) 8370230*
*4 rooms, Double: €85\**
*\*Breakfast not included*
*Open: all year*
*Other languages: very little English*
*Region: Campania, Michelin Map: 564*
*karenbrown.com/italy/vuotto.html*

The Ombria farmhouse nestles amidst the foothills just 30 kilometers from both beautifully austere Bergamo and Lecco on Lake Como. Bed-and-breakfast/restaurant activity in this 1613 stone house began after meticulous restoration by owner Luciano Marchesin, who has now retired, leaving the business in the capable hands of the Vergani brothers, part of his staff from the beginning. An arched entryway leads into a stone courtyard with gazebo and open grill, where tables are set for summer meals. The Ombria is well known for its exceptional restaurant where locals enjoy candlelit regional cuisine at long tables in the intimate stone-walled dining room—as long as they make reservations three months in advance! For those retiring to bed early, it would be best to avoid weekends. The spacious double bedrooms, which accommodate up to four persons, are decorated with country antiques and wrought-iron beds. Original fireplaces, exposed beams, warm wood floors, and stone walls make them very appealing and cozy. Special attention has been given to bathrooms, which are beautifully tiled and rather luxurious. Readers give Ombria a high rating. *Directions:* From autostrada A4, exit at Dalmine and follow signs for Lecco on route 36. After Pontida, turn right at the sign for Celana and continue on to Celana, then Ombria (total 15 km).

*OMBRIA*
*Hosts: Alberto & Giuseppe Vergani*
*Localita: Celana*
*Caprino Bergamasco (BG) 24030, Italy*
*Tel & fax: (035) 781668*
*3 rooms, Double: €100*
*Dinner Thur to Sun only*
*Open: all year*
*Other languages: some English*
*Region: Lombardy, Michelin Map: 561*
*karenbrown.com/italy/ombria.html*

Between the cities of Bergamo and Brescia is a vast commercial area that incorporates the wine region known as Franciacorta—or "land of bubbles." The Ricci Curbastro vineyards, made up of almost 80 acres, are located in the heart of the area based at the foot of Lake Iseo. The family is one of the most renowned producers of top-quality (D.O.C.G.) Franciacorta Brut champagne, among 12 other varieties of wine. The large and busy family estate just on the main road is made up of a complex of houses, which include the family's villa, wine cellars, a wine-tasting showroom, an antiques store, and an interesting agricultural museum and library filled with ancient farm tools and wine presses. Across the street is the farmhouse, transformed into guest apartments of various sizes (studio, one and two bedrooms), each with living area and kitchenette facilities. Rooms are simply decorated with country antiques and stenciled borders around windows and doorways. Here you have the advantage of being close to town while having views of the flat vineyards from bedroom windows. Sports facilities in the area include golf, horseback riding, and biking. This is a conveniently located accommodation for independent travelers. *Directions:* Exit at Palazzolo from the A4 autostrada and follow signs to Capriolo (2 km). Turn right in town at the sign for Adro. After half a kilometer the farm is on the left-hand side of the road.

*AZIENDA AGRICOLA RICCI CURBASTRO*
*Host: Ricci Curbastro family*
*Via Adro 37*
*Capriolo (BS) 25031, Italy*
*Tel: (030) 736094, Fax: (030) 7460558*
*7 apartments: €50–€75 daily*
*Minimum nights required: 2*
*Open: all year, Credit cards: all major*
*Other languages: good English*
*Region: Lombardy, Michelin Map: 561*
*karenbrown.com/italy/curbastro.html*

Although many think of Sardinia as purely a sailors' paradise (which it is), the development and widespread publicity of the chic Emerald Coast has robbed the island of its true identity. The beauty of ancient Sardinia (dating back to the Neolithic and Bronze Age periods) lies in its stark and rugged windswept landscapes and its relatively simple lifestyle. With the strategic location of Monti Tundu, the traveler can take advantage of both coast and mountain excursions, exploring this corner of the island. Making your way up the steep dirt road, you are rewarded with mountaintop views over the rocky Mediterranean terrain stretching out to the Cugnana Gulf. Meals incorporating local delicacies such as the island's famed Percorino cheeses are served in the simple circular dining room with windows looking out over the striking vistas. A separate one-story L-shaped stone house contains the guestrooms, each with independent entrance from the exterior and more sweeping views. Newly refurbished double rooms (all of which can become triples) and bathrooms have soft pastel color schemes, beige tiled floors, and simple and practical furnishings. Hosts Gianni and Giuseppina offer warm Sardinian hospitality. *Directions:* 10 km from Olbia (airport and ferry port). From Olbia take the S.S.125 regional road towards Arzachena/Palau. Monti Tundu is marked on the right side of the road. Follow the very rough, steep road up to the very end.

*MONTI TUNDU*
*Hosts: Gianni Spolittu & Giuseppina Serra*
*Localita: Casagliana*
*Via Francoforte 4, Casagliana, Olbia (SS) 07026, Italy*
*Tel & fax: (0789) 613072 or 58001*
*Cellphone: (336) 9608389*
*10 rooms, Double: €70–€90*
*Open: all year*
*Other languages: French, Spanish*
*Region: Sardinia, Michelin Map: 566*
*karenbrown.com/italy/tundu.html*

After 20 years of managing guided tours throughout Italy, Welsh-born Maureen, along with husband, Roberto, brought her expertise "home" to La Torretta. Restoration work on the three-story 15th-century building, tucked away in this yet-undiscovered medival hilltop village, took three years to complete. The entrance stairway leads to a large open and elegant living room with a collection of the family's paintings, stone fireplace, and 16th-century frescoes discovered during the restoration process. All seven bedrooms are individually and tastefully decorated in soft beige tones, which harmonize with travertine bathrooms, and have stunning views over the town's rooftops. Meals are served upstairs in a dining area with panoramic terrace overlooking olive groves and the wooded Sabine hills. This virgin territory is filled with hilltop villages to explore, besides being on the border of Umbria, and is just a 45-minute train ride from Rome. Maureen and her daughters customize itineraries for guests and organize cooking courses, while Roberto specializes in ancient Roman architecture and archaeology. A separate self-catering apartment across the street is available. *Directions:* From Rome or Florence exit the A1 at Ponzano-Soratte (a new exit not marked on maps). Go straight then turn right at the T-junction. Turn left and follow signs to Casperia (20 mins). Cars are easily parked on the street below and luggage is delivered by special vehicle.

*LA TORRETTA*
*Hosts: Maureen & Roberto Scheda*
*Via Mazzini 7*
*Casperia (RI) 02041, Italy*
*Tel & fax: (0765) 63202, Cellphone: (338) 1451859*
*7 rooms, Double: €80–€90*
*1 apartment: €75–€90 daily*
*Minimum nights required: 2*
*Other languages: fluent English*
*Region: Lazio, Michelin Map: 563*
*karenbrown.com/italy/torretta.html*

A stay at the Villa Aureli with Count di Serego Alighieri (descendant of Dante) can only be memorable. With its back to the town and looking out over the Italian Renaissance garden and surrounding countryside, the imposing brick villa has been standing for the past 300 years. When it was bought by the di Serego family in the 18th century, it was meticulously restored and embellished with plasterwork, decorative painted ceilings, richly painted fabrics on walls, ornately framed paintings and prints, colorful tiles from Naples, and Umbrian antiques. Left intentionally intact by the Count, who disdains overly restored historical homes, the elegant apartments for guests maintain their original ambiance. They can accommodate from four to six persons and are spacious, having numerous sitting rooms with fireplaces; although do not expect updated bathrooms or kitchens. A small swimming pool set against the villa's stone walls is a refreshing spot for dreaming. The villa serves as an ideal base from which to explore Umbria and parts of Tuscany, as well as special local itineraries prepared for guests by the Count. *Directions:* Exit from the Perugia highway at Madonna Alta and follow route 220 for Citta della Pieve. After 6 km, turn left for Castel del Piano Umbro.

*VILLA AURELI*
*Host: Sperello di Serego Alighieri family*
*Via Cirenei 70*
*Castel del Piano (PG) 06071, Italy*
*Tel: (340) 6459061, Fax: (075) 514 9408*
*2 apartments: €950–€1,200 weekly*
*Heating extra*
*Open: all year*
*Other languages: good English, French, German*
*Region: Umbria, Michelin Map: 563*
*karenbrown.com/italy/villaaureli.html*

Castelfiorentino is 40 kilometers from Florence, Siena and Pisa, and although its outskirts are very commercial, it is a strategic touring base and the surrounding countryside is lovely. Continuing a long tradition of making guests feel at home—their hotel in Florence has been in the family for four generations—Massimo and Susanna opened this bed and breakfast five years ago after major restoration of two hilltop farmhouses. The completely refurbished rooms, with many modern amenities new bathrooms, fresh landscaping, and recently installed swimming pool and tennis court, have a very new feeling. Spacious bedrooms are appointed with authentic and reproduction antiques and have colorful Sicilian ceramic tiles above beds, with matching ones in bathrooms. The former barn was converted into a small restaurant decorated with contemporary art, a kitchen with viewing window, and a common living room/library upstairs. The preparation of delectable Tuscan fare using ancestral recipes is another strong tradition and cooking lessons are happily arranged for those eager to take home family secrets. A buffet breakfast is served. The side terrace, overlooking soft hills, is where guests can both enjoy breakfast and watch the sunset in the evening. *Directions:* From Castelfiorentino turn off at signs for Renai (this can be tricky to locate) and follow signs for Locanda Country Inn Le Boscarecce (5 km).

*LE BOSCARECCE*
*Hosts: Susanna Ballerini & Massimo Ravalli*
*Via Renai 19, Castelfiorentino (FI) 50051, Italy*
*Tel: (0571) 61280, Fax: (0571) 634008*
*14 rooms, Double: €130–€145*
*Restaurant closed on Tuesdays*
*Minimum nights required: 2*
*Open: all year, Credit cards: all major*
*Other languages: good English*
*Region: Tuscany, Michelin Map: 563*
*karenbrown.com/italy/boscarecce.html*

The Villa Gaidello farm has been written up several times (in Bon Appetit, Cuisine, Eating in Italy), mostly for its superb cuisine. There is nothing extravagant about hostess Paola Bini's recipes—rather, the secret to her success seems to lie in the revival of basic traditional dishes using the freshest possible ingredients. Pasta is made daily (a great treat to watch) and features all the local variations on tagliatelle, pappardelle, and stricchettoni. Reservations for dinner must be made several days in advance. Paola is one of the pioneers in agritourism, transforming her grandmother's nearly-200-year-old farmhouse into a guesthouse and restaurant more than 30 years ago. One to five guests are accommodated in each of the eight apartments, which include kitchen and sitting room. The apartments are cozy and rustic with exposed-brick walls, country antiques, and lace curtains. Two double bedrooms are found in a fourth house on the property, San Giacomo, each decorated in the style of Paola's two favorite countries, France and the U.S. The dining room, set with doilies and ceramic, is situated in the converted hayloft and overlooks the vast garden and a small pond. This is a convenient stopover just off the Bologna-Milan autostrada. *Directions:* Exit the A1 autostrada at Modena Nord (or Bologna Nord from the south). Follow Via Emilia/route 9 towards Castelfranco. Turn left at the stop light (or right) on Via Costa (hospital) and follow signs to Gaidello.

*VILLA GAIDELLO*
*Host: Paola Bini*
*Via Gaidello 18*
*Castelfranco Emilia (MO) 41013, Italy*
*Tel: (059) 926806, Fax: (059) 926620*
*2 rooms, Double: €93*
*8 apartments: €86–€228 daily B&B*
*Closed: Aug, Credit cards: all major*
*Other languages: very little English*
*Region: Emilia-Romagna, Michelin Map: 562*
*karenbrown.com/italy/villagaidello.html*

There is no doubt that the spectacular Amalfi coast must be seen, but in high season when the traffic is unbearable and Positano's streets are packed, a welcome retreat is the coast farther south at Castellabate. This is a very quiet and modest resort area where the majority of summer tourists are Italians. The winding road climbs up to the medieval village of Castellabate and La Mola, the summer home of the Favilla family, is right on the road entering town. Rather nondescript from the roadside entrance, the four-story former olive-press building, perched on the cliffside, faces out to the bay. Each room takes in some angle of this amazing panorama, two having balconies and the two-bedroom suite having a terrace. With an occasional antique, the bedrooms and living room with spiral staircase are pleasantly uncluttered so as not to detract from the inspiring sea views. On a clear day the Amalfi coastline and even Capri are visible. Hostess Loredana takes care of guests, preparing cakes and bread for breakfast, which is served on a table made from the old stone press on the main terrace. It is difficult to tear oneself away to try one of the interesting itineraries with an emphasis on either nature or ancient history (temples of Paestum, Certosa, or Padula). *Directions:* 60 km from Salerno. Take the road up to the town center and La Mola is marked on the side of the gray building on the right, the first house as you enter town on Via Cilento.

*LA MOLA*
*Host: Francesco Favilla*
*Via A. Cilento 2*
*Castellabate (SA) 84048, Italy*
*Tel: (0974) 967053, Cellphone: (335) 1292800*
*Fax: (0974) 967714*
*5 rooms, Double: €114–€124*
*Open: Apr to Oct, Credit cards: all major*
*Other languages: some English*
*Region: Campania, Michelin Map: 564*
*karenbrown.com/italy/lamola.html*

While wandering in Umbria through picture-perfect landscapes, we came upon the Giardino degli Ulivi bed and breakfast and were immediately intrigued. The absolutely charming accommodation is actually part of a 12th-century stone village and faces out to the rolling hills splashed with bright patches of yellow sunflowers. The scenery per se is enough to leave one in awe, let alone Maria Pia's marvelous cuisine with its Michelin rating. The carefully restored building, left ingeniously intact, thanks to her architect husband, Sante, includes the stone-walled restaurant with its many intimate nooks, centered around the ancient wine-making press. The five bedrooms upstairs off two sitting rooms with fireplace have wrought-iron beds, antique bedside tables, and beamed ceilings. The favorite corner bedroom (at a higher rate) has a large arched window taking in the breathtaking view. A small apartment for two persons with living area and kitchenette has been incorporated within the large house. While their son, Francesco, tends to the breeding of horses, daughter Raffaele assists guests with the many interesting itineraries in the area (Camerino, San Severino, Matelica, and Fariano—famous for its paper industry). A real sense of discovery is experienced in this region, which keeps its traditions and folklore intact. *Directions:* From Castelraimondo follow route 256 towards Matelica, turning first left for Castel S. Maria then Castel S. Angelo.

*IL GIARDINO DEGLI ULIVI*
*Host: Sante Cioccoloni family*
*Localita: Castel S. Angelo*
*Castelraimondo (MC) 62022, Italy*
*Tel: (0737) 642121, Fax: (0737) 642600*
*5 rooms, Double: €90–€130, 1 apartment: €89 daily*
*Reduced rates for 3 or more nights*
*Closed: Jan 8 to Mar 7, Credit cards: AX, VS*
*Other languages: good English*
*Region: Marches, Michelin Map: 563*
*karenbrown.com/italy/ilgiardino.html*

Tucked away off a winding mountain road in the enchanting Siusi Alps is a typical Tyrolean farmhouse where the Jaider family has resided ever since the 15th century, traditionally running a dairy farm. Their inviting home, with its authentic ambiance of the past, is colorfully accented with green shutters and flower-laden windowboxes. Two wooden barns are connected to the residence via a stone terrace. Paula Jaider runs her home with the hotel efficiency expected by visitors to this predominantly German-speaking area. Meals are served either out on the vine-covered terrace or in the original dining room, whose charm is enhanced by the low, wood-paneled ceiling and little carved wooden chairs. Be sure to reserve dinner: the food is excellent and it is just too far to go out for a meal. Cuisine in this region has an Austrian flavor, featuring speck ham, meat and potatoes, and apple strudel, and regulars come from afar to this well-known restaurant. Lovely country antiques are dispersed throughout the house and the eight very nice bedrooms, which are wood-paneled from floor to ceiling and all have balconies with pretty valley views. A real charmer and a bargain. Book well in advance. *Directions:* Exit from the Bolzano-Brennero autostrada at Klausen and drive south to Ponte Gardena where you turn left across the river and first right towards Castelrotto. After 3.5 km make a sharp right for San Osvaldo and follow the narrow road for 2.5 km.

*TSCHOTSCHERHOF*
*Host: Jaider family*
*San Osvaldo 19*
*Castelrotto (BZ) 39040, Italy*
*Tel: (0471) 706013, Fax: (0471) 704801*
*8 rooms, Double: €58–€67.20*
*Per person half board: €33–€35*
*Open: Mar to Nov, Credit cards: all major*
*Other languages: very little English, German*
*Region: Trentino-Alto Adige, Michelin Map: 562*
*karenbrown.com/italy/tschotscherhof.html*

Il Loghetto is located 10 kilometers east of Bologna and is a combination of converted farmhouse and the efficiency and service of a small hotel. Run by Ulicia and her son, Andrea, the yellow house surrounded by a large garden and then flat fields has ten beamed bedrooms upstairs and a restaurant downstairs. There is a reception area at the entrance and also an elevator up to the rooms, which are all new with rather standard wood furniture and amenities such as television and air conditioning. The dining room with fireplace and hanging brass pots, where fresh pasta dishes and other local specialties are served, is filled with a variety of antiques collected by Andrea. Beyond is an enormous living room with arched glass doors overlooking the garden and outdoor tables, a bar, billiard table, piano, and two sitting areas. There may be minimal noise from the nearby road. Transfers are arranged to Bologna or the airport. Besides this being a convenient stopover, marvels such as Ravenna, Ferrara, and Faenza (ceramic museum) can be visited from here. *Directions:* From the ring highway of Bologna, exit at S. Vitale (N11) and continue towards Villanova. After the commercial area of Castenaso, turn left for Budrio. Il Loghetto is indicated on the left.

*IL LOGHETTO*
*Host: Mazza family*
*Via Zenzalino Sud 3-4*
*Castenaso (BO) 40050, Italy*
*Tel: (051) 6052218, Fax: (051) 6052254*
*10 rooms, Double: €95*
*Closed: Jan & Aug, Credit cards: MC, VS*
*Other languages: some English*
*Region: Emilia-Romagna, Michelin Map: 562*
*karenbrown.com/italy/loghetto.html*

The lesser-known area of Tuscany south of Siena makes a delightful discovery and the variety of landscapes within an 8-kilometer drive provides one of the most fascinating excursions in the region. Besides the charming hilltowns of Montepulciano, Pienza, and Montalcino, there are the abbeys of Monte Oliveto and Sant'Antimo, plus the thermal baths of Bagno Vignoni. A perfect base in this richly historical and natural area is the magnificent castle of the Aluffi Pentini family, theirs for the past 400 years or so and practically a village in itself. The family resides in the upper reaches of the castle while guests are accommodated in several separate farmers' houses divided into a combination of apartments with one or two bedrooms, living room, and kitchenette, plus six simply and characteristically appointed bedrooms with country furniture. Rooms facing out have absolutely breathtaking views over the virgin valley. Downstairs is the dining room with wood tables covered with cheery checked cloths, where breakfast and dinner are served using homegrown products. A common space for guests is the old granary, converted into a large cozy reading room with fireplace. This is truly like a place out of a fairy-tale. *Directions:* The castle is well marked at 5 km from San Quirico d'Orcia. Ripa d'Orcia is marked on most maps.

*CASTELLO DI RIPA D'ORCIA*
*Host: Aluffi Pentini family*
*Via della Contea 1/16*
*Castiglione d'Orcia (SI) 53023, Italy*
*Tel: (0577) 897376, Fax: (0577) 898038*
*6 rooms, Double: €99–€135*
*8 apartments: €500–€850 weekly*
*Minimum nights required: 2, 7 in apartments*
*Open: Mar to Nov, Credit cards: MC, VS*
*Region: Tuscany, Michelin Map: 563*
*karenbrown.com/italy/castellodiripadorcia.html*

This bed and breakfast has been added to the new group of agritourism accommodation in the Aosta Valley region. It offers a pleasant place to stay right in the center of charming Champoluc and is associated with the agritourism cheese farm, La Tchavana, up on the mountainside overlooking town. In the summer months the two establishments offer a very worthwhile four-day itinerary featuring a country lunch and tour of the Bagnod family's fontina cheese farm, a visit to an ancient mountain village with sabotier artisans, and two other mountain hikes. The scenic ride up through the valley leading to Champoluc takes you by many picturesque villages, ending at the ski/summer resort. Raul and Lorena took over the family's early-19th-century home in the center of town and recently had it refurbished into a small bed and breakfast. The prim white house with wood-trim balconies, conveniently located right next to the cable-car lift entrance, contains nine (non-smoking) bedrooms divided among the top two floors, decorated plainly and practically with new tiled flooring and wood-beamed mansard ceilings. The main entrance to the home opens directly into a welcoming living room with dark-wood furniture, burgundy armchairs, and combination wood and slate floors. A loft balcony overlooks the room. Breakfast is served downstairs in the dining room. *Directions:* On the main road in Champoluc.

*LO MIETE VIEI*
*Hosts: Raul Chasseur & Lorena Blondin*
*Rue Prabochon 6*
*Champoluc (AO) 11020, Italy*
*Tel: (0125) 308713, Fax: (0125) 308449*
*9 rooms, Double: €80–€110*
*Open: all year, Credit cards: MC, VS*
*Other languages: some English, French*
*Region: Aosta Valley, Michelin Map: 561*
*karenbrown.com/italy/lomiete.html*

In the hills between Tuscany and Umbria, overlooking the Tiber and Chiana valleys, you find the Nannotti family's typical farm property. Renato and Maria Teresa used to run a restaurant nearby before deciding to open a bed and breakfast and serve delicious Tuscan-Umbrian recipes at home. The two adjacent red-stone houses include five guestrooms, one apartment, and the family's private quarters. Two rooms are on the ground floor, another has an upstairs terrace, and all are decorated in a simple, pleasant country style with a mix of armoires, wrought-iron beds, and some modern pieces. Renato specializes in organic produce and makes his own honey, jams, grappa, D.O.C. red wine (Colli del Trasimeno), and extra-virgin olive oil, which are brought directly to their little restaurant Le Due Valli for Maria Teresa to use in her cooking. She creates an easy, informal ambiance and young daughter Aureliana and son Ernesto both help out. Being close to the charming, historical village and having easy access to the autostrada make this a super touring location. There are also bikes, a swimming pool, hiking trails, a special spa package at nearby thermal waters, a park for children, many farm animals, a fitness track, and horses to ride. *Directions:* Exit at Chiusi from the north or Fabro from the south and follow signs for Citta della Pieve. In town follow signs for Ponticelli—the bed and breakfast is signposted.

*MADONNA DELLE GRAZIE*
*Host: Renato Nannotti family*
*Via Madonna delle Grazie 6*
*Citta della Pieve (PG) 06062, Italy*
*Tel: (0578) 299822, Fax: (0578) 297749*
*6 rooms, Double: €90–€130*
*2 apartments: €600–€1000 weekly*
*Minimum nights required: 7 in Jul & Aug*
*Other languages: some English, German, French*
*Open: all year, Region: Umbria, Michelin Map: 563*
*karenbrown.com/italy/madonna.html*

Il Caggio is a delightful agriturismo farm, distinguishing itself from the many others by the sincere and warm hospitality of its owners, Gabriella and Paolo, and the superb quality of the meals. Conveniently located close to the main autostrada, guests have this corner of Chianti at their fingertips, from Siena, Cortona, Chianti, to Arezzo. Two bedrooms and two apartments are in part of the main stone house and an adjacent house. All are carefully appointed in a creative, country-style with great attention to details and the comfort of guests. All accommodations have private entrances from the exterior. In the rustic main house, the ambience really warms up around Gabriella's dinner table where a non-stop series of aperitifs, pasta specialities, and a dessert buffet are served, accompanied by good local wine. An abundant breakfast with more of Gabriella's homemade, baked cakes awaits guests in the morning. A swimming pool behind the house bordering the woods is available, as well as a six-person hot hydrojet pool. Convinced that their guests will enjoy their stay, their brochure warns: An extended stay here generates a sense of well-being with a tendency to forget about problems, tempting one to postpone going back home! *Directions:* From the A1 autostrada exit at Monte Savino and turn left continuing for 6.7 km to Ciggiano. Turn right and then left at abandoned farmhouse and follow up to the house.

*CASALE IL CAGGIO          New*
*Hosts: Gabriella & Paolo Magini*
*Località: Ciggiano*
*Civitella in Val di Chiana (AR) 52040,*
*Tel & fax: (0575) 440022*
*2 rooms, 3 suites, Double: €75–€130*
*2 apartments €560–€1,250\**
*\*Breakfast not included, 5,00 euro*
*Open: all year, Credit cards: all major*
*Other languages: good English, Region: Tuscany*
*karenbrown.com/italy/ilcaggio.html*

The Villa Alpina is another good choice for an efficient and moderately priced family-run bed and breakfast (or meublè, as they are called) right in Cortina. The inviting white stucco house with front bay windows has a large veranda on one side lined with flowerboxes where a buffet breakfast is set out for guests. Tables and umbrellas are set up outside in the summer months. Elio and his mother reside in a part of the large home, which was recently renovated, with the addition of an elevator up to the bedrooms. Each carpeted room (standard and superior) is decorated individually in characteristic style using mostly wood furniture and paneling. Some have balconies in the back looking over town and up to the mountains, and all have satellite TV and telephones. There is also a comfortable sitting room with Tyrolean printed fabrics on sofas and curtains whose focus is the ceramic-tiled wood-burning stove heater so typical in this mountain area. *Directions:* Just a few minutes' walk to the pedestrian-only main street (Corso Italia) with all its famous shops. Follow signs through town to Via Roma—Villa Alpina is well marked.

*VILLA ALPINA*
*Host: Elio Zardini*
*Via Roma 72, Cortina d'Ampezzo (BL) 32043, Italy*
*Tel: (0436) 2418, Cellphone: (335) 1244801*
*Fax: (0436) 867464*
*12 rooms, Double: €80–€220*
*Junior suite: €75–€240*
*Open: all year, Credit cards: all major*
*Other languages: good English*
*Region: Veneto, Michelin Map: 562*
*karenbrown.com/italy/villaalpina.html*

Cortina has enjoyed a long-standing reputation as one of the most "in" resorts of the Dolomites, helped also by its center-stage location. Prominent politicians, stars of television and cinema, socialites, and nobility have vacation homes here and congregate three times a year at Christmas, Easter, and during the month of August. In town, there is a large range of accommodation available, but if you want to be part of the scene yet desire a quiet place to sleep, the Menardi family's Baita Fraina is the perfect choice. A baita is a typical chalet farmhouse where home and barn are incorporated into one building. Overlooking mountains to the back and a large park for children to the front, the Fraina is primarily a well-established and esteemed restaurant cited in top restaurant guides and specializing in pastas with fresh mushrooms as well as the exquisite local fartaies dessert with wild-berry sauce. Three paneled and intimate dining rooms have ceramic-tiled stove heaters, lace curtains, antique kitchen tools, and dried flower arrangements. The six simply decorated bedrooms done in pinewood were added later on the top two floors. A sauna, Jacuzzi, and sun terrace are extra features of this characteristic bed and breakfast. *Directions:* Entering Cortina on route 48, turn left before town for Fraina and take the road for 1.2 km.

*BAITA FRAINA*
*Host: Adolfo Menardi family*
*Localita: Fraina*
*Cortina d'Ampezzo (BL) 32043, Italy*
*Tel: (0436) 36 34, Fax: (0436) 87 62 35*
*6 rooms, Double: €80–€130*
*Closed: Apr 1 to June 26, Sept 22 to Dec 1*
*Credit cards: MC, VS*
*Other languages: good English*
*Region: Veneto, Michelin Map: 562*
*karenbrown.com/italy/fraina.html*

Cortina is one of the most frequented spots for travelers passing through the Dolomites on their way up to Austria, or those who just want to get a taste of a mountain resort Italian-style. The multitude of ski lifts and variety of slopes along with the absolutely gorgeous scenery make it an easy winner. For shorter stays, accommodation right in town is convenient to restaurants, ski slopes, and hiking trails. The Meublè Oasi is a pleasant, recently updated bed and breakfast on the outskirts of town (easily reached by foot) at the beginning of a pretty residential street. This former private residence dating to 1925 has ten rooms located on the ground and first floors, while the Luchetta family, the original owners, reside on the top floor. New bedrooms are comfortably appointed with pinewood beds topped with fluffy comforters and soft-pea-green curtains and matching chairs. Amenities include satellite TV and phones in the rooms. A good buffet breakfast is served in the downstairs breakfast room with bay window. A small garden to the side of the house offers a restful spot. This is an efficient little hotel maintaining the warmth of a home and the Seppis are true hosts. *Directions:* The Meublè Oasi is in town on the road leaving Cortina towards Dobbiaco and well marked.

*MEUBLÈ OASI*
*Hosts: Lorenza Seppi & Tranquillo Luchetta*
*Via Cantore 2*
*Cortina d'Ampezzo (BL) 32043, Italy*
*Tel: (0436) 862019, Cellphone: (340) 7383 822*
*Fax: (0436) 879476*
*10 rooms, Double: €65–€120*
*Open: all year, Credit cards: MC, VS*
*Other languages: German, good English*
*Region: Veneto, Michelin Map: 562*
*karenbrown.com/italy/meubleoasi.html*

Borgo Elena, located in the hills outside one of our favorite Tuscan towns, Cortona, belongs to Mario Baracchi, whose brother owns the gorgeous inn, Il Falconiere (listed in our Inns guide). In fact, you can reach Borgo Elena by passing through the Falconiere property (stop in for an exquisite meal) on a narrow, steep gravel road that ends at the cluster of stone houses bordered by dense chestnut woods. Here you are totally immersed in nature and complete silence, with hilltop Cortona to one side and the immense Chiana Valley spread out before you. Seven quaint apartments, each with independent entrance, are dispersed among the various stone houses, which were the quarters for the farmhands of the Falconiere estate a century ago. Their original rustic ambiance remains while convenient modern utilities and amenities have been incorporated. The apartments, all charmingly appointed with Tuscan country pieces, accommodate from two to six persons and are all different in layout, most being on two levels. A lovely swimming pool sits higher up and takes in even more of the expansive view. The Borgo Elena is an ideal base for independent travelers who want to settle in one place for easily touring Tuscany's highlights. *Directions:* Instead of going into the center of Cortona, follow signs for Arezzo and drive past Camucia on the outskirts of town to Tavarnelle. Turn right at San Pietro a Cegliolo and drive 2 km up to Borgo Elena.

*BORGO ELENA*
*Host: Mario Baracchi*
*Localita: San Pietro a Cegliolo*
*Cortona (AR) 52042, Italy*
*Tel & fax: (0575) 604773, Cellphone: (333) 9319320*
*7 apartments: €490–€560 weekly,*
*€40 per person per night*
*Minimum nights required: 3, Open: all year*
*Other languages: very little English*
*Region: Tuscany, Michelin Map: 563*
*karenbrown.com/italy/borgoelena.html*

The charming medieval etruscan town of Cortona that gained international fame through Frances Mayes' bestseller, "Under the Tuscan Sun", has subsequently responded to the increased demand for tourist accommodation. The Mancini family decided to completely refurbish their lovely old farm (a village in itself on the site of an Etruscan settlement) to accommodate a variety of needs for the more demanding traveller. The 17th century private home sits in the middle of its meticulously landscaped gardens boasting 2,500 rose plants and surrounded by ten other stone houses which are now home to the comfortable hotel, Locanda. Featuring a voluminous breakfast room, eight spacious one, two and three-bedroom apartments on two floors of the former olive oil mill and farmer's quarters, there are also two excellent restaurants, a wine bar, a stunning swimming pool with hydro-massage, and a chapel. The décor of all the rooms is in keeping with an air of elegant country ambience. A complete country resort. *Directions:* Exit from autostrada A1 at Valdichiana, proceed towards Perugia. Exit from this highway at second exit for Cortona. Strategically located, Il Melone is well-marked on the main street leading to Arezzo, below Cortona center.

*BORGO IL MELONE*      *New*
*Host: Carlo Livraga Mancini family*
*Il Sodo, Case Sparse 38*
*Cortona (AR) 52042, Italy*
*Tel: (0575) 603330, Fax: (0575 )630001*
*12 rooms, Double: €125–€260*
*8 apartments: € 1,200–€2,700 weekly*
*Minimum nights required: 7*
*Open: Open all year, Credit cards: all major*
*Other languages: good English, Region: Tuscany*
*karenbrown.com/italy/ilmelone.html*

For British couple, Scarlett and Colin, the fantasy of restoring a farmhouse in the Tuscan hills and enjoying a slower-paced life became reality when they found their dream property, Stoppiacce. Set amongst the lush green mountains separating Tuscany and Umbria beyond Cortona, the ancient stone farmhouse was meticulously restored and tastefully appointed with country antiques and matching fabrics. Within are the hosts' quarters plus three lovely guestrooms, the "tower" room having its own independent entrance. Scarlett, an excellent cook, prepares dinners, by prior arrangement, accompanied by top-choice local wines (€46 per person). Below the main house is a cozy nest for two (Il Castagno) with sitting room and kitchenette, terrace on the first floor, and bedroom with bathroom on the second floor. This is an ideal place for those who like to combine leisurely local touring with pure relaxation. Take advantage of the lovely swimming pool with the most incredible views over the valley. *Directions:* Exit the A1 autostrada at Val di Chiana and follow the highway towards Perugia. Exit at second turnoff for Cortona, pass the city, and continue for Citta del Castello on a small winding road. After 7 km turn left at Portole and continue for 10 km until San Pietro a Dame. Drive through the village and look for mailbox on the right marked "Stoppiacce", turn left down stone road for 1 km.

*STOPPIACCE*
*Hosts: Scarlett & Colin Campbell*
*Localita: San Pietro a Dame*
*Cortona (AR) 52044, Italy*
*Tel & fax: (0575) 690058, Cellphone: (349) 8657088*
*3 rooms, Double: €130*
*1 apartment: €575–€680 weekly*
*Minimum nights required: 3*
*Open: Apr to Oct, Other languages: fluent English*
*Region: Tuscany, Michelin Map: 563*
*karenbrown.com/italy/stoppiacce.html*

The Antica Fattoria came highly recommended by several readers who stayed there in the first year it opened. It is indeed a delightful combination of pretty countryside, strategic touring position, comfortable rooms, excellent meals, and warm hospitality. Following the increasingly popular lifestyle trend of abandoning the city for a rural pace, Roman couple Alessandro and Anna left their offices to become, essentially, farmers. They bought and restored two connected stone farmhouses and incorporated a combination of seven rooms and two apartments, decorated pleasantly with a characteristic country flavor, for guests. While Alessandro tends to the crops and farm animals, Anna lives out her passion for cooking, much to guests' delight. Meals are served either outside at one long table or in the transformed cow stalls below with cozy sitting area and fireplace. At times the allegria and good food keep guests at the table until the wee hours. A lovely swimming pool looks over the wooded hills to the valley. The busy hosts take time to assist guests with the many local itineraries and organize a wide variety of games. Perfect for families and a great base for exploring Umbria. The town of Deruta is world-famous for its painted ceramic pottery and filled with workshops and stores. *Directions:* From Perugia (18 km), exit from E45 at Casalina. Take the first right and follow signs to the Santuario Madonna dei Bagni and then to the Fattoria.

*ANTICA FATTORIA DEL COLLE*
*Hosts: Anna & Alessandro Coluccelli*
*Strada Colle delle Forche 6*
*Deruta (PG) 06053, Italy*
*Tel & fax: (075) 972201, Cellphone: (329) 9897272*
*7 rooms, Double: €76–€106*
*2 apartments: €780–€1,035*
*Minimum nights required: 2, 7 Aug*
*Open: Easter to Jan 10, Other languages: good English*
*Region: Umbria, Michelin Map: 563*
*karenbrown.com/italy/anticafattoriadelcolle.html*

At the edge of the Mugello area north of Florence is the property of Enrico and Elisa Lippi and their growing family. The primary activity on the farm is the production of the highest-grade quality (D.O.C.G.) Chianti Rufina, something that guests can observe up close as the cantinas, guests' farmhouses, and main villa are closely integrated, forming a borgo. Independent houses have from one to three bedrooms, living room, kitchen, and small garden with sitting area. They have been freshly redone, retaining wood-beamed ceilings and some exposed brick features. Country antiques were also restored and fit in well with the general ambiance. Rosmarino and Bosco, within or attached to the ancient medieval tower, are most characteristic of all the apartments. Il Cavaliere is designed for longer stays and is a nice base for exploring this lesser-known part of northern Tuscany and Emilia-Romagna, divided by the Apennines with their villages of medieval and even Etruscan origins. Mountain bikes can be rented, a pool is open to guests from June through September, and courses in Italian wine and olive-oil production are arranged. *Directions:* From Florence head for Pontassieve and continue to Dicomano. At 1 km before town, turn right for Frascole and follow signs to Il Cavaliere.

*FRASCOLE-IL CAVALIERE*
*Hosts: Elisa & Enrico Lippi*
*Via di Frascole 27*
*Dicomano (FI) 50062, Italy*
*Tel & fax: (055) 8386340, Cellphone: (339) 3050554*
*Double: €60–€110*
*5 apartments: €70–€150 daily (high season)*
*Open: all year, Credit cards: VS*
*Other languages: some English, French*
*Region: Tuscany, Michelin Map: 563*
*karenbrown.com/italy/frascole.html*

The prestigious Luigi Einaudi wine estate (he was the first president of the Italian republic), established in 1897, is the oldest in the area and extends over 300 acres of land of which some 60 acres are covered entirely with vineyards. Today, Luigi's granddaughter Paola and husband Giorgio Ruffo continue this strong family tradition as leading producers of top Barolo, Barbera, and Dolcetto wines. They have transformed one of the family residences dating to the 18th century into a refined bed and breakfast that preserves an authentic essence of the past. The very attractive and spacious bedrooms, all on the first floor and appointed with fine antiques and gorgeous fabrics, are joined by an elegant common living room where plenty of material on what the region offers is readily available. There is also a large terrace for guests on this same floor and a full country breakfast is served in the sunny dining room off the kitchen. Corner rooms and the one suite have terraces and all rooms have splendid views of the undulating hillsides with a backdrop of the Alps in the distance. Elvira, who takes care of guests, lives with her family in the apartment downstairs next to the cantina. In various stages of completion is the addition of six more bedrooms opposite the main house with arched glassed-in living room, swimming pool, and tennis court. *Directions:* The Foresteria dei Poderi is 2 km outside of Dogliani on the road towards Belvedere.

*FORESTERIA DEI PODERI*
*Host: Elvira Raimondi family*
*Localita: Borgata Gombe 31*
*Dogliani (CN) 12063, Italy*
*Tel: (0173) 70414, Fax: (0173) 742017*
*10 rooms, Double: €114*
*Open: all year, Credit cards: MC, VS*
*Other languages: some English*
*Region: Piedmont, Michelin Map: 561*
*karenbrown.com/italy/enaudi.html*

The Villa Goetzen is an excellent choice as a base for visiting the villas of Palladio and the stunning historical centers of Verona and Padua (plus being 20 minutes from Venice). With a long tradition in hospitality, the local Minchio family bought the peach-colored home (dating from 1739) sitting on the Brenta Canal in town and transformed it into an elegant bed-and-breakfast accommodation. Although the house borders the main road, silence reigns within. You enter the iron gates into a courtyard, where on the right is a miniature coach house with two of the twelve rooms. These are the favorites and most romantic, with beamed mansard ceilings, parquet floors, and canal view. All rooms are decorated with classic good taste in the selection of antique pieces, wrought-iron beds, and coordination of fabrics and individual color schemes. Immaculate bathrooms have black-and-white checked tiles. Fortunate guests can sample delectable Venetian meals prepared by Paola and her son, Massimiliano, in one of the three intimate dining rooms. Brother Cristian receives guests and attends to their needs with great charm and finesse. It would be virtually impossible to find a hotel with similar standards in Venice at this rate. *Directions:* Exit at Dolo from the A4 autostrada and go straight into town until you arrive at the canal. Turn left and follow signs for Venezia. The villa is on the right.

*VILLA GOETZEN*
*Host: Minchio family*
*Via Matteotti 6*
*Dolo (VE) 30031, Italy*
*Tel: (041) 5102300, Fax: (041) 412600*
*12 rooms, Double: €103–€130*
*Restaurant closed Aug*
*Open: all year, Credit cards: all major*
*Other languages: good English*
*Region: Veneto, Michelin Map: 562*
*karenbrown.com/italy/goetzen.html*

Picturesque Courmayeur, on the Italian side of the tunnel cutting through Mont Blanc into France, is a popular ski and summer resort. In the summer months comfortable temperatures and spectacular mountain scenery along with activities such as hiking, golf, horseback riding, and kayaking attract many visitors. The warm Berthod family have been offering hospitality to guests for some time, greeting them by name as they return "home" year after year. The old stone chalet and barn, squeezed between other houses in the center of the centuries-old village of Entreves, outside Courmayeur, has been restored using old and new materials. The cozy reception area maintains its original rustic flavor with flagstone floors and beams, hanging brass pots, typical locally made pine furniture, and homey touches like dried-flower arrangements and lace curtains. The 23 simply appointed rooms, divided between two buildings, offer the amenities of a standard hotel. A hearty breakfast is the only meal served; however, half-board arrangements can be made with local restaurants for longer stays. La Grange is an efficiently run bed and breakfast right at the foot of the snow-capped Alps. *Directions:* From Aosta where the A5 autostrada ends, continue on route 26 to Courmayeur. Entreves is 5 km beyond.

*LA GRANGE*
*Host: Berthod family*
*Entreves (AO) 11013, Italy*
*Tel: (0165) 869733, Fax: (0165) 869744*
*23 rooms, Double: €100*
*Closed: May, Jun, Oct, Nov*
*Credit cards: all major*
*Other languages: good English*
*Region: Aosta Valley, Michelin Map: 561*
*karenbrown.com/italy/lagrange.html*

Although the Apulia region is decidedly one of the most intriguing and unusual areas of the less-traveled Italy, it is short of accommodation with that combination of comfort, charm, and history we search high and low for. The 350-year-old Masseria Marzalossa, however, is a true exception, being a romantic inn strategically placed between the highlights of the region with its unique trulli cone-shaped houses. The stunning 100-acre property, which produces top-quality olive oil, has belonged to the Guarini family since its origins and they take pride in sharing their piece of paradise with world travelers. A wall surrounding the ancient masseria conceals several inner courtyards leading to the massive stone main house and connecting houses where the elegant, ground-level bedrooms enjoy their own private courtyard entrances. The tastefully decorated rooms are appointed with period antiques in harmony with the stone floors and vaulted or beamed ceilings. Also available is a magnificent suite with high, vaulted ceilings, frescoes, and a marble bathroom. A passageway from the front garden leads to a divine enclosed swimming pool surrounded by columns, lemon trees, bougainvillea vines, potted geraniums, and utter silence. Full country breakfasts and occasional dinners are served in the intimate dining room. This property is impeccable. *Directions:* Two km from Fasano on the S.S.16 going towards Ostuni, turn right at their sign.

❄ ⚓ ☕ 🍽 💳 🏕 ☎ 🕺 👫 🏇 ♈ Ψ P ≈ 🚶 ⚓ 🍇

*MASSERIA MARZALOSSA*
*Hosts: Mario & Maria Teresa Guarini*
*Contrada da Pezze Vicine 65*
*Fasano (BR) 72015, Italy*
*Tel & fax: (080) 4413780 or (080) 4413024*
*5 rooms, Double: €156–€228*
*Minimum nights required: 3*
*Open: all year, Credit cards: VS*
*Other languages: some English*
*Region: Apulia, Michelin Map: 564*
*karenbrown.com/italy/marzalossa.html*

The countryside between Bologna, Parma, and Piacenza south of the A1 autostrada is unexpectedly scenic and intact. This is the home of Italy's most famous cheese, Parmesan (cheese factories can be visited in the mornings), as well as balsamic vinegar and most of the country's salami production. Excellent restaurants abound both in the city and outside as the region prides itself on its longstanding reputation for superior cuisine. Father-and-son team, Mauro and Federico, bought and restored the stately 6th-century stone convent and offer hospitality within 12 guestrooms on the upper two floors of the home, several of which become family suites when adjoined. Past the front foyer off to the right is a beamed sitting room for guests and the breakfast room. As in a private home, no two bedrooms are identical and are rather casually appointed with various pieces from the family's period antiques. Guests are made to feel right at home in this informal atmosphere. Besides Parma, day trips include Modena, Reggio, Mantova, Cremona, and down to the Cinque Terre. Also nearby at only 4 kilometers is La Rocca golf club. *Directions:* Exit from autostrada A1 at Parma and head directly south through the city and on towards Langhirano. After 8 km turn right for Felino and then first left at the sign for Torre. (15 km from Parma's city center.)

☕ 🏍 CREDIT ☎ P

*TORRE*
*Hosts: Federico & Mauro Pelizzoni*
*Via Ghirardi 8*
*Felino (PR) 43030, Italy*
*Tel: (0521) 831491, Fax: (0521) 337540*
*12 rooms, Double: €93*
*Open: all year, Credit cards: all major*
*Other languages: good English*
*Region: Emilia-Romagna, Michelin Map: 562*
*karenbrown.com/italy/torre.html*

Casa Palmira, directly north of Florence, was originally a group of rural buildings attached to an 11th-century tower guarding the road to the Mugello area of Tuscany. Stefano and Assunta, the amiable hosts, named their bed and breakfast after the old lady who lived in the house her entire life. She represents perhaps the spirit of the place, reminding everyone of the basic values of simple country living. The seven bedrooms on the top floor are decorated in a fresh, simple, country style, with hardwood floors, dried and fresh flowers, patchwork quilts, botanic prints, and local country antiques. Rooms are accessed by a large open sitting area with skylights and green plants. The hosts' naturally informal style of hospitality has guests feeling so at home that they can't resist assisting as Assunta works wonders in the open kitchen. This is part of a multi-functional space incorporating kitchen, dining room, and cozy living area with wicker chairs and large fireplace. Meals based on fresh vegetables are served either here or out in the garden under the portico. Daily cooking lessons for individuals or weekly cooking courses for small groups are arranged. Transfers from train station or airport are also offered. *Directions:* Halfway between Borgo S. Lorenzo and Florence on route 302 (Via Faentina), 2 km after Olmo coming from Florence (16 km). Casa Palmira is on the right at the sign for Ristorante Feriolo. From the north leave the A1 at Barberino del Mugello.

*CASA PALMIRA*
*Hosts: Assunta & Stefano Mattioli*
*Via Faentina–Polcanto*
*Feriolo (FI) 50030, Italy*
*Tel & fax: (055) 8409749, Cellphone: (339) 3331190*
*7 rooms, Double: €75–€95,*
*apartments from €500–€800 weekly*
*Minimum nights required: 3, Open: Mar to Dec*
*Other languages: French, good English*
*Region: Tuscany, Michelin Map: 563*
*karenbrown.com/italy/casapalmira.html*

The stunning ancient cities of Ferrara, Ravenna, and Mantova have recently become part of the more curious traveler's itinerary and Il Bagattino could not be a more perfect base for exploring this triangle of Emilia-Romagna as well as making day trips to Bologna or Venice. Congenial hostess Alessandra left a ten-year restaurant business and opened her six-room bed and breakfast in the apartment next door to her own. Just off the main square of the historic center with its impressive fortress Castello Estense, Il Bagattino is on the second floor (with elevator) of a completely refurbished brick building dating to the 1400s. You are warmly greeted in the cheery yellow front room where a breakfast of fresh croissants and homemade cakes is served at one table. The six bedrooms are divided on both sides of the main room, with a small sitting room for extra privacy. Each comfortable, identically-sized bedroom, with air conditioning, television, mini-bar, and hairdryer, has its own color scheme reflected in matching bedspreads and curtains, and a new checked-tiled bathroom. The entire historic center of this fascinating ancient city is closed off to traffic and is a cyclist's haven (bikes can be rented through Alessandra). Ferrara is a city not to be missed! *Directions:* Although this is a restricted traffic area, you can unload luggage in front of the bed and breakfast. Follow signs for the city center and Duomo—Corso Porta Reno begins from the piazza at the clock tower.

✳ 🍵 CREDIT ☎ 🛗 🚶 🚶‍♂️ 🏇 ⅄ 🖼

IL BAGATTINO
*Host: Alessandra Maurillo*
*Corso Porta Reno 24*
*Ferrara 44100, Italy*
*Tel: (0532) 241887, Cellphone: (349) 8696683*
*Fax: (0532) 217546*
*6 rooms, Double: €90–€100*
*Open: all year, Credit cards: all major*
*Other languages: good English*
*Region: Emilia-Romagna, Michelin Map: 562*
*karenbrown.com/italy/bagattino.html*

Best friends Luciano and Tommaso, refugees from city life, have over the past dozen or so years transformed the 1,000-acre property, La Casella, made up of woods, rivers, and valleys, into a veritable countryside haven for vacationers. Foremost attention has been given to the 32 rooms, which are divided between three separate stone houses. The Noci house contains seven doubles upstairs appointed with country antiques, and a large vaulted room downstairs used for small meetings or dining. La Terrazza, originally a hunting lodge, has nine rooms, one with namesake terrace looking over the poplar woods. On the highest point sits San Gregorio, with small chapel, where guests revel in the utter silence and a spectacular 360-degree view over the entire property. The lively dining room offers delectable cuisine, with ingredients direct from the farm. The many sports facilities include a beautiful big swimming pool, tennis, and an equestrian center where numerous special outings and events are organized. There is also a spa program with natural treatments. Well-marked trails lead the rider, biker, or hiker to such marvels as Todi, Orvieto, or even Perugia. *Directions:* Exit at Fabro from the Rome-Florence A1 autostrada. Follow signs for Parrano (7 km), turning right at the Casella sign, and continue for another 7 km on a rough gravel road.

*LA CASELLA*
*Hosts: Luciano Nenna & Tommaso Campolmi*
*Localita: La Casella*
*Ficulle (TR) 05016, Italy*
*Tel: (0763) 86588 or (0763) 86684, Fax: (0763) 86684*
*32 rooms, Double: €90–€105*
*Apartment €90–€115*
*Open: all year, Credit cards: all major*
*Other languages: fluent English*
*Region: Umbria, Michelin Map: 563*
*karenbrown.com/italy/lacasella.html*

The latest arrival in the group of independent, city bed & breakfast properties, managed by Lea, is the very charming Antica Dimora. Located in part of an ancient palazzo owned by the Pandolfini family, just 5 blocks north of the Duomo Cathedral, it has similiar characteristics to the other three bed & breakfasts found in the same area (Johanna, Johlea I and II) owned by the same cordial owner, but offers a touch more. Six rooms are located on the top floor of the ancient, residential building. Each room is individually and tastefully appointed as in a true home, with great attention to detail and guest comfort. A cozy living/reception room with inviting, striped burgundy sofas awaits guests. Breakfast is served in this same reception room or privately in the bedrooms. It is difficult to choose a preference among the six romantic rooms, each completely different in soft pastel color schemes and a unique, additional feature. There are two lovely corner rooms and two quiet ones with small back terraces. All have antique pieces, silk or hand-woven Busatti fabrics and linens, and canopy beds. The color-coordinated bathrooms have marble or brick floors. All are delightful giving the feeling of having your own private apartment in Florence, including the key to the front door! *Directions:* 3 blocks north of San Marco church and square.

*ANTICA DIMORA        New*
*Host: Lea Gulmanelli*
*Via San Gallo 72*
*Florence 50129, Italy*
*Tel: (055) 462 7296, Fax: (055) 463 4450*
*6 rooms, Double: €125–€140*
*Open: all year*
*Other languages: some English, French*
*Region: Tuscany*
*karenbrown.com/italy/dimora.html*

The Hotel Aprile, owned by the Cantini Zucconi family for almost four decades, is located in a 15th-century Medici palace behind the Piazza Santa Maria Novella, near the train station and many fine restaurants and shops. The historical building was restored under the strict ordinance of Florence's Commission of Fine Arts. The small and charming hotel is full of delightful surprises: from 16th-century paintings and a bust of the Duke of Tuscany to the frescoed breakfast room and quiet courtyard garden. The old-fashioned reception and sitting areas are invitingly furnished with Florentine Renaissance antiques, comfy, overstuffed red armchairs, and Oriental carpets worn with time. There are 35 bedrooms, all with private bathrooms. The wallpapered rooms include telephones and mini-bars, and feature parquet floors and high vaulted ceilings, but vary widely in their size and decor—some are too basic and modern. A recent extensive renovation has made improvements in facilities while maintaining the original overall charm. Request one of the quieter rooms at the back of the hotel, overlooking the garden. At the desk you find Roberto Gazzini and Sandra Costantini looking after guests' needs. *Directions:* Use a detailed city map to locate the hotel, three blocks north of the Duomo. There is a parking garage.

*HOTEL APRILE*
*Host: Riccardo Zucconi*
*Via della Scala 6*
*Florence 50123, Italy*
*Tel: (055) 216237, Fax: (055) 280947*
*35 rooms, Double: €200*
*Open: all year, Credit cards: all major*
*Other languages: good English*
*Region: Tuscany, Michelin Map: 563*
*karenbrown.com/italy/aprile.html*

Another nice discovery in the category of small, renovated hotels in Florence is the Botticelli, hidden away on a narrow back street behind the Central Market. Many original features of this 16th-century building, once a private home, have been preserved including evidence of a tiny alley that divided the two now-united buildings. Guests enter into a painted, vaulted reception area appointed with large blue and gold armchairs and side sitting room. Other architectural features so typical of the Renaissance period in Florence are the austere gray stone doorways, beamed ceilings in bedrooms, and the delightful open loggia terrace on the second floor lined with terra-cotta vases of cascading red geraniums. The bedrooms are situated on the three upper floors, with two being up in the mansard and enjoying the best views, and are comfortably and practically decorated with clean wooden furniture and an occasional antique piece blending well with the pea-green fabrics. A full buffet breakfast is offered in the breakfast room with bar just behind the reception area. All the necessary modern amenities such as air conditioning, elevator, modern telephone system, and satellite TV were incorporated during the recent renovation. Fabrizio and his American wife, Janet, run two other hotels in Florence, one being the Villa Carlotta near Piazzale Michelangelo. *Directions:* The hotel is one block north of Piazza San Lorenzo and the Medici Chapels.

*HOTEL BOTTICELLI*
Hosts: Fabrizio & Janet Gheri
Via Taddea 8
Florence 50123, Italy
Tel: (055) 290905, Fax: (055) 294322
34 rooms, Double: €110–€225
Minimum nights required: 3 during fairs & New Year
Open: all year, Credit cards: all major
Other languages: good English
Region: Tuscany, Michelin Map: 563
karenbrown.com/italy/botticelli.html

In the center of the city and around the corner from the Accademia Gallery where Michelangelo's David has stood for the past 400 years or so, you find the pleasant and intimate Hotel delle Arti. The Budini Gattai family, owners of the nearby Hotel Loggiato dei Serviti, just recently took over the reigns of this small B&B type hotel. Comfort, quiet, and a feeling of being pampered guests in a friend's home were the foremost objectives in the renovation process and the decorating was handled with the same care and attention one would give to a private home. Three tasteful bedrooms are located on each of the three upper floors reached by an elevator or green-carpeted staircase. Rooms with fresh color-tiled bathrooms are furnished with antique pieces, parquet floors, and amenities such as air conditioning, satellite TV, and a safe. On the top floor you find a cozy living room and a breakfast room with small balcony looking out over rooftops where a full buffet breakfast is offered. Warm and gracious hostess Cinzia is personally on call for guests and is a marvelous source of information on special less-touristy places to visit and what is happening in the city. *Directions:* Four blocks north of the Duomo cathedral.

HOTEL DELLE ARTI
Host: Budini Gattai family
Via dei Servi 38/a
Florence 50122, Italy
Tel: (055) 2645307, Fax: (055) 290140
9 rooms, Double: €154–€185
Open: all year
Credit cards: all major
Other languages: good English
Region: Tuscany, Michelin Map: 563
karenbrown.com/italy/arti.html

The Hotel Hermitage is a dream of a small, well-manicured hotel housed in a 13th-century palazzo with efficient service and breathtaking views over the city's most famous monuments. The location could not be more central—on a small street between the Uffizzi Gallery and the River Arno. The fifth-floor reception area looking out to the Ponte Vecchio bridge has a cozy living-room feeling with selected antique pieces, Oriental rugs, and corner fireplace. Across the hall is the veranda-like breakfast room dotted with crisp yellow tablecloths and topped with fresh flowers where privileged guests view the tower of Palazzo Signoria. Color-coordinated, air-conditioned rooms, some with hydrojet baths, have scattered antiques, framed etchings of the city, and more views. However, the highlight of a stay at the Hermitage is spending time dreaming on the rooftop terrace. The view embraces not only the previously mentioned marvels of Florence, but also the famous dome of the Duomo cathedral and Giotto's tower. Guests are served a continental breakfast under the ivy-covered pergola and among the many flower-laden vases lining its borders. Reserve well in advance. *Directions:* Consult a detailed city map. There is a parking garage in the vicinity. Call for instructions as car traffic in this part of the city is strictly limited.

*HOTEL HERMITAGE*
*Host: Vincenzo Scarcelli*
*Piazza del Pesce*
*Florence 50122, Italy*
*Tel: (055) 287216, Fax: (055) 212208*
*23 rooms, Double: €233–€245*
*Open: all year*
*Credit cards: MC, VS*
*Other languages: good English*
*Region: Tuscany, Michelin Map: 563*
*karenbrown.com/italy/hermitage.html*

The bed and breakfast In Piazza della Signoria is a dream of a B&B hidden away on the corner of Florence's most famous square hosting the imposing city hall, Palazzo della Signoria. Sonia and Alessandro initially bought the four-story ancient building as an investment but were touched by the magic spell of this very special historic spot just up the street from the house of Dante and decided to restore it and share it with friends. The fascinating restoration project became something of an archaeological adventure, with documents discovered dating back to 1427 along with a pair of woman's shoes from that same period, and 18th-century frescoes uncovered. Up one flight from street level, Sonia, Alessandro, and their three young sons greet guests in a small living room with tables where breakfast is served. The eight bedrooms, named after Renaissance masters, are spread about the two floors, with the top floor being crowned with three apartments for those able to enjoy this marvelous city for a full week. To-die-for views from this level include the piazza, Giotto's tower, and Brunelleschi's cupola. Impeccably styled rooms with unique personalities display the architectural discoveries, lovely antique furnishings, parquet floors, and rich colors of teal, peach, and rust. None of the innovative bathrooms are identical. A real treat. *Directions:* On the northeast corner of the square at the beginning of Via dei Magazzini.

*IN PIAZZA DELLA SIGNORIA*
*Hosts: Sonia & Alessandro Pini*
*Via dei Magazzini 2*
*Florence 50122, Italy*
*Tel: (055) 2399546, Fax: (055) 2676616*
*8 rooms, Double: €200–€260*
*3 apartments:€320–€380 daily, €1200–€1400 weekly*
*Open: all year, Credit cards: all major*
*Other languages: good English*
*Region: Tuscany, Michelin Map: 563*
*karenbrown.com/italy/piazza.html*

Orto de'Medici was named for the Medici family's extensive gardens and orchards that once existed on the site of this hotel. Capable father-and-son team Emilio and Giacomo Bufalini recently took over the reins and took on the challenge of completely refurbishing the family's prim, centuries-old palazzo. Public areas maintain the ambiance of an elegant private home—the frescoed foyer and sitting rooms are graced with portraits, chandeliers, overstuffed armchairs, and Oriental carpets—while services and facilities in bedrooms conform to European Community standards. The spacious upper-floor guestrooms are reached by an elevator and are decorated with classic style. They have matching armoires and beds and all but ten have smart new gray-and-white-marble bathrooms. Several rooms on the top floor have a terrace or balcony with dreamy views over red Florentine rooftops. Perhaps the architectural highlight is the gracious breakfast room (breakfast is a buffet), with high ceilings, original parquet floors, and frescoed panels depicting garden scenes all around. French doors lead from this area to an outdoor terraced flower garden with wrought iron chairs and tables and a lovely view of San Marco church. Wine and cheese tastings are held here in the late afternoon. Dynamic young host Giacomo and his efficient and friendly staff ensure a perfect city sojourn. *Directions:* Four blocks north of the Duomo.

*HOTEL ORTO DE'MEDICI*
*Host: Giacomo Bufalini family*
*Via San Gallo 30*
*Florence 50129, Italy*
*Tel: (055) 483427, Fax: (055) 461276*
*31 rooms, Double: €130–€240*
*Open: all year, Credit cards: all major*
*Other languages: good English*
*Region: Tuscany, Michelin Map: 563*
*karenbrown.com/italy/demedici.html*

Accommodations in Italy's major art cities has transformed dramatically over the past five years, offering everything from the classic and boutique type hotels, urban bed & breakfasts, and hospitality in historic homes—in all price ranges. The Palazzo Ruspoli is an example of one of Florence's centrally located historic family residences converted into an charming accommodation. Literally around the corner from the Duomo cathedral, one enters the palazzo on a side street, and takes the elevator up one flight to the reception area. Guestrooms are laid out on two wings off this area. An adjacent breakfast room is very inviting with crisp, white linen chairs and French print drapes. The spacious bedrooms with high ceilings have parquet floors, canopy headboards and matching red or blue checked bedspreads, and new bathrooms. Many rooms have views of the famed Brunelleschi cupola. Getting around the city's dense art center is certainly not a problem from this location as you are within easy walking distance to almost everything. The friendly staff is always ready to assist with personal sight seeing arrangements. *Directions:* Half block north of the Duomo cathedral.

*PALAZZO RUSPOLI*        *New*
*Owner: Enrico Ponzall*
*Via de' Martelli 5*
*Florence 50129, Italy*
*Tel: (055) 2670563, Fax: (055) 2670525*
*20 rooms, Double: €130–€220*
*Open: all year, Credit cards: all major*
*Other languages: good English, French, German*
*Region: Tuscany*
*karenbrown.com/italy/ruspoli.html*

The country residences of wealthy Florentine families dating back to Renaissance times were all concentrated on the hills above the city. Villa Poggio San Felice is one of these, reached by way of a labyrinth of narrow (unbelievably two-way) winding roads past stone-walled gardens concealing magnificent villas. Livia inherited not only the actual property of her great-grandfather but also a long-standing tradition in the hospitality field—he was the founder of two of Florence's most prominent hotels, today called the Grand and the Excelsior. This bed and breakfast is special indeed as guests are given full run of the main part of the two-story villa with its library, gracious, portrait-lined sitting rooms, and high-ceilinged dining room where a full buffet breakfast is served overlooking the formal gardens through French doors. Enthusiastic Livia and her husband Lorenzo's desire was that their guests experience the true flavor of a noble villa and consequently minimum possible modifications were made. This authentic ambiance prevails throughout the bedrooms, which are spread out on the upper floor and contain the family's original furniture. The romantic I Sposi honeymoon bedroom has fireplace, parquet floors, and hunter-green color scheme, while the spacious room Nonni features a large terrace looking out over hills to the famous dome of Florence's cathedral. *Directions:* Ten minutes from the center of Florence. A detailed map is provided.

*VILLA POGGIO SAN FELICE*
*Hosts: Livia Puccinelli & Lorenzo Magnelli*
*Via San Matteo in Arcetri 24*
*Florence 50125, Italy*
*Tel: (055) 220016, Fax: (055) 2335388*
*5 rooms, Double: €200–€250*
*Open: Mar to Dec, Credit cards: all major*
*Other languages: good English*
*Region: Tuscany, Michelin Map: 563*
*Abitare la Storia*
*karenbrown.com/italy/borgosanfelice.html*

In the past two years, a new breed of bed and breakfasts has developed in Italy's favorite cities, especially in Florence and Rome. In order to keep costs down and be a competitive alternative to hotels, fewer amenities are offered and breakfast is self-service style in rooms (coffee, tea, breads, jam, cakes) and therefore is more adapted to an independent type of traveler. In fact, it is like having your own home in Florence with keys to the front door. Hostess Lea Gulmanelli had such success with her first B&B that she opened three additional places at a superior level, all in the same neighborhood. At the Johlea three floors of two neighboring 19th-century buildings were restored, producing twelve bedrooms of varying sizes for guests (Johlea I and II). Lea has a real flair for decorating and, as in someone's home, each well-proportioned bedroom retains its own character. All are very cozily appointed in muted soft colors, with an occasional antique, Oriental carpets, paintings by the owner, and original tiled or parquet floors. There is someone on duty all day to assist guests with their needs. Both I and II have a common living room for guests, with Johlea I having a delightful flower-potted terrace with dreamy views over Florence's rooftops to the cupola of the Duomo. Tasteful and very economical. *Directions:* The B&B is located between San Marco Square and Piazza della Libertà, directly north of the Duomo, reached in 12 minutes on foot.

❄ ☕ ☎ 👪 🍴 👫 P 🍇

*LE RESIDENZE JOHLEA*
*Host: Lea Gulmanelli*
*Via San Gallo 76 & 80*
*Florence 50129, Italy*
*Tel: (055) 4633292, Fax: (055) 4634552*
*12 rooms, Double: €95–€105*
*Open: all year*
*Other languages: good English*
*Region: Tuscany, Michelin Map: 563*
*karenbrown.com/italy/johlea.html*

The refurbished Hotel Silla is located on the left bank of the River Arno opposite Santa Croce, the famous 13th-century square and church where Michelangelo and Galileo are buried. This position offers views from some of the rooms of several of Florence's most notable architectural attractions—the Duomo, the Ponte Vecchio, and the tower of the Palazzo Vecchio. Housed on the second and third floors of a lovely 15th-century palazzo with courtyard entrance, 36 new and spotless double rooms (non-smoking upon request) with private baths are pleasantly decorated with simple dark-wood furniture and matching bedspreads and curtains. Air conditioning and an elevator were recently added necessities. The fancy, cream-colored reception area is appointed in 17th-century Venetian style, with period furniture, a chandelier, and large paintings. Breakfast is served on the splendid and spacious second-floor outdoor terrace or in the dining room overlooking the Arno. The Silla is a friendly, convenient, and quiet hotel, near the Pitti Palace, leather artisan shops, and many restaurants. It offers tourists a good value in pricey Florence. A parking garage is available. *Directions:* Refer to a detailed city map to locate the hotel.

*HOTEL SILLA*
*Owner: Gabriele Belotti*
*Via dei Renai 5*
*Florence 50125, Italy*
*Tel: (055) 2342888, Fax: (055) 2341437*
*36 rooms, Double: €150–€175*
*Open: all year, Credit cards: all major*
*Other languages: good English*
*Region: Tuscany, Michelin Map: 563*
*karenbrown.com/italy/hotelsilla.html*

La Torricella, just on the outskirts of Florence, offers travelers the advantage of staying in a Tuscan home in a quiet residential area, yet with the city easily accessible by public transportation. Marialisa completely restored her great-grandfather's home and converted it into a comfortable and efficient lodging. She decided to offer all the trimmings of a hotel, with amenities such as satellite TVs, mini-bars, and telephones in rooms, plus daily cleaning service. The terraced front of the pale-yellow villa is lined with terra-cotta vases of flowers and intoxicating wisteria vines. Upon entering the home, you pass through a small reception area with brick arches and equestrian prints into the luminous breakfast room where a buffet is served in the morning. Accommodations are scattered about the large, pristine home on various levels and are each similarly appointed in soft-green and mustard hues with sparkling new white bathrooms. Reproduction armoires and desks and wrought-iron beds harmonize well with the brick floors and high, beamed ceilings. Marialisa offers cooking classes, teaching secrets of genuine Tuscan dishes, and is a rich source of information on the area. There is a small pool at the back of the house. *Directions:* From the Certosa exit of the A1, head for the center of the city, turning right at the stoplight in Galluzzo at Piazza Acciaiuoli. Take Via Silvani for several blocks, turning right on Via Vecchia di Pozzolatico just before the fork in the road.

*LA TORRICELLA*
*Host: Marialisa Manetti family*
*Via Vecchia di Pozzolatico 25*
*Florence 50125, Italy*
*Tel: (055) 2321808, Fax: (055) 2047402*
*7 rooms, Double: €113–€130,*
*1 apartment: €600–€800 weekly*
*Minimum nights required: 2*
*Open: Mar 1 to Nov 20, Credit cards: VS*
*Other languages: good English, Region: Tuscany*
*karenbrown.com/italy/torricella.html*

The Fontanasalsa is a restored farm within a historic baglio farm complex in the countryside outside Trapani, where ferry boats depart for the beautiful Egadi islands. The vast property of the Burgarella family headed by Signora Maria Caterina, a retired pediatrician, is made up mostly of citrus and olive groves (10,000 trees!), the source of their award-winning olive oil. Cordial hospitality is offered within inviting bedrooms in a section of the quad-shaped structure which includes the wine cellars, olive oil press, a small agricultural tool museum, and the lofty beamed dining room with fireplace. Outside the courtyard, beyond a citrus grove, is the swimming pool and outdoor dining area. Individually decorated rooms appointed with family heirloom furniture and olive print curtains and bedspreads contribute to the feeling of being a truly doted upon houseguest of Signora, exactly what she had in mind. The farm continues with its daily business. Guests get a first hand look (and taste!) at Sicilian country life. This is also an excellent location for exploring the Mozia salt islands, the majestic temple of Segesta, hilltop Medieval Erice, and Trapani. *Directions:* From Palermo on autostrada A29 to Trapani, follow for Marsala-Birgi airport and exit at Fontanasalsa. At first stop light turn right and continue for a half km to the farm entrance.

*BAGLIO FONTANASALSA*     *New*
*Host: Maria Caterina Burgarella*
*Via Cusenza, 78*
*Fontanasalsa, Sicily 91020, Italy*
*Tel & fax: (0923) 591001*
*9 rooms, Double: €92–€100*
*Per person half board: €67-€75*
*Open: all year, Credit cards: all major*
*Other languages: good English*
*Region: Sicily, Michelin Map: 565*
*karenbrown.com/italy/fontanasalsa.html*

The bed and breakfast boom of the last decade in Italy has brought about a vast variety of accommodation from classic, in-home hospitality to places with many amenities that more resemble small hotels. Il Torrino brings us back to the more traditional example, with four bedrooms offered within the hostess's home. The large, old-fashioned family home of Signora Cesarina's grandparents is located in the Montechiari hills between Florence and Pisa east-west and between Volterra and Lucca north-south—a prime touring location. Here you will not find standardized rooms all decorated alike, but rather individual rooms filled with the family's personal belongings, heirloom furniture, and the authentic feeling of a Tuscan home. With her children grown and residing in various parts of the world, the very sweet hostess, Cesarina Campinotti, opened her home to travelers and welcomes guests into the downstairs living room and upstairs breakfast room where an abundant meal is served. A separate garden apartment for two persons has glass doors overlooking the small pool and countryside beyond. The four bedrooms with living room and kitchen can also be rented separately. Here you are in the center of Tuscany and there is a golf course 12 kilometers away. *Directions:* From Forcoli follow signs for Montechiari and Montacchita, continuing past Montacchita up to the group of houses called Montechiari (2 km). Il Torrino has the black iron gate and no sign.

*IL TORRINO*
*Host: Cesarina Campinotti*
*Montechiari*
*Forcoli (PI) 56030, Italy*
*Tel & fax: (0587) 629181, Cellphone: (347) 3643411*
*4 rooms, Double: €93–€104*
*1 apartment: €440– €490 weekly*
*Minimum nights required: 3, Open: all year*
*Other languages: French, Spanish, very little English*
*Region: Tuscany, Michelin Map: 563*
*karenbrown.com/italy/iltorrino.html*

The Locanda San Rocco is located in the heart of the Marches region, in spectacularly unspoilt countryside virtually unknown to international tourists. Here you have a chance to experience at first hand the beauty and simplicity of Italian country life. Nearby you can explore the historic hilltop towns of Camerino, Jesi, Osimo, Macerata, Loreto, and Recanati. The Pirri family from Rome return to their native Marches in the summer months and gracious hostess Signora Gisla opened her summer bed and breakfast business in order to share her love for this beautiful piece of the country. She offers very charming accommodation within an 18th-century stone farmhouse, part of a small village near their 132-acre property. Guests have full run of the house, which includes a large living area in a cozy exposed-stone and wood-beamed room, billiard room, and dining room looking out to a patio and garden at the back. The home is very tastefully appointed with fine country antiques, crisp striped fabrics on overstuffed armchairs, and sofas in sea-green and burgundy tones. The six bedrooms, divided between two floors and reached by an elevator, have wrought-iron beds, fine linens, and original brick floors. *Directions:* From Castelraimondo head towards San Severino and after 2 km turn left for Gagliole. The Locanda San Rocco is located in a small group of houses in Collaiello, before Gagliole.

*LOCANDA SAN ROCCO*
*Host: Gisla Pirri Conforti*
*Frazione Collaiello 2*
*Gagliole (MC) 62020, Italy*
*Tel: (0737) 642324, Fax: (0737) 642324*
*6 rooms, Double: €89, €470 weekly*
*Minimum nights required: 2*
*Closed: Oct to May, Credit cards: MC, VS*
*Other languages: some English*
*Region: Marches, Michelin Map: 563*
*karenbrown.com/italy/rocco.html*

In the heart of the beautiful Chianti wine region, a cypress-lined lane leads up to the handsome, 13th-century Castello di Meleto, set upon a gentle hill just outside Gaiole. The fairytale-perfect castle with its imposing round watchtowers and arched stone doorway embraced by fragrant roses makes an enchanting stop while exploring the back roads of Tuscany. There is a double treat in store because you can not only sample delicious wines in the attractive tasting room, but also visit the interior of this splendid castle with its walls and ceilings lavishly enhanced by superb frescoes, lovely antique furnishings, and even an adorable baroque theater dating back to the mid-1700s (call ahead for tour times). The castle also offers nine attractively decorated guestrooms with antique furnishings, five within the castle and four in the chapel house. Breakfast is served each morning in the cozy kitchen with huge open fireplace. The castle gardens stretch out to a line of lacy trees that frame a superb vista of the idyllic Tuscan countryside. There is also a stunning view from the swimming pool, which is bordered on three sides by a flagstone terrace and on the fourth flows seamlessly into the horizon. If you are traveling with friends or family and want a place for a longer stay, the castle offers 11 beautifully furnished stone cottages with well-equipped kitchens and from one to three bedrooms. *Directions:* From Gaiole in Chianti, follow signs to the castle.

*CASTELLO DI MELETO*
*Hosts: Lucia Pasquini & Roberto Garcea*
*Gaiole in Chianti (SI) 53013, Italy*
*Tel & fax: (0577) 749129*
*9 rooms, Double: €125–€148*
*11 cottages: €791–€1,700 weekly*
*Minimum nights required: 2, 7 in apartments*
*Open: all year, Credit cards: all major*
*Other languages: fluent English, German*
*Region: Tuscany, Michelin Map: 563*
*karenbrown.com/italy/castellomeleto.html*

The Castello di Tornano, a strategically situated hilltop tower dating back almost 1,000 years, has a 360-degree vista of the surrounding valley and has been of great historical significance in the seemingly endless territorial battles between Siena and Florence. The owners are the Selvolini family and it is Patrizia who welcomes guests to the expansive wine estate. Nine charming suites are situated in the actual castle and its monumental tower. Patrizia has personally taken care of the décor of the house using many of the family's own antiques. The piece d'resistance is the superior suite on the top floor of the tower, offering a unique architectural style and a magnificent view from eight large windows. The tower-top terrace has a 6-person hydrojet pool, a view not easily forgotten. In the stone farmhouse, in front of the tower, 7 one- and two-bedroom apartments are offered guests, each appointed in the typical rustic style of Tuscany. The restaurant serves authentic, traditional meals. The spectacular pool was built inside the ancient moat of the castle. Trails cut across the vineyards and the surrounding woods, enjoyable for walks. It is also possible to ride the owners' horses through the scenic countryside. *Directions:* From the A1 exit at Valdarno, follow the sign to Gaiole. Take the S.S.408 towards Gaiole and pass through the village, following signs for Siena. After 6 km you see the sign for Tornano on the left.

※ ▬ ⚗ ♨ 📇 ☎ 🍴 🚶🚶 🐎 ⛾ P 🍴 🚭 ≈ 🚶 🏞 🐾 🍇

*CASTELLO DI TORNANO*
*Hosts: Patrizia Selvolini & Francesco Gioffreda*
*Gaiole in Chianti (SI) 53013, Italy*
*Tel: (0577) 746067, Fax: (0577) 746094*
*9 rooms, Double: €160–€390*
*7 apartments: €80–€250 daily*
*Minimum nights required: 2*
*Open: Mar to Dec, Credit cards: VS*
*Other languages: good English*
*Region: Tuscany, Michelin Map: 563*
*karenbrown.com/italy/castelloditornano.html*

The heel of Italy offers a wealth of natural beauty but, because of its remoteness, few really charming places to stay. The Masseria Lo Prieno is run by the delightful Castriota family, whose crops are representative of the staples of the Apulia region, and include olives, almonds, fruits, and grains. Spartan accommodations are offered in bungalows scattered among the pine woods and palms on the family property. Each mini guesthouse includes one bedroom, kitchenette, bathroom, and an eating area containing basic necessities. Nine simply decorated rooms with bathrooms are now available within a newly constructed house on the property. Former animal stalls have been converted into a large dining space rustically decorated with antique farm tools and brass pots. Along with warm hospitality, the family makes meals a top priority and it is the food that makes the stay here special. For an exquisite and authentic traditional meal, the restaurant here is incomparable. Both Maria Grazia, the energetic daughter who runs the show, and her charming mother take pride in demonstrating how local specialties are prepared. This is a budget choice for touring this area. *Directions:* From Taranto take N174 to Galatone, then follow signs for Secli. From Bari take the Gallipoli-Galatone road. After the first traffic light, continue to the sign on the right for Masseria and follow signs to the farm.

*MASSERIA LO PRIENO*
*Host: Francesco Castriota family*
*Localita: Contrada Orelle*
*Galatone (LE) 73044, Italy*
*Tel: (0833) 865898, Fax: (0833) 861879*
*9 rooms, Double: €58–€72, 5 bungalows: €64–€74 daily*
*Per person half board: €51, Minimum nights required: 2*
*Open: Apr to Sep, Credit cards: all major*
*Other languages: some English*
*Region: Apulia, Michelin Map: 564*
*karenbrown.com/italy/masserialoprieno.html*

On the extreme outskirts of Florence, the Fattoressa offers a location for dual exploration of both the city and the Tuscan countryside. One of the many marvelous attractions of Florence is how the countryside comes right up to the doors of the city and just behind the magnificent Certosa monastery you find the 15th-century stone farmhouse of the delightfully congenial Fusi-Borgioli family. They have transformed the farmer's quarters into guest accommodations: four sweetly simple bedrooms plus two triples, each with its own spotless bathroom. Angiolina and Amelio, who have tended to this piece of land for many years, treat their guests like family and, as a result, enjoy receiving some of them year after year. Daughters-in-law Laura and Katia, who speak English, have been a great help in assisting guests with local itineraries. Visitors take meals en famille at long tables in the cozy, rustic dining room with a large stone fireplace (€31 for dinner). Here Angiolina proudly serves authentic Florentine specialties using ingredients from her own fruit orchard and vegetable garden. *Directions:* Entering Florence from the Certosa exit off the Siena superstrada, turn left one street after the Certosa monastery stoplight onto Volterrana. After the bridge, turn right behind the building. The house is just on the left.

*LA FATTORESSA*
*Hosts: Angiolina Fusi & Amelio Borgioli*
*Via Volterrana 58*
*Galluzzo (FI) 50124, Italy*
*Tel & fax: (055) 2048418*
*6 rooms, Double: €90*
*Minimum nights required: 2*
*Open: all year*
*Other languages: some English, French, German*
*Region: Tuscany, Michelin Map: 563*
*karenbrown.com/italy/lafattoressa.html*

Gangi                    Villa Raino                    Map: 12

Wandering off the main tourist trail in Sicily is recommended for the traveler who truly enjoys contact with local people and their culture (best to have some command of Italian) and is curious and open to new experiences, without being tied to rigid schedules. If you leave yourselves in the hands of the Contes, you will certainly be rewarded with a once-in-a-lifetime stay. Reaching Gangi is an adventure in itself, taking you far away from the main route through the scenic Madonie Mountains, which cut across the mid-northern part of Sicily. Villa Raino is just outside Gangi, with its tightly packed houses covering the tip of a mountaintop. Genuine host, Aldo, left the family hotel business in town and restored this 100-year-old brick house once owned by a noble family, offering an excellent countryside restaurant for local families and city people coming from as far away as Palermo. On the first and second floors there are ten unique guestrooms with mansard ceilings, some having a small balcony. A mix of family antiques is scattered about the rooms, which have Tiffany bedside lamps and walls stenciled using an ancient technique that gives the effect of floral wallpaper. Bathrooms have brightly colored tiles. All in all Villa Raino provides a delightful opportunity to explore. *Directions:* From A19 exit at Tre Monzelli and follow S.S.120 to Gangi for 38 km. A sign before town takes you down a rough, unpaved road to the property.

*VILLA RAINO*
*Hosts: Nina & Aldo Conte*
*Contrada Raino*
*Gangi, Sicily (PA) 90024, Italy*
*Tel: (0921) 644680, Fax: (0921) 644424*
*10 rooms, Double: €70–€75*
*Open: all year, Credit cards: all major*
*Other languages: some English*
*Region: Sicily, Michelin Map: 565*
*karenbrown.com/italy/raino.html*

Casa Mezzuola is part of a small group of farmhouses atop a hill 3 kilometers outside Greve where the land was divided into separate smaller properties. Friendly hosts, Riccardo, an antiques and jewelry dealer, Nicoletta, and their two girls live in the main house while hospitality is offered within three apartments for two to four persons in the adjacent stables and fienile where the hay was once stored. The stone walls, beams, and original brick openings to allow air into the barn were all preserved in the tower-like construction housing two of the apartments. A two-story apartment has a tiled kitchen/living area on one floor and bedroom and bathroom upstairs, while the snug studio apartment crowns the top of the tower. They are all nicely furnished with colorful rugs, local country furniture, satellite TV, and fully equipped kitchens. Breakfast is served within the apartments or outside under one of the pergola terraces. Just below the apartments is a swimming pool, which enjoys the expansive vistas, and there are bikes for guests' use. This is a convenient base for travelers in the heart of Chianti. Greve has a full program of festivals, concerts, and events, especially during the summer. *Directions:* Entering Greve from the north (Florence), turn right at the Esso Petrol Station. Follow signs for Mezzuola, Cologne, not Montefioralle. After 3 km of unpaved, bumpy road, you will come across the marked property.

*CASA MEZZUOLA*
*Host: Riccardo Franconeri family*
*Via S. Cresci 30, Greve in Chianti (FI) 50022, Italy*
*Tel & fax: (055) 8544885, Cellphone: (347) 6135920*
*Double: €80–€120*
*3 apartments: €400–€850 weekly, €90–€130 daily*
*Minimum nights required: 3, 7 Jun to Sep*
*Open: all year, Credit cards: MC, VS*
*Other languages: good English*
*Region: Tuscany, Michelin Map: 563*
*karenbrown.com/italy/mezzuola.html*

In the northern reaches of Lazio, bordering Umbria and Tuscany, is the stately, 17th-century castle of the noble Mancini Caterini family. Sociable hosts Antonello and Cristina decided to transfer their young family from Rome and reside permanently on the vast wooded property, overseeing the agricultural activity as Antonello's ancestors once did. They have done an admirable job of restoring the large, ivy-covered farmhouse just below the family's residence and creating four charming apartments plus twelve bedrooms for guests. The bi-level apartments maintain their original rustic flavor and are cheerfully decorated with antique armoires and dressers, country fabrics for curtains and bedspreads, and wrought-iron beds. Accommodation in low season and for shorter stays is offered in the Granaio 1 and 2, with four bedrooms on each floor and individual living rooms, which can also be used as separate apartments. On the ground floor you find outdoor and indoor eating areas, billiard room, and game room overlooking a lovely swimming pool. Activities include tennis, horseback riding, wine itineraries, and boat rides and sailing on nearby Lake Bolsena, besides exploration of the many ancient Etruscan towns in this very beautiful countryside. *Directions:* From the A1 autostrada exit at Orvieto and follow signs first for Bolsena then Castel S. Giorgio-S. Lorenzo Nuovo-Grotte di Castro. Just past town turn right at the Castello sign.

⚓ 💺 🍴 🍲 ⛺ 👥 🏇 P ⚓ 🏃 ⛵ 🍇

*CASTELLO DI S. CRISTINA*
*Hosts: Cristina & Antonello Mancini Caterini*
*Grotte di Castro (VT) 01025, Italy*
*Tel & fax: (0763) 78011*
*Cellphone: (339) 8605166*
*12 rooms, Double: €80–€120*
*6 apartments: €450–€1250 weekly*
*Open: all year*
*Region: Lazio*
*Michelin Map: 563*
*karenbrown.com/italy/cristina.html*

The Aosta mountain area is known primarily as a ski resort, sharing the majestic Alps with France and Switzerland. Tourism during the rest of the year is in the developing stages and offers a myriad of attractions in a beautifully unspoilt environment, including mountain hikes on well-marked trails (the famous Walser trail stretches straight across the region starting on the Swiss border and ending on the French border), medieval castles, quaint villages, Roman archaeological sites, local artisans, artisan cheese production, and wine tours. Lo Triolet offers a strategic point from which to visit these treasures within two comfortable apartments in the restored 16th-century house with cantina next door. The group of stone houses near the road includes the family's own house, the guesthouse, and surrounding neighbors all backed by the hillside and woods. Everything in the one- and two-bedroom apartments—tiles on floors, kitchenettes, bathrooms, and furniture—is brand new. The immediate area lends itself well to the production of various grapes and Marco took advantage of this climate for the production of various Pinot Gris, which he enthusiastically explains to guests. His wife's family owns another winery in the next valley. *Directions:* Exit from A5 at Aosta Ovest, driving towards Courmayeur. After 5 km, just after the village of Villeneuve, follow signs for Introd. After another 2 km, Lo Triolet is marked on the right.

*LO TRIOLET*
*Hosts: Marco Martin & Paola Bionaz*
*Fraz. Junod 7*
*Introd (AO) 11010, Italy*
*Tel & fax: (0165) 95437, Cellphone: (339) 1387092*
*2 apartments: €40–€75 daily (2 people)*
*Minimum nights required: 3, 7 (Jul & Aug)*
*Open: all year*
*Other languages: French*
*Region: Aosta Valley, Michelin Map: 561*
*karenbrown.com/italy/triolet.html*

La Morra is a quaint village dominating the Langhe wine valley with spectacular views over undulating layers of striped hillsides. The village, dating back to the 12th century, has six historic churches and a bell tower from the 1600s. There is a comprehensive enoteca in town where most regional wines are presented and sold, plus five other wine bars and six restaurants. The Vibertis have returned to their farm property after living in Alba for some years and now the retired couple enjoys hosting guests from around the world in their pristine white brick farmhouse dating to 1885. Signora Teresa has done a wonderful job of maintaining an authentic ambiance of the farmer's home. Rooms with worn brick floors retain all the original country antiques, are decorated with embroidered curtains and bedspreads, and have immaculate new bathrooms. All four bedrooms face the road and are off a hallway up on the first floor of one half of the house, while the hosts' quarters remain separate on the opposite side. A country breakfast with fresh-baked cakes is served downstairs in the guests' common room. Son Franco speaks English well and is present mostly in the afternoons and weekends, while brother Bruno has just opened his own 14-room hotel in La Morra. Genuine hospitality and ambiance. *Directions:* Leaving Alba, follow signs for Barolo. At the town of Gallo d'Alba, turn right for La Morra-Santa Maria. Casa Bambin is right on the road 2 km before La Morra.

*CASA BAMBIN*
*Host: Teresa Viberti family*
*Frazione Santa Maria 68*
*La Morra (CN) 12064, Italy*
*Tel & fax: (0173) 50785*
*4 rooms, Double: €55–€60*
*Minimum nights required: 2*
*Closed: Dec to Mar*
*Other languages: good English*
*Region: Piedmont, Michelin Map: 561*
*karenbrown.com/italy/bambin.html*

Among the many identical, perfectly practical chalet-style accommodations available throughout the Dolomites, we gratefully came upon a unique treasure. Easily spotted on the hillside above the main road from La Villa to Corvara, the 16th-century castle with its surrounding stone wall, rock foundation, and two corner lookout towers is the most important and best-preserved monument of its kind remaining in the Badia Valley. Ciastel Colz is something very magical and intimate and has been restored and tastefully decorated with the utmost attention to detail and to the preservation of the castle's rich history. The upstairs floor is dedicated entirely to the restaurant where traditional local dishes are served. Set up like a private home, you find a very cozy rust-and-gray-colored breakfast room with a wood-burning oven where fresh bread is made, a comfortable sitting room, and two simply elegant dining rooms. These luminous paneled rooms, decorated in pastel colors accented with green and rust, have a light and airy ambiance, which contrasts with the building's massive volume. One large bedroom is found on the next floor while the other three are located in the external towers and offer extra privacy. The castle offers guests an authentic ambiance in a most romantic setting. *Directions:* Leave the A22 at Val Gardena and drive through Ortisei, Selva, and Corvara to La Villa. Follow signs to the Ciastel Colz before reaching La Villa center. (A total of 45 km.)

*CIASTEL COLZ*
*Hosts: Wilma & Stefan Weiser*
*Strada Marin 80*
*La Villa (BZ) 39030, Italy*
*Tel: (0471) 847511, Cellphone: (348) 224 4547*
*Fax: (0471) 844120*
*4 rooms, Double: €128–€268*
*Closed: May & Nov, Credit cards: all major*
*Other languages: good English*
*Region: Trentino-Alto Adige, Michelin Map: 562*
*karenbrown.com/italy/colz.html*

An outstanding alternative to the city hotels of Venice is the perfectly charming Gargan bed and breakfast situated in the countryside just 30 kilometers away. The Calzavara family renovated the family's expansive 17th-century country house and opened the restaurant and guestrooms, offering four sweetly decorated bedrooms each with its own bathroom on the top floor plus two suites consisting of bedroom, sitting room, and bathroom. Signora Antonia, son Alessandro who looks after the farm, and his wife Nicoletta enjoy making their guests feel as "at home" as possible by having fresh flowers in the cozy, antique-filled bedrooms. The downstairs sitting and dining rooms display the family's country antiques as well as a large fireplace and nice touches such as lace curtains and paintings. Guests are treated to a full breakfast of home-baked cakes and exceptional four-course dinners prepared especially for guests by Signora Antonia herself, using all ingredients from the farm. The Gargan is an ideal choice in this area, being a short drive from such marvels as Padua, Venice, Treviso, Vicenza, Verona, and Palladian villas plus many smaller medieval villages. *Directions:* From Venice take route 245 to Scorze, turning right for Montebelluna at the stoplight 1 km after town. After the town of S. Ambrogio turn left at the stoplight. Turn right at the church in Levada up to the house.

*GARGAN*
*Host: Calzavara family*
*Via Marco Polo 2*
*Levada di Piombino Dese (PD) 35017, Italy*
*Tel: (049) 9350308, Fax: (049) 9350016*
*6 rooms, Double: €65–€85*
*Dinner: €20 per person*
*Closed: Jan & Aug*
*Other languages: some English*
*Region: Veneto, Michelin Map: 562*
*karenbrown.com/italy/gargan.html*

When Lois Martin, a retired teacher, spotted the lovely restored farmhouse at San Martino, she knew it literally had her name on it and immediately purchased it. She has been running a bed and breakfast for the past eight years and offers travelers all possible amenities of home. The house is completely open to guests, from the upstairs cozy living room with large stone fireplace, which divides the four bedrooms, to the downstairs country kitchen and eating area. Abundant ingredients for a full country breakfast await you in the kitchen with its impressive display of Deruta ceramics. One bedroom with king bed is joined by a bathroom to a small room with twin beds, ideal for a family. Each of the other two doubles has a bathroom, with one being en suite. Besides a swimming pool overlooking the wooded hills and valley, other extras are satellite TV, a travel library, American washer and dryer, bikes, guest bathrobes, and dinner upon request, served out on the back porch where tobacco was once hung to dry. Being right on the border of Umbria and Tuscany, Lake Trasimeno and towns such as Gubbio, Perugia, Cortona, Assisi, and Deruta are all easily accessible. The entire house can also be rented weekly for a group of up to eight persons. *Directions:* From Lisciano square, pass the bar and turn left for San Martino. Continue for 2 km and take a right up the hill at the sign for San Martino for just over 1.5 km to the house.

*CASA SAN MARTINO*
*Host: Lois Martin*
*Localita: San Martino 19*
*Lisciano Niccone (PG) 06060, Italy*
*Tel: (075) 844288, Fax: (075) 844422*
*4 rooms, Double: €145*
*1 house: €2,500–€3,000 weekly*
*Minimum nights required: 3, Open: all year*
*Other languages: fluent English, German, Spanish*
*Region: Umbria, Michelin Map: 563*
*karenbrown.com/italy/casasanmartino.html*

The attractive Le Vescovane bed and breakfast up in the wooded Berici hills just outside the Vicenza city limits is a lovely base for enjoying Veneto. The three-story stone hunting lodge dating back to the 15th century has eight very comfortable and tastefully decorated guestrooms. All have views and many amenities, and all are enhanced by the original stone, wood, and brick building materials. The Savoia family antiques are found in the cozy living room with large fireplace and in the breakfast room. Well-known by locals for its high-quality country cuisine using products from Le Vescovane's farm, the attractive restaurant was created from the original barn with loft ceilings and enormous windows overlooking this wondrous, bucolic spot. From here, guests can choose various hiking trails, also visiting prehistoric caves in the woods. Besides vegetables, fruits, and cereals, the farm produces its own olive oil and DOC-level Cabernet, Chardonnay, Barbarano, and Sauvignon wines. Aside from the famous Palladian villas, you can explore many interesting itineraries in Vicenza and its surrounding areas-the Barbarano wine area, Asolo, Basssano, and Marostica (with its annual human chess game). *Directions:* Exit the A4 autostrada at Vicenza Est, heading for Rivera Berica. From Longare (on the southern edge of Vicenza) follow signs for Le Vescovane-Villa Balzana, turning right at the church onto the Via S. Rocco. Follow the road up to the left for 3 km.

*LE VESCOVANE*
*Hosts: Luigi & Rita Maria Savoia*
*Via S. Rocco 19*
*Longare (VI) 36023, Italy*
*Tel: (0444) 273570, Fax: (0444) 273265*
*8 rooms, Double: €74–€94*
*apartment: €700–€1050 weekly*
*Open: all year, Credit cards: all major*
*Other languages: good English*
*Region: Veneto, Michelin Map: 562*
*karenbrown.com/italy/vescovane.html*

Mario and Gabriella Tortella left an intense corporate life and returned to their peaceful Abruzzo region with the intention of concentrating on organic farming and hospitality. They have succeeded and today the 90-acre property overlooking the Apennines is made up of olive groves, woods, a kiwi plantation, orchards, pastures for farm animals, and fields of grain and cereals. Guests are welcomed like old friends and are accommodated within the six country-style bedrooms upstairs in the main 300-year-old house or in one of the more independent apartments next door. Very much in keeping with the simple rustic features of the farmhouse, they have wrought-iron beds, antique armoires, new tiled bathrooms, and a common living room. The largest has a fireplace and kitchenette. Guests convene in the evening for conversation and an excellent regional meal prepared with ingredients straight from the farm by Gabriella's mother, Olga, either out on the covered porch or in one of the vaulted brick dining rooms. This is a very pleasant base for exploring Loreto, Penne, Pescara, Atri, and three national parks, among other attractions. Alternatively, you can relax poolside and just enjoy the views, the tranquillity, and superb meals. *Directions:* Exit the A25 at Pescara-Villanova and drive towards Penne on S.S.81. Six km before Penne, just before S. Pellegrino, turn right after a bar (or call from there) onto a gravel road up to Le Magnolie. (18 km total from exit.)

*LE MAGNOLIE*
*Hosts: Mario & Gabriella Tortella*          chapel for 5
*Contrada Fiorano 83*
*Loreto Aprutino (PE) 65014, Italy*
*Tel & fax: (085) 8289534, Cellphone: (335) 384180*
*2 rooms, Double: €60–€80,*          $75 each
*6 apartments: €80–€120 daily*
*Minimum nights required: 2, Credit cards: MC, VS*
*Other languages: good English, French, Spanish*
*Region: Abruzzo, Michelin Map: 563*
*karenbrown.com/italy/magnolie.html*

Still another undiscovered area is the peaceful countryside northeast of Todi, where you find the Castello di Loreto. After having meticulously restored part of this medieval fortress castle as a country home, Nino Segurini now coordinates restoration work on ancient buildings, besides continuing his own business as a consultant to antiques dealers. Nino is very knowledgeable on many subjects, and delights in introducing guests to the undiscovered treasures he has found in the immediate area. Nino and Francesca's home is a veritable museum, with collections of ancient artifacts naturally inhabiting the historical building. Within the base of the thick-walled fortress you find the main living room, two small bedrooms (one twin, one double) connected by a sitting area, and three bathrooms. The kitchen leads outside to the spacious patio with grape pergola overlooking the landscaped garden and swimming pool. The preferred and largest bedroom, arranged as a suite with its own sitting room, is reached by two flights of stairs past another living room with fireplace, appointed with antique armour and weaponry and an enclosed loggia. A fourth guestroom features a 16th-century carved, gilded bed of a noble Venetian family who once had Napoleon as a houseguest. *Directions:* Leave highway E45 at Todi/Orvieto, heading for Pian di Porto, then San Terenziano. After 2 km, fork right towards Loreto for another 4 km. The entrance gate is opposite the church.

*CASTELLO DI LORETO*
*Hosts: Nino & Francesca Segurini*
*Loreto-Todi (PG) 06059, Italy*
*Tel & fax: (075) 8852501, Cellphone: (335) 6249734*
*3 rooms, Double: €110–€130*
*Minimum nights required: 2*
*Open: all year*
*Other languages: good English, Spanish, French*
*Region: Umbria, Michelin Map: 563*
*karenbrown.com/italy/loreto.html*

Lucca is decidedly one of the loveliest cities of Italy with its historical churches and circular piazzas interspersed among beautiful shops featuring original storefronts and signage. Besides the well-known summer Puccini Festival (this is his birthplace), there are antiques markets, artisan fairs, and some of the most beautiful formal gardens and villas in Italy surrounding the city. In March the villas and gardens open for a special tour when the area's famed flower, the camellia (tree size), is in bloom. Over the years we have patiently awaited the arrival of a charming place to stay within the city walls and we were eventually rewarded with the Alla Corte degli Angeli. The Bonino family, already very familiar with the hospitality business, took over a private residence in the very heart of Lucca and created ten spacious bedrooms with guests' comfort in mind. The ground-floor reception area includes a lovely dining room with fireplace where an abundant buffet breakfast is served, if not in your own room. Bedrooms on the upper two floors are reached by an elevator, and all follow a specific flower theme, with pastel-colored walls giving an overall fresh feeling. Complementing the well-put-together decor are antique dressers, parquet floors, and amenities such as air conditioning, Jacuzzi tubs, mini-bars, TVs, and internet access. *Directions:* In the pedestrian-only center of Lucca near the famous Piazza Anfiteatro. Private garage parking can be arranged.

*ALLA CORTE DEGLI ANGELI*
Host: Pietro Bonino
Via degli Angeli 23
Lucca 55100, Italy
Tel: (0583) 469204, Fax: (0583) 991989
10 rooms, Double: €155
Open: all year, Credit cards: all major
Other languages: some English
Region: Tuscany, Michelin Map: 563
karenbrown.com/italy/allacorte.html

A few years ago the Luz family of Luino refurbished another home, creating a second, more economical accommodation just 2 kilometers up the road from their hotel on Lake Maggiore. The Colmegna is run by their young and energetic daughter Lara and caters well to families—in fact, there is no charge for children under four. The two pale-yellow buildings run right along the waterfront bordered by an old stone port. There are several terraces for dining outdoors and another with a lawn for sunning or relaxing and enjoying the view. Beyond this is a gorgeous shaded park with romantic trails, tall trees, and wildflowers at one of the prettiest points of the lake. Simply appointed bedrooms are all situated lakeside on the two floors and accommodate from two to four persons. Swimming, sailing, and windsurfing sports can be arranged. Luino is famous for its open market on Wednesdays, a long-standing tradition since 1541. Within touring distance are the lakes of Lugano and Como, the ferry from Laveno across Lake Maggiore, and the Swiss border. *Directions:* Luino is halfway up the lake on the eastern side near the Swiss border. Heading north, Colmegna is on the left-hand side of the main road just past the town of Luino.

*CAMIN HOTEL COLMEGNA*
*Host: Lara Luz*
*Localita: Colmegna*
*Luino (VA) 21016, Italy*
*Tel: (0332) 510855, Fax: (0332) 501687*
*25 rooms, Double: €125–€140*
*Open: Mar to Dec, Credit cards: all major*
*Other languages: good English*
*Region: Lombardy, Michelin Map: 561*
*karenbrown.com/italy/caminhotelcolmegna.html*

The noble Albertario family have four large countryside properties in Umbria and Tuscany that they have opened up to accommodate travelers. Macciangrosso, bordered by ancient cypress trees, is the most beautiful, with its hilltop position overlooking the sweeping valley. The large stone villa, which has been added on to at various times throughout its long history (15th-century origins), belonged to the noble Piccolomini ancestors. You enter through the side gate, walk over a large patio looking onto the delightful rose garden, and climb an external stairway up to the six bedrooms. These are all accessed by a main living room, more like a museum with its rare antique pieces and gilded frame paintings. Bedrooms, each with a small bathroom, are simpler, appointed with wrought-iron beds and coordinated bedspreads and curtains. Other common living areas are the transformed cantina and dining and game rooms. The swimming pool is bordered by a stone wall from the Etruscan period and a tennis court is nearby. Ten apartments of various sizes are found in the rest of the home and in a nearby house next to the chapel. Close to the thermal spas, Macciangrosso is on the edge of Umbria and Tuscany, offering easy access to the highlights of both regions. *Directions:* From Chiusi drive 3 km towards Chianciano. Turn right at the grocery store and go 1.5 km to the house.

*MACCIANGROSSO*
*Hosts: Sonia & Luigi Albertario*
*Macciano (SI) 53044, Italy*
*Tel & fax: (0578) 21459, Cellphone: (347) 3204472*
*6 rooms, Double: €135*
*10 apartments: €440–€950 weekly*
*Heating extra, Minimum nights required: 2*
*Closed: Nov, Credit cards: MC, VS*
*Other languages: French, good English*
*Region: Tuscany, Michelin Map: 563*
*karenbrown.com/italy/macciangrosso.html*

Ca'delle Rondini opened its doors first as a restaurant and then six years ago as a bed and breakfast. The typical rectangular-shaped, pale-yellow farmhouse with incorporated barn, built in 1800, faces out to the main road in town and at the back to acres of flat fields, fruit orchards, and horse stables. In a section of the long house live gregarious host Ilo and his brother Alessandro, who helps Mamma in the kitchen with the creation of delectable local fare whose ingredients come directly from the farm. Entering the lofty restaurant with fireplace, gray-stone floors, beamed ceilings, and large arched windows, one has the sense of being part of a truly authentic local gathering place—especially for Sunday lunch. Guests sit down in one of the two dining rooms and are offered a variety of inventive antipasti served on cutting boards. The comfortable bedrooms upstairs and one below (with access for the handicapped) all have telephones and air conditioning, and are very pleasantly appointed in typical country style with mansard beamed ceilings, pine-wood floors, and country antiques. Outings by bike or horseback are arranged in the nearby nature park reserve. Ilo can suggest many original itineraries, including a tour of Venice's abandoned islands on a friend's boat. Ca'delle Rondini is a great base for visiting Venice, Padua, Treviso, Verona, and Vicenza. *Directions:* Ca'delle Rondini is in the town of Maerne, northwest of Mestre, just 10 km from Venice.

❄ ☕ 🚴 CREDIT ☎ 🐎 ⑪ 🍴 ♿

*CA'DELLE RONDINI*
*Host: Silvestri family*
*Via Ca' Rossa 26*
*Maerne (VE) 30030, Italy*
*Tel & fax: (041) 641114*
*6 rooms, Double: €85*
*Restaurant open Thu to Sun*
*Open: all year, Credit cards: MC, VS*
*Other languages: none*
*Region: Veneto, Michelin Map: 562*
*karenbrown.com/italy/rondini.html*

Mantova is a delightful discovery on the trail of lesser-known art cities of Italy, exceptional for its position on four miniature lakes, which are found right in the historic center. On the outskirts of the city is the San Girolamo property of the Mantovani family where guestrooms are also situated in a part of the former convent and watermill dating to the 17th century, complete with the sound of waterfalls. Four very simply appointed bedrooms are found above the breakfast room (two with en suite bathrooms and two sharing a bathroom) where Kim your host greets you in the morning with fresh cakes and coffee and makes suggestions on the many itineraries in the area. After years of world travel, he has come back to assist in the management of the family agricultural and hospitality business. Ten new guestrooms have been added on one level with individual entrances in the converted barn just across from the family's home. The almost 200 acres of cultivated land are divided up in various surrounding areas. An interesting bike or boat excursion starts from San Girolamo and follows the Mincio Park Preserve and river all the way to Lake Garda (20 kilometers). Bikes can also be used to ride into Mantova as the locals do, an excellent way to view the ancient monuments and squares. *Directions:* From Mantova center take the 62 north towards Villafranca-Verona, turn left at Cittadella, then left again at the sign for San Girolamo. (3 km from the city.)

■ ⚞ P ♿

*CORTE SAN GIROLAMO*
*Host: Kim Mantovani family*
*Strada S. Girolamo 1*
*Mantova (MN) 46100, Italy*
*Tel: (0376) 391018, Cellphone: (347) 8008505*
*Fax: (0376) 391018*
*14 rooms, Double: €70*
*Open: all year*
*Other languages: good English*
*Region: Lombardy, Michelin Map: 561*
*karenbrown.com/italy/sangirolamo.html*

It would be difficult for anyone with a passion for the outdoors to resist the challenge offered Federico when he inherited this 1,000-plus-acre estate in the wilderness of Maremma. He and his energetic wife, Elisabetta, plunged in and in two years made this dream come true. The results are notable and very ambitious, with the complete restoration of four stone farmhouses scattered about the vast property comprised of wooded hills, olive groves, and cultivated fields of grain and sunflowers. Guests first arrive at the imposing 1850s main villa, which houses the reception office and private family quarters. Comfortable apartments and rooms (divided among the various farmhouses) are nicely furnished with country pieces old and new and can accommodate from two to ten persons. Guests have the use of four swimming pools, mountain bikes, sauna, exercise and game rooms, Jacuzzi, and massage therapy. They convene at Podernovo where Tuscan meals are served in the exposed-stone dining room with fireplace, or on the patio looking out over the valley and up to Massa Marittima. The Etruscan towns of Massa Marittima, Volterra, Vetulonia, and Populonia are waiting to be explored and you are also close to the seaside. The summer months offer a rich musical program of operas and classical concerts in the main piazza and villas. *Directions:* Drive for 2 km on the gravel road from Massa Marittima where signs indicate Il Cicalino.

*TENUTA IL CICALINO*
*Hosts: Elisabetta & Federico Vecchioni*
*Localita: Cicalino, Massa Marittima (GR) 58024, Italy*
*Tel: (0566) 902031, Cellphone: (347) 6444130*
*Fax: (0566) 904896*
*7 rooms, Double: €75–€85*
*23 apartments: €82–€323 daily*
*Minimum nights required: 2, Open: Mar to Nov*
*Credit cards: MC, VS, Other languages: some English*
*Region: Tuscany, Michelin Map: 563*
*karenbrown.com/italy/cicalino.html*

La Biancarda is the beautiful country home of the Florio family of Ancona, overlooking the colorful hilly countryside. Just south of Ancona begins one of the prettiest coastlines of the eastern Adriatic shores, with a combination of seaside villages, hilly countryside, and dramatic mountains cascading into the sea, making up the Conero National Park. Signora Giovanna had the salmon-colored farmhouse dating to 1760 restored to provide her family with a relaxing country retreat, and adorned it with many of the family's precious antiques. The impressive, stone-walled living room upstairs with enormous fireplace, plus cozy library and billiard room are all open to guests. Six guest bedrooms are divided between the two floors of the home. A real treat is breakfast in the delightful country kitchen with fireplace, long family table, beamed ceilings, and collection of hanging brass pots. Exquisite dinners based on fresh fish and local produce can also be arranged. Outdoor activities in the area include golf, tennis, horseback riding, and swimming (beaches are ten minutes away). The historical towns of Macereto, Loreto, and Urbino are nearby. *Directions:* From the A14, exit at Ancona Sud, following signs for Numana. Keep on this road for several kilometers to Coppo, turning left onto a dirt road just after the bar—follow it to the end.

*LA BIANCARDA*
*Hosts: Giovanna Florio & family*
*Via Biancarda 129, Coppo di Sirolo*
*Massignano (AN) 60125, Italy*
*Tel & fax (summer) (071) 2800503*
*Tel & fax (winter): (071) 34331*
*6 rooms, Double: €105–€170*
*Minimum nights required: 2*
*Open: May to Sep, Other languages: good English*
*Region: Marches, Michelin Map: 563*
*karenbrown.com/italy/biancarda.html*

The simple and economical Oasi Verde "green oasis" is just that: a convenient roadside stop for those traveling between Umbria and the Marches region. Carla and Andrea Rossi inherited the sprawling 200-year-old stone farmhouse and surrounding land, ideally located midway between Perugia and Gubbio (a not-to-be-missed medieval stone village set high up in the hillside), and decided to convert it to a bed and breakfast and restaurant. The eight rooms in the main house, each with its own bathroom, have been decorated like model room number 3, with its original beamed ceiling and country-antique bed and armoire. White-tiled floors may be out of character, but give a sense of cleanliness nonetheless. Another wing of the complex houses three simply furnished suites (two bedrooms and a bathroom) for longer stays, perfect for a family of four. Additional rooms, each with separate ground-floor entrance, are found in a wing renovated within the last few years. The windows at the back of the house open out to green hills with alternating patches of woods and sunflower fields. Facilities tempting you to linger for a while include a swimming pool and bikes available for rent. *Directions:* Traveling from Perugia on route 298, after 25 km you find the bed and breakfast on the left-hand side, at Mengara, 10 km before Gubbio.

❄ ☕ 🏍 💳 ☎ 🚶 👫 🏇 P 🍴 🏊 🍇

*OASI VERDE MENGARA*
*Hosts: Andrea & Carla Rossi*
*Localita: Mengara 1, Mengara (PG) 06020, Italy*
*Tel: (075) 9227004, Cellphone: (335) 1225738*
*Fax: (075) 920049*
*19 rooms, Double: €60–€76*
*Minimum nights required: 4 in high season*
*Open: Mar to Dec, Credit cards: MC, VS*
*Other languages: some English*
*Region: Umbria, Michelin Map: 563*
*karenbrown.com/italy/oasiverde.html*

Florentine sisters Francesca and Beatrice Baccetti eagerly accepted the challenge of converting the family's country home and vineyards into an efficient bed and breakfast. Restoration work began immediately on the two adjacent stone buildings dating back to 1400. All original architectural features were preserved, leaving the five guestrooms and eleven apartments (for two to four people) with terra-cotta brick floors, wood-beamed ceilings, and mansard roofs, and many with generous views over the tranquil Tuscan countryside. The very comfortable and tidy rooms are furnished with good reproductions in country style and feel almost hotel-like with their telephones and modern bathrooms. A beautiful swimming pool with hydro-massage, tennis court, billiards room, and nearby horse stables are at guests' disposal, although finding enough to do is hardly a problem with Florence only 18 kilometers away and practically all of Tuscany at one's fingertips. Breakfast is served at wooden tables in the stone-walled dining room or out on the terrace. Readers give Salvadonica a high rating for service and warm hospitality. *Directions:* From Florence take the superstrada toward Siena for 6 km, exiting at San Casciano Nord. Follow signs for town, turning left at the sign for Mercatale. Salvadonica is on this road and well marked.

*SALVADONICA*
*Hosts: Francesca & Beatrice Baccetti*
*Via Grevigiana 82*
*Mercatale Val di Pesa (FI) 50024, Italy*
*Tel: (055) 8218039, Fax: (055) 8218043*
*5 rooms, Double: €108–€115*
*11 apartments: €125–€260 daily B&B*
*Open: Mar to Nov, Credit cards: all major*
*Other languages: good English*
*Region: Tuscany, Michelin Map: 563*
*karenbrown.com/italy/salvadonica.html*

In an industrial city where the word "charm" is practically nonexistent, the Hotel Regina, although not inexpensive, came as a pleasant surprise among the rather nondescript modern hotels in Milan. For those flying in and out of Milan, with a desire to catch a glimpse of the city center (and newly restored Last Supper of Da Vinci—by advance reservation only), this is an ideal selection. The attractive, typically 18th-century façade and entrance invite guests into a luminous reception area, converted from the original courtyard, with stone columns, arches, marble floors, large plants, and a small corner bar with sitting area and tables. Completely refurbished rooms (non-smoking upon request) include all modern amenities and are very quiet, being set off the street. Decorated comfortably and uniformly with identical furniture, rooms are warmed with soft-pastel-colored walls, parquet floors, and scattered Oriental rugs. A full buffet breakfast is served below and is included in the room rate. Manager Michela is helpful in satisfying guests' requests and bicycles are available for visting the city's historical center. Linate airport is easily reached by cab in 20 minutes, while the Malpensa airport can be reached by bus from the train station. *Directions:* Via Correnti is just off the Via Torino, which leads to Milan's famous cathedral and shopping area, and is between the basilicas of San Lorenzo and San Ambrogio.

*HOTEL REGINA*
*Host: Michela Barberi*
*Via Cesare Correnti 13*
*Milan 20123, Italy*
*Tel: (02) 58106913, Fax: (02) 58107033*
*43 rooms, Double: €171–€260*
*Open: all year, Credit cards: all major*
*Other languages: good English*
*Region: Lombardy, Michelin Map: 561*
*karenbrown.com/italy/hotelregina.html*

A recent and long-overdue updating of the regional agritourism laws of Veneto has paved the way for many farm property owners to offer accommodation. Villa Mocenigo is one such place and along with being an economical and pleasant choice, first and foremost it has the advantage of an ideal location right outside of Mirano. At just 20 kilometers from Venice (a bus for the 20-minute ride leaves in front of the farm every 20 minutes), guests have the marvels of Veneto at their fingertips: Padua, Vicenza, Treviso, Brenta and Palladian villas, Chioggia, Asolo. The Ribon family resides in the historic 16th-century villa, while the ten guestrooms are located within two other adjacent buildings, originally the farmer's quarters and converted stalls, one being all on ground level and each having an independent entrance from the garden. Damask fabrics and the family's antique beds and armoires adorn the rooms in contrast with the simplicity of the building. Cultivated fields and vineyards line the flat fields in the back and come right up to the house. Locals convene at the authentic country restaurant with checked green tablecloths to be treated to one of Luigina's famed meals with fresh pastas, breads, and their own choice of meats. *Directions:* Exit the A4 autostrada at Dolo-Mirano and drive 5 km to Mirano. Turn left at the stoplight on Via Cavin di Sala and after 1 km, left again on Via Viasana to the house.

*VILLA MOCENIGO*
*Hosts: Giorgio & Luigina Ribon*
*Via Viasana 59*
*Mirano (VE ) 30035, Italy*
*Tel & fax: (041) 433246*
*10 rooms, Double: €52–€60*
*Restaurant: guests only weekdays*
*Open: all year*
*Other languages: some English*
*Region: Veneto, Michelin Map: 562*
*karenbrown.com/italy/villamocenigo.html*

The Alcala farm, made up of citrus and olive groves extends over 75 acres of fertile plain backdropped by the Etna volcano—a picture-perfect setting. Cordial hostess Anna Sapuppo and her young family have taken over the family's agricultural business and have added hospitality activity as well. The main house is a hundred-year-old masseria, built in several sections. Guests are situated nearby in four different apartment setups (one has handicapped facilities) for two to six persons. Two of them are separate houses and all have terraces of varying dimensions. They include living room areas and kitchenettes simply decorated with floral sofas and a mix of modern and old family furniture. Although breakfast is not served, guests can help themselves in season to plenty of oranges, tangerines, and grapefruit. An occasional Sicilian dinner is served in the rustic wine cantina with its enormous wooden wine barrels or by request in your apartment. Anna, a native Sicilian, gladly assists her guests with touring suggestions, which include Catania city (important where not to go), Syracuse, Etna National Park, and the temples of Agrigento. *Directions:* Take the Palermo-Catania autostrada A19 and leave at the exit Motta S. Anastasia. Access is on S.S.192 at km 78. Turn left, backtracking towards Catania on route 192, pass the U.S. army base, then turn left again at the Alcala sign (milestone 78). Go to the end of the private road.

ALCALA
Host: Anna Sappupo family
Casella Postale 100-S.S.192 at km 78
Misterbianco, Sicily (CT) 95045, Italy
Tel & fax: (095) 7130029, Cellphone: (368) 3469206
4 apartments: €44–€60 daily per person
Minimum nights required: 3, 7 Jul, Aug, Easter & Xmas
Open: all year, Credit cards: MC, VS
Other languages: good English, French
Region: Sicily, Michelin Map: 565
karenbrown.com/italy/alcala.html

Just 20 kilometers from Siena, at the foot of Chianti is the Godiolo stone farmhouse with its double loggia and cupola dating back to 1350. Red geraniums cascade from every one of the balconies and terra-cotta urns. While Signor Giuliano tends to the acres of vineyards and wine production, gracious Signora Bianca dedicates her time to making their guests feel very much at home. What used to be the children's rooms are now four charming guestrooms with nice, homey touches such as embroidered linen sheets, dried flower arrangements, and heirloom furnishings. Breakfast in the typical tiled kitchen consists of homemade baked goods to which guests help themselves. Signora, with her Roman-Tuscan origins, is an excellent cook and guests can treat themselves to a delightful dinner with the family upon request. Downstairs is a large informal living and game room for guests. Nearby are the thermal baths of Rapolano where massages, mud baths, and other spa services are available—true relaxation—and the stark and fascinating crater-like landscapes (Le Crete Senesi) south between Rapolano and Montalcino. *Directions:* Exit from the A1 autostrada at Val di Chiana and head towards Siena on route 326 towards Serre di Rapolano, but turn right up to Godiolo rather than left into town.

*GODIOLO*
*Hosts: Giuliano & Bianca Perinelli*
*Modanella (SI) 53040, Italy*
*Tel & fax: (0577) 704304*
*4 rooms, Double: €130*
*Open: all year*
*Other languages: some English*
*Region: Tuscany*
*Michelin Map: 563*
*karenbrown.com/italy/godiolo.html*

While many agritourism farms are run by transplanted urbanites, many are still owned and operated by farmers whose families have worked the land for generations. Such is the case with Onofrio Contento and his family, proprietors of Masseria Curatori, not far from the city of Monopoli and the Adriatic Sea, where, for five generations, the family has produced olives, almonds, and cattle. Inside the main coral-color house are very modest and immaculate quarters for guests, consisting presently of a large three-bedroom apartment with kitchen and living room, plus two doubles with private bathrooms. Old and new family furniture has been combined to decorate the rooms. The view is pleasingly pastoral, overlooking olive-tree-studded hills. Two apartments for two to four persons are found in a nearby one-story building overlooking a lovely stone-walled garden and fruit orchard. Breakfast and extra meals are taken together with the hospitable family in their dining room where Lucrezia delights guests with local dishes. Horseback riding can be arranged for guests. Curatori is an excellent base from which to visit the highlights of this unique region of Italy. *Directions:* 40 km from Bari. Take coastal route S.S.16 south, leaving at the sixth exit for Monopoli called Monopoli-San Francesco da Paola. Turn right for 300 meters and then left on S.C. Conchia Road, to a pink house on your right.

*MASSERIA CURATORI*
*Hosts: Onofrio & Lucrezia Contento family*
*Contrada Cristo delle Zolle 227 (S.C. Conchia)*
*Monopoli (BA) 70043, Italy*
*Tel & fax: (080) 777472, Cellphone: (338) 6242833*
*2 rooms, Double: €50–€60*
*3 apartments: €110–€130 daily*
*Open: all year*
*Other languages: very little English*
*Region: Apulia, Michelin Map: 564*
*karenbrown.com/italy/masseriacuratori.html*

A well-kept secret among off-the-main-road travelers is the countryside north of Rome known as "Sabina" after the mountain range. It is unusual that agritourism has not developed close to Rome compared to what has occurred around Florence, but locals are beginning to wake up. Ancestors of the Gabbuti family came from this area and the principal palazzos in both medieval towns of Casperia and Montasola, plus a large farm with olive groves, have been in the family for generations. One of the daughters, Letizia, decided to leave a law career in Rome to work on restoration of these properties and offer hospitality in the form of apartments and one bedroom within her home. Spacious apartments include one to three bedrooms, living room, kitchen, and bathrooms, all warmly decorated with the family's own antiques. Characteristic architectural features have been preserved, and two apartments have terraces with a breathtaking panoramic view (our favorite is the mansard Le Stelle). There is something very special indeed about being a "resident" of an intact medieval village with its narrow stone alleyways. Guests can lounge under the shady trees of a stone-walled garden close by and dine at the characteristic osteria in the village. Other charming villages dot the area, Umbria is nearby, and Rome is just a 45-minute train ride away. Suitable for independent explorers. *Directions:* Arrangements to be met should be made at the time of reservation.

*MONTEPIANO*
*Host: Maria Letizia Gabbuti*
*Via dei Casalini 8, Montasola (RI) 02040, Italy*
*Tel: (330) 749221, Cellphone (328) 3813145*
*Fax: (0765) 63252*
*1 room, Double: €70–€100*
*4 apartments: €100–€204 daily*
*Minimum nights required: 2*
*Open: all year, Other languages: some English*
*Region: Lazio, Michelin Map: 563*
*karenbrown.com/italy/montepiano.html*

Lucca, one of our favorite Italian cities, is well situated near Pisa, with the beautiful Valdera countryside to the south, the Apuane mountain range to the north, the seaside 20 kilometers away, and many splendid villas and famous gardens scattered in the vicinity. The city, however, is directly surrounded by a heavily commercial area until you get to the wine country around the charming hilltop town of Montecarlo, 15 kilometers east of town. This medieval stone village with fortress walls has several restaurants and cafés, its own theater where Puccini was known to put on operas, and many olive-oil-producing farms and wineries close by. All but two have en suite bathrooms and are simply appointed with wrought-iron beds and floral bedspreads. A rich and tasty breakfast, made with local and homemade products, is served either out on the patio where you can observe the daily life of the locals, or in the miniature breakfast room to the left of the reception and living room area where a wine and coffee bar is open all day. *Directions:* From the A11 autostrada, take the Altopascio exit. Head towards Pescia (3 km) and turn left for Montecarlo for another 2 km.

*ANTICA CASA DEI RASSICURATI*
*Hosts: Antonella Romanini, Marta Giusti & Miriam Kell*
*Via della Collegiata 2*
*Montecarlo (LU) 55015, Italy*
*Tel: (0583) 228901, Fax: (0583) 22498*
*8 rooms, Double: €70–€75*
*Open: all year, Credit cards: MC, VS*
*Other languages: good English, French, German*
*Region: Tuscany, Michelin Map: 563*
*karenbrown.com/italy/rassicurati.html*

Within the same quaint village as the previous listing is an alternative kind of accommodation that allows the traveler to stay in one of Montecarlo's private, historical homes. The large building on the main street of town with Pompeiian-red worn façade (a color that is predominant in the interior) dates back to the 1500s and its foundation was part of the original walls of the castle. Gracious hostess Bianca's desire was to bring back life to the ancient, antique-filled home by offering unique accommodation to travelers. Even though space would allow it, she has made no alterations or added extra rooms, preferring to keep the original architectural features of her ancestral home intact. Limited accommodation, therefore, is offered either within an enormous double bedroom with en suite bathroom overlooking the street, or in a family suite incorporating three sleeping areas (separate double bedroom plus two sleeping alcoves for an additional three people), bathroom, and grand hall with French windows looking out over the lovely terraced garden. Breakfast is served in the formal dining room with antique tapestries or in the absolutely charming country kitchen with open fireplace and French plates adorning the walls. Take a step back in time in this castlelike home filled with precious antiques and paintings. *Directions:* From the A11 autostrada, take the Altopascio exit. Head towards Pescia (3 km) and turn left for Montecarlo for another 2 km.

*CASA SATTI*
*Host: Bianca Satti Tori*
*Via Roma 31*
*Montecarlo (LU) 55015, Italy*
*Tel: (0583) 22347, Fax: (0583) 22007*
*2 rooms, Double: €120–€230*
*Minimum nights required: 2*
*Open: Apr to Nov 15*
*Region: Tuscany, Michelin Map: 563*
*karenbrown.com/italy/casasatti.html*

The scenic approach to the Fattoria di Vibio passes through lush green hills, by picturesque farms, and is highlighted by a romantic view of the quaint town of Todi, 20 kilometers away. Two handsome brothers from Rome run this top-drawer bed and breakfast consisting of several recently restored stone houses. The houses sit side by side and share between them 14 double rooms with private baths. Common areas for guests include a cozy, country-style living room with fireplace, games room, and country kitchen. The accommodations are enhanced by preserved architectural features such as terra-cotta floors and exposed-beam ceilings, and typical Umbrian handicrafts such as wrought-iron beds, renovated antiques, and Deruta ceramics. On the assumption that guests may find it difficult to leave this haven, the hosts offer half board plus lunch and snacks, along with spa facilities (massages and Turkish bath) indoor and outdoor heated swimming pools, tennis, hiking, horseback riding, fishing, and biking. Signora Gabriella, with a passion for cooking, gets all the richly deserved credit for the marvelous meals served either poolside or on the panoramic terrace. Two houses are also available for rent. *Directions:* From either Todi or Orvieto follow route S448 until the turnoff for Vibio at the sign for Prodo-Quadro and follow the well-marked dirt road for 10 km up to the farmhouse.

*FATTORIA DI VIBIO*
*Hosts: Giuseppe & Filippo Saladini*
*Localita: Buchella-Doglio*
*Montecastello di Vibio (PG) 06057, Italy*
*Tel: (075) 8749607, Fax: (075) 8780014*
*14 rooms, Double: €140–€200*
*2 houses: €800–€1,800 weekly\**
*\*Includes breakfast & dinner, Open: all year*
*Credit cards: all major, Other languages: good English*
*Region: Umbria, Michelin Map: 563*
*karenbrown.com/italy/fattoriadivibio.html*

Surprisingly, one of the least visited regions in Italy is the Marches, an area rich in culture, nature, and history bordering on the Adriatic. Just 7 kilometers from the coast in the heart of this gentle, hilly countryside you find the Campana farm, run by ten families of professionals and artists who came here from Milan in search of an alternative lifestyle. The farm, made up of four pale-peach stone houses dating from 1700, has been restored with great care and taste, making space for private quarters, a refined restaurant, wine cellar, studio, music room, and, for guests, nine rooms, a few large enough for a family of four. Some have lovely terraces looking across vineyard-covered hills to the distant sea, and are decorated with a combination of old and new furnishings. Others are situated within a separate two-story, recently renovated farmhouse. Drawing on the considerable pool of available talent, an unusual variety of activities is offered, including workshops in crafting leather and silk, and wool dyeing with plant extracts. Guests have the use of a swimming pool and tennis courts, as well as bikes for local touring. *Directions:* From Ancona go south on the A14 autostrada, exit at Pedaso, continue south to Cupramarittima, then turn right at the sign for Carassai. After 6 km, turn right for Montefiore, then left after 1.5 km at the small sign for La Campana.

*LA CAMPANA*
*Host: Coop Agricola*
*Via Menocchia 39*
*Montefiore dell'Aso (AP) 63010, Italy*
*Tel: (0734) 939012, Fax: (0734) 938229*
*9 rooms, Double: €90–€148*
*Open: Mar to Dec, Credit cards: MC, VS*
*Other languages: good English*
*Region: Marches, Michelin Map: 563*
*karenbrown.com/italy/lacampana.html*

It is only logical that the Antinori family, one of the most famous wine producers in Italy, has joined the ranks of landowners offering top-quality, agriturismo accommodation. They have done it in grand style, restoring and creating twenty apartments and seven guestrooms within the eight stone houses scattered about the vast property in the center. Chianti is composed of hills, woods, and, of course, infinite vineyards. In keeping with the general countryside ambience, the high-level accommodation is appointed with wood furniture, smart striped or checked fabrics that harmonize well with the brick floors and beamed ceilings. While three of the ancient farmhouses are located up a road across the vineyards, the others are grouped together at the main entrance near the reception room, swimming pool, tennis courts, small gym, and restaurant serving typical Tuscan fare. The Fonte de Medici is heads above the rest with an offering of a wide range of amenities including air conditioning, kitchenette, fireplaces, dishwasher, barbeque, satellite TV, and internet access. Enjoy the classic, Tuscan landscapes coupled with classic Chianti wine and the marvels of this region surrounding you. *Directions:* Exit from A1 at Certosa-Firenze and follow the highway for Siena. Exit at San Casciano and follow for Montefiridolfi, then Badia di Passignano. Follow signs for Fonte de Medici-Antinori to the front gate.

❄ 🍺 🏊 CREDIT ☎ 🐕 🏋 🚶 👫 ⛤ P 🍴 🚭 🏊 🏖 ♿ 🍇

*FONTE DE MEDICI*     **New**
*Manager: Gilberto Nori*
*Località S. Maria a Macerata*
*Montefiridolfi (FI) 50020, Italy*
*Tel: (055) 8244700, Fax: (055) 8244701*
*7 rooms, Double: €150–€350*
*20 apartments: €150–€350*
*Open: all year, Credit cards: all major*
*Other languages: good English*
*Region: Tuscany, Michelin Map: 563*
*karenbrown.com/italy/medici.html*

La Loggia, built in 1427, was one of the Medici estates during the centuries of their rule. Owner Giulio Baruffaldi, weary of urban life in Milan, transplanted himself and his wife here and succeeded in reviving the wine estate's splendor while respecting its past, enhancing its architectural beauty while giving utmost attention to the preservation of the historic property. Their informal yet refined hospitality is reflected in the care given to retaining the rustic ambiance of the former farmers' homes, each containing one to three bedrooms, living room, and kitchen, some with fireplace, and adorned with country antiques and original paintings from the Baruffaldis' own art collection. In fact, many important bronze and ceramic sculptures by international artists are displayed throughout the gardens of the villa. Four double rooms have been added, some having a fireplace or hydro-massage bath and steam room. Apart from just basking in the pure romance and tranquillity of this place, you can enjoy a heated seawater swimming pool, horseback riding, and nearby tennis and golf facilities. Other activities include the occasional cooking or wine-tasting lesson, and impromptu dinners in the cellar. The charming hostess Ivana personally takes care of guests' needs. *Directions:* Leave the Florence-Siena autostrada after San Casciano at Bargino. Turn right at the end of the ramp, then left for Montefiridolfi (3.5 km). La Loggia is just before town.

*FATTORIA LA LOGGIA*
*Hosts: Giulio Baruffaldi & Cuca Roaldi*
*Via Collina*
*Montefiridolfi, San Casciano (FI) 50026, Italy*
*Tel: (055) 8244288, Fax: (055) 8244283*
*4 rooms, Double: €100–€160*
*11 apartments: €110–€190 daily*
*Open: all year, Credit cards: MC, VS*
*Other languages: French, Spanish, good English*
*Region: Tuscany, Michelin Map: 563*
*karenbrown.com/italy/laloggia.html*

Just opposite the lovely Fattoria La Loggia is a bed and breakfast that was actually one of the farmhouses belonging to the vast vineyard property. Gracious Signora Nadia fell in love with the ancient house and decided to retire here after having the entire place restored, leaving the ground floor for herself and the guests' breakfast room while the upstairs provides apartments of flexible configurations for travelers. The two adjoining apartments to the right (yellow and blue color schemes) can become a three-bedroom apartment with three colorful bathrooms, living room, kitchen, and large fireplace. The two one-bedroom apartments in green hues can be rented separately or adjoined as well. Rooms have a clean, country feeling to them with antique armoires, simple wrought-iron beds blending in nicely with stone walls, wood-beamed mansard ceilings and brick floors so typical in Tuscany. A lovely swimming pool sits close to the house overlooking the soft valley. This is a very easy base from which to visit most of the region's highlights besides being only 20 minutes from Florence and 30 from Siena. *Directions:* Exit at Bargino from the Florence-Siena highway and turn right and then immediately left at the sign for Montefiridolfi. After 3 km look for a stone house with large arched windows on the left side of the road before town.

*MACINELLO*
*Host: Nadia Ciuffetti*
*Via Collina 9*
*Montefiridolfi,*
*San Casciano Val di Pesa (FI) 50020, Italy*
*Tel & fax: (055) 8244459*
*4 apartments: €210–€225 daily*
*Minimum nights required: 3, 7 Jun to Aug*
*Open: all year*
*Region: Tuscany, Michelin Map: 563*
*karenbrown.com/italy/macinello.html*

Poggio Miravalle is a peaceful and panoramic haven located atop a hill between the regions of Umbria and Tuscany. Reserved hostess Rita has developed the hospitality end of her farm business (organic olive oil and wine) over the past years and today offers accommodation within six apartments, all but two inside the main restored stone farmhouse. A firm believer in the healing benefits of country living, she offers an oasis of silence for true lovers of nature, defined as "ecotourists." Each apartment (among them four named Sun, Moon, Earth, and Sky) has an independent entrance through French doors overlooking the garden and can comfortably accommodate from two to five guests. Pleasantly decorated with a mix of old and new country-style furniture, they include a living area and kitchenette. The barn has been transformed into a common area where breakfast and an occasional dinner are served and nearby is a swimming pool taking advantage of the most scenic and breezy spot overlooking the sweeping valley. Rita is full of interesting itinerary suggestions following gastronomic, cultural, recreational, or nature themes. *Directions:* Exit from the A1 autostrada at Fabro and travel towards Monteleone. After S. Lorenzo turn right for Miravalle (1.5 km).

*POGGIO MIRAVALLE*
*Host: Rita Trincia*
*Localita: Cornieto 2*
*Monteleone d'Orvieto (TR) 05017, Italy*
*Tel & fax: (0763) 835309*
*Cellphone: (333) 5254620 or (340) 7736315*
*6 apartments: €60–€110 daily*
*Open: Mar 15 to Oct 30*
*Credit cards: all major*
*Region: Umbria, Michelin Map: 563*
*karenbrown.com/italy/miravalle.html*

The hilltop home of the Lacetera family is equidistant to both Perugia and Lake Trasimeno with its small islands. The characteristic stone farmhouse is large enough to accommodate guests within six bedrooms and includes upstairs and downstairs living rooms with fireplace, a large dining room, and the family's private quarters. There are two regular doubles with en suite bathrooms (one in a separate little house just in front) plus two sets of two rooms with one bathroom making a perfect setup for families or two couples. Luminous, comfortable rooms are warmly decorated in peach and soft-yellow tones with traditional country furniture. Excellent light evening meals are prepared by Francesca's mother, Renata, and served in the attractive rustic dining room or out on the patio overlooking the scenic wooded hills. Beautiful views are captured as well from the stone-bordered swimming pool overlooking the valley and castle in Montemelino. Activities include biking, hiking, or horseback riding in the immediate area and you are close to the highlights of both Umbria and Tuscany. Guests easily become friends in the informal and very convivial atmosphere here. *Directions:* From Perugia (12 km) take the highway towards Lake Trasimeno and exit at Corciano. Follow signs for Montemelino and from there continue up through woods on a dirt road for 2 km to the house.

*LA LOCANDA DELLE FONTANELLE*
*Hosts: Angelo & Francesca Lacetera*
*Vocabolo Fontanelle 25*
*Montemelino (PG ) 06063, Italy*
*Tel: (075) 8472674, Fax: (075) 8478287*
*6 rooms, Double: €90–€94*
*Open: all year, Credit cards: all major*
*Other languages: good English*
*Region: Umbria, Michelin Map: 563*
*karenbrown.com/italy/locandafontanelle.html*

One result of increasing interest in the singular attractions of the Maremma, or southern Tuscany, is the opening or expansion of several noteworthy places to stay. The Villa Acquaviva, once owned by nobility and a small family hotel for some years, was extensively remodeled to include eight guestrooms named for and painted in the colors of local wildflowers. The bedrooms all have private baths and are decorated with country antiques and wrought-iron beds. Breakfast of homemade cakes, breads, and jams can be eaten in the breakfast room near the enoteca. There are ten newer rooms in a stone farmhouse on the property plus eight in another, joined together by a glassed-in reception area. These are our favorites, with beautiful local antiques and colorful matching fabrics adorning beds and windows. Tennis courts and a swimming pool with bar service are attractive features of the complex. In the center of the park, in a scenic position by the swimming pool, the restaurant presents typical Maremman dishes made with fresh products from the farm. *Directions:* From Rome, take the Aurelia coastal road, exiting at Vulci. Follow signs for Manciano, then Montemerano. Acquaviva is well marked just outside the village.

*VILLA ACQUAVIVA*
*Hosts: Valentina di Virginio & Serafino d'Ascenzi*
*Localita: Acquaviva, Montemerano (GR) 58050, Italy*
*Tel: (0564) 602890, Cellphone: (335) 7509100*
*Fax: (0564) 602895*
*25 rooms, Double: €103–€160*
*Minimum nights required: 3*
*Open: all year, Credit cards: all major*
*Other languages: French, good English*
*Region: Tuscany, Michelin Map: 563*
*karenbrown.com/italy/acquaviva.html*

Le Fontanelle country house sits in the heart of the Maremma area of Tuscany where, besides being pleasant and well run, it fills a need for the growing interest in this off-the-beaten-track destination. Signor Perna and his two lovely daughters, originally from Rome, searched and found this peaceful haven from the stress of city life, promptly transferring themselves and undertaking major restoration work. Looking over a soft green valley up to the nearby village of Montemerano, the stone farmhouse with its rusty-red shutters offers four comfortable rooms with spotless private bathrooms. The converted barn houses five rooms while the last room is in a separate cottage set in the woods. Sunlight pours into the front veranda-like breakfast room where coffee and cakes are taken together with other guests at one large table. The Pernas assist guests in planning local itineraries including visits to artisan workshops. With due notice, guests can find a wonderfully prepared dinner awaiting them under the ivy-covered pergola in the rose garden. The property is part of a reserve with deer, wild boar, and various types of wildlife, where Porcini mushrooms, wild asparagus, and berries are found in season. *Directions:* From Rome, take the A12 autostrada. Continue north on Aurelia route 1, turning off at Vulci after Montalto. Follow signs for Manciano then Montemerano. Turn left at the bed-and-breakfast sign before town and follow the dirt road for 1 km.

*LE FONTANELLE*
*Hosts: Daniela & Cristina Perna*
*Localita: Poderi di Montemerano*
*Montemerano (GR) 58050, Italy*
*Tel & fax: (0564) 602762*
*Cellphone: (335) 6559699 or (338) 9205641*
*10 rooms, Double: €82*
*Open: all year, Credit cards: MC, VS*
*Other languages: some English*
*Region: Tuscany, Michelin Map: 563*
*karenbrown.com/italy/fontanelle.html*

A pleasant alternative to a countryside bed and breakfast is one right in the historical center of the marvelously preserved medieval town of Montepulciano. Most famous for its prized Rosso di Montepulciano wines, its striking charm of the past rivals that of its hilltop neighbors, Pienza and Montalcino. Here Cinzia Caroti offers bed and breakfast on the first floor of a 16th-century palazzo on the main street of town, which is lined with shops and restaurants and is off limits to cars, which adds much to its medieval aura. One flight of wide stairs takes you up to L'Agnolo's reception area. There are three bedrooms off this area and another two off the frescoed dining room with wrought-iron chandelier. The spacious, high-ceilinged rooms have a subdued ambiance, with wrought-iron beds, family antiques, and new white-tiled bathrooms. Better lighting could be used to show off lovely original frescoed ceilings and painted borders. A classic breakfast of cappuccino and fresh croissants is served in the coffee shop below the home, making one feel like a true local resident. Cinzia lives two doors down and is present throughout the day to assist guests and make suggestions from the many sightseeing possibilities in this rich area of Tuscany, bordering Umbria. *Directions:* Park your car nearby (north or east lot) outside the village walls and follow Via di Gracciano running north-south to the middle. There is a small gold name plaque at the door.

*L'AGNOLO*
*Host: Cinzia Caroti*
*Via di Gracciano nel Corso 63*
*Montepulciano (SI) 53045, Italy*
*Tel: (0578) 717070, Cellphone: (339) 2254813*
*Fax: (0578) 757095*
*5 rooms, Double: €83*
*Open: all year, Credit cards: MC*
*Other languages: very little English*
*Region: Tuscany, Michelin Map: 563*
*karenbrown.com/italy/agnolo.html*

Montepulciano, ancient hilltop town and home of the prized Rosso di Montepulciano wine, is one of Tuscany's best-preserved marvels. The scenic countryside leads to other enchanting towns, such as Pienza, Montalcino, Sarteano, and San Quirico. Set below the town, behind the Basilica, taking in upwardly sweeping views of Montepucliano, is the lovely San Bruno property. The owners from Milan restored a typical stone farmhouse, drenched in pink cascading geraniums, and found themselves (naturally) with so many houseguests that they created two additional, one-story guesthouses across the informal garden dotted with lavender plants and roses. With guest comfort foremost in mind, large doubles have spacious, travertine bathrooms with hydrojet tub and separate shower. They are impeccably appointed in a refined country décor, using the finest materials and reflecting the innate beauty of these famed landscapes. A borderless, swimming pool awaits guests with a small, side gym and massage room. Home-baked goods are served in the morning until 11:00 in the dining room—located in a separate house incorporating the reception office and a soft-peach/yellow-colored living room with fireplace, inviting white sofas, and enormous glass doors with views. All extras are included in the room rate. *Directions:* From Montepulciano, follow for Basilica San Biagio. Behind church, turn a sharp left on Via Pescaia, then into second gate on left.

*RELAIS SAN BRUNO*     **New**
Hosts: Danilo Morales & Alberto Pavoncelli
Via di Pescaia, 5/7
Montepulciano, Tuscany (SI) 53045, Italy
Tel: (0578) 716 222, Fax: (0578) 715 084
7 rooms, Double: €280–€340
Open: Mar to Nov, Credit cards: all major
Other languages: good English
Region: Sicily, Michelin Map: 563
karenbrown.com/italy/sanbruno.html

After years of working in a hotel in Siena, then owning a wine bar, Marcello and his wife Maria Pia decided to put their hospitality experience into practice and opened the charming Bolsinina bed and breakfast. This is a perfect location for travelers, being so close to Siena (18 km) and having easy access to the main road, which passes through the magical Crete Senesi landscapes with their low, rolling clay hills punctuated by an occasional cypress tree against the horizon, to the hilltowns of Montalcino, Pienza, and Montepulciano. The 18th-century brick house has a courtyard where meals are served in season. To one side are the apartments of varying sizes, and to the other is the large house where the beamed guestrooms are located upstairs, along with a large common living room and loggia terrace with splendid views. Downstairs is an open multi-use space rotating around the center staircase with billiard table, cozy living room with fireplace and two large brick arches, and dining room. Guests reserve in the morning for dinner accompanied by excellent local wines. The house and rooms are filled with local antique country furniture and armoires and there is an immediate "at-home," informal air about the place. An inviting swimming pool is an added bonus. *Directions:* From Siena on the S.R.2, pass Monteroni d'Arbia, Lucignano, and before Buonconvento turn left at Casale-Gaggiolo (km 209). Take the gravel road up to the house.

*CASA BOLSININA*
*Hosts: Marcello & Maria Pia Mazzotta*
*Localita: Casale, Monteroni d'Arbia (SI) 53014, Italy*
*Tel & fax: (0577) 718477, Cellphone: (338) 2705153*
*6 rooms, Double: €80–€150,*
*4 apartments: €410–€1000 weekly*
*Cleaning & heating extra for apartments*
*Closed: Jan 15 to Mar 15, Credit cards: all major*
*Other languages: good English*
*Region: Tuscany, Michelin Map: 563*
*karenbrown.com/italy/bolsinina.html*

Hostess Silvana's claim to fame is her innate ability to please guests at the dining table and she did this for years in her own restaurant in Alba, which was written up in many culinary guides. Now she concentrates on her privileged guests who can sample her regional specialties right at home. Gracious Silvana and her journalist husband, Gianni, have transformed the grandparents' farmhouse, a group of three attached wings forming a U, into an intimate bed and breakfast with just two rooms. Their idea was to offer couples maximum space and privacy in junior suites (Rosa and Azzurra). Each room has its own entrance from the garden, sitting area, bedroom, and bathroom and Azzurra also has a small loft with two extra beds. The most extraordinary feature here is the soul-soothing panoramic views encompassing layers and layers of unspoilt landscapes dotted with villages and farmhouses all the way to the distant Alps on the horizon. All this accompanied by silence or the occasional chirping of birds. At sunset the only thing that can possibly tear guests away from the patio with its huge pots of hydrangeas overlooking the deep-green countryside is the call to dinner for another one of Silvana's fabulous meals served on the veranda. *Directions:* From Murazzano follow signs for Dogliani. After 1 km turn left at a small chapel on the road marked Cichetti and follow it to the end. 35 km from Alba, 70 km from Turin.

*CASCINA CICHETTI*
*Hosts: Silvana Faggio & Gianni Galli*
*Frazione Mellea 69*
*Murazzano (CN) 12060, Italy*
*Tel: (0173) 798501, Fax: (0173) 798921*
*2 rooms, Double: €95*
*Minimum nights required: 2*
*Open: all year, Credit cards: VS*
*Other languages: fluent English*
*Region: Piedmont, Michelin Map: 561*
*karenbrown.com/italy/cichetti.html*

The Albergo Sansevero Degas belongs to the Sansevero properties, a group of small hotels in Naples that are within prestigious palaces dating to the 1700s. Our favorite, of the three more basic hotels in the affiliation, is the Albergo Sansevero Degas. As the name implies, the palace at one time belonged to the family of the painter Edgar Degas, who also stayed here. The location couldn't be more ideal; the hotel is located just off of the Piazza Gesú Nuovo, a gem of a small square in the historic heart of Naples. The charm of the Albergo Sansevero Degas is not immediately apparent. You enter through a handsome portal into a dreary courtyard, then up an elevator to the hotel, where you step out into a pleasant reception area. The Sanservero affiliation has done an excellent job in staffing personnel, since every property we visited had exceptionally friendly, knowledgeable hosts at the front desk. The Albergo Sansevero Degas is a simple hotel, but offers great value. The décor is not pretensiously antique, but instead offers fresh and pretty rooms decorated with bamboo furniture. Our favorite, room 305, looks out to the colorful Piazza Gesú Nuovo. Not all of the rooms are with a private bathroom, so be sure to specify a private bath when making reservations. Also, remember that the reservation telephone represents all the hotels in the group, so ask for the Albergo Sanservero Degas by name. *Directions:* Located just off of the Piazza Gesú Nuovo.

*ALBERGO SANSEVERO DEGAS*     **New**
*Manager: Armida Auriemma*
*Calata Trinit à Maggiore 53, Piazza Gesù Nuovo*
*Naples (NA) 80138, Italy*
*Tel: (081) 79 01 000, Fax: (081) 21 16 98*
*9 rooms, Double: €95–€110*
*Open: all year*
*Region: Campania, Michelin Map: 564*
*karenbrown.com/italy/sanseverodegas.html*

In a small pocket of land in the southernmost point of Umbria is the Podere Costa Romana property, immersed in the green hillsides south of ancient Narni. Dynamic hostess Anna Maria left her native Naples for the peace and quiet of the Umbrian hills and meticulously restored the stone 18th-century farmhouse where she now hosts guests within six well-appointed apartments. Rooms have been thoughtfully decorated with antique country furnishings, which harmonize perfectly with the rustic quality of the original farmhouse. Each individual apartment (named for women) can accommodate from two (Giovanna is an adorable love nest) to five guests (Paola has two bedrooms) and is equipped with a kitchenette. Soft-peach and pale-yellow walls highlight exposed stones, beamed ceilings, and brick floors. The large main living room with fireplace and double arches opens out to the surrounding garden and swimming pool overlooking the hills. Travelers can easily reach many lesser-known Umbrian villages as well as the cities and from Orte frequent trains depart for either Rome or Florence. *Directions:* Exit the A1 autostrada at Magliano Sabina and turn right for Otricoli. 8 km after Otricoli turn right at the Narni-Testaccio-Itieli sign and then right again for the Podere Costa Romana.

*PODERE COSTA ROMANA*
*Host: Anna Maria Giordano*
*S.S. Flaminia, Strada per Itieli*
*Narni (TR) 05035, Italy*
*Tel: (0744) 722495, Cellphone: (335) 5738210*
*Fax: (0823) 797118*
*6 apartments: €550–€750 weekly, €118–€136 daily*
*Minimum nights required: 2, Open: all year*
*Other languages: some English*
*Region: Umbria, Michelin Map: 563*
*karenbrown.com/italy/romana.html*

La Magioca is a wonderful discovery in the wine country of Valpolicella, close to Lake Garda and historic Verona. The elegant 17th-century country home of the Merighi family was transformed into a luxurious bed and breakfast under the direction of the family's youngest son, Matteo, who runs the operation with flair and efficiency. No detail has been overlooked in this ivy-covered home where many decorating ideas were inspired by innumerable trips to the French countryside. A golden-yellow hue prevails, giving common areas luminosity and warmth. A large living room with enormous arched windows gives access to the surrounding garden and extended lawns, which lead to a private 13th-century chapel and a hidden hydrojet pool for six people. Three double bedrooms, two junior suites, and a suite, all very individually appointed with fine antiques and each more delightful than the other, are divided among the top floors. Rich fabrics, carpets, and paintings harmonize perfectly with wood-beamed mansard ceilings and parquet floors. Matteo's mother, Signora Marisa, is on hand as well and oversees the buffet breakfast. Romantic and peaceful and a great splurge. *Directions:* From Milan exit the A4 autostrada at Verona and follow signs for the city center (centro) for 3.5 km. After passing under a highway, turn left at the sign for the Valpolicella area and Negrar just after Pedemonte. From Negrar, follow signs for La Magioca just 1 km away.

*LA MAGIOCA*
*Host: Matteo Merighi*
*Via Moron 3*
*Negrar (VR) 37024, Italy*
*Tel: (045) 6000167, Fax: (045) 6000840*
*6 rooms, Double: €180–€240*
*Open: all year, Credit cards: all major*
*Other languages: good English*
*Region: Veneto, Michelin Map: 562*
*karenbrown.com/italy/magioca.html*

Right next door to the Grazia farm is the very similar property of the Lignana family. Again, a long, straight road takes you off the busy coastal Aurelia highway back to the 700-plus-acre farm and hunting reserve looking out to the distant sea and Mount Argentario. Gracious Signora Marcella and husband Giuseppe live in the ivy-covered ancient stone tower and attached villa, while guests reside within seven comfortable self-catering apartments in a converted barn down the road. Spacious apartments have two bedrooms and two bathrooms, living/dining area, and kitchenette. Some apartments have the bedrooms on a second floor, while others have them split between the main floor and an open loft space. They are nicely appointed in a clean and easy style, with fresh white walls, smart plaid cushions on built-in sofas, framed prints, wicker furniture, and wrought-iron beds. An alternative to sea bathing is a dip in the swimming pool, guarded by olive trees. For nature lovers, the area is full of marvelous expeditions on foot or bike, including the National Park of Uccellina, various forts on Mount Argentario, and the islands of Giglio and Giannutri, not to mention the Saturnia thermal spa. *Directions:* From Rome take the Aurelia Highway 1 and turn right at the sign "Piante-Vivaio" (140.5 km after the turnoff for Ansedonia). From the north you must exit at Ansedonia and return to the highway heading towards Grosseto. 140 km from Rome's Fiumicino airport.

*IL CASALONE*
*Hosts: Marcella & Giuseppe Lignana*
*S.S. Aurelia sud km 140.5*
*Orbetello Scalo (GR) 58016, Italy*
*Tel: (0564) 862160, Cellphone: (329) 2167397*
*Fax: (0564) 866308*
*7 apartments: €600–€1,300 weekly*
*Minimum nights required: 2, 7 in Jul & Aug*
*Open: all year, Other languages: good English*
*Region: Tuscany, Michelin Map: 563*
*karenbrown.com/italy/casalone.html*

The expansive Grazia farm is uniquely located at 3 kilometers from the sea. Gracious and warm hostess Signora Maria Grazia divides her time between Rome and the 300-acre property she inherited from her grandfather. The long cypress-lined driveway takes you away from the busy Aurelia road past grazing horses up to the spacious, rust-hued edifice with its arched loggia. The hosts' home, office, guest apartments, farmhands' quarters, and horse stables are all housed within the complex, which is encased by superb country and has peeks of the sea in all directions. From here one can enjoy touring Etruscan territory: Tuscania, Tarquinia, Sovana, Sorano, and the fascinating Roman ruins of Cosa, or stay by the coast on the beaches of Feniglia on the promontory of Argentario. Comfortably modest accommodations, including living area, kitchen, and breakfast basket, pleasantly decorated with homey touches, are offered within five apartments for two to four persons. Maria Grazia can suggest a myriad of local restaurants specializing in seafood or local country fare. Tennis and horseback riding lessons are available. Altogether a delightful combination. *Directions:* Take the coastal Aurelia road from Rome and after the Ansedonia exit turn right into an unmarked driveway immediately after the Pitorsino restaurant.

*GRAZIA*
*Host: Maria Grazia Cantore family*
*Localita: Provincaccia, 110, S.S. Aurelia sud km 140.1*
*Orbetello Scalo (GR) 58016, Italy*
*Tel & fax: (0564) 881182 or (06) 483945*
*5 apartments: €95–€140 daily B&B*
*Minimum nights required: 3*
*Open: all year*
*Other languages: good English, French*
*Region: Tuscany, Michelin Map: 563*
*karenbrown.com/italy/grazia.html*

The location of La Chiocciola bed and breakfast, minutes from the main tollway from Rome to Florence and on the border of the Lazio and Umbria regions, is ideal. Added bonuses are the warm hospitality, deliciously prepared regional meals (set rate of €21), and lovely country-style bedrooms. Roberto and Maria Cristina from Rome bought the stone farmhouse dating back to 1400 several years ago and began restoration work while living in the newer house next door. The results of their efforts are six perfectly neat and spotless bedrooms and two separate private suites divided between the two houses, and a large stone-walled dining room with outdoor veranda. Obvious care and attention has been put into the decorating of the air-conditioned bedrooms with wrought-iron canopy beds, crisp, white linen curtains, and botanical prints. The scenic 50-acre property with fruit orchards and olive trees is part of the Tiber river valley and woods. A swimming pool, spa facilities and excercise room are there for guests to enjoy. Innumerable day trips and itineraries of special interest are offered in the area of Umbria and Lazio and it's a 40-minute train ride to Rome. *Directions:* From Rome or Florence on the A1 autostrada, exit at Orte and turn immediately left for Orte, passing under the tollway. Continuing towards Orte, turn again for Amelia and repass over the tollway, taking the first left towards Penna in Teverina. La Chiocciola is 5 km along this road.

*LA CHIOCCIOLA*
*Hosts: Roberto & Maria Cristina de Fonseca Pimentel*
*Localita: Seripola*
*Orte (VT) 01028, Italy*
*Tel: (0761) 402734, Cellphone: (348) 5108309*
*Fax: (0761) 490254*
*8 rooms, Double: €100–€120*
*Open: all year, Credit cards: MC, VS*
*Other languages: good English, French*
*Region: Lazio, Michelin Map: 563*
*karenbrown.com/italy/lachiocciola.html*

Whether you want to take advantage of some of the best skiing in the country or prefer invigorating hikes up lush green mountain trails in summertime, the Dolomite mountain range will leave you spellbound. Ortisei is one of the main towns of the Siusi Alps area and a busy place, especially when Italians flock there during their Christmas and August vacations. This is a region with a distinct Austrian-Tyrolean flavor where more German is spoken than Italian and more wurstel served than pasta. The Stuflesser family, naturals in the hospitality business, have put an impressive addition onto their house near the old barn of the farm as a result of their success as a bed and breakfast. In fact, everything about the place is crisp and new, from the white exterior to the pinewood-paneled entrance, bar, and dining room, modeled after the typical stuben style, with a wood-burning ceramic heater where Signora Stuflesser creates traditional meals. Comfortable bedrooms with balconies to the back overlooking green wooded hills, the town below, and distant mountains are slightly higher in rate. Typical of this area, they have built-in wooden furniture and white down covers on the beds. Your jovial host divides his time between guests and the agricultural duties. The Hotel Digon offers all the amenities of a hotel with the warmth of a family home. *Directions:* From Ortisei, take the road towards Castelrotto. The Hotel Digon is on the right-hand side of the road after 2 km.

❄ ☕ 🛷 💳 ☎ 🍷 👫 🚶 🐎 P 🍴 🎿 🖼

*HOTEL DIGON*
*Host: Stuflesser family*
*Via Digon, Ortisei (BZ ) 39046, Italy*
*Tel: (0471) 797266, Fax: (0471) 798620*
*10 rooms, Double: €60–€130*
*Includes breakfast & dinner*
*Closed: April 15 to May 25 & Oct 15 to Dec 5*
*Credit cards: all major*
*Other languages: some English, German, Italian*
*Region: Trentino-Alto Adige, Michelin Map: 562*
*karenbrown.com/italy/digon.html*

After following directions up to the village of Bulla where the winding mountain road ends (1,400 meters up), 5 kilometers from Ortisei below, we thought this accommodation was in just a little too remote a location. Our opinion quickly changed, however, when we entered the Uhrerhof, a very special haven indeed. The Zemmer family have done a remarkable job of combining old and new in their recently renovated hotel, which just exudes warmth and welcome. Spacious antique-filled common rooms with fireplaces or stuben burners are strewn about the first floor, many opening out to terraces taking in the glorious mountaintop views. Walter treats guests to one of his divine five-course meals, using mostly organic ingredients, in typical stuben dining rooms, thoughtfully divided between families and couples in consideration of noise level. Spacious bedrooms and suites, many with balconies for the uplifting views, are divided between the original house and the new addition and are traditionally appointed in light pinewood with white comforters. A beautiful mosaic-tiled wellness center below includes everything: sauna, whirlpool, Turkish bath, and other special treatments. This place is all about serenity, slowing down, and pampering of the body and soul. *Directions:* From Ortisei, take the road for Castelrotto and after 1 km, turn left up to the road's end at Bulla.

*HOTEL UHRERHOF*
*Host: Walter Zemmer family*
*Localita: Bulla, Ortisei (BZ ) 39046, Italy*
*Tel: (0471) 797335, Fax: (0471) 797457*
*10 rooms, Double: €140–€208*
*Includes breakfast & dinner*
*Minimum nights required: 3*
*Closed: Nov, Credit cards: all major*
*Other languages: good English, German*
*Region: Trentino-Alto Adige, Michelin Map: 562*
*karenbrown.com/italy/uhrerhof.html*

A convenient stopover while heading either north or south along the main artery—the A1 autostrada—is the Villa Ciconia inn. Located below the historical center of Orvieto, in the newer commercial outskirts, the property maintains its tranquil setting thanks to the fortress of trees protecting the 16th-century stone villa. The first floor includes reception area, breakfast room, and two large high-ceilinged dining rooms. These latter, with their somber gray-stone fireplaces, tapestries, heavy dark-wood beams, and subdued-color frescoes depicting allegorical motifs and landscapes, give the place a medieval castle's air. The 12 air-conditioned bedrooms on the second floor are appointed either in appropriate style, with antique chests and wrought-iron beds, or with more contemporary furnishings (lower rates) and all the amenities of the four-star hotel that this is. Most rooms are quiet and look out onto the 8 acres of woods behind the villa. There are also two enormous beamed sitting rooms on this floor for guests and a beautiful new swimming pool. The restaurant has a solid reputation for creating excellent Umbrian specialties. Manager Anna Glena Petrangeli is always on hand to assist guests. *Directions:* Exiting from the autostrada, turn right towards Orvieto and right again where marked Arezzo, Perugia, passing under the tollway. The Ciconia is just after the river on the left-hand side of the road.

※ ☕ ✕ CREDIT ☎ 🚶 🐎 Y P ♍ ≋ 🏞 ♫ ♈

*VILLA CICONIA*
*Host: Petrangeli family*
*Via dei Tigli 69*
*Orvieto (TR) 05019, Italy*
*Tel: (0763) 305582, Fax: (0763) 302077*
*12 rooms, Double: €130–€155*
*No dinner Mon*
*Open: all year, Credit cards: all major*
*Other languages: French, good English*
*Region: Umbria, Michelin Map: 563*
*karenbrown.com/italy/villaciconia.html*

A very high rating goes to the Locanda Rosati on the border of Umbria and Lazio, and just steps away from Tuscany. Giampiero and sister, Alba, with their respective spouses, Luisa and Paolo, sold their cheese production business in Lucca and returned to Orvieto to transform the family farmhouse into a bed and breakfast. The results are splendid and guests, taking priority over the agricultural activity in this instance, are treated with extra-special care. The downstairs common areas include two cozy living rooms with fireplace and a large stone-walled dining room divided by a brick archway leading down to the "tufo" stone cellar. Seven bedrooms upstairs (one with access and bathroom for the handicapped) have been decorated with an animal theme evident in the carvings on bedboards and lamps. Three more bedrooms were added for guests on the top floor with mansard ceilings, leaving the entire home to the bed and breakfast business. Although the house is right on the road, most rooms face the countryside to the back where a large open lawn space leads to the inviting swimming pool. Paolo produces appetizing pastas, soups, and other specialties all written up in a recipe book for guests. *Directions:* Exit from the A1 autostrada at Orvieto and follow signs for Viterbo-Bolsena. Skirt town and continue towards Bolsena for about 8 km on route 71. After a series of sharp curves, the locanda comes up on the right.

*LOCANDA ROSATI*
*Host: Rosati family*
*Localita: Buonviaggio 22*
*Orvieto (TR) 05018, Italy*
*Tel & fax: (0763) 217314*
*10 rooms, Double: €110–€130*
*Closed: Jan & Feb*
*Credit cards: MC, VS*
*Other languages: good English*
*Region: Umbria, Michelin Map: 563*
*karenbrown.com/italy/locandarosati.html*

Claudia Spatola does a great job of single-handedly running a bed and breakfast in the complex of stone houses known as Borgo Spante, which dates back to the 15th century and has been in her family since 1752. Consisting of a main villa, connecting farmers' houses, chapel, barns, swimming pool, and garden, it is isolated in 500 acres of woods and hills, yet is located only 16 kilometers from Orvieto and not far from Assisi, Todi, and Perugia. Guests stay in a combination of rooms or apartments in the former farmers' quarters with their irregular-sized rooms, sloping worn-brick floors, and rustic country furnishings—very charming in its way. Authentic Umbrian meals, prepared by local women, are served in the dining room with long wooden tables and fireplace. A larger dining area has been added in the former barn, along with four additional mini-apartments, simply and characteristically decorated. Memorable evenings are spent in the garden or poolside conversing with other guests or listening to an impromptu concert or lecture. *Directions:* From the A1 autostrada exit at Orvieto and follow signs for Arezzo on route 71. After 7 km, turn right at Morrano and proceed for 12 km to the sign for Spante. Turn left and continue for 2 km.

*BORGO SPANTE*
*Host: Claudia Spatola*
*Ospedaletto (TR) 05010, Italy*
*Tel: (075) 8709134, Fax: (075) 8709201*
*5 rooms, Double: €130\**
*8 apartments: €130 (2 persons)\**
*\*Includes breakfast & dinner*
*Minimum nights required: 2, Open: all year*
*Other languages: some English*
*Region: Umbria, Michelin Map: 563*
*karenbrown.com/italy/borgospante.html*

The Belfiore farm property certainly stands out among a very bland choice of bed and breakfasts in the area between the well-preserved Renaissance city of Ferrara and Ravenna with its extraordinary mosaics. The flat countryside is characterized by marshland and the National Delta del Po Park, a paradise for birdwatchers and bikers, where many excursions are organized. The Bertelli sisters, Fiorenza and Daniela, from Ferrara, transformed their farm into a country restaurant with 18 bedrooms on the upper two floors. They are identically appointed with rustic wooden beds painted with a floral motif and matching armoires. Guests can feel right at home in the spacious living room with antiques and enormous open fireplace. The restaurant, where locals come for excellent local fare based on organically produced fruits and vegetables, is divided among several beamed dining rooms and guests are invited into the kitchen for a demonstration of making various types of pastas and breads. Italian lessons are also offered free of charge. A neat garden surrounds the simple rectangular-shaped house with burgundy shutters and a swimming pool sits invitingly in one corner. A mini-spa center includes facial and body treatments, sauna, and massage. *Directions:* Exit from the Ferrara-Comacchio highway at Ostellato and pass through the rather nondescript town to the tall bell tower at the corner of Via Pioppa, following signs to Belfiore.

※ ⚓ ☕ 🎿 ☕ CREDIT ☎ 🏋 🚶 👫 🐎 P 🍴 🏊 ⛵ 🐕 ♿ 🍇 🍸

*BELFIORE*
*Host: Tullio Bertelli family*
*Via Pioppa 27*
*Ostellato (FE) 44020, Italy*
*Tel: (0533) 681164, Cellphone: (335) 275702*
*Fax: (0533) 681172*
*18 rooms, Double: €90–€100*
*Open: all year, Credit cards: all major*
*Other languages: some English*
*Region: Emilia-Romagna, Michelin Map: 562*
*karenbrown.com/italy/belfiore.html*

Armando and Rosalba left behind a corporate life in order to bring this 72-acre property back to its original state as a self-sufficient farm where they could offer very special hospitality. Numerous articles written about this magical spot and a guestbook overflowing with happy travelers' praise testify to the success of their labor of love. Eight lovely bedrooms, a large dining room, living room, game room, library, bird sanctuary, lemon grove, chapel, and agricultural museum are all part of the ancient whitewashed masseria complex. Outside the walls are horse stables, farm animals, fruit orchards, and a vegetable garden, then acres and acres of olive trees divided by rows of low stone walls, so typical of Apulia. No detail has been overlooked in the decor of the bedrooms, which are appointed with selected antiques, wrought-iron beds, fine linens and lace, and paintings. Many have an adjoining room for families and there is an extra kitchen for guests. Dinner, either out in the candlelit courtyard or by the fire, is a very special time and requires full sensory attention. Courses after course of unique culinary combinations are served and explained with anecdotes, poetry, or stories by Armando while Rosalba guides her team of local women in the kitchen. Enchanting! *Directions:* Three km from the sea and close to Alberobello, Castellana Locorotondo, and Martina Franca. Il Frantoio is well marked at km 874 on S.S.16 between Fasano and Ostuni.

*MASSERIA IL FRANTOIO*
*Hosts: Armando & Rosalba Balestrazzi*
*S.S.16, km 874*
*Ostuni (BR) 72017, Italy*
*Tel & fax: (0831) 330276*
*8 rooms, Double: €196–€365*
*Minimum nights required: 2*
*Open: all year, Credit cards: MC, VS*
*Other languages: good English*
*Region: Apulia, Michelin Map: 564*
*karenbrown.com/italy/frantoio.html*

With her children grown and traveling around the world, Christine, an expatriate from England, decided to offer hospitality to travelers in her country home. Situated an hour north of Rome by train or car, the pretty countryside home made of typical local tufo brick is a short distance from the ancient village of Otricoli with its ancient Roman origins. It is one of many villages centered in the Tiber river valley, historically an important area for trade and commerce with Rome. A long wing off the main house, reserved for guests, offers three beamed bedrooms decorated with country furniture and overlooking the garden and hills. An order-as-you-like breakfast is served either in the kitchen or out on the patio. The cozy living room with open fireplace invites guests to relax after a day in the city. Being at the edge of Umbria and Lazio, she can suggest a myriad of local itineraries and destinations, known and not so well known, as well as town festivals throughout the region and concentrated in the months of May and June. This is a very informal, at-home accommodation just 7 kilometers from the main Rome-Florence autostrada. *Directions:* Exit at Magliano Sabina and turn left for Otricoli-Terni. Turn off for Otricoli and take the first road to the right—Strada Crepafico. Gates to Casa Spence are on the corner.

*CASA SPENCE*
*Host: Christine Spence*
*Strada Crepafico 29*
*Otricoli (TR) 05030, Italy*
*Tel & fax: (0744) 719758, Cellphone: (329) 0832886*
*3 rooms, Double: €75–€80*
*Open: all year*
*Other languages: fluent English*
*Region: Umbria, Michelin Map: 563*
*karenbrown.com/italy/casaspence.html*

For those who wish to become better acquainted with the real Sardinia, head inland where the natives live, the scenery is striking, and the food authentic. Sardinia presents travelers with its own unique scenery, layers of history, artisans' craftwork and folklore, traditional cuisine, and delightfully warm hospitality (not one single place we stopped at neglected to offer us refreshment). The 150-acre property of the Corda Altana family is isolated and completely immersed in the typical Sardinian landscape where huge time-worn granite rocks emerge on the horizon surrounded by cork trees and Mediterranean brush vegetation. Roads are bordered by low stone walls and the base of the family's prim white house was built on the granite foundation. The six bedrooms (two are adjoining for families), all on the first floor and separate from the family's quarters, are new and immaculate like the rest of Maria's house. Breakfast and dinner are served either out on a large granite table or within the spacious dining room, which caters to non-guests as well (Maria is well known for her homemade gnocchetti and soups). Innumerable hiking or horseback-riding excursions are organized from the property. *Directions:* From Olbia head south for San Teodoro and after 10 km turn right for Padru. After Padru drive another 8 km towards Buddusò, turning left for Pedra Bianca-Sas Concas. The house is marked on the right after 3 km.

⏫ 🍷 ♿ 👫 🏇 P 🍴

*TONINO CORDA*
*Host: Maria Sabina Altana family*
*Localita: Sas Concas-Pedra Bianca*
*Padru (SS) 07020, Italy*
*Tel & fax: (0789) 49125*
*6 rooms, Double: €85–€100\**
*\*Includes breakfast & dinner*
*Minimum nights required: 2*
*Open: all year, Other languages: none*
*Region: Sardinia, Michelin Map: 566*
*karenbrown.com/italy/corda.html*

45 kilometers south of the Amalfi coast is the archaeological site of Paestum with its three well-preserved Greek temples. The area is surrounded by unattractive commercial strips and much new construction, although farther south are the lovely Cilento National Park and the coast. Here the Seliano farm provides an oasis of peace and tranquillity very near the sea. Baroness Cecilia, her two sons, Ettore and Massimino, and manager, Nicola, are wonderful hosts and make the managing of this busy farm, the horseback riding center, restaurant, and bed and breakfast look like a delightful game. The emphasis here is on the preparation of meals using local recipes and their own produce, including fresh mozzarella, most famous in this area. In fact, the Baroness conducts week-long cooking classes including excursions to local cultural and gastronomic highlights. Pleasantly decorated rooms with tiled floors and family antiques are situated in the farmhouse or adjacent yellow house, with two comfortable living rooms for guests. Truly delectable meals are served out on the covered terrace or in the long dining/living room with fireplace and historic paintings. There is an inviting swimming pool for guests. *Directions:* Leave the A3 at Eboli (less traffic than Battipaglia) and head for Paestum. Turn right off the main road (S.S.18) at Paestum and after 1 km turn into the driveway marked Seliano. Pass the main villa (uninhabited) to the main gate.

*SELIANO*
*Host: Baroness Cecilia Bellelli Baratta*
*Localita: Seliano*
*Paestum (SA) 84063, Italy*
*Tel: (0828) 723634, Cellphone: (335) 6674200*
*Fax: (0828) 724544*
*13 rooms, Double: €80–€130*
*Closed: Jan & Feb, Credit cards: MC, VS*
*Other languages: good English*
*Region: Campania, Michelin Map: 564*
*karenbrown.com/italy/seliano.html*

We look all over for bed and breakfasts that radiate a natural charm like that of Fagiolari, just outside Panzano. Cordial hostess Giulietta has seemingly unintentionally created a haven for travelers just by letting her home be a home. The unique stone farmhouse on three levels is brimming with character and has been restored with total respect for its innate simplicity using stone, terra-cotta brick, and chestnut-wood beams. Entering the front door into the cozy living room with large fireplace, I was impressed by the refreshingly authentic ambiance of this Tuscan home. Two bedrooms are just off this room, the larger having an en suite bathroom of stone and travertine. The main house and former barn, where you find two other good-sized bedrooms, are united by a connecting roof, left open in the middle to allow for an enormous fig tree. Bedrooms hold lovely antiques, book-lined shelves, collections of framed drawings and artwork, embroidered linens, and views of the delightful garden and cypress-lined paths. Overlooking the swimming pool, an adorable one-bedroom house on the property with a bookcase dividing the kitchen and living area is rented out weekly. Giulietta also teaches cooking classes lasting from one to four days *Directions:* From the piazza in Panzano follow signs to centro and take the left fork for Mercatale. At a half km from the piazza turn left after a pale-green building and follow the gravel road downhill to the end.

*FAGIOLARI*
Host: Giulietta Giovannoni
Case Sparse 25, Panzano in Chianti (FI) 50020, Italy
Tel & fax: (055) 852351, Cellphone: (335) 6124988
4 rooms, Double: €100–€120
1 cottage: €840– €910  weekly
Minimum nights required: 3 in cottage
Open: all year, Credit cards: all major
Other languages: some English
Region: Tuscany, Michelin Map: 563
karenbrown.com/italy/fagiolari.html

As you wind your way up a steep unpaved road through thick woods, you will no doubt wonder as we did how English couple Sonia and Edward ever found the secluded 70-acre property set above the Sieve river valley to the east of Florence. Upon arrival you will be greeted and rewarded with a glass of fresh spring water from the fountain "shower" (la doccia). It is understandable that long ago the farmhouse was originally a farm for the monks of the local abbey—the views are inspirational and the positions of both the house and the swimming pool take full advantage of the expansive panorama encompassing the Rufina wine valley nature reserve. Original features remain intact after a complete restoration of the house that created a variety of high-level accommodation in the form of four bedrooms, three suites with individual kitchenettes, and two attached houses with two bedrooms each for weekly stays. The perfectly charming home is filled with lovely antiques (local and imported from England), queen- or king-sized beds, and beautiful linens and tiled bathrooms. Guests can wander about the many common rooms and have a glass of wine in front of a spectacular sunset while Edward works Mediterranean wonders in the kitchen. Prepare to be pampered. *Directions:* 40 minutes from Florence, 5 km from Pelago. Detailed directions are supplied at the time of reservation.

*LA DOCCIA*
*Hosts: Sonia & Edward Mayhew*
*Localita: Paterno, Ristonchi 19/20, Pelago (FI) 50060*
*Tel: (055) 8361387, Fax: (055) 8361388*
*7 rooms, Double: €130–€250*
*2 apartments : €800–€1,275 weekly*
*Minimum nights required: 3*
*Open: all year, Credit cards: all major*
*Other languages: fluent English*
*Region: Tuscany, Michelin Map: 563*
*karenbrown.com/italy/doccia.html*

Located on a southwest corner of Sicily, 14 km from Marsala (not a particularly scenic area), is a historic Baglio farm estate, owned forever by the Montalto Spano family. The typical, 18th-century, fortified construction with two inner courtyards includes the main house, farmer's quarters, wine cellars, and barns and stalls; all in the center of more than a thousand-acres of flat land—primarily vineyards from which the famous Marsala wines derive. A long, dirt road through the vineyards and citrus groves leads to the front gate, where one passes through the first seemingly abandoned and dilapidated work area to the second courtyard, where the restored home is situated. On the ground floor of the owner's villa is a rustically styled dining room, where guests can enjoy a typical home-cooked, Sicilian country meal. A rooftop terrace off the main living room offers views to the not so distant sea. Ten guestrooms are found on two floors off the main living room, each individually decorated with original, patterned-tile floors and family heirlooms, giving turn-of-the-century ambience. New bathrooms have been added to each bedroom. There are the Mozia salt and wine islands, the fascinating seaside archaeological site of Selinunte with temples still-standing and vast areas of fallen columns (best seen at sunset), and many wineries to visit in the area. *Directions:* Take the A29 from Palermo to Mazara then SS 115 towards Marsala. After 7 km, follow signs to Baglio Spano.

*BAGLIO SPANO*      **New**
*Host: Federico Montalto*
*Contrada Triglia Scaletta*
*Petrosino, Sicily (TP) 91020, Italy*
*Fax: (0923) 989840*
*10 rooms, Double: €60–€95*
*Open: all year, Credit cards: all major*
*Other languages: good English*
*Region: Sicily, Michelin Map: 565*
*karenbrown.com/italy/bagliospano.html*

The coastal stretch from Messina to Cefalu has special appeal to the off-the-beaten-track traveler who will find the perfect place to stay at Casa Migliaca, a 200-year-old farmhouse nestling in the wooded hills 7 kilometers off the main road. This stone house just outside town, owned by Maria Teresa and Sebastiano, who left the city several years ago in favor of a rural lifestyle, offers a lovely sweeping view over olive and citrus groves down to the sea. The very congenial hosts love to converse with guests around the kitchen table or down in the cool dining room (originally the oil-press room) around the press wheel. A special effort was made to keep everything possible intact, giving the house its own very distinct charm, maintaining all original floors, ceilings, beams, kitchen tiles, and furniture, although new bathrooms have been incorporated in most of the rooms. There are even extra showers out in the garden! Guests are offered a choice of three double bedrooms upstairs or five downstairs. For those who desire direct contact with Sicilian culture, Casa Migliaca is a truly memorable experience. *Directions:* From coastal route 113, just 25 km after Cefalu, turn right at the sign for Pettineo and follow it right past town. Just after a gas station, turn right on a descending gravel road to the house (unmarked) 300 meters from Pettineo.

*CASA MIGLIACA*
*Host: Maria Teresa Allegra*
*Contrada Migliaca, Pettineo, Sicily (ME) 98070, Italy*
*Tel: (0921) 336722, Cellphone: (335) 8430645*
*Fax: (0921) 391107*
*8 rooms, Double: €136\**
*\*Includes breakfast & dinner*
*Open: all year, Credit cards: all major*
*Other languages: good English*
*Region: Sicily, Michelin Map: 565*
*karenbrown.com/italy/casamigliaca.html*

The southernmost, "heel-side" of Italy's boot-shaped peninsula, known as Puglia, presents another facet of the country's many-sided culture. It is a land with spectacular coastlines, villages with distinct Greek and Turkish influence, endless lines of olive groves, fields of wildflowers, and a rich history of art including baroque (Bari's Santa Nicola church is exquisite). All of this plus delectable cuisine and a warm and open people await in Puglia (Apulia), as does the Masseria Salamina, a 16th-century fortified farmhouse between Bari and Brindisi covering 100 acres of land and producing primarily olive oil. The long driveway leads to the sand-colored castle with turreted tower with expansive vistas over olive groves to the sea. The seven rooms, each with a separate courtyard entrance, are decorated with basic reproductions and wicker furniture, and are a notch up in level but not as luminous as the upstairs apartments. These eight one-bedroom apartments are available for longer stays, with simple and practical furnishings. Host Gianvincenzo and family live in the main wing and run their masseria like a small hotel. A lofty, vaulted restaurant with terra-cotta floors provides all meals for guests. In the low season a week-long stay including Mediterranean cooking lessons and local excursions for small groups is arranged. *Directions:* From the S.S.16 exit at Pezze di Greco. Just before town take the first right for 1 km to the masseria.

*MASSERIA SALAMINA*
*Host: Gianvincenzo de Miccolis Angelini*
*Pezze di Greco (BR) 72010, Italy*
*Tel: (080) 4897307, Fax: (080) 4898582*
*7 rooms, Double: €90–€110*
*8 apartments: €600–€750 weekly*
*Minimum nights required: 7 in Jul & Aug*
*Open: all year, Credit cards: MC, VS*
*Other languages: some English*
*Region: Apulia, Michelin Map: 564*
*karenbrown.com/italy/salamina.html*

Right along the road connecting the hilltowns of Pienza and Montepulciano is the conveniently positioned farm of Felice and Giulia, transplanted from their hometowns in the regions of Marches and Campania respectively. The 18th-century stone farmhouse forms a U with inner courtyard from which you gain access to the breakfast room/bar, stone-walled restaurant with large dividing arch, living room, and upstairs bedrooms divided on both sides. Bedrooms are luminous and spacious, with immaculate bathrooms, pretty bedspreads, and country furniture. The bedrooms on the right side overlook the hilly countryside, swimming pool, and the 100-acre property of woods and fields, which produces its own wine and olive oil. Ancient Pienza can be seen at a distance. The real treat here is Giulia's cooking using the farm's own fresh produce. She has a flair for combining local traditional recipes with her own personal inventions, having homemade pastas as her base. Hard-working Felice relaxes and jokes with guests, often ending the evening playing the guitar. This is an easy-access touring base for the endless itineraries available, including Siena Montalcino and tours of the d'Orcia wine valley, and a great value. *Directions:* Exit from the autostrada at Chiusi and follow signs for Montepulciano, then Pienza. After a total of 25 km, well before Pienza, the iron gates of the Santo Pietro are on the left.

*SANTO PIETRO*
*Hosts: Felice d'Angelo & Giulia Scala*
*Strada Statale 146, No. 29, Pienza (SI) 53026, Italy*
*Tel: (0578) 748410, Fax: (0578) 749877*
*11 rooms, Double: €85–€93*
*Per person half board: €67*
*Minimum nights required: 3*
*Open: Mar to Dec, Credit cards: all major*
*Other languages: some English*
*Region: Tuscany, Michelin Map: 563*
*karenbrown.com/italy/santopietro.html*

The most striking images of southern Tuscany are in the Orcia Valley—enchanting landscapes with soft, rolling hills topped with rows of cypress trees silhouetted against the sky. This alternating with the area called Le Crete Senesi—barren hills made of clay and resembling moon craters—makes for fascinating scenery. Le Traverse, at 4 kilometers from Pienza, is submersed in this peaceful countryside to which your gracious hosts, Pinuccia and Enrico, retired from Milan. Their charming home has been very tastefully restored and all the right touches (such as terry bathrobes and the finest-quality bedlinens) added to make guests feel right at home. The stone farmhouse with front courtyard is divided between the couple's own quarters, rooms for their visiting children, and an apartment for guests with independent entrance. The other two bedrooms are situated in the one-level converted barn nearby and are enhanced with the family's country antiques and prints. Huge terra-cotta vases overflowing with geraniums, trailing roses, and azalea plants dot the 50-acre property, which includes a swimming pool. Olive oil is produced as well as jams using homegrown fruit. The intimacy of the place with its three rooms makes you feel like a true houseguest and the area is full of delightful day trips. *Directions:* Follow signs for Monticchiello from Pienza (circular piazza). After 3.3 km turn left on an unpaved road up to a group of cypress trees and the house.

*LE TRAVERSE*
*Host: Pinuccia Barbier Meroni*
*Localita: Le Traverse, Pienza (SI) 53026, Italy*
*Tel: (0578) 748198, Cellphone: (333) 4708789*
*Fax: (0578) 748949*
*3 rooms, Double: €155*
*Minimum nights required: 2*
*Closed: Jan 22 to 30, Credit cards: all major*
*Other languages: good English, French*
*Region: Tuscany, Michelin Map: 563*
*karenbrown.com/italy/traverse.html*

The San Teodoro Nuovo property offers the "way-off-the-beaten-track" traveler a delightful base for exploring the southernmost reaches of Italy. In the Basilicata region, just 5 kilometers from the beaches of the Gulf of Taranto, this 400-acre farm specializing in citrus fruits and olive oil has been in the noble Xenia Doria family for generations and the family resides here all year, offering guest accommodation in a variety of renovated buildings. Two apartments appointed with the house's original furniture are found in a wing of the large main brick villa covered with bougainvillea vines, while another five, simpler in decor, are just below on the ground floor facing out to the back orchards. These can accommodate from two to four persons and have a kitchen. The remaining four very pleasant apartments, for two to four people, are in the same building as the restaurant on the property and and are appointed with the family's own furniture, with accents of color from the fresh country fabrics used. Meals at the restaurant are based on local traditional recipes and the farm's own products. In the vicinity are the highlights of Apulia and many Greek archaeological ruins, as well as two 18-hole golf courses and horse riding. *Directions:* From Taranto take the S.S.106 coastal highway and pass the S.S.407 for Potenza. Turn right at the sign for San Teodoro Nuovo at the km 442 sign of the S.S. 106.

*SAN TEODORO NUOVO*
*Host: Maria Xenia Doria family*
*Localita: Marconia*
*Pisticci (MT) 75020, Italy*
*Tel & fax: (0835) 470042, Cellphone: (338) 5698116*
*11 apartments: €100–€120 double B&B*
*Minimum nights required: 2*
*Open: all year, Credit cards: all major*
*Other languages: good English, French, German*
*Region: Basilicata, Michelin Map: 564*
*karenbrown.com/italy/teodoro.html*

As more and more Italians reclaim family property in the countryside or buy and restore their own abandoned castles, people such as the Baccheschi family are moving into more affordable, lesser-known areas. They left behind a successful fashion business to come to the quiet southern part of Tuscany where they bought the ruins of a 13th-century stone castle/ex-convent and have completed putting its pieces back together to form their own private residence and rooms for guests. Two adjacent stunning stone guesthouses are available, plus three suites in the main castle. The smaller house, I Sassi, has one bedroom, a large bathroom, and glassed-in living room taking in the sumptuous view of virgin territory. La Chiesina has a kitchen and spacious living room with intarsia parquet flooring, two bedrooms, and two bathrooms. They are appointed sophisticatedly with family antiques and colonial pieces from Indonesia, and are worthy of an article in Architectural Digest. The suites, decorated in the same vein, share a large kitchen and living room. The travertine swimming pool hangs on the edge of the manicured garden, which drops down into untamed landscapes. *Directions:* From the Grosseto-Siena highway 223, exit at Paganico. After 3 km turn right for Sasso d'Ombrone, and right again for Poggi del Sasso. In town watch for street sign Via de Vicarello on the right and follow the dirt road, keeping left at the fork for 7.5 km to the gray iron gate on the right.

*CASTELLO DI VICARELLO*
Hosts: Aurora & Carlo Baccheschi Berti
Via di Vicarello 1
Poggi del Sasso (SI) 58043, Italy
Tel & fax: (0564) 990718, Cellphone: (328) 8720670
4 rooms, Double: €250–€350
1 house: €600 daily
Minimum nights required: 3, Open: all year
Region: Tuscany, Michelin Map: 563
Abitare la Storia
karenbrown.com/italy/vicarello.html

The picturesque countryside dotted with medieval hilltowns north of Rome called Sabina is finally getting some recognition after centuries of being just a sleepy rural area. Bed and breakfasts are springing up right and left and at long last the tourist, inexplicably foreign to this lovely area so close to the capital city, has the opportunity to explore this virgin territory with its ancient traditions still in practice. Maria Vittoria, the warm and enthusiastic hostess of Wonderland, as her bed and breakfast translates, is another newcomer to Sabina. She offers a very comfortable level of accommodation in her own home set down below the main road outside of town and facing out to an impressive panorama of hills covered with olive groves and distant mountains. Four bedrooms are found in the main house, elegantly appointed with precious antiques, paintings, and various collections from Maria's travels. Some have terraces from which you can watch sunsets over the magnificent valley. Two suites have been built into the hillside in front of the home. One has a loft bedroom with sitting area and kitchenette below. There's a swimming pool for guests to enjoy. A homemade breakfast is served on the front patio. *Directions:* From the Rome-Rieti Via Salaria (route SS4), turn right and left at km 52. Two hundred meters later turn left on the road called SP42 and continue for 5km and you see the Paese delle Meraviglie sign and an iron gate on the right.

*PAESE DELLE MERAVIGLIE*
*Host: Maria Vittoria Toniolo*
*Via Mirtense km 5*
*Poggio Nativo (RI) 02030, Italy*
*Tel & fax: (0765) 872599, Cellphone: (328) 6642954*
*4 rooms, Double: €78–€90*
*1 apartment: €460–€540 weekly*
*Minimum nights required: 2, Open: all year*
*Other languages: good English, French*
*Region: Lazio, Michelin Map: 563*
*karenbrown.com/italy/paese.html*

Thirty-five kilometers northeast of Florence, in a beautiful, hilly area of Tuscany, lies the Rufina Valley, famous for its robust red wine. Crowning a wooded slope is one of the many residences of the noble Galeotti-Ottieri family. The interior of the 15th-century main villa reveals spacious high-ceilinged halls with frescoes depicting family history. The family has also restored several stone farmhouses on the vast property, one of which is the Locanda Praticino whose upper floor contains lovely, simple double rooms with countryside views down one long hall, each named after its color scheme. Downstairs is a large rustic dining and living room with vaulted ceiling, enormous stone fireplace, worn brick floors, and casual country furniture. Full country-fresh Tuscan meals are only €15. A swimming pool and tennis courts, plus the enchanting landscape, make it difficult to tear oneself away for touring. In order to retain the characteristic flavor of farmers' quarters, the properties have an intentionally unrestored, natural air to them. Available for longer stays are three very tastefully decorated apartments. The Petrognano is a tranquil spot where guests may enjoy the gracious hospitality of this historically important Florentine family. *Directions:* From Florence head toward Pontassieve. Continue to Rufina, turning right at Castiglioni-Pomino. Follow the winding road to the property, marked just before Pomino (12 km from Pontassieve).

*FATTORIA DI PETROGNANO*
*Host: Cecilia Galeotti-Ottieri family*
*Localita: Pomino, Pomino, Rufina (FI) 50060, Italy*
*Tel: (055) 8318867, Fax: (055) 8318812*
*8 rooms, Double: €75–€95*
*3 apartments: €350–€800 weekly*
*Minimum nights required: 2*
*Open: Apr 15 to Oct, Credit cards: all major*
*Other languages: good English, French*
*Region: Tuscany, Michelin Map: 563*
*karenbrown.com/italy/petrognano.html*

In the undiscovered valley of Champorcher, Mauro and his wife Piera took over the ancient town grain mill and have reopened its doors as a bed and breakfast. The plain exterior on the road gives no clue to the fascinating interior where enormous dining-room windows look right out over the rushing torrents of Ayasse, which cut directly through this lush valley. In the middle of this spacious room is an antique carpenter's sawing machine, once part of the mill. Restoration work on the stone mill, just off the dining room, is being completed with the hopes of continuing the grain production activity using original methods. A loft living room with fireplace and burgundy sofas looks over the main room. Piera prepares the nightly meal for guests using traditional recipes from this mountain area. The Gontiers' agriculture activity produces various vegetables, berries, and chestnuts. The four sweetly decorated new bedrooms are located on the same floor and all have water views (and sounds!), brand-new bathrooms, lace curtains, and carved pinewood beds. Hiking trails in the valley take you up to the many waterfalls. This is a perfect spot for nature lovers wanting to explore. *Directions:* Exit at Verres from the A5 from the north, heading for Verres, then Bard. At Bard turn right for Hone, Champorcher. After 7 km, just after Pontboset, Le Moulin is located just before the stone bridge on the left-hand side of the road.

*LE MOULIN DES ARAVIS*
*Hosts: Mauro Gontier & Piera Chanoux*
*Fraz. Savin 55, Pontboset (AO) 11020, Italy*
*Tel: (0125) 809831, Cellphone: (329) 8013184*
*Fax: (0125) 834982*
*4 rooms, Double: €42–€46*
*Per person half board: €30–€37*
*Open: all year*
*Other languages: very little English, French*
*Region: Aosta Valley, Michelin Map: 561*
*karenbrown.com/italy/pontboset.html*

The Taticchi family warmly welcome guests to their corn, sunflower, and horse-breeding farm above Perugia, a rambling villa owned by the family since 1600. The former farmer's quarters near the main house contain a breakfast room and guestrooms with wood-beamed ceilings and brick floors, furnished in simple country style. Additional rooms are within the villa. Ceramic bathroom tiles (and lamps), handmade by their talented daughter, depict horses, ducks, roses, butterflies, and the like, for which the rooms are named. The main villa's dramatic entrance foyer with arched stairway leads up to a glassed-in veranda overlooking a neglected garden and woods through which the River Tiber flows. Annabella serves her specialties in the old-style dining room with chandelier and frescoes. Time stands still in the original library/billiard room and the two living rooms with piano, Oriental carpets, and period paintings. Horses are available for lessons in the indoor/outdoor ring or excursions in the area. Weeklong courses with special all-inclusive rates are available in cooking, ceramics, and riding. Il Covone is a busy and informal place for families. *Directions:* Take route E45 from Perugia, exiting at Ponte Pattoli. Turn right at the T-junction and continue for 1 km. The farm is just after the tennis/sport complex.

*IL COVONE*
*Hosts: Elena & Cesare Taticchi*
*Strada della Fratticiola 2*
*Ponte Pattoli (PG) 06085, Italy*
*Tel & fax: (075) 694140*
*10 rooms, Double: €80–€92*
*Per person half board: €60–€70*
*Minimum nights required: 2*
*Open: all year, Credit cards: all major*
*Region: Umbria, Michelin Map: 563*
*karenbrown.com/italy/ilcovone.html*

Just north of Spoleto is the tiny 14th-century village of Poreta and farther up on the hillside are the remains of the walls of the castle that once dominated the valley. It is here that a group of friends, Luca and American Pam being the omnipresent, genial hosts, restored what was left of the ancient castle and transformed it into a country bed and breakfast. Their idea was to provide not only accommodation but also a special place offering a variety of cultural events such as classical concerts, art shows, poetry reading, and dinners with particular local food themes. The cluster of stone houses where the eight bedrooms are located includes a church restored in the baroque period with original frescoes and faux-marble borders. The small restaurant is made up of two cozy rooms with beamed ceilings, fireplace, and cheery yellow walls. A clean and pleasant country style pervades the bedrooms with their soothingly soft beige tones and occasional country antiques. They need no elaborate paintings for decoration as the views out the windows suffice. The buildings are united by an expansive brick terrace overlooking olive groves and sweeping views of the valley—a wonderful spot for watching the spectacular sunsets while enjoying a pre-dinner drink. *Directions:* From the N3 Spoleto-Perugia road turn right after 8 km at Poreta and follow signs up to the castle.

*IL CASTELLO DI PORETA*
*Hosts: Luca Saint Amour di Chanaz & Pam Moskow*
*Localita: Poreta*
*Poreta–Spoleto (PG) 06049, Italy*
*Tel: (0743) 275810, Cellphone: (335) 7371838*
*Fax: (0743) 270175*
*8 rooms, Double: €99–€114*
*Open: all year, Credit cards: all major*
*Other languages: good English*
*Region: Umbria, Michelin Map: 563*
*karenbrown.com/italy/poreta.html*

The Vecchio Convento is a real gem, offering quality accommodation for a moderate price. Its several dining rooms are brimming with rustic country charm and serve delicious meals prepared from local produce. There are 15 guestrooms tastefully decorated with antiques. The town of Portico di Romagna is like the inn, inviting yet unpretentious—an old village surrounded by wooded hills and clear mountain streams. A stroll through medieval pathways, which twist down between the weathered stone houses, leads you to an ancient stone bridge gracefully arching over a rushing stream. The inn, too, is old, but was not (as you might expect from its name) originally a convent. According to its gracious owner, Marisa Raggi, it was named for a restaurant located in a convent that she and her husband Giovanni (the chef) used to operate—when they moved here they kept the original name. The restaurant is still their primary focus, as its fine, fresh cuisine reflects. Italian lessons are also organized. *Directions:* Because of the winding, two-lane mountain highway that leads to the village, it takes about two hours to drive the 75 km from Florence. The inn is located 34 km southwest of the town of Forli.

*ALBERGO AL VECCHIO CONVENTO*
*Hosts: Marisa Raggi & Giovanni Cameli*
*Via Roma, 7*
*Portico di Romagna (FO) 47010, Italy*
*Tel: (0543) 967053, Fax: (0543) 967157*
*15 rooms, Double: €90–€100*
*Closed: Jan 12 to Feb 12*
*Credit cards: all major*
*Other languages: some English*
*Region: Emilia-Romagna, Michelin Map: 562*
*karenbrown.com/italy/vecchioconvento.html*

On the outskirts of historical Mantova sits the Villa Schiarino Lena, one of the magnificent estates formerly belonging to the Gonzaga family, once among the most powerful nobility in Lombardy. The very cordial Lena Eliseo family, the present owners, have taken on the enormous task of restoring the 15th-century palace room by room. With high vaulted ceilings, completely frescoed rooms, wrought-iron chandeliers, and original terra-cotta floors, the seemingly endless parade of rooms reveals one delight after another. Besides being a museum, the villa is used for large parties, weddings, and business meetings, and guestrooms are also available. Surrounding the villa are small houses, once inhabited by farmhands, which are now offered to travelers on a daily or weekly basis. The three modest but spacious and comfortable apartments are appointed with a mixture of antique and contemporary furniture and can accommodate up to four persons. Each apartment has its own living area and one includes a kitchenette. A golf practice range is available on the property. This location is the ideal spot to base yourself while exploring less-touristy Ferrara, Cremona, Verona, and Mantua, which are filled with medieval and Renaissance buildings (Palazzo del Te and Palazzo Ducale are "must sees"). *Directions:* From Mantova take route N62 north past the church and turn left on Via Gramsci. Follow it for 1 km to the villa.

*VILLA SCHIARINO LENA*
*Host: Giuseppe Lena Eliseo family*
*Via Santa Maddalena 7*
*Porto Mantovano (MN) 46047, Italy*
*Tel: (0376) 398238, Fax: (0376) 393238*
*2 rooms, Double: €110–€120*
*3 apartments: €100–€120 daily*
*Minimum nights required: 2, Open: all year*
*Credit cards: MC, VS, Other languages: good English*
*Region: Lombardy, Michelin Map: 561*
*karenbrown.com/italy/schiarino.html*

All types of acccommodation are available in Positano: from five-star luxury to simple bed and breakfasts like Casa Cosenza, with its sunny yellow façade. Sitting snug against the cliff side, halfway down to the beach, it is reached by descending one of the variety of stairways found in this unique seaside town. The front arched entranceway, lined with terra-cotta pots overflowing with colorful local flora, leads to an enormous tiled terrace overlooking the pastel-color houses of Positano and the dramatic coastline. Seven guestrooms on the second floor, each with a balcony and air conditioning, enjoy the same breathtaking panorama. The residence dates back 200 years, as evidenced by the typical cupola ceilings, originally designed to keep rooms cool and airy. Guestrooms have bright, tiled floors and are simply and sweetly decorated with old-fashioned armoires, desks, and beds. Room 7 (at a slightly higher rate), although smaller and with an older bathroom, has a lovely large terrace, as do two suites behind the main house that can accommodate three to four persons. Two apartments located in the back and above the B&B also have lovely views. A continental breakfast is served on the terrace. The helpful Cosenza family assures visitors of a pleasant stay. *Directions:* Park your car in F. lli Milano parking near the center of Positano and ask for directions to Cafe Positano. It is next to the stairway that takes you to Casa Cosenza. Remember to pack light!

*CASA COSENZA*
*Host: Salvatore Cosenza family*
*Via Trara Genoino 18, Positano (SA) 84017, Italy*
*Tel: (089) 875063, Fax: (089) 8122391*
*9 rooms, Double: €120–€150*
*2 apartments: €1,500–€1,700 weekly*
*Minimum nights required: 3 in high season*
*Open: all year, Credit cards: all major*
*Other languages: some English*
*Region: Campania, Michelin Map: 564*
*karenbrown.com/italy/casacosenza.html*

The spectacular Amalfi coast offers a wide variety of accommodation, yet few as special as La Fenice—as fantastic as the mythological bird for which it is named. Guests leave their cars on the main road and climb the arbored steps to discover the white villa hidden amid lush Mediterranean vegetation. Costantino and Angela heartily welcome new arrivals on the shady front terrace, where a basic continental breakfast is served each clement morning. Seven luminous bedrooms, three with terrace and marvelous sea views, the others with lateral sea or no sea view, are simply and sparsely furnished with an occasional antique armoire or bureau in a wing off the family's home. Eight more rooms of varying dimensions, most with terraces, reached by many steps down from the road, are built separately into the side of the cliff and have colorful, tiled floors and similar furnishings. Descending yet more steps, you'll come to the curved seawater pool and Jacuzzi carved against the rock (open June to October), where an occasional salad or sandwich is served during summer months (at an extra cost). A coastal boat tour (pick-up at La Fenice's beach) including a stop for lunch can be arranged. This property has few or no amenities in the rooms, but is a natural wonder, cascading down to the sea and a small private beach. *Directions:* Located on the coastal highway south of Positano towards Amalfi. Two curves after town, watch for gates on both sides of the road.

*LA FENICE*
*Hosts: Angela & Costantino Mandara*
*Via Marconi 4*
*Positano (SA) 84017, Italy*
*Tel: (089) 875513, Fax: (089) 811309*
*15 rooms, Double: €130*
*Open: all year*
*Other languages: some English*
*Region: Campania, Michelin Map: 564*
*karenbrown.com/italy/lafenice.html*

The Villa La Tartana, owned by the same delightful owners of the Villa Rosa, deserves more than a full page write-up. Very different than the Villa Rosa, which is located high above on the hillside above the main road of town, the Tartana is down at the seaside where one has easier access to restaurants, ferries to Capri, stores, and lounging on the popular beach. A three-story white house snuggled in between others, the bed & breakfast offers comfortable rooms each with its own terrace, many amenities, and the warm hospitality of the Caldiero family. In keeping with the seaside ambience, local hand-painted tiles from Vietri are used in cool blue tones throughout. A main living room with bright, yellow sofas and colorful paintings of nautical themes is where guests are greeted and daily itineraries are arranged to Amalfi, Sorrento, or Ravello. The best way to get a real taste of Positano is to rent a gozzo boat (with or without a skipper) and view the dramatic coastline from the sea, stopping to swim at various beaches and coves or lunching at one of the delectable, waterside trattorias serving pasta with seafood and other local specialities. *Directions:* Arriving in Positano, take the main road down into town and continue until you reach a small fork. You can park the car here in the garage and call the hotel for assistance with baggage. The hotel is down at the beach reached by a pedestrian path.

*VILLA LA TARTANA*        *New*
*Owners: Franco & Virginia Caldiero family*
*Via Vicolo Vito Savino, 6/8*
*Positano (SA) 84017, Italy*
*Tel: (089) 812 193, Fax: (089) 812 2012*
*12 rooms, Double: €140–€150*
*Minimum nights required: 3*
*Open: Mar to Oct*
*Other languages: some English*
*Region: Campnia*
*karenbrown.com/italy/tartana.html*

Villa Rosa opened its doors six years ago after restoration work by local couple Virginia and Franco who own a clothing store and ceramic store in town (the house has always been in Virginia's family). The 150-year-old villa, built into the cliffside and hidden behind bougainvillea vines high above the road right in town, is on three levels. Taking the stairs up to the first level, you find the reception area where guests are greeted. The twelve bedrooms are spread over all three floors, each having access to the large front terraces which are divided by plants and grapevine-covered pergolas for privacy. Picturesque views of Positano's colorful houses and the spectacular coastline are enjoyed from any point. Breakfast is served either in rooms or out on individual terraces adorned with large terra-cotta vases laden with cascading pink and red geraniums, in sharp contrast to pure white walls. Bedrooms maintain original tiles and vaulted ceilings and are furnished with simple antiques, while bathrooms display typical yellow and blue hand-painted tiles from Vietri. Air conditioning is an exceptional amenity offered along with satellite TV, mini-bar, telephone, and safe. Easy day trips include Amalfi, Ravello, and the ruins of Pompeii, Paestum, or Herculum. *Directions:* Following the main road through town, you find Villa Rosa almost at the end just before the famous Sirenuse Hotel. Parking is possible in a nearby public garage only.

❄ ⚓ ☕ 🚲 [CREDIT] ☎ 🏃 🍸 🖼 🏄

*VILLA ROSA*
*Hosts: Virginia & Franco Caldiero*
*Via C. Colombo 127*
*Positano (SA) 84017, Italy*
*Tel: (089) 811955, Fax: (089) 812112*
*12 rooms, Double: €140–€270*
*Minimum nights required: 3*
*Open: Mar to Oct, Credit cards: all major*
*Other languages: some English*
*Region: Campania, Michelin Map: 564*
*karenbrown.com/italy/rosa.html*

From the moment you enter the grand foyer looking out over the classical Italian garden of this 16th-century country villa, all sense of time and place is lost. The Rucellais' devotion to their estate (in the family since 1759) is apparent, as is their warm hospitality. Guests are given the run of the rambling old home, from the cozy bedrooms, varying in size and decor; antique-filled library; and spacious living room with fireplace, old comfortable sofas, and family portraits to a gracious buffet breakfast room where guests are served at a long table. At the entrance is a duck pond, a large shady area with tables and a 15th-century swimming pool. Francesca and Frank enjoy helping their guests with their itineraries, as well as suggesting cultural events such as art courses, concerts, and tours. Villa Rucellai serves as an excellent base for visiting Florence, Siena, Lucca, and Pisa. The nearby town with its many restaurant choices is conveniently just a fifteen minute walk away. *Directions:* From Florence take the A11 autostrada, exiting at Prato Est. Follow signs towards Vaiano-Vernio and the railway station. Turn right at the Contemporary Art Museum and follow Viale della Republica. Go over the river and under the railway. Circle left onto Borgo Valsugana, keeping the river and railroad to the left. Follow signs all the way to the Trattoria La Fontana, then go another 1.5 km on the very narrow Via di Canneto to the entry gate.

❄ ☕ 🛷 🏌 👫 P ≈ 🍇

*VILLA RUCELLAI DI CANNETO*
*Host: Rucellai Piqué family*
*Via di Canneto 16*
*Prato (FI) 59100, Italy*
*Tel & fax: (0574) 460392, Cellphone: (347) 9073826*
*11 rooms, Double: €80–€90*
*Open: all year*
*Other languages: fluent English*
*Region: Tuscany, Michelin Map: 563*
*karenbrown.com/italy/rucellai.html*

The fascinating Castello di Proceno is in the Lazio region bordering Tuscany and Umbria. This unique accommodation combines historical context, authentic ambiance, unspoiled landscapes, regional foods and wines, and congenial hosts. The Cecchini Bisoni family, owners of this 12th-century hilltop fortress for many generations, have done an outstanding job of restoring some of the farmers' quarters that make up part of the village grouped around the tower. They modernized plumbing, electricity, and heating systems without disturbing the innate quaintness of these stone dwellings. In addition, Signora Cecilia is a passionate decorator and has found very clever ways of displaying many of the family's antique collections and restored furniture throughout the comfortable apartments. The restaurant, complete with cantina and fireplace, leads to a labyrinth of tunnels and stairways connecting to four of the apartments, while the remaining three are located in the fortress attached to the ancient pentagonal walls of the tower and castle, in a wooded area leading down to the swimming pool. All apartments have one or two bedrooms and a kitchenette and all feature both a fireplace and garden area or terrace. *Directions:* The castello is in the village of Proceno, 16 km north of Lake Bolsena. Follow S.S.2 from the lake to Acquapendente and after 3 km turn left for Proceno.

*CASTELLO DI PROCENO*
*Host: Cecilia Cecchini Bisoni family*
*Corso Regina Margherita 155, Proceno (VT) 01020*
*Tel: (0763) 710367, Fax: (0763) 710072*
*3 rooms, Double: €90–€100*
*7 apartments: €110–€150 daily*
*No dinner Mon & Tue, Minimum nights required: 2*
*Open: all year, Credit cards: MC, VS*
*Other languages: good English*
*Region: Lazio, Michelin Map: 563*
*karenbrown.com/italy/proceno.html*

Weary of life in the intense financial world of Milan, Guido and Martina packed up and headed for the hills of Chianti and the "good life" that attracts so many there. After a long search they chose the scenic property where La Locanda now stands, primarily for its magnificent position facing out to medieval Volpaia and an endless panorama filled with layers of virgin hills. The results of their meticulous restoration of three simple stone farmhouses are formidable and today fortunate guests can share in their dream. Its remote location among woods and olive groves guarantees total silence and tranquillity and the comfortable, decorator-perfect common rooms and luminous colors harmonize divinely with this idyllic setting. An understated elegance permeates the six bedrooms and suite divided among one of the two-story farmhouses. They are tastefully appointed with antiques and smart plaid curtains, and four have the advantage of the views. Breakfast and dinner (except Sundays and Thursdays) are served out on the terrace above the swimming pool whose borderless edge disappears into the landscape. Guido and Martina, natural and gregarious hosts, exude a contagious enthusiasm for their new surroundings. *Directions:* From Radda follow signs for Florence and turn right for Volpaia. Continue on the unpaved road for another 3.8 km after Volpaia village, following signs to La Locanda/Montanino.

*LA LOCANDA*
*Hosts: Guido & Martina Bevilacqua*
*Localita: Montanino, Radda in Chianti (SI) 53017, Italy*
*Tel: (0577) 738833, Fax: (0577) 739263*
*7 rooms, Double: €200–€280*
*Minimum nights required: 2*
*Open: Apr to Nov, Credit cards: MC, VS*
*Other languages: good English*
*Region: Tuscany, Michelin Map: 563*
*Abitare la Storia*
*karenbrown.com/italy/lalocanda.html*

Podere Terreno combines idyllic location and authentic, charming ambiance with delightful hosts Sylvie and Roberto, a Franco-Italian couple, and son, Francesco. The 400-year-old rustic stone farmhouse is surrounded by terra-cotta flower vases, a grapevine-covered pergola, a small lake, and sweeping panoramas of the Chianti countryside. Inside are seven sweet double bedrooms with very small bathrooms, each decorated differently with country antiques and the family's personal possessions, which make the feeling very informal and homelike. Guests convene in the main room of the house around the massive stone fireplace on floral sofas for a glass of house wine before sitting down to a sumptuous candlelit dinner prepared by your hosts. This is a cozy, stone-walled room, filled with country antiques, brass pots, dried-flower bouquets hanging from the exposed beams, and shelves lined with bottles of the proprietors' own Chianti Classico wine. Wine tastings take place within the new cantina. The hosts are experts at suggesting local itineraries and directing guests to the many quaint villages waiting to be explored. *Directions:* From Greve follow signs to Panzano, then go left for Radda and on to Lucarelli. After 3 km turn right at Volpaia and after 5 km turn right at the sign for Podere Terreno.

*PODERE TERRENO*
*Hosts: Marie Sylvie Haniez, Roberto Melosi*
*Via della Volpaia, Radda in Chianti (SI) 53017, Italy*
*Tel: (0577) 738312, Fax: (0577) 738400*
*7 rooms, Double: €190\**
*\*Includes breakfast & dinner*
*Minimum nights required: 2*
*Open: all year, Credit cards: all major*
*Other languages: good English*
*Region: Tuscany, Michelin Map: 563*
*karenbrown.com/italy/podereterreno.html*

Both Radda and Greve are excellent bases from which to explore the scenic Chianti wine country with its regal castles and stone villages, in addition to Siena, Florence, and San Gimignano. Radda in particular offers a myriad of possibilities for accommodation, including many private homes with rooms or apartments. The Val delle Corti is the home and vineyard property of gracious hostess Eli Bianchi and her son Roberto where they produce a high-quality Chianti Classico wine. The cozy pale-stone house with white shutters tops a hill overlooking the quaint town. The hosts, who moved here over 27 years ago from Milan, are extremely active in community affairs and are a superb source for area information. The guest accommodation is a lovely separate little house called il Fienile (hay barn), simply appointed with family antiques and newer pieces, which has a large open kitchen and living space looking out to the vineyards, and two bedrooms and one bathroom on the first floor. Meals can be taken at one of the excellent restaurants right in nearby Radda. *Directions:* Equidistant from Florence and Siena off the N222 Chianti road. Before entering Radda, turn right toward Lecchi-San Sano, then take the first left at Val delle Corti.

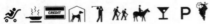

*PODERE VAL DELLE CORTI*
*Host: Bianchi Family*
*Localita: La Croce*
*Radda in Chianti (SI) 53017, Italy*
*Tel: (0577) 738215, Fax: (0577) 739521*
*1 apartment: €700–€800 weekly, €110 daily*
*heating extra, Minimum nights required: 3*
*Open: all year, Credit cards: MC, VS*
*Other languages: good English*
*Region: Tuscany, Michelin Map: 563*
*karenbrown.com/italy/poderevaldellecorti.html*

In the very heart of Chianti between Radda, Castellina, and Vagliagli sits the Pornanino farm surrounded by 90 acres of wooded hills and olive groves. Hosts Franco and Lia have carefully restored the main house for themselves plus two stone barns for guests, appointed with the same warm country style as their own home, with antique furniture enhancing beamed ceilings and cotto floors. Il Capannino is completely refurbished and offers a large central room with open kitchen at an upper level, dining room/living room with open fireplace, and two bedrooms with two bathrooms. A large arched glass door opens onto the pergola-covered terrace for outside meals. Il Leccino is similar but has just one bedroom. Guests can also take advantage of the lovely swimming pool overlooking the olive groves. Franco and Lia are part of the increasing breed of "neo-farmers" migrating from major cities in search of a slower-paced lifestyle where the basic values of life are emphasized in everyday living. Franco has become a passionate producer of top-quality olive oil and even conducts small seminars and tastings on the subject. The Lombardis are part of a group of family and friends (called Case Spante) offering similar rentals in the area. *Directions:* The farm is located 9 km south of Radda, 5 km from Castellina, and 4 km north of Vagliagli on route 102 but the turnoff is not marked, so it is best to call ahead. 18 km from Siena and 54 km from Florence.

*PORNANINO*
*Hosts: Lia & Franco Lombardi*
*Localita: Pornanino 72, Radda in Chianti (SI) 53017*
*Tel: (0577) 738658, Cellphone: (347) 7980012*
*Fax: (0577) 738794*
*2 houses: €725–€1,100 weekly*
*Heating extra, Minimum nights required: 7*
*Open: all year, Credit cards: MC, VS*
*Other languages: good English, French*
*Region: Tuscany, Michelin Map: 563*
*karenbrown.com/italy/pornanino.html*

On the opposite side of town from the Podere Val delle Corti live relatives Lele Bianchi Vitali and her family, who offer a two-bedroom apartment in a stone tower dating from 1832. This unique accommodation, perfect for a family of four, has an enchanting view of Radda and the countryside. The three-story tower has terra-cotta floors and beamed ceilings, a living room/kitchenette on the ground floor, one bedroom and a bath on the second floor, and a second bedroom on top. Furnishings are simple and in keeping with the tower's rustic features. A small olive grove separates the tower from the Vitalis' Tuscan farmhouse, where a swimming pool bordered by lavender plants awaits road-weary guests and a double bedroom with bathroom is offered. Lele is a vivacious hostess who divides her time between guests, her three sons and grandchildren, and cooking lessons with several other bed and breakfast owners in the area whose success has brought them to the States to teach as well. Meals at the nearby restaurant Le Vigne are arranged at a special rate. *Directions:* From either Siena or Florence, follow signs for Radda off the spectacular Strada del Chianti N222. Go through town until you reach the hotel/restaurant Villa Miranda (not recommended), after which turn right at the sign for Canvalle and follow the dirt road up to the tower.

*TORRE CANVALLE*
*Hosts: Enrico & Lele Bianchi Vitali*
*Localita: La Villa*
*Radda in Chianti (SI) 53017, Italy*
*Tel & fax: (0577) 738321*
*1 room, Double: €100*
*1 tower apartment: €800 weekly*
*Minimum nights required: 3, Open: all year*
*Other languages: good English*
*Region: Tuscany, Michelin Map: 563*
*karenbrown.com/italy/torrecanvalle.html*

Nicoletta Innocenti is the delightful owner and hostess of La Palazzina, one of our favorite bed and breakfasts. The stately 18th-century villa has 11 lovely guestrooms appointed with antiques, each having its own cool pastel color scheme. The large dining room with checked black-and-white tiled floors looks out to the garden and expansive lawns. A swimming pool hugs the side of the hill overlooking sweeping panoramas. Two of the three apartments within a 17th-century stone farmhouse, Colombaio, have two double bedrooms each, living area with kitchenette, fireplace, and bathroom. The third is a studio apartment for two persons. They are rustically furnished with local antiques and offer gorgeous valley views. The lovely Villa Fonte Emerosa, appointed with period antiques, has three bedrooms, three bathrooms, large living rooms with fireplace, garden, and swimming pool and faces out to the mountains. The 18th-century farmhouse, Casa di Terra, is set among the vineyards and includes three bedrooms, two bathrooms, kitchen, living room, and dining room. This southeast corner of Tuscany offers a rich variety of sites to explore, including the Amiata Mountains and the hilltowns of Montepulciano, Pienza, and Montalcino. *Directions:* From Florence on the A1 autostrada, exit at Chiusi and drive towards Sarteano on route 478, turning left for Radicofani. After 14 km turn left for Celle Sul Rigo then right at the sign for La Palazzina.

*LA PALAZZINA*
*Host: Innocenti family*
*Localita: Le Vigne, Radicofani (SI) 53040, Italy*
*Tel: (0578) 55771, Cellphone: (335) 8253937*
*Fax: (0577) 899647*
*11 rooms, Double: €98–€118, 2 nights minimum*
*3 apartments: €345–€600 weekly*
*2 houses: €414–€2,582 weekly, Open: Apr to Oct*
*Credit cards: all major, Other languages: good English*
*Region: Tuscany, Michelin Map: 563*
*karenbrown.com/italy/palazzina.html*

The Villa Maria is perhaps best known for its absolutely delightful terrace restaurant, which has a bird's-eye view of the magnificent coast. Whereas most of Ravello's hotels capture the southern view, the Villa Maria features the equally lovely vista to the north. The hotel is easy to locate, being on the same walking path that winds its way from the main square to the Villa Cimbrone gardens. After parking a level below the main square (or at the owner's other hotel, Giordano, where porters can handle your luggage and a heated pool can be used), look for signs for the Villa Maria, perched on the cliffs to your right. The building is a romantic old villa with a garden stretching to the side where tables and chairs are set, a favorite place to dine while enjoying the superb view. Inside, there is a cozy dining room overlooking the garden. The bedrooms are air-conditioned and furnished with antique pieces including brass beds. The bathrooms have been freshly remodeled and some have Jacuzzi tubs. Ingredients for excellent Mediterranean dishes come directly from the property's organic vegetable garden and for those wishing to know more about this regions's fine cuisine, weekly cooking courses have become very popular here. A private garden down the road is another relaxing spot for guests who fill the comments book with appreciation of the warm hospitality. *Directions:* Ravello is about 6 km north of Amalfi on a small road heading north from the highway.

*VILLA MARIA*
*Host: Vincenzo Palumbo*
*Via San Chiara 2*
*Ravello 84010, Italy*
*Tel: (089) 857255, Cellphone: (338) 6764540*
*Fax: (089) 857071*
*22 rooms, Double: €220–€440*
*Open: all year, Credit cards: all major*
*Other languages: good English*
*Region: Campania, Michelin Map: 564*
*karenbrown.com/italy/maria.html*

Ravenna is a splendid small city boasting one of the world's most prized collections of Byzantine mosaics housed within eight of its churches, basilicas, and mausoleums. The city comes alive in the summer months with a full program of theater, opera, and outdoor concerts, and also evening opening hours of churches to view the mosaics by night. There are lovely shops and the historical center of Ravenna is quiet since most residents get around by bicycle. Since we found bed and breakfast possibilities in the surrounding area to be much too spartan, the Hotel Diana with its yellow façade, in the center of Ravenna, is the best accommodation choice. A very friendly staff welcomes you into the luminous reception area with various sofas and armchairs arranged around a faux-marble fireplace, and a small patio outside. A buffet breakfast is served downstairs and an elevator takes you up to the second and third floors where the renovated bedrooms are located. These are rather standard but pleasant, with cream-colored walls and bedspreads, carpeting, and reproduction furniture. All have satellite television, air conditioning, and nice new bathrooms. The recommended superior doubles afford more space. Within a drive of an hour or less are Venice, Padua, Ferrara, Bologna, and the ancient ceramic center of Faenza. *Directions:* Follow signs for city center (Centro) then follow yellow hotel signs. Near the San Vitale Basilica.

*HOTEL DIANA*
*Manager: Filippo Donati*
*Via G. Rossi 47*
*Ravenna 48100, Italy*
*Tel: (0544) 39164, Fax: (0544) 30001*
*33 rooms, Double: €83–€125*
*Open: all year*
*Credit cards: all major*
*Other languages: good English*
*Region: Emilia-Romagna, Michelin Map: 562*
*karenbrown.com/italy/diana.html*

Highly recommended for those desiring to roam around a lesser-known part of Italy is the central section of the Marches region, an enchanting area offering something for every possible interest. The ancient town of Recanati with its redbrick houses and monumental main square was home to one of Italy's most famous poets, Giacomo Leopardi. Today the palazzo where the 18th-century poet lived is a museum incorporating a library with over 20,000 volumes, 15th-century wine cellars, and an exhibit highlighting his biography. Descendents of Leopardi, the Count Vanni and his daughter, Olimpia, currently live on the palazzo's upper floors, besides owning over 300 acres of farmland in the immediate vicinity. Across the street from the palazzo is a small two-story brick home where at one time artisans used to weave fabrics and where four comfortable independent apartments are now offered to guests. Apartments have a bedroom, bathroom, and living room with kitchenette (concealed in furniture), and one has a small rooftop terrace. In stages of restoration are several farmhouses on the family's surrounding property including Tre Ulivi, a typical farmhouse of the area with four bedrooms. For more independent travelers (no breakfast served), this is an ideal base rich with history from which to explore. *Directions:* Exit the A14 at Loreto and drive towards Recanati center, then follow signs for Casa Leopardi.

*IL TELAIO*
*Hosts: Vanni & Olimpia Leopardi di San Leopardo*
*Piazzuola Sabato del Villaggio 5*
*Recanati (AN) 62019, Italy*
*Tel & fax: (071) 7573380, Cellphone: (338) 6568989*
*4 apartments: €65–€85 daily*
*Open: all year*
*Other languages: good English, French*
*Region: Marches*
*Michelin Map: 563*
*karenbrown.com/italy/telaio.html*

With passion and determination, Daniela and her architect husband, Piero, brought back to life the family's ancient property with total respect for its 9th-century origins. This very special place has a rich historical past and a Romanesque church within the home where concerts are held. A nature lover's paradise, the complex of stone houses is surrounded by lush vegetation, vineyards, woods, and olive groves (from which the family's prestigious olive oil comes), and a garden including a collection of antique English roses. Hospitality is offered within seven apartments attached to the main house accommodating from two to five persons, impeccably decorated with the family's refined antiques, which live harmoniously with their perfectly preserved centuries-old environment. The dwellings feature living room with fireplace, balconies taking in either the sweeping countryside views down to the sea or out to the woods, wrought-iron beds, and original paintings by Daniela's father, a renowned fresco painter. Daniela, a world traveler, is a hostess par excellence. During May and October, they offer a week of painting classes. Besides Siena and Montalcino, there are plenty of off-the-beaten-track sights to see and bikes can be rented. *Directions:* From Grosseto take Aurelia route 1 north and exit at Braccagni. Continue towards Montemassi and before town turn right for Caminino and Roccatederighi. After 1 km turn right at the gate for Caminino.

*PIEVE DI CAMININO*
*Hosts: Daniela Locatelli & Piero Marrucchi*
*Via Provinciale di Peruzzo*
*Roccatederighi (GR) 58028, Italy*
*Tel: (0564) 569737, Fax: (0564) 2568756*
*Double: €120–€150*
*4 apartments: €600–€1,100 weekly, €120–€150 daily*
*Minimum nights: 7 Jun to Sep, Open: all year*
*Credit cards: all major, Other languages: good English*
*Region: Tuscany, Michelin Map: 563, Abitare la Storia*
*karenbrown.com/italy/caminino.html*

With the momentous occasion of the Millenium combined with the Holy Year celebration at the Vatican, a myriad of bed and breakfasts popped up in Rome, among them Villa Delros. Offering hospitality to foreigners is nothing new to Rosemarie Diletti, whose daughter, Patrizia, took over the family's Hotel Venezia in Rome (see listing). With the children grown and busy with their own careers, and because she misses the daily contact with international guests, Rosemarie decided to offer accommodation in the family home on the outskirts of the city. The sprawling, very modern home built in the sixties is located on a small road with other large estates and the property extends to the back overlooking lush green countryside. Two spacious air-conditioned guest suites on the upper floor each have a double bedroom, bathroom, corner kitchenette, sitting room, and large terrace. A third suite is located at garden level. Rosemarie, being a collector of antiques, fills the house with pieces from the baroque period, both in the common rooms downstairs and in guestrooms. Breakfast is served out on the terrace looking out to the garden and a swimming pool. Transportation to the local train station is provided and the center of Rome is just 15 minutes away. The rate indicated is already reduced for our readers only. *Directions:* North of Rome 4 km from the GRA ring highway, Via Livigno is just off the Via Flaminia. Call in advance to arrange pickup at a nearby meeting point.

❄ ⚓ ☕ ☎ 🍴 👫 🍸 P 🍽 ≈ 🖼 ⛵ 🔔 🍇

*VILLA DELROS*
*Host: Rosemarie Truninger Diletti*
*Via Livigno 166*
*Rome 00188, Italy*
*Tel: (06) 33679837, Cellphone: (340) 9295488*
*Fax: (06) 4957687*
*Double: €170, 3 suites, €800 weekly*
*Minimum nights required: 2, Open: Mar to Dec*
*Other languages: good English*
*Region: Lazio, Michelin Map: 563*
*karenbrown.com/italy/delros.html*

The Due Torri, a small and charming city hotel, dates to the early 1800s and is tucked away on a tiny, narrow cobblestone street in the historical heart of Rome very near the Navona Square with its Bernini fountains. The 26 rather petite bedrooms, decorated with period antiques and matching burgundy drapes and bedspreads, are accompanied by newly tiled bathrooms. Amenities include an elevator and air conditioning, which provides welcome relief on hot Roman summer days. The contained reception and sitting area have Oriental carpets, pieced marble floors, brocaded draperies, gilt-framed mirrors and paintings, and red-velvet chairs accenting the cream-colored walls. The fifth-floor mansard rooms (even smaller size) have small terraces and fourth-floor rooms have balconies with enchanting views over typical tiled rooftops and terraces. A buffet breakfast is served in a windowless room made cheery with painted borders and paintings. Super hostess Cinzia (owner as well of the newer Fontanella Borghese, also featured in this book) and her courteous staff are very helpful at arranging everything from advance ticketing for museums to transfers and restaurant and itinerary suggestions. *Directions:* Use a detailed city map to locate the hotel, north of Navona Square in a maze of winding streets.

*HOTEL DUE TORRI*
*Owner: Cinzia Pighini Giordani*
*Vicolo del Leonetto 23*
*Rome 00186, Italy*
*Tel: (06) 6876983, Fax: (06) 6865442*
*26 rooms, Double: €170–€235*
*Open: all year, Credit cards: all major*
*Other languages: good English*
*Region: Lazio, Michelin Map: 563*
*karenbrown.com/italy/duetorri.html*

Many hotels in Rome can boast panoramic views over the city, but few have such a close-up view of a world-famous monument as the Hotel Fontana. Located directly on the square containing the magnificent Trevi Fountain, the Fontana's windows look out on to its gushing waters—you can practically toss a coin from your room. The sleek black-and-white breakfast room with wrought-iron chairs and tables is situated on the top floor of the 14th-century building, giving a bird's-eye view over the square from an enormous picture window. The small bedrooms are sweetly done with pastel-floral wallpaper, bedspreads, and white curtains and vary in size and decor. Bathrooms were incorporated into each room later, and are quite small. Narrow, vaulted-ceilinged halls leading to the guestrooms are adorned with antique prints of Rome. Signora Elena and her staff at the desk attend to guests' every need. The noise commonly associated with a city hotel is not a problem here as the square is closed to traffic, although loud voices of tourists lingering into the early hours can be a problem in the summer. There is a supplement for air conditioning in rooms without a fountain view. *Directions:* Use a detailed city map to locate the hotel right in the Piazza di Trevi (at the fountain) off the Via Tritone.

*HOTEL FONTANA*
*Host: Elena Daneo*
*Piazza di Trevi 96*
*Rome 00187, Italy*
*Tel: (06) 6791056, Fax: (06) 6790024*
*25 rooms, Double: €200–€450*
*Minimum nights required: 2*
*Open: all year, Credit cards: all major*
*Other languages: good English*
*Region: Lazio, Michelin Map: 563*
*karenbrown.com/italy/fontana.html*

The many travelers who have enjoyed staying at the Due Torri can also experience the same charismatic hospitality offered by Cinzia in her other hotel very close by. The hotel has the same name as the triangular-shaped piazza where it is located, directly in front of the imposing Palazzo Borghese leading to the Spanish Steps. The enormous doors of the 17th-century building open up to a courtyard where you take the elevator up to the second floor. The small lobby has a sitting corner and a sweeping spiral staircase up to additional rooms on the next floor. Guestrooms have sparkling new bathrooms and modern amenities such as satellite TV and air conditioning, and are appointed with either an antique desk or armoire, green or blue matching bedspreads and draperies, and prints of Rome. An effort was made to preserve the original gray-marble floors in some rooms, while parquet flooring was put in the others. Most have a view on a narrow and very characteristic cobblestone street, or on the inner courtyard, offering rare silence. The reception area leads to the breakfast room with marble floors and matching faux-marble doorways. Cinzia oversees every detail in both hotels and the secret to her success is that she obviously has guests' comfort foremost in mind. Even extra assistance such as securing advance reservations to certain museums is offered. *Directions:* Largo Fontanella Borghese is at the end of the Via Condotti leading from the Spanish Steps.

*HOTEL FONTANELLA BORGHESE*
*Owner: Cinzia Pighini Giordani*
*Largo Fontanella Borghese 84*
*Rome 00186, Italy*
*Tel: (06) 68809504, Fax: (06) 6861295*
*29 rooms, Double: €180–€260*
*Open: all year, Credit cards: all major*
*Other languages: good English*
*Region: Lazio, Michelin Map: 563*
*karenbrown.com/italy/fontanellaborghese.html*

The Hotel Locarno is centrally located on the corner of a rather busy street, only two blocks from bustling Popolo Square. Its downtown location makes noise unavoidable, so it is advisable to request a room away from the street, even though the installation of thermal windows has helped. Even with the extensive renovations it has undergone, the hotel, dating from 1925, retains the art-deco flavor it originally had. The red-carpeted reception area leads to a cozy bar and long, mirrored sitting room lined with cushioned banquettes and café tables. There is also a side patio with shady canvas umbrellas where guests can have breakfast in warm weather, if not in the cheery breakfast room looking out to the patio. A very special feature of the hotel is the rooftop garden where you can gaze over Rome's tiled roofs and terraces to St. Peter's dome and the Villa Borghese Park. The comfortable rooms (regular and superior doubles), decorated with antiques, gold-framed mirrors, and pretty floral wallpaper, are air-conditioned. Two two-bedroom apartments (no kitchen) are offered to guests in the building directly across the street. The Locarno offers such extras as a parking garage and free use of bicycles with which you might tour the Villa Borghese Park. It is no wonder that this has always been a favorite among artists and writers. Reserve well in advance. *Directions:* Use a detailed city map to locate the hotel one block east of the River Tiber at the Flaminia Square sign.

*HOTEL LOCARNO*
*Host: Caterina Valente*
*Via della Penna 22*
*Rome 00186, Italy*
*Tel: (06) 3610841 or 3610842, Fax: (06) 3215249*
*66 rooms, Double: €200–€310*
*2 apartments: €510 weekly B&B*
*Open: all year, Credit cards: all major*
*Region: Lazio, Michelin Map: 563*
*karenbrown.com/italy/hotellocarno.html*

Marco and Giulia Di Tillo are young and enterprising hosts who have adopted the family hotel tradition with their Hotel Modigliani. Leaving their careers as musician and writer (Marco just wrote a guide on seven romantic itineraries in Rome), they totally renovated a centuries-old building with the goal of offering comfortable and practical accommodation with many amenities (air conditioning, satellite TV, mini-bar, laundry service, motorbike and car rental, city tour excursions, nearby garage), topped off with an efficient but friendly staff. With its unbeatable central location close to Via Veneto and the Spanish Steps, they have all the elements for success. The front desk, sitting area, and breakfast room make up the ground-floor common spaces and have a clean, contemporary ambiance. A personalized touch has been given to the breakfast room with framed black-and-white photos of the couple's children and friends artwork. Bedrooms on the three upper floors, reached by an elevator, are decorated along the same clean lines with wood floors and olive-green-striped spreads and drapes. Most desirable are the top-floor rooms with balconies and views over rooftops including St. Peter's cupola while others face the inner courtyard (where breakfast can be enjoyed in warm seasons) or quiet street. Next door to a convent, quiet is guaranteed! *Directions:* Via della Purificazione is a side street just north of the Piazza Barberini.

*HOTEL MODIGLIANI*
*Hosts: Marco & Giulia Di Tillo*
*Via della Purificazione 42, Rome 00187, Italy*
*Tel: (06) 42815226, Cellphone: (338) 9269528*
*Fax: (06) 42814791*
*23 rooms, Double: €198–€280*
*1 apartment: €430–€618*
*Open: all year, Credit cards: all major*
*Other languages: good English*
*Region: Lazio, Michelin Map: 563*
*karenbrown.com/italy/modigliani.html*

Trastevere, literally translated as "across the Tiber", is the most authentically Roman neighborhood of the city's historic center. Tourists flock here to stroll down the narrow cobblestone streets, visit artisans' shops, dine in one of the many excellent sidewalk trattorias, or just watch the daily life of locals. What pleasure to have discovered the new Hotel Santa Maria, the first accommodation to speak of in the area, which has proved already to be a true winner. Native Romans Paolo and Valentina had the ingenious idea of transforming a plot of open land between the jumble of ancient apartment buildings into a unique one-story hotel with rooms looking out to two courtyards with orange trees. The couple welcomes travelers as private houseguests, serving a buffet breakfast with freshly baked cakes either out in the courtyard or in the breakfast room/wine bar. Before going out for dinner in one of many nearby favorite restaurants, guests enjoy a glass of wine with nibbles from a nearby bakery. Bedrooms, each with its own entrance to the outside, are identically decorated in pale yellow, with a splash of color on matching bedspreads and curtains, and enjoy amenities such as air conditioning, mini-bar, and TV. Bikes are available for guests to use. Identify yourself as a Karen Brown reader and receive a 10% discount. *Directions:* In the heart of Trastevere just behind the famous Piazza Santa Maria, on the tiny Vicolo del Piede. Garage parking is available.

*HOTEL SANTA MARIA*
*Hosts: Paolo & Valentina Vetere*
*Vicolo del Piede 2*
*Rome 00153, Italy*
*Tel: (06) 5894626, Fax: (06) 5894815*
*20 rooms, Double: €145–€230*
*Open: all year, Credit cards: all major*
*Other languages: good English*
*Region: Lazio, Michelin Map: 563*
*karenbrown.com/italy/santamaria.html*

A delightful alternative to our other accommodations in Rome is Casa Stefazio, the only true in-home bed and breakfast. The location and setting are as perfect as the dedication and warm hospitality offered by Stefania and Orazio in their large, ivy-covered suburban home, just 16 kilometers from the very center of the city, surrounded by several acres of manicured garden and utter silence. On the lower level, with a separate entrance, are one bedroom and two spacious suites (with sauna) accommodating a family of four, each with its own immaculate bathroom, satellite TV, air conditioning, and mini-bar. The main areas include living room, large American-style kitchen, where the Azzolas work wonders, and eating area overlooking the expansive lawn and distant woods. Dinner is served on request under the pergola. Their style, in both decorating and easy entertaining, has obviously been influenced by their yearly winter sojourn in the States, which they adore. Sports activities such as horseback riding, tennis, golf, and swimming are easily arranged. The hosts also organize excursions for groups of friends throughout Italy. Highly recommended by readers. *Directions:* Located north of Rome just outside the circular highway around the city (GRA), close to the tollway north to Florence and south to Naples. Call one day ahead for detailed directions.

*CASA STEFAZIO*
*Hosts: Stefania & Orazio Azzola*
*Via della Marcigliana 553*
*Rome 00138, Italy*
*Tel: (06) 87120042, Cellphone: (338) 2180612*
*Fax: (06) 87120012*
*3 rooms, Double: €220–€275*
*Open: Apr to Nov*
*Other languages: good English*
*Region: Lazio, Michelin Map: 563*
*karenbrown.com/italy/casastefazio.html*

Hotel Venezia is part of the group of select family-run city hotels, efficiently run and owned by brother-and-sister team, Patrizia and Francesco. Although hotels near train stations are generally less desirable, the area around Rome's Termini station has experienced dramatically positive changes—there is a high concentration of hotels and offices within refurbished turn-of-the-century-style buildings. Even though the Venezia has 60 rooms, it has the feeling of a small and friendly place the moment you enter its doors. Patrizia and Francesco inherited the hotel from their parents and their mother's passion for collecting antiques such as Orientals rugs and rich period paintings is evident throughout the spacious sitting rooms. A buffet breakfast is served in a room with peach tablecloths and fresh flowers topping tables. Upstairs the spotless rooms are decorated uniformly in white and rose hues with Venetian glass chandeliers, and offer all modern amenities, including Internet access. Patrizia has purposely decorated predominantly with white so that any sign of dirt can be spotted immediately. The corner rooms are the most spacious and those on the top floor have small balconies. Centrally located, the hotel is a 15-minute walk to Rome's historical center. In the exact same style is the family's nearby 45-room Hotel Columbia with its lovely rooftop terrace. *Directions:* Consult a detailed city map—the hotel is to the right of the Termini train station.

*HOTEL VENEZIA*
*Hosts: Patrizia & Francesco Diletti*
*Via Varese 18*
*Rome 00185, Italy*
*Tel: (06) 4457101, Fax: (06) 4957687*
*60 rooms, Double: €143–€160*
*Open: all year, Credit cards: all major*
*Other languages: good English*
*Region: Lazio, Michelin Map: 563*
*karenbrown.com/italy/venezia.html*

Beyond the city gates of Porta Pia, whose ancient walls lead from the Via Veneto, is tranquil, tree-lined Via Nomentana, once a luxurious residential street. Many elegant pastel-colored villas remain (including the last residence of Mussolini), but most have been converted into embassy-owned apartments over the years, while in 1956 the Villa del Parco was transformed into a lovely, quiet hotel with a bed-and-breakfast feel to it. A flower-edged driveway leads to the villa, passing by tables set up for breakfast in the small front garden. When you enter the pleasant lobby scattered with antiques and comfy sofas, you feel that you've arrived home. Three cozy sitting rooms invite guests to sit and relax. All of the 30 guestrooms, each with private bath, have been renovated and vary greatly in size and decor, which tends to be a mixture of old and new furnishings. The Bernardini family and the friendly staff are happy to make restaurant and itinerary suggestions. Special features are an elevator, central air, and five nice new bedrooms on the top floor with beamed mansard ceilings. A 24-hour snack bar service is available. *Directions:* Rely on a detailed city map to locate the hotel in a residential district, a 15-minute walk from the city center.

❄ ⚓ ☕ ✏ 💳 ☎ 👫 🏌 ⍓ P 🚭 🖼 ♿

*HOTEL VILLA DEL PARCO*
*Host: Alessandro Bernardini*
*Via Nomentana 110*
*Rome 00161, Italy*
*Tel: (06) 44237773, Fax: (06) 44237572*
*30 rooms, Double: €120–€180*
*Open: all year, Credit cards: all major*
*Other languages: good English, French*
*Region: Lazio, Michelin Map: 563*
*karenbrown.com/italy/villadelparco.html*

The spectacular 2,500-acre hilltop farm property of Montestigliano is a rich combination of woods, cultivated fields, olive groves, and open meadows all surrounding the hamlet dating from 1730. British-born hostess Susan makes sure guests are comfortable in one of the ten independent apartments within the various houses scattered about the property. All retain their original Tuscan character in furnishings and have a combination of two or three bedrooms, kitchen, living room (some with fireplace), and essential modern amenities like washing machines and telephones. The granary has been restored and converted into a farm shop, recreation room, and dining room where meals are served upon request from Monday to Friday. Groups of up to 12 persons have the opportunity to reside in the main villa. Two swimming pools are at guests' disposal, plus many paths and trails. Montestigliano is a marvelous base for getting to know in depth a part of Tuscany whose traditions and lifestyles have remained intact, while still having Siena, San Gimignano, Pienza, Montalcino, and the Chianti area at one's fingertips. Plenty of places to dine are available in Rosia and Sovicille. Susan has also recently arranged weddings in this idyllic setting for groups staying at Montestigliano. *Directions:* From Siena (12 km) take S.S.223 (towards Grosseto). After 12 km, just after a gas station, turn right and after 2 km turn left for Brenna and drive up the unpaved road to the end.

*MONTESTIGLIANO*
*Host: Susan Pennington*
*Rosia (SI) 53010, Italy*
*Tel: (0577) 342189, Fax: (0577) 342100*
*10 apartments: €454–€1,622 weekly*
*1 villa: €1,382–€2,957 weekly*
*Minimum nights required: 5*
*Open: all year, Other languages: fluent English*
*Region: Tuscany, Michelin Map: 563*
*karenbrown.com/italy/montestigliano.html*

The climb up to L'Abri is worth the trip just for the spectacular view over the valley and for the warm welcome given by amiable hostess Antonella, a young, enterprising woman who opened her sweet and simple bed and breakfast within her grandmother's home in order to be able to live in her native area. The typical stone house with slate roof is part of a miniature village with just a few other houses, restaurant, church, and school. A collection of grandmother's lace and domestic work adorns the entrance to the left of a small breakfast room. Six small bedrooms are dispersed about this compact home's upper three floors, including the attic. Three have small balconies decorated with cascading geraniums and all are identically appointed using local pine for beds and wall paneling, accented with colorful Provençal curtains. A nice extra is the possibility of sampling local fare at the family's trattoria next door. For two generations traditional dishes such as polenta with meat, rice (no pasta served in this region!), soups, crêpes, and scrumptious desserts made with apples from their own orchards have been served in the cozy dining room covered with black-and-white photos of decades past. Enthusiastic Antonella is an expert on local tourism and can suggest many interesting itineraries for the area. *Directions:* Exit the A5 at Aosta-Ovest and follow signs for Saint Pierre (1 km) and then up to Vetan where L'Abri is located (15 km).

*L'ABRI*
*Host: Antonella Montrosset*
*Fraz. Vetan Dessous 83*
*Saint Pierre (AO) 11010, Italy*
*Tel: (0165) 908830, Cellphone: (333) 2095679*
*Fax: (0165) 908228*
*6 rooms, Double: €55–€60, Minimum nights required: 2*
*Open: all year, Credit cards: VS*
*Other languages: some English, French*
*Region: Aosta Valley, Michelin Map: 561*
*karenbrown.com/italy/labri.html*

The Aosta mountain valley has just recently joined the agritourism trend in Italy, with 40 farms in the region currently offering hospitality. Les Ecureuils was one of the first to open, well ahead of the trend, and is the most established of the group. The Gontiers' large property—a cheese farm—overlooks the valley surrounding the capital city of the region, Aosta. The main chalet, which dates to the mid-1800s, houses five double bedrooms and a characteristic dining room adorned with ceramic plates, brass pots, and locally fashioned sabots. A modern barn for the goats and three typical stone houses make up the farm complex. The three front bedrooms have small balconies and valley views, while the remaining two look into the pine woods. The individually decorated, homelike rooms have floral wallpaper and carpeted or wood floors. Each room is equipped with a shower and sink and has a private toilet just outside. Plans to renovate and add full bathrooms are projected for the next season. Half board is required here and meals are based for the most part on fresh products from the farm including various salamis, vegetables, poultry, and their primary production of high-quality goat cheeses. The Gontiers organize half- and full-day nature walks and picnics in the back woods accompanied by the family mule. *Directions:* After the A5 autostrada ends at Aosta, continue 6 km to Sarre and turn right, following the winding road for 6 km up to the end.

*LES ECUREUILS*
*Hosts: Pepe & Glori Gontier Ballauri*
*Fraz. Homené Dessus 8*
*Saint Pierre (AO) 11010, Italy*
*Tel: (0165) 903831, Fax: (0165) 909849*
*5 rooms, Double: €44–€60*
*Closed: Jan & Dec*
*Other languages: some English, French*
*Region: Aosta Valley, Michelin Map: 561*
*karenbrown.com/italy/ecureuils.html*

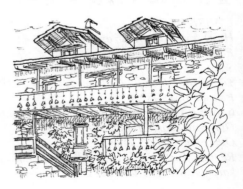

Parma is without doubt the city internationally most known for its Parmesan cheese and prosciutto ham, which you should not fail to sample while you're in the region. Thirty kilometers from Parma are found the curative thermal waters of Salsomaggiore and just beyond town is the Antica Torre, the ancient 13th-century tower that majestically crowns a hilltop overlooking the gorgeous soft green countryside. The hard-working Pavesi family, proprietors of the ancient property and surrounding farm, offer warm hospitality to its guests within the tower where one bedroom with bath is located on each of the four floors. In addition, there are five characteristic suites on two floors in the main stone residence, including a large two-bedroom suite with fireplace, which is ideal for a family. Rooms are simply decorated and have lovely views over the valley. The original barn has been converted into a pleasant dining room where fortunate guests sit down together to a hearty, homemade, Emiliana-style meal, including fresh pastas, vegetables, meat, and poultry direct from the farm (drinks not included in half-board rate). Amenities include a swimming pool, bicycles, and horses. *Directions:* From Salsomaggiore, go through town, following signs for Cangelasio and then Antica Torre, 3.5 km from Salsomaggiore.

*ANTICA TORRE*
*Host: Francesco Pavesi family*
*Localita: Cangelasio-Case Bussandri 197*
*Salsomaggiore Terme (PR) 43039, Italy*
*Tel & fax: (0524) 575425*
*9 rooms, Double: €80–€100,*
*Minimum nights required: 7 in Jul & Aug*
*Open: Mar to Nov*
*Other languages: good English, French, Spanish*
*Region: Emilia-Romagna, Michelin Map: 562*
*karenbrown.com/italy/anticatorre.html*

In the southeastern corner of Tuscany is a delightful, yet-undiscovered pocket of absolutely stunning countryside. It was only natural that Andrea, with his expert culinary skills, and his lovely wife, Cristina, a born hostess, should open a bed and breakfast close to their vast 1,000-acre countryside property producing olive oil, wine, cereals and vegetables. La Crocetta sits at the crossroads leading up to the charming town of San Casciano, offering eight guestrooms above the restaurant. You enter the small restaurant by way of a front porch, where meals are also served outdoors, into the cozy reception area set around a large sit-in fireplace. Here within the two dining rooms with soft-pink-colored walls Andrea presents his delectable creations featuring homemade pastas with vegetable fillings and other regional dishes using the best local ingredients available. His success has been noted in several restaurant guides. Small guestrooms with varying color schemes, each with a new bathroom, are pleasantly appointed with canopy beds and fresh country fabrics used for bedspreads and curtains. A pool has been added in the front garden. Thermal hot springs with spa treatments and horse-riding facilities are located nearby. Orvieto, Perugia, Siena, and the hilltowns of Montepulciano and Montalcino are all at easy touring distance. *Directions:* From the A1 autostrada, exit at Fabro from the south or Chiusi from the north, traveling towards Sarteano-Cetona, then San Casciano.

*LA CROCETTA*
*Hosts: Cristina & Andrea Leotti*
*Localita: La Crocetta*
*San Casciano dei Bagni (SI) 53040, Italy*
*Tel: (0578) 58360, Fax: (0578) 58353*
*8 rooms, Double: €121–€130*
*Per person half board: €75*
*Minimum nights required: 2, Open: Mar 30 to Nov 12*
*Credit cards: MC, VS, Other languages: good English*
*Region: Tuscany, Michelin Map: 563*
*karenbrown.com/italy/lacrocetta.html*

Perched atop a hill and enjoying a 360-degree view of perfectly unspoiled landscape, including a stunning medieval castle, sits the Le Radici farmhouse. Partners and ex-urbanites Marcello and Alfredo carefully chose this peaceful spot in order to offer accommodation to those who truly appreciate nature and the sense of well-being it inspires. The two farmhouses have been restored, maintaining most of the original rustic flavor, and divided into seven double rooms, three suites, and two apartments. The apartments include one or two bedrooms, living room with fireplace, kitchenette, and bathroom. The tastefully appointed rooms in muted colors are adorned by wrought-iron beds and antique furnishings, complemented by wood-beam and brick ceilings. Special attention has been given to landscaping around the immediate property, which includes vineyards and olive groves. The real treat is the absolutely gorgeous "borderless" swimming pool with cascading water, which fits harmoniously into its surroundings. A romantic candelit dinner showing off Alfredo's passion for cooking is served in the dining room or out on the terrace, using fresh ingredients from the property. The hosts suggest many interesting itineraries in this area, which borders Umbria. One can relax in the thermal waters of San Casciano or venture out to the towns of Orvieto, Todi, or Pienza, among others. *Directions:* From San Casciano follow signs for Le Radici (4 km).

*LE RADICI*
*Hosts: Alfredo Ferrari & Marcello Mancini*
*San Casciano dei Bagni (SI) 53040, Italy*
*Tel: (0578) 56033, Fax: (0578) 56038*
*10 rooms, Double: €150–€204*
*2 apartments: €1,078–€1,281 weekly (utilities extra)*
*Minimum nights required: 2*
*Open: Apr 1 to Nov 6, Credit cards: MC, VS*
*Other languages: good English*
*Region: Tuscany, Michelin Map: 563*
*karenbrown.com/italy/leradici.html*

Agritourism and bed-and-breakfast-type accommodations are virtually nonexistent in the northern lake district, so coming across the enchanting Villa Simplicitas was a special treat. The pale-yellow country house of Milanese family Castelli, run by sister-in-law Ulla, sits isolated high up in the hills between Lakes Como and Lugano and is surrounded by thick woods. There is a wonderful old-fashioned charm to the place, enhanced by many heirloom turn-of-the-century antiques scattered about the cozy living and dining rooms. Pretty floral fabrics cover sofas and armchairs, in perfect harmony with the soft-yellow walls bordered with stenciled designs. The same warmth is spread among the ten guest bedrooms with their pinewood floors and trompe l'oeil paneled walls, antique beds, and lace doilies adorning dressers. Innovative meals prepared by local chef Maurizio are served either inside or out on the veranda with green-and-white-striped awnings and matching director's chairs. In the evening, impeccably set tables are candlelit for a romantic dinner for two—simply heavenly. *Directions:* From Como head north to Argegno. Turn left, passing through S. Fedele, then just after town at the first bus station, turn left—it is just 2 km up to the house.

*VILLA SIMPLICITAS*
*Host: Curzio Castelli family*
*Localita: Simplicitas*
*San Fedele d'Intelvi (CO) 22028, Italy*
*Tel: (031) 831132 or (02) 460421, Fax: (02) 460407*
*10 rooms, Double: €120–€150*
*€500–€800 weekly*
*Open: May to Oct, Credit cards: all major*
*Other languages: good English*
*Region: Lombardy, Michelin Map: 561*
*karenbrown.com/italy/simplicitas.html*

Il Casale is a highly efficient and very popular bed and breakfast, thanks to warm and dedicated host, Alessandro, who has combined his extensive hospitality experience with a desire to see his great-grandfather's lovely country property restored properly. Six double rooms and two small apartments including bedroom, kitchen/eating area, and bathroom are all housed within the extended stone farmhouse. Another section is reserved for Alessandro and the family who looks after the wine estate. Access to the guest entrance is through a well-kept garden around the back with a small chapel and lovely views over the soft hills. Main areas include a sitting room and beamed breakfast room with fireplace. The spotless home is appointed with scattered antiques and the very comfortable guestrooms, each with a different color scheme, have new bathrooms and either countryside views or garden or interior patio entrance. Infinite attention to details in both the esthetics and service offered is given to guests. The entrepreneurial Alessandro has also restored the stone barn and cantina over in the olive grove, Rocca degli Olivi, creating an apartment, five lovely bedrooms with either mansard or vaulted ceilings and gorgeous views, and a breakfast room. An inviting swimming pool is hidden among the olive trees. Plenty of tourist information is on hand. *Directions:* From San Gimignano follow signs for Certaldo for 3 km. Il Casale is on the left and well marked.

*IL CASALE DEL COTONE*
*Host: Alessandro Martelli*
*Localita: Cellole 59*
*San Gimignano (SI) 53037, Italy*
*Tel & fax: (0577) 943236, Cellphone: (348) 3029091*
*11 rooms, Double: €93–€108*
*3 apartments: €93–€130 daily*
*Minimum nights required: 3 in apartments*
*Open: all year, Credit cards: all major*
*Region: Tuscany, Michelin Map: 563*
*karenbrown.com/italy/casaledelcotone.html*

Due to the ever-increasing popularity of the stunning medieval village of San Gimignano, accommodations in the surrounding countryside have flourished. The Casanova is a typical square stone farmhouse with wood shutters and red-tile roof, which you'll grow accustomed to seeing throughout Tuscany. The bed and breakfast's exceptional feature is that it enjoys a privileged view of the towers of San Gimignano, an ancient town referred to as the "Manhattan" of the year 1000. Roberto and his wife Monica, who aim to offer quality accommodation at competitive rates, have the bed and breakfast, adding amenities in rooms such as air conditioning, satellite TV, and telephone, and have also installed a swimming pool. Breakfast is served on the outside patio where guests are immersed in breathtaking scenery, before heading out to visit intriguing San Gimignano and the many surrounding villages. This is an authentic wine-producing farm with eight double rooms with private baths and one apartment for two persons. Country furniture characteristic of the region decorates the rooms, whose original architectural features have been preserved. *Directions:* From San Gimignano take the road toward Volterra. After 2 km, turn left at the sign for Casanova, not Hotel Pescille.

*CASANOVA DI PESCILLE*
*Hosts: Monica & Roberto Fanciullini*
*Localita: Pescille, San Gimignano (SI) 53037, Italy*
*Tel & fax: (0577) 941902*
*8 rooms, Double: €90–€100*
*1 apartment: €100–€110 daily*
*Minimum nights required: 2*
*Open: Mar to Dec, Credit cards: MC, VS*
*Other languages: very little English*
*Region: Tuscany, Michelin Map: 563*
*karenbrown.com/italy/casanovadipescille.html*

Accidentally coming upon the Casolare, tucked away in the unpopulated hills 8 kilometers past medieval San Gimignano, was a delightful surprise. Just before reaching the bed and breakfast, you'll see a half-abandoned stone convent dating back to 1100. The attractive renovated farmhouse, hosted by Andrea, a former art and antiques dealer, and his Spanish wife, Berta, retains all the features characteristic of the original structure. The five double rooms are extremely comfortable and tastefully appointed. Rooms are divided between the two floors of the house, with one being an independent structure poolside. The suites for two to four persons with terrace and living room have been decorated with refined antiques as well. Original watercolor paintings by a local artist adorn an entire wall in the inviting double living room. An extra bonus is the breathtaking swimming pool, with sweeping countryside panorama, surrounded by a manicured lawn, fruit trees, and terra-cotta pots overflowing with pink geraniums. It provides refreshment after a hot day of sightseeing, while you anticipate another appetizing candlelit meal at dusk under the pergola. Berta is an excellent cook and prepares very special Tuscan menus accompanied by an impressive wine list. This is a truly tranquil haven. *Directions:* From San Gimignano follow signs for Montaione. Staying left at the fork, turn left for Libbiano and take the dirt road to the end.

*CASOLARE DI LIBBIANO*
*Hosts: Berta & Andrea Bucciarelli*
*Localita: Libbiano 3, San Gimignano (SI) 53037, Italy*
*Tel & fax: (0577) 946002, Cellphone: (349) 8706933*
*8 rooms, Double: €164–€206*
*Half board €164–€206 daily (per person)\**
*\*Includes breakfast & dinner*
*Open: Apr to Nov, Credit cards: all major*
*Other languages: good English*
*Region: Tuscany, Michelin Map: 563*
*karenbrown.com/italy/casolaredilibbiano.html*

Leaving San Gimignano on the road north towards Pancole-Certaldo, you come across La Fonte, the property of the Bergamasco family. Their daughter Maria now runs it after selling her nearby bed and breakfast, Il Vicario, previously in this guide. This typical Tuscan farmhouse with cupola is surrounded by a nature reserve, vineyards, olive groves, and woods, yet is very close to many major sights and cities. Within the large main house are four fully-equipped apartments with coveted views for longer stays. Three have two bedrooms each with en suite bathrooms and one has one bedroom. Depending on guests' requests, Maria uses the seven bedrooms separately for bed-and-breakfast guests or as four apartments. Maria has enhanced the natural beauty of the home's original features—brick vaulted ceilings and floors—with appropriate country furnishings and smart, colorful fabrics. The cypress-backed swimming pool is nearby, and several patios within the English garden with its extensive lawns offer quiet places for relaxing after touring the many sights of the area. At your fingertips are Volterra, Lucca, the Chianti area, Siena, and many other Tuscan delights. Breakfast can be served outdoors or a pre-ordered tray is brought directly to rooms. *Directions:* 8 km from San Gimignano, 4 km from Certaldo. From Certaldo, take the road south (there are three) towards San Gimignano-Pancole, and at Il Monte turn in at the sign for La Fonte.

*LA FONTE*
*Host: Maria Bergamasco*
*Via Canonica 4, San Gimignano (SI ) 53037, Italy*
*Tel: (0577) 944845, Fax: (0577) 945635*
*Double: €110*
*7 rooms, 4 apartments: €90–€165 daily*
*Minimum nights required: 3*
*Open: all year, Credit cards: all major*
*Other languages: fluent English*
*Region: Tuscany, Michelin Map: 563*
*karenbrown.com/italy/lafonte.html*

The increasing popularity of this perfectly intact medieval town and the resulting availability of accommodations have made San Gimignano a hub from which tourists fan out to visit nearby, lesser-known treasures such as Volterra, Colle Val d'Elsa, and Monteriggioni. A pleasant, informal stay can be had at the Podere Villuzza, run by friendly young Sandra and Gianni Dei who opened the doors of their 150-year-old stone farmhouse to guests after extensive modification. Chairs are set up in front where visitors can enjoy the view of vineyard-covered hills leading up to the impressive multi-towered town. Common areas include the rustic living room with ceramic-tiled tables and fireplace where guests convene after a day of touring. While gregarious Sandra pampers guests, Gianni occupies himself with the production of top-quality olive oil. Six double rooms on ground and first floors accessed by several different entrances are furnished in true country style with a mix of wrought-iron beds and antique armoires, complemented by mansard beamed ceilings and stone walls. Rooms have views out over the countryside and town or over back hills. Also available for weekly stays are three small apartments within the house that include a living area and kitchen. A swimming pool just to the left of the farmhouse is a great bonus for guests. *Directions:* Go through town and follow signs for Certaldo. After 2 km turn right and follow signs for Villuzza.

*PODERE VILLUZZA*
*Hosts: Sandra & Gianni Dei*
*Strada 25, San Gimignano (SI) 53037, Italy*
*Tel: (0577) 940585, Cellphone: (335) 7118172*
*Fax: (0577) 942247*
*6 rooms, Double: €95–€102*
*3 apartments: €752 weekly*
*Open: all year, Credit cards: MC, VS*
*Other languages: good English*
*Region: Tuscany, Michelin Map: 563*
*karenbrown.com/italy/poderevilluzza.html*

The countryside around San Gimignano is becoming like the Alto Adige mountain area where practically every house offers some kind of accommodation, and the competition has created bed and breakfasts with high standards of quality and service. Among these, Il Rosolaccio (the local name for the poppies that cover the hill in springtime) is an 18th-century typical Tuscan farmhouse perched high above the road between Certaldo and San Gimignano. As expected, the view over the vineyards and hillsides is absolutely breathtaking. After a 30-year career running a hotel in Rome, Ingrid Music, with her son Steven and his Russian wife, Natalie, bought and very carefully restored the house which, by tradition, was added on to each time someone in the family got married. All the right ingredients are included for a perfectly delightful stay, with tastefully decorated bedrooms and apartments perfectly in tune with the simple beauty of the preserved farmhouse, warm and discreet hospitality, and marvelous views to be enjoyed either poolside or at sunset with a glass of wine. Common areas include the vaulted dining room and cozy upstairs living room with huge open fireplace and family antiques. *Directions:* From San Gimignano follow signs for Certaldo and after 7 km, turn right at the sign up to Il Rosolaccio. From Certaldo drive in the direction of San Gimignano for 5 km and turn left at Rosolaccio.

*IL ROSOLACCIO*
*Hosts: Ingrid, Natalie & Steven Music*
*Localita: Capezzano Basso, San Gimignano (SI) 53037*
*Tel: (0577) 944465, Fax: (0577) 944467*
*6 rooms, Double: €96–€110*
*6 apartments: €660–€1,090 weekly*
*No dinner Tues, Minimum nights required: 2*
*Open: Mar to Oct, Credit cards: all major*
*Other languages: fluent English, French, German*
*Region: Tuscany, Michelin Map: 563*
*karenbrown.com/italy/rosolaccio.html*

La Locanda del Castello is a dreamy place to stay recently opened by Silvana Ravanelli, who took on the ambitious project of restoring part of the village's 13th-century castle (the municipal hall is housed in the other half) and transforming it into charming accommodations and a restaurant. The success she had with her previous, much smaller bed and breakfast in this guide created the desire to offer additional, more upscale rooms. She has a real talent for decorating and each individual room has been thoughtfully appointed with the family's antiques, gorgeous fabrics, and beautiful travertine bathrooms. Most have king-sized beds, double sinks, and generous showers. The golden hue chosen for the rooms' walls harmonize perfectly with the surrounding wheat-covered hillsides dotted with cypresses. The brick-vaulted restaurant, originally the olive press, is accessed through a delightful garden with dining tables right at the historic walls of the castle. The chef adds his own creativity to ancient Tuscan recipes using local percorino cheeses, white truffles, and other fresh local products. San Giovanni is right in the middle of some of Tuscany's most picture-perfect scenery. *Directions:* 35 km south of Siena, exit from autostrada A1 at Bettolle-Sinalunga and follow signs for San Giovanni d'Asso. Stairs from the town's main parking lot lead up to the inn.

*LA LOCANDA DEL CASTELLO*
*Piazza Vittorio Emanuele II, 4*
*San Giovanni d'Asso (SI) 53020, Italy*
*Tel: (0577) 802939, Fax: (0577) 802942*
*9 rooms, Double: €100–€150*
*Half board: €160–€220 daily (per person)*
*Minimum nights required: 3 for half board*
*Open: all year, Credit cards: all major*
*Other languages: good English*
*Region: Tuscany, Michelin Map: 563*
*karenbrown.com/italy/locandadelcastello.html*

For those seeking a base for exploring the hilltowns of Tuscany while sojourning in very characteristic accommodation with a rich historical past, the Lucignanello is a sublime choice. Imagine residing in one of the cluster of stone houses that make up the quaint village immersed in the type of picture-perfect, timeless Tuscan landscape seen in Renaissance paintings. The illustrious Piccolomini family still owns the 15th-century property where lovers of Italy can live out a dream. Five two-bedroom houses have been masterfully restored, preserving the original architectural features while ensuring modern facilities. The irregularly shaped interiors are filled with lovely antiques, Oriental carpets, beautifully tiled bathrooms, and kitchens with travertine counters, and all but one have large fireplaces. High above the village is a pool set among olive trees with inspiring views. Although breakfast ingredients are supplied, guests are self-sufficient (they find the hamlet's grocery shop and osteria most convenient) but a permanent staff is at their disposal for any suggestions or assistance. A separate five-bedroom farmhouse with private swimming pool is rented out by the week. Country charm exudes from every corner and the ambiance is so authentic you will feel almost Tuscan before you leave! *Directions:* From San Quirico go towards Siena, taking the first right to San Giovanni d'Asso. Two km before town, turn right for the 2-km drive to Lucignano d'Asso.

*LUCIGNANELLO BANDINI*
*Host: Angelica Piccolomini Naldi Bandini*
*Localita:Lucignano d'Asso*
*San Giovanni d'Asso (SI) 53045, Italy*
*Tel: (0577) 803068(0577) 803062, Fax: (0577) 803082*
*5 apartments: €1,100–1,700 weekly*
*1 villa: €4,000 weekly, Minimum nights required: 3*
*Open: all year, Credit cards: MC, VS*
*Other languages: good English, Region: Tuscany*
*Michelin Map: 563, Abitare la Storia*
*karenbrown.com/italy/lucignanello.html*

Hidden away from the nearby fashionable beaches of the Emerald Coast of Sardinia is the Ca'La Somara farm where warm hosts Laura and Alberto offer alternative hospitality in nine guestrooms. The 20-acre property stretches up a rocky granite mountainside where the rare Sardinian mules bred here are seen grazing. The bougainvillea-covered one-story main house next door to the owners' quarters has a large, beautiful dining room looking out to a walled, untamed garden and a swimming pool, rare in the area, has a view of the countryside. Rustically decorated in typical Sardinian style, an interior wooden balcony spans the length of the room with colorful hand-woven rugs, baskets, and mule saddles decorating the walls. Guest bedrooms are in a separate house (seven with private bathrooms) and are painted in bright colors with matching bedspreads. A breakfast of homemade breads and cakes is served outdoors under the portico and a superlative vegetarian dinner is available upon request. The hosts' warm and informal hospitality puts guests immediately at ease. The location allows visitors to see two sides of Sardinia: spectacular seaside and inland villages. Many archaeological sites are in the area and activities, such as biking, sailing, diving, horseback riding, and hiking can be arranged. This is a nature lovers' paradise. *Directions:* From Arzachena head for Porto Cervo and turn right for San Pantaleo. After 1 km, turn left for Ca'La Somara.

*CA'LA SOMARA*
*Hosts: Laura & Alberto Lagattolla*
*San Pantaleo, Arzachena (SS) 07021, Italy*
*Tel & fax: (0789) 98969*
*9 rooms, Double: €60–€126*
*Minimum nights required: 2*
*Closed: Jan 25 to Feb 28*
*Other languages: fluent English, French*
*Region: Sardinia, Michelin Map: 566*
*karenbrown.com/italy/cala.html*

The beautiful countryside surrounding the hilltown of Montalcino unfortunately does not offer much in the way of accommodation. Descending from Montalcino towards the Amiata Mountains and Grosseto, one comes across the picturesque hilltop town of S. Angelo in Colle, still undiscovered by tourists, and just below is the scenic 5-acre vineyard property and stone farmhouse where the Girardi family offer bed and breakfast hospitality within six double rooms. Four bedrooms decorated identically with wooden country furniture are upstairs while the other two are on the ground floor, with their own exterior entrances, next to the breakfast room. The large windows of this room look out over a small manicured lawn and lavender-lined garden. Just about everything about the property is impeccable, and for this reason and the fact that return clients come for the peacefulness and privacy of this haven, it is not ideal for small children. To the back of the house is a covered terrace with spectacular valley views, while to the front, through the olive groves, you find a lovely secluded swimming pool. Settle in for a week or so and make this your base for visiting Sant'Antimo Abbey, San Galgano, Montalcino, Pienza, and Siena (50 km). *Directions:* 10 km south of Montalcino. From Grosseto on the S.S.223 to Siena, exit at Paganico and follow signs for Montalcino. After 16 km, Il Poderuccio is on the right-hand side of the road before the town of S. Angelo in Colle.

*IL PODERUCCIO*
*Host: Giorgio Girardi family*
*Sant'Angelo in Colle, SI 53024, Italy*
*Tel: (0577) 844052, Fax: (0577) 844150*
*6 rooms, Double: €85*
*Minimum nights required: 3*
*Open: Easter to Nov, Credit cards: MC, VS*
*Other languages: good English*
*Region: Tuscany, Michelin Map: 563*
*karenbrown.com/italy/poderuccio.html*

During the 18th century under the rule of Leopoldo II, the flat plains to the south of Cortona were divided into equal farm lots, each having a rectangular-shaped farmhouse topped with pigeon loft, called "case Leopoliane". Sister-brother team Diletta and Dimitri found the Agrisalotto property already restored with the former stables transformed into a large restaurant with veranda for special events and eight guest apartments and rooms next to the restaurant and on the floor above. The comfortable apartments for two to six persons are of varying dimensions and include either one or two bedrooms, bathroom, and living room with kitchenette. Each is decorated individually with a mix of country antiques and newer reproductions. A garden lined with overflowing terra-cotta vases of flowers leads to a swimming pool with surrounding lawn. Agrisalotto prides itself also on serving genuine Tuscan cuisine, rich in tradition and naturally fresh flavors, accompanied by vintage wines. The Jacomoni family owns a successful fashion business and manages to take time personally to follow the production and bottling of wine sold at the farm. Cooking and wine lessons along with organized daily itineraries are arranged for groups of six or more. An excellently located base for both Umbria and parts of Tuscany. *Directions:* Exit from autostrada A1 at Valchiana and head towards Perugia. Leave this road at Foiano-Cortona and follow signs to Agrisalotto.

*AGRISALOTTO*
*Hosts: Diletta & Dimitri Jacomoni*
*Localita: Burcinella 88*
*Santa Caterina di Cortona (AR) 52040, Italy*
*Tel & fax: (0575) 617417, Cellphone: (338) 7378393*
*3 rooms, Double: €120–€150*
*5 apartments: €110–€250*
*Closed: Nov, Credit cards: all major*
*Other languages: some English, French*
*Region: Tuscany, Michelin Map: 563*
*karenbrown.com/italy/agrisalotto.html*

A delightful find on our recent tour of Sicily is the newly restored Villa Cefalà, conveniently located on the coastline just east of Palermo. The family came back to their ancestral home, dating from 1778, to bring it back to its original splendor, open it up to guests, and oversee the production of organic wine, olive oil and the citrus groves. Cordial and enthusiastic Paola offers her guests accommodation in comfortable apartments or bedrooms, set in four different cottages surrounding the stately, main white villa with its rooftop terrace looking out to the sea. The Limonaia, overlooking the citrus groves, contains 4 well-decorated two-bedroom apartments divided on two floors, complete with living room and kitchenette: Nespolo is a separate 3-bedroom house with sea views. Casetta Rosa and Atrio are separate guesthouses, each containing a lovely 2-bedroom apartment. Oliveto holds four individual bedrooms, all with their own entrance. Wrought iron canopy beds, country furniture, and country fabric curtains furnish the very pleasant rooms. Breakfast and dinner are served, upon request, in the rustic dining room in the villa. A great location for touring Palermo, Monreale and the northern coastline. *Directions:* 40km from the Palermo airport and 15 km from the city, take the A19 Palermo-Catania, exiting at Casteldaccia. Follow S.S.113 and at the junction take a left on S.S.113 at sign for Villa. The Villa is on the left side of the road.

*VILLA CEFALA     New*
*Host: Paola Tedesco family*
*Via SS 113, 48*
*Santa Flavia, Sicily (PA) 90017, Italy*
*Tel: (091) 325927, Fax: (091) 941616*
*3 rooms, Double: €64–€160* 80 – 200 plus meals
*7 apartments: €98–€148*
*Open: all year, Credit cards: all major*
*Other languages: good English*
*Region: Sicily, Michelin Map: 565*
*karenbrown.com/italy/cefala.html*

Right in the heart of the chic (and expensive) Italian Riviera is a small jewel of a bed and breakfast hugging the hillside high above the ports of Portofino and Santa Margherita. The young host, Roberto, has restored almost single-handedly the two small stone farmhouses on a piece of his grandfather's property. Nine tastefully decorated double rooms are divided between the two houses, each with private bath, scattered antiques, and lovely panoramic views over the olive trees and fruit orchards and down to the sea. A cozy living room, inviting one to curl up with a book or to converse, gives visitors the feeling of being at the home of friends. The ambiance is intimate and welcoming. In the small, beamed dining room or out in the panoramic terraced garden, breakfast and dinner (featuring local specialties such as the famous fresh pesto sauce) are served and prepared by Roberto himself while his darling wife, Simona, serves and attends to guests. From Genoa to the marvels of Cinque Terre, the Ligurian coast holds some very special treasures, and the Gnocchi makes a perfect and very reasonable place from which to discover them. Arrival accepted without notice before 1:30 pm or after 5 pm. *Directions:* From Santa Margherita follow signs to Genova/S. Lorenzo uphill for about 4 km to a blue intersection sign. Just after the sign, about 90 meters before the intersection, take the narrow, winding road on the left with the red-and-white gate down to the end.

*VILLA GNOCCHI*
*Hosts: Simona & Roberto Gnocchi*
*Via Romana 53*
*Santa Margherita (GE) 16038, Italy*
*Tel & fax: (0185) 283431, Cellphone: (333) 6191898*
*9 rooms, Double: €100* ~ *130*
*Per person half board: €70*
*Open: mid-Apr to mid-Oct*
*Other languages: good English*
*Region: Liguria, Michelin Map: 561*
*karenbrown.com/italy/villagnocchi.html*

Within the charming, medieval town of Sarteano, just south of the famed Tuscan hilltowns of Montepulciano, Pienza, and Montalcino, is the historic 16th-century home of gracious hostess, Signora Liboria. Although uninhabited for forty years and in dire need of restoration, she fell in love with the home and purchased it eight years ago, complete with frescoed-ceilings, private chapel, and formal garden. A meticulous restoration followed; the prime objective to preserve the home's original flavor and offer three guestrooms for her bed & breakfast activity. Signora thoroughly enjoys walking visitors through the historic, museum-like rooms, each with a mythical theme portrayed in the frescoed-ceilings (Venus, Cupid, Bacchus). Pastel-colored rooms are appointed with a selection of antiques, small object collections, family heirloom paintings, and lace curtains (one made from a wedding veil!), to create a feminine, romantic ambience. The theme continues in the three bedrooms with immaculate bathrooms, tiled rooftop, and hillside views. Royal blue and yellow are the predominant colors in the Contessa room, red in the canopied-bed of the Cardinal room, and roses decorate every object in the third, smallest bedroom. An abundant, country breakfast is served guests, while daily itineraries are arranged for this scenic area. *Directions:* Exit A1 at Chiusi-Chianciano, follow signs for Sarteano, and continue directly into the historic center.

*PALAZZO FANELLI*     *New*
*Host: Liboria Albanese*
*Via dei Lecci 25*
*Sarteano (SI) 53047, Italy*
*Tel: (0578) 268130 (0578) 268130, Fax: (0578) 268130*
*3 rooms, Double: €120–€140*
*Open: all year*
*Region: Tuscany*
*karenbrown.com/italy/fanelli.html*

As more travelers realize how close together destinations of interest throughout Italy are, weekly house rentals to use as a home base for excursions have become more popular. One such ideal base is La Sovana, bordering Tuscany and Umbria and equidistant to Siena, Perugia, Assisi, Arezzo, and many other smaller hilltowns such as Montepulciano, Pienza, and Montalcino—the area where Italy's finest wines are produced. Two stone farmhouses were carefully restored to provide comfortable suites for two to six people. Tastefully decorated with local antique beds and armoires, matching floral bedspreads and curtains, each has a fully equipped kitchenette and eating and living area. Guests can dine by candlelight in the dining room in the main house, whose enormous arched window takes in the expansive view of vineyards, wheat fields, and impeccable landscaping. Giovannella and Giuseppe Olivi, dedicated and amiable hosts, and their two grown children, Riccardo and Francesca, dine with their guests each evening. Potted flowers abound around the pool and jacuzzi where on Saturday nights a sumptuous barbecue is organized to enable guests to meet one another. Two tennis courts, a small fishing lake, and bikes are available. There are more bi-level suites in a large converted barn in the woods a short walk away from the main farmhouse. *Directions:* Just 2 km from the Chiusi exit of the A1 autostrada. La Sovana is just before Sarteano on the right.

*LA SOVANA*
*Host: Giuseppe Olivi family*
*Localita: Sovana*
*Sarteano (SI) 53047, Italy*
*Tel: (0578) 274086, Fax: (075) 5158098*
*15 rooms, Double: €134–€192*
*Minimum nights required: 3, 7 in high season*
*Open: Jan 1 & Mar 20 to Nov 3*
*Other languages: good English*
*Region: Tuscany, Michelin Map: 563*
*karenbrown.com/italy/lasovana.html*

Tenuta La Bandita is set amid 150 acres of woods, olive groves, orchards, and meadows within a beautifully undisturbed area south of Livorno near the sea. Dino and Daniela, with their former business and hotel experience, bought the estate not too long ago and are in the process of gradually bringing it back to its past splendor. There is certainly plenty to keep them busy since the property includes six additional farmhouses surrounding the 17th-century main villa where most of the guest bedrooms are situated. Their idea was to transform the villa into a bed and breakfast while leaving as much as possible of the original structure and atmosphere of the private residence intact. This was made easier by the fact that the home came with ten furnished bedrooms with bathrooms, situated down one long corridor. The rooms are appointed with original period furniture, chandeliers, and matching drapes and bedspreads. Guests can lounge on the front terrace or in the spacious arched living and dining room downstairs with gray-stone fireplace and framed portraits. Fifteen additional rooms are divided within two adjacent houses, between the villa and swimming pool. *Directions:* Exit from S.S.1 at Donoratico and head for Sassetta/Castagneto for 11 km on a winding mountain road. Take the turnoff left for Laderello/Monteverdi (not Sassetta) for 1 km to the La Bandita property. Pass through the gate and go past the first group of houses to the villa.

*TENUTA LA BANDITA*
*Hosts: Daniela & Dino Filippi*
*Via Campagna Nord 30*
*Sassetta (LI) 57020, Italy*
*Tel: (0565) 794224, Fax: (0565) 794350*
*25 rooms, Double: €90–€165*
*Minimum nights required: 2*
*Open: Mar 19 to Nov 6, Credit cards: all major*
*Other languages: some English, German, French*
*Region: Tuscany, Michelin Map: 563*
*karenbrown.com/italy/tenutalabandita.html*

Saturnia's thermal waters have been gushing from an underground volcano for over 2,000 years, yet only recently have it and the enchanting surrounding Maremma area become internationally famous, leading to new accommodations springing up. One such is the charming Villa Clodia, once home to nobility, now run by former restaurateur Giancarlo Ghezzi. The villa is a curiosity, seemingly built out of the limestone rock, one side overlooking the street and the other an expansive valley of grapevines and olive trees. Because of its unusual proportions, each room is unique in size and decor. A small winding stairway takes guests up or down to rooms, some of which have been literally carved out of the rock. All bedrooms feature scattered antiques, new bathrooms, and valley views, and a fortunate few boast a terrace. Amenities include air conditioning, TVs, and mini-bars. Breakfast is offered in a sweet, luminous room next to the sitting room. A lush rose garden and fruit orchard surround the inviting star-shaped pool. Advance reservations are a must and weekly stays preferred. *Directions:* From Rome take the Aurelia highway north, turning off to the right at Vulci following signs for Manciano, Montemerano, and Saturnia. Villa Clodia is in the middle of town.

*VILLA CLODIA*
*Host: Giancarlo Ghezzi*
*Via Italia 43*
*Saturnia (GR) 58050, Italy*
*Tel: (0564) 601212, Fax: (0564) 601305*
*12 rooms, Double: €90–€105*
*Minimum nights required: 4*
*Closed: Dec 1 to 20, Credit cards: VS*
*Other languages: good English*
*Region: Tuscany, Michelin Map: 563*
*karenbrown.com/italy/clodia.html*

North of the beautifully austere ancient city of Bergamo, at the foothills of the Ortighera mountain range right on the River Brembo is the farm property of young local couple, Cinzia and Ferdy Quarteroni. They bought the stone farmhouse at the edge of thick woods, which dates to 1850, and completely restored it to include four guestrooms, their private quarters, dining rooms, and small store where they sell their home-produced goat cheeses. The cabin-like bedrooms on the two upper floors are simply decorated in tune with the natural features of the house: stone walls, wood-beamed ceilings, and brick floors. Downstairs in the cozy, arched, stone-walled dining room with large fireplace, gregarious Cinzia serves excellent local fare and an ample breakfast with freshly baked cakes and breads. This is a nature lover's paradise where Ferdy sees to the goats and organizes itineraries by mountain bike, horse, or foot while nearby there are several ski resorts. This is a perfect vacation spot for families. *Directions:* From the A4 autostrada exit at Dalmine (35 km), heading north for Villa d'Almè, San Pellegrino, San Giovanni, and Scalvino. Ten km after San Pellegrino, the source of the famous mineral water, park on the right-hand side of road at the agriturismo sign and cross over the footbridge up to the house.

*FERDY*
*Hosts: Cinzia & Ferdy Quarteroni*
*Scalvino (BG) 24010, Italy*
*Tel & fax: (0345) 82235*
*4 rooms, Double: €62–€80*
*Per person half board: €47–€55*
*Open: all year, Credit cards: MC, VS*
*Other languages: good English*
*Region: Lombardy, Michelin Map: 561*
*karenbrown.com/italy/ferdy.html*

The Locanda Strada della Marina, another answer to the increasing request for charming accommodation in this infrequently visited region, is just 20 kilometers north of Ancona in the northern section of the Marches area. In the summer this part of the flat Adriatic coast is normally inundated with Italian and northern European tourists who flock to the shores for sun and entertainment. Gianmarco had the family's house in the nearby countryside restored into a peaceful bed and breakfast with emphasis on excellent dining. The converted tobacco-drying barn is a restaurant with a menu inspired by traditional, regional recipes, meat and fish, using top quality ingredients seasonally available. There is also an extensive wine list. The bedrooms in the pale-yellow main house have many amenities. Decorated with a fresh country flavor, they have parquet floors and sparkling bathrooms, and some enjoy a loft sitting space or extra bed. Common spaces are found both in the ground-floor living area where breakfast is served and a cozy upstairs corner with fireplace. Surrounding the house is an open lawn space and garden with heated swimming pool. The Beccis are friendly hosts who can suggest many interesting local itineraries. *Directions:* Leave the A14 at Senigallia and drive through the city to the Strada della Marina, which leads to Scapezzano. The Locanda Strada della Marina is on this road before town.

*LOCANDA STRADA DELLA MARINA*
*Hosts: Stefania & Gianmarco Becci*
*Strada della Marina 265*
*Scapezzano di Senigallia, (AN) 60010, Italy*
*Tel: (071) 6608633, Fax: (071) 6611727*
*9 rooms, Double: €140–€160*
*Open: all year, Credit cards: all major*
*Other languages: good English*
*Region: Marches, Michelin Map: 563*
*karenbrown.com/italy/dellamarina.html*

For those who prefer the intimacy of a small pension, native Salvatore and his amiable Panamanian wife Marisin await you with open arms. The pale-yellow three-story house sits in the quaint town of Scopello with its piazza and three streets. From ancient times this was an important fishing center especially for tuna, and the Tonnara stone fishing station down by the sea still stands as proof. The entrance hall is a combination breakfast and dining room with a sitting area in the corner around the fireplace. A central staircase leads up to guestrooms, a few with balconies facing out to the distant sea. The rooms are simply appointed with light-wood armoires, wrought-iron beds, and crocheted white bedspreads. In the evening after a day at the seaside or touring, you come "home" to a delicious three-course home-cooked meal of fresh fish or meat and vegetables from their garden. Enthusiastic Marisin spends time chatting with her guests and advising them what to visit in this culturally rich area. "Must sees" include the ancient town of Erice, the ruins of Segesta, Selinunte, and Agrigento. Well-marked hiking trails cover the spectacularly beautiful Zingaro Nature Reserve along the northern coast (one of its kind in Sicily). *Directions:* From Palermo, exit from autostrada A29 at Castellammare and follow signs for Scopello. The Tranchina is found just after the bar with outdoor tables.

*PENSIONE TRANCHINA*
*Hosts: Marisin & Salvatore Tranchina*
*Via A. Diaz 7*
*Scopello, Sicily (TP) 91014, Italy*
*Tel & fax: (0924) 541099*
*10 rooms, Double: €69–€88*
*Per person half board: €54–€68*
*Open: all year, Credit cards: all major*
*Other languages: fluent English*
*Region: Sicily, Michelin Map: 565*
*karenbrown.com/italy/pensionetranchina.html*

Another one of Italy's best-kept secrets is the Monte Amiata area in the southern part of Tuscany, offering some of the most spectacular naturalistic landscapes in all of Italy. The mountain's peak reaches a height of 1800 meters and is surrounded by one enchanting village after another, untouched by tourism. Enrico Casini and his wife Stefania took over a vast countryside property here, transforming the four scattered ancient farmhouses into fourteen very comfortable apartments for guests. Appointed in true Tuscan country style, they have either one or two bedrooms, living room, and kitchenette. The main house is the heart of the place where Enrico, a well-known chef and sommelier with international experience, thoroughly expresses himself. His extraordinary dishes combine the freshest produce and top-quality cheeses and salamis of the area with traditional recipes and his own creative touch. The estate also produces top-rated extra-virgin olive oil using ancient methods. Meals are served in one of two attractive dining rooms or out on the porch overlooking an open lawn leading to the swimming pool. *Directions:* 15 km from Montalcino. From the Cassia route 2, exit from the north at S. Quirico or from the south at Radicofani and drive towards Seggiano-Castel del Piano. Turn right 4 km before town at Poggio Ferro-Le Casacce.

*LE CASACCE*
*Hosts: Enrico & Stefania Casini*
*Localita: Casacce*
*Seggiano (GR ) 58038, Italy*
*Tel: (0564) 950895, Fax: (0564) 950970*
*14 apartments: €465–€1,290 weekly (Jul & Aug)*
*Per person half board: €72*
*Open: all year, Credit cards: all major*
*Other languages: good English*
*Region: Tuscany, Michelin Map: 563*
*karenbrown.com/italy/casacce.html*

Luciana and Luigi from Rome are pioneers in offering accommodation in Sabina, bringing back to life a lovely inherited piece of property. Gregarious Luciana is the hostess par excellence: she goes out of her way to see that guests' needs are taken care of and suggests many fascinating local itineraries and events. Accommodation is offered in a variety of apartments divided between the main villa and the well-restored farmhouse with adjacent scenically positioned pool down the hill. Each has one or two bedrooms, bathroom, kitchenette, and eating area, while a double living room with enormous stone fireplace is reserved for all guests. The cozy country decor, with its stenciled borders and mix of family antiques, is the result of Luciana's good taste. Apartments on ground and second floors (some with terraces) take in views of the sweeping valley below. Rooms in the villa are more elegant, with frescoed ceilings, panoramic terraces, and antique furnishings. In addition to producing wine, olive oil, and fruit, Luigi raises thoroughbred horses. On request, Luciana also arranges interesting walking tours and courses in Italian and cooking. *Directions:* From Rome, leave the A1 at Ponzano Romano/Soratte (a new exit and not marked on maps) after the Fiano exit. Turn right at the next intersection, then left at Forano intersection, continue until the turnoff left for Forano. Before the church, turn right for Selci, then right before town at Via Vallerosa.

*VILLA VALLEROSA*
*Hosts: Luciana Pancera & Luigi Giuseppi*
*Via di Vallerosa 27*
*Selci Sabino (RI) 02040, Italy*
*Tel & fax: (0765) 519179, Cellphone: (339) 1226213*
*7 apartments: €690–€1,075 weekly, €114–€190 daily*
*Minimum nights required: 2, 7 in high season*
*Open: all year*
*Other languages: good English*
*Region: Lazio, Michelin Map: 563*
*karenbrown.com/italy/vallerosa.html*

So very close to Siena, yet having the advantage of countryside tranquillity, is the elegant Villa dei Lecci of the Albuzza sisters from Milan. The enterprising and energetic pair left their city careers to resettle in Tuscany, totally renovating an abandoned 17th-century country home to create an upscale bed and breakfast and an intimate and romantic retreat for couples. The yellow bedroom downstairs is a suite with large bathroom adjacent to the frescoed dining room where a generous breakfast is served. A candlelit dinner can also be had upon request here or out in the garden gazebo. Upstairs, where the noble proprietors once lived, the quarters are more elaborate, with painted, wood-paneled ceilings and a large living room and library filled with fine antiques. The Victorian-style Peach Room has floral wallpaper, lace curtains, and silver-framed family photos, while the Alcove Suite is done in golden tones and rich fabrics. Adding to guests' indulgence are a hot tub, exercise room, and sitting area on a frescoed veranda. A weeklong cooking program is organized in off-season months. An excellent touring base. *Directions:* Exit the A1 at Val di Chiana and take 326 to Siena. Continue straight on to the Siena Est exit, arriving at Due Ponti. Take a sharp right at Bar Due Ponti onto Strada Pieve al Bozone for 2.5 km, turning left at the crucifix onto an unpaved road, Strada di Larniano. Continue 1.8 km to the end of the road and up to the gate of the stone villa.

*VILLA DEI LECCI*
*Hosts: Miki & Marika Albuzza*
*Strada di Larniano 21/1*
*Siena 53100, Italy*
*Tel & fax: (0577) 221126, Cellphone: (339) 1543743*
*4 rooms, Double: €180–€230*
*Minimum nights required: 3*
*Open: mid-Mar to Dec*
*Other languages: good English*
*Region: Tuscany, Michelin Map: 563*
*karenbrown.com/italy/lecci.html*

The fascinating Marches region has been justifiably receiving great press recently as one of Italy's last undiscovered treasures. Certainly one of the most interesting areas from which to begin exploring is that of Monte Conero, which boasts the most spectacular coastline on the Adriatic, with white cliffs plunging into the sea. Here you find many historic villages and churches in scenic countryside, the highest concentration of historic theaters in Italy, and a summer opera festival in Macerata and Pesaro. Just slightly inland is the 80-acre agritourism property of the noble Nembrini Gonzaga family, producers of top-quality Rosso Conero wine and virgin olive oil. Next to the family's elegant 18th-century villa is a restored grain mill converted into guest apartments. An extensive two-story structure of white stone typical of the area, it contains pleasant, practical accommodation for two to five persons consisting of one or two bedrooms, bathroom, and living room with kitchenette. Adjacent to the apartments and surrounded by a large garden is a recently built house with eight very tastefully decorated bedrooms. A wide variety of sports including sailing, golf, hiking on national-park trails overlooking the sea, and horseback riding can all be arranged. *Directions:* Exit the A14 autostrada at Ancona Sud heading for Sirolo-Numana. In Coppo (on most maps), 2 km before Sirolo, turn right on the road opposite the bar and follow the Via Valcastagno up to the property.

*RELAIS VALCASTAGNO*
*Host: Francesca Nembrini Gonzaga family*
*Via Valcastagno 10, Sirolo (AN) 60026, Italy*
*Tel: (071) 7391580, Fax: (071) 7392776*
*8 rooms, Double: €70–€150*
*10 apartments: €285–€750 weekly*
*Minimum nights required: 2*
*Open: all year, Credit cards: all major*
*Other languages: fluent English, French*
*Region: Marches, Michelin Map: 563*
*karenbrown.com/italy/granaio.html*

There is a beautiful stretch of coastline on the Adriatic Sea just south of Ancona, dramatically different from the more flat, uninteresting shoreline to the north and south with its modern hotels and condos. The 14th-century quaint stone village of Sirolo sits high above the water on a mountainside looking down to the beaches of the Riviera Conero. Delightful seafood restaurants dot the shore, where you might enjoy a plate of pasta with fresh clams while watching the tide come in. Here Isabella and Giorgio offer seven guestrooms above their small, quaint, peach-colored restaurant. The Locanda, dating to 1300, being actually part of the town's walls and arched entryway, is of great architectural and historical importance, so it has taken them many years to acquire permits to restore and renovate rooms. Their patience has paid off and their bed and breakfast, respecting the original structure, is a true charmer. Bedrooms, most with sea views, have exposed stone walls and terra-cotta floors showing off wrought-iron beds and antique armoires. Amenities such as air conditioning, telephones, TVs, mini-bars, and hairdryers were added for guests' comfort. They also have two apartments nearby overlooking the park and sea for stays of four nights or more. Isabella's highly praised meals feature seafood dishes. *Directions:* The Rocco sits at the edge of the town of Sirolo, after Portonovo.

❄ ⚓ ☕ ☄ 🆑 ☎ 🛗 🧍 🏃 🐎 🍸 P 🍴 ⛵ 🍇

*LOCANDA ROCCO*
*Hosts: Isabella & Giorgio Tridenti*
*Via Torrione 1*
*Sirolo (AN) 60020, Italy*
*Tel & fax: (071) 9330558, Cellphone: (339) 5205519*
*7 rooms, Double: €120–€180*
*2 apartments: €700–€800 weekly*
*Open: Apr to Nov, Credit cards: MC, VS*
*Other languages: some English*
*Region: Marches, Michelin Map: 563*
*karenbrown.com/italy/locandarocco.html*

The real fascination about the gorgeous Val Gardena mountain resort area is that you can actually ski from one connecting valley to the next and finish up at the end of the day over near Cortina. Siusi is a convenient place to set up camp in any season and the Aquila Nera with its excellent restaurant and amenities of a hotel is steps up from the very economical bed and breakfast choices of the region. The very cordial Mutschlechner family, with a long tradition in the hospitality business, renovated most of the former private home whose origins date back to 1518. A second building was added on, creating additional rooms (and an elevator), which are very fresh with light-wood furnishings and cheerful fabrics. Downstairs common rooms include a luminous sitting area, a stube, a breakfast room completely paneled in wood including floor and ceiling, and a large contemporary dining room where five-course dinners are served based on a combination of Italian and southern Tyrolean recipes. A small swimming pool at the back, plus sauna, steam bath, and free shuttle to the lifts are nice added extras. *Directions:* Turn into the main street of town, Via Santner, and take the first right to Via Laurin.

*AQUILA NERA (SCHWARZER ADLER)*
*Host: Mutschlechner family*
*Via Laurin 7, Siusi allo Sciliar (BZ) 39040, Italy*
*Tel: (0471) 706146, Fax: (0471) 706335*
*21 rooms, Double: €100–€176\**
*\*Includes breakfast & dinner*
*Closed: Apr 3 to May 22, Oct 23 to Dec 25*
*Credit cards: all major*
*Other languages: some English*
*Region: Trentino-Alto Adige, Michelin Map: 562*
*karenbrown.com/italy/aquilanera.html*

In yet another lesser-known pocket of Tuscany halfway between Siena and the sea is the absolutely stunning 1,000-acre property of the Visconti family. Dating back to the 1400s, in its heyday it was a village in itself, complete with the noble family's main villa, farmers' houses, church, nuns' quarters, oil press, and blacksmith and carpenter's shops. These stone buildings are all attached to the villa in a U-shape formation with a beautiful formal garden within. Terra-cotta pots with lemon trees and red geraniums give spots of color among the greenery. Vitaliano and Vittoria, whose home has been in the same family since its origins, welcome guests in the restored part of the villa where nine bedrooms with private bathrooms have been created including three large triples. All with beamed ceilings and brick floors, they are simply appointed with beds and armoires, looking out either to the garden or woods at the back. Common areas are the living room with enormous fireplace, the dining room where delectable Tuscan country meals are served (€20), and an upstairs loggia with a panoramic view over the countryside, which seems to take in all of Tuscany. Three apartments are available for weekly stays. For those who enjoy spectacular scenery in a very special, historical setting, this is the place. *Directions:* From the Florence-Siena highway exit at Colle Val d'Elsa Sud. Follow signs for Grosseto-Radicondoli-Castelnuova Val di Cecina, then Fattoria Solaio.

*FATTORIA SOLAIO*
*Hosts: Vittoria & Vitaliano Visconti*
*Solaio–Radicondoli (SI) 53030, Italy*
*Tel: (0577) 791029, Fax: (0577) 791015*
*9 rooms, Double: €90–€115*
*3 apartments: €630– €750 weekly*
*Minimum nights required: 3*
*Open: Mar to Nov, Credit cards: all major*
*Other languages: good English*
*Region: Tuscany, Michelin Map: 563*
*karenbrown.com/italy/fattoriasolaio.html*

Le Sorgive, near Lake Garda, is a vast agritourism property, an oasis that offers a wealth of activities connected with nature and agriculture. Anna and her brother, Vittorio, both passionate advocates for the environment, divide the duties, with Anna operating a large country restaurant, Le Volpi, and a major equestrian center where locals convene, and Vittorio running the hospitality end. The 60 acres are made up of cultivated fields, vineyards, and woods with plenty of farm animals within the triangle of flat countryside between Brescia, Mantova, and Verona. The extensive yellow main house with cupola and arched portico contains the family's private quarters, dining room, and eight well-appointed guestrooms, some with loft beds for two children, spread about the three floors. For longer stays, there are also two lovely apartments. An ample country breakfast is served in the rustic beamed dining room with fireplace. Anna's busy restaurant highlights recipes specifically from the Mantova area, using the variety of organic produce, cheeses, and salamis. Other facilities offered are a fully-equipped gym, swimming pool, and mountain bikes. *Directions:* Exit the A4 autostrada at Sirmione, turn left for Pozzolengo (3 km) and then to Solferino (7 km). Turn left at the first crossroads, then keep to the right towards Castiglione delle Stiviere (1.5 km) until you reach a sign indicating the farm entrance.

*LE SORGIVE*
*Hosts: Vittorio & Adriana Serenelli*
*Localita: Sorgive, Solferino (MN ) 46040, Italy*
*Tel: (0376) 854252, Fax: (0376) 855256*
*8 rooms, Double: €85–€105*
*2 apartments: €550–€900 weekly*
*Restaurant closed Mon & Tues*
*Open: all year, Credit cards: all major*
*Other languages: good English*
*Region: Lombardy, Michelin Map: 561*
*karenbrown.com/italy/lesorgive.html*

The town of Spoleto has gained international fame thanks to the July Due Mondi festival, a month-long series of cultural events including ballet, theater, opera, and concerts with renowned artists, which attracts a worldwide audience. Accommodations are reserved from one year to the next. For the rest of the year, however, Spoleto holds its own along with nearby Assisi, Spello, Todi, and Perugia as an enchanting medieval stone town, rich in its historical past. The 14th-century Palazzo Dragoni, situated on a quiet little street in the heart of the town near the famous cathedral, was completely renovated by the Diotallevi family and offers charming accommodation within 15 bedrooms. Son Roberto manages the bed and breakfast while his parents reside in a section of the palazzo. The spacious bedrooms (larger ones are considered suites) are spread out among the three floors, reached by elevator, and have new bathrooms and many modern amenities including air conditioning. Everything possible has been done to maintain the original architecture and ambiance of a private home, with vaulted and frescoed high ceilings, antique furnishings, Oriental carpets, and Murano chandeliers. The real treat is breakfast served in the glassed-in loggia, taking in splendid views of the tiled rooftops and bell tower of the Duomo. *Directions:* Follow signs for the center of Spoleto, by way of Via P. Bunilli, passing the football field (campo sportivo). Follow white signs for the hotel.

*PALAZZO DRAGONI*
*Host: Roberto Diotallevi family*
*Via del Duomo 13*
*Spoleto (PG) 06049, Italy*
*Tel: (0743) 222220, Fax: (0743) 222225*
*15 rooms, Double: €120–€150*
*Open: all year, Credit cards: MC, VS*
*Other languages: some English*
*Region: Umbria, Michelin Map: 563*
*karenbrown.com/italy/dragoni.html*

On the border of Liguria and Piedmont and conveniently located near the Genoa-Milan autostrada sits the hillside property of friendly hosts, Domenico and Rosanna, national vice president of the regional agritourism association. The house is immersed in woods at the end of a long gravel road and is barely visible through the ivy and rose vines that conceal it—a true spectacle in late May. This gives just a hint of one of Rosanna's two passions: cooking and gardening, both of which guests can participate in by taking lessons. Two bedrooms are situated in the main farmhouse dating to 1714 and in Rosanna's family since that time. The apartments with exposed beams are located next door in the converted barn and are all decorated in pleasant country style with antiques and family memorabilia. Guests sit down together en famille at a long table to taste one of Rosanna's delectable meals prepared with their own fresh, organically-grown produce from the garden (Domenico's passion). Guests/friends are made to feel right at home in this informal and tranquil atmosphere, where silence and privacy are highly respected and guests become a natural part of the farm's everyday life. A small pool is hidden in lush vegetation just behind the house. *Directions:* Exit the A7 autostrada (Milano-Genova) at Vignole Borbera, following the sign for Stazzano (4 km). Turn right in town at the traffic light and follow the bed and breakfast sign for 2 km on an unpaved road.

*LA TRAVERSINA*
*Hosts: Rosanna & Domenico Varese*
*Localita: Traversina 109, Stazzano (AL) 15060, Italy*
*Tel & fax: (0143) 61377, Cellphone: (335) 494295*
*2 rooms, Double: €84–€100*
*4 apartments: €105–€170 daily*
*Per person half board: €62–€85*
*Open: all year, Credit cards: all major*
*Other languages: some English*
*Region: Piedmont, Michelin Map: 561*
*karenbrown.com/italy/traversina.html*

The well-preserved medieval village of Stroncone sits on the southernmost edge of Umbria bordering Lazio, 7 kilometers from Terni. It is here that Cristiana from Genoa and her husband, Massimiliano, whose parents were originally from this area, bought and restored an ancient building in the stone village and opened a charming bed and breakfast. The eight bedrooms are divided among the top three floors of the medieval building, which centuries ago was once the police station. The old wooden doors of the cells remain intact and are part of the small reception and breakfast room where a buffet table holds breads and cakes each morning. Each bedroom is unique in size and pastel color scheme, with stenciled borders, new bathrooms, and variations according to the original architecture, with either brick-vaulted or wood-beamed ceilings. A mansard bedroom on the top floor offers privacy and rooftop views over the village, besides being the only bedroom with air conditioning (the others remain naturally cool with the thick stone walls). The hosts organize a week-long painting course with daily excursions taking advantage of the scenic surrounding landscapes and villages. The Brunellis have just opened an agritourism business with apartments near Orvieto. *Directions:* Stroncone is 9 km directly south of Terni. The B&B is on Via del Sacramento, the main street of the village.

*LA PORTA DEL TEMPO*
*Hosts: Cristiana & Massimiliano Brunelli*
*Via del Sacramento 2*
*Stroncone (TR) 05039, Italy*
*Tel: (0744) 608190, Fax: (0744) 609034*
*8 rooms, Double: €83–€120*
*Open: all year, Credit cards: all major*
*Other languages: good English*
*Region: Umbria, Michelin Map: 563*
*karenbrown.com/italy/portadeltempo.html*

The Limoneto was recommended to us by a reader who raved about the "open arms" hospitality, excellent meals, comfortable accommodations, and proximity to fascinating Syracuse. We have to agree. At just 10 kilometers from the historical center of Syracuse with its Greek and Roman influences, the orange- and olive-grove farm is a perfectly delightful, safe, and economical base from which to explore Sicily's southeastern corner. Adelina, Alceste, and son, Francesco, make guests part of their family. Guestrooms are split between the refurbished barn and part of the main house, all with individual entrances. Air-conditioned rooms, some for up to four persons, are new, with pleasant modern decor and spotless bathrooms. Dinner is served either in the spacious dining room where locals come for a Sunday meal, or out in the back garden. You are welcome into Adelina's kitchen to observe and participate in the making of typical regional meals. The warmth exudes and when the evening is just right and the limoncello flowing, she might even read some poetry. Truly unique is the boat tour on the river among the Papiro trees of Egyptian origin. *Directions:* From Catania, take the autostrada to Syracuse and exit at Palazzolo (km 152) after a brown sign for the Limoneto B&B. Drive on the S124 and turn left at the first intersection for Canicattini B. At the T-junction turn right again for Canicattini: the house is on the left after 4 km.

*LIMONETO*
*Hosts: Alceste & Adelina Norcia*
*Via del Platano 3, Mailing address: Viale Teracati 142*
*Syracuse, Sicily (SR) 96100, Italy*
*Tel: (0931) 717352, Fax: (0931) 717728*
*8 rooms, Double: €80–€90*
*Minimum nights required: 3*
*Closed: Nov, Credit cards: MC, VS*
*Region: Sicily, Michelin Map: 565*
*karenbrown.com/italy/limoneto.html*

Nowadays the owners of agritourism operations are increasingly city people rather than local farmers but Il Tondino, by contrast, goes back to tradition, with informal hospitality and board offered on the farmland of a local family. Andrea, his two brothers, and his father divide up the chores on the ranch between them, attending to guests, cooking, caring for the horses, and producing cereal and grains. The property is comprised of three buildings: the family's brick house with attached restaurant in the former barn, the stables with guest living room/game area above, and a small guesthouse with three pleasant air-conditioned bedrooms with quilts, rustic wood furniture, and new bathrooms. Five new rooms have been created within the main house and have wrought-iron beds and characteristic beamed ceilings. All pasta and breads are homemade and served at long tables in the cheery dining room with yellow-sponged walls and brick-vaulted ceilings. The small swimming pool captures the sweeping countryside views of this very scenic area, famous for the production and worldwide distribution of Parmesan cheese and Parma prosciutto. The castles of Parma are among the many treasures in the area to explore. *Directions:* Exit from the A1 at Fidenza and head towards Salsamaggiore until the sign for Tabiano. After 3 km turn left at the Il Tondino sign and drive for another 4.5 km to the farm.

※ ➠ ✗ ⚖ ⅂ P ⅋ ≈ ⚕ ⚘

IL TONDINO
Host: Andrea Bertoletti
Tabiano (PR) 43036, Italy
Tel & fax: (0524) 62106
8 rooms, Double: €80–€100
1 apartment
Minimum nights required: 2, Open: Mar to Oct
Other languages: some English
Region: Emilia-Romagna, Michelin Map: 562
karenbrown.com/italy/tondino.html

Taormina is on what could be referred to as the Amalfi coast of Sicily and, although the town is lovely and rich with history, it is very touristy. This of course means that rates are on the high side but, happily, the Villa Schuler makes it affordable and its location and service are superb. The villa was converted from a private residence to a hotel by the Schuler family a century ago and now grandson Gerardo is the proud owner. The pink façade faces out to the street and has a large raised terrace with potted flowers, palms, and cypresses, where a large suite with two bathrooms, Jacuzzi, kitchenette, and garden area has been added. A continental or full breakfast is served either here or in the gazebo where you can enjoy open views encompassing the coastline and the peak of the Etna volcano. To the back is an enchanting botanic garden filled with a profusion of jasmine, bougainvillea, and geraniums with several quiet places to sit in the shade. The garden gives directly onto the main street of town and it is just a short walk to the cable car that takes you down to the beach where guests gain free entrance (or you may take the shuttle service). Inside are the luminous bedrooms, some with sea views, and five mansard junior suites that have everything, including air conditioning, satellite TVs, safes, and terraces with sea views. For its efficient service, ideal location, and incredibly low rate, the Villa Schuler is a winner. *Directions:* Follow hotel signs through town.

*VILLA SCHULER*
*Host: Gerardo Schuler family*
*Via Roma 2*
*Taormina, Sicily (ME) 98039, Italy*
*Tel: (0942) 23481, Fax: (0942) 23522*
*32 rooms, Double: €114–€220*
*Minimum nights required: 3*
*Open: Mar to Nov, Credit cards: all major*
*Other languages: good English*
*Region: Sicily, Michelin Map: 565*
*karenbrown.com/italy/villaschuler.html*

Halfway between Florence and Siena in the heart of the Chianti region is the Sovigliano farm, restored by a gracious couple from Verona, Claudio Bicego and his wife, Patrizia, and daughter, Claudia. Guests have an independent entrance to the four bedrooms with kitchenette, each very much in keeping with the pure simplicity of this typical farmhouse. Exposed-beam ceilings and worn terra-cotta floors, antique beds and armoires, and bucolic views make time stand still here. Besides three apartments (two with air conditioning) in a separate farmhouse, there is also a spacious two-bedroom apartment within the house with kitchen and dining area and fireplace. At guests' disposal are a living room, kitchen with country fireplace, TV, large surrounding garden with swimming pool and hydrojet, exercise trail, and outdoor eating area overlooking the characteristic hills of Chianti. Signor Bicego is actively involved in the production of top Tuscan wines in conjunction with several other wine estates, and also coordinates with other area residents to organize lessons in language, history, and culinary arts with local professors. *Directions:* From Siena, exit the superstrada at San Donato in Poggio; from Florence at Tavarnelle Val di Pesa. Drive through the village of Tavarnelle following the directions to Certaldo-Marcialla. At the end of Tavarnelle, at the fourth traffic circle, veer to the left (blue sign says Magliano), following signs for Sovigliano.

*SOVIGLIANO*
*Hosts: Patrizia & Claudio Bicego*
*Via Magliano 9, Tavarnelle Val di Pesa (FI) 50028*
*Tel: (055) 8076217, Fax: (055) 8050770*
*4 rooms, Double: €130–€160*
*4 apartments: €870–€1,130 weekly B&B*
*Minimum nights required: 3*
*Closed: Jan 15 to 31, Credit cards: MC, VS*
*Other languages: good English*
*Region: Tuscany, Michelin Map: 563*
*karenbrown.com/italy/sovigliano.html*

With their hearts set on running a bed and breakfast in the Liguria region, the Giani family searched hard and long before finding Giandriale. Set high up in the remote mountains above the coast, the 18th-century stone farmhouse is surrounded by a low range of mountains covered with thick woods as far as the eye can see. Utter silence prevails. There are just two guestrooms within their home and five others plus two apartments in the refurbished stone barn, simply decorated with country-style wooden furniture. Guests can relax in one of two comfortable living rooms. Meals are enjoyed in the downstairs dining room with its old-fashioned country stove, which is used occasionally in winter for making polenta. Lucia prepares coffee cakes and jams for breakfast and uses mostly regional recipes in her cooking, taking advantage of their own organic produce. Classic sightseeing destinations in the area include the Riviera (Portofino, Santa Margherita, Chiavari) and the Cinque Terre, 45 minutes away. Nereo can also suggest several interesting off-the-beaten-track itineraries beyond Giandriale. Hiking trails and mountain bikes are available. *Directions:* From autostrada A14, exit at Sestri Levante and follow signs for Casarza Ligure, Castiglione, then, after 2 km and many curves, Missano. After a long tunnel turn right for Tavarone and just before town follow B&B signs for 2.5 km.

*GIANDRIALE*
*Hosts: Lucia Marelli & Nereo Giani*
*Localita: Giandriale, Tavarone di Maissana (SP) 19010*
*Tel: (0187) 840279, Fax: (0187) 840156*
*7 rooms, Double: €60–€70*
*2 apartments: €42–€57 daily per person*
*Minimum nights required: 3 in Jul & Aug*
*Open: all year, Credit cards: all major*
*Other languages: some English*
*Region: Liguria, Michelin Map: 561*
*karenbrown.com/italy/giandriale.html*

In order to stand out among the crowd of recently opened bed and breakfasts in Italy, many hosts have begun to specialize according to their own personal interests. This is true for enthusiastic and friendly hosts, Alberto and his Brazilian wife Luzia, who opened a gourmet vegetarian bed and breakfast on their isolated 27-acre farm up on a mountain ridge between Perugia and Lake Trasimeno, the first of its kind in Umbria. A 4-kilometer gravel road ends at the panoramic property with its main house, two stone guesthouses, and cultural center where courses on yoga and meditation and ethnic music concerts are held. An informal ambiance prevails and the total respect for nature and tranquillity is evident among guests who take hikes in the surrounding woods or read poolside, enjoying both sunrise and sunset over the opposite valleys. The ten neat rooms with independent outside entrances are comfortably decorated with teak-wood beds and armoires and the paintings of a reputed artist. The sun-filled dining room is where guests convene for Luzia's and Alberto's famed fare based on strictly organic produce from the farm. So unique is this bed and breakfast that the BBC did a special documentary on it, and it received the Best Hotel Award 2002. *Directions:* From Perugia follow route 220 for approximately 22 km and turn right before Tavernelle at Colle San Paolo.

*MONTALI*
*Hosts: Luzia & Alberto Musacchio*
*Via Montali 23*
*Tavernelle di Panicale (PG) 06068, Italy*
*Tel: (075) 8350680, Fax: (075) 8350144*
*10 rooms, Double: €170–€200\**
*\*Includes breakfast & dinner*
*Minimum nights required: 3, Open: Mar to Oct*
*Credit cards: MC, VS, Other languages: good English*
*Region: Umbria, Michelin Map: 563*
*karenbrown.com/italy/montali.html*

The Cinque Terre coastline of southern Liguria bordering Tuscany has earned notable popularity in the past years. Its five quaint stone villages hugging the hillside as it sweeps down to the sea were, until recently, accessible only by boat or by foot and are a delight to explore. Just 40 minutes south of the area right on the Poets Gulf is the adorable seaside town of Tellaro hugging the rock over the sea, where visitors make a point of stopping to have a memorable meal at the Miranda restaurant. Husband-and-wife team Giovanna and Angelo have their own inimitable and ever-varying style of cooking based exclusively on fresh seafood (no meat), which is present in the inexhaustible series of antipasti and pasta plates. Angelo has received plenty of press and praise for these extraordinary dishes. Meals are served in one of the newly renovated dining rooms, pleasantly appointed with scattered antiques. In the same vein are the bedrooms, most with gulf views. Aunt Miranda used to rent them out in the Sixties, and they are now in the capable hands of son, Alessandro. Guests have a cozy living room with fireplace for relaxing. This is an exclusive "residents only" area. If questioned by the local police, declare that you are guest of the Locanda Miranda. Reserve well in advance. *Directions:* Leave the A12 autostrada at Sarzana, following signs for Lerici on route 331. Tellaro is 2.5 km down the coast and the Miranda is on the main road before town.

*LOCANDA MIRANDA*
*Hosts: Angelo & Giovanna Cabani*
*Via Fiascherino 92, Tellaro (SP) 19030, Italy*
*Tel: (0187) 968130 or 964012, Fax: (0187) 964032*
*7 rooms, Double: €120–€194\**
*\*Includes breakfast & dinner*
*Minimum nights required: 2*
*Closed: Jan, Credit cards: all major*
*Other languages: fluent English, French*
*Region: Liguria, Michelin Map: 561*
*karenbrown.com/italy/locandamiranda.html*

The remote L'Agnata property is truly unique and mystic. After leaving the main road, you follow a seemingly endless country road dense with cork trees and their curious shaved trunks. Never fear—you are delightfully rewarded at last when you come into the world of silence at L'Agnata. You leave your car parked at the entrance near a lake down a ravine and walk up the arbored path to the main 100-year-old ivy-covered house. Host Piero greets guests at the reception house and shows them to their rooms either upstairs in the main stone house where the owners, the De Andre family, reside during the summer months or in the guesthouse at the back across an expansive green lawn. An inviting swimming pool sits at the side of the house and looks perfectly natural with its surrounding large rocks sitting up straight like sculptures. Rooms are well appointed with antiques and warm colors in the rich fabrics and walls. The manicured lawn spreads around both houses and represents the taming of nature while the rest of the 400-acre property is immersed in the more wild and rugged mountain landscapes so typical of Sardinia. In the corner of the magical garden is a little waterfall creating soothing sounds which break the silence. Excellent dishes of this area called Gallura are served in the muraled dining room. *Directions:* From Tempio, follow the S.S.392 towards Oschiri. After 4.5 km turn right for S. Bachisio and take the unpaved road all the way to the end.

*L'AGNATA*
*Host: Ugo Pedrazzini*
*Localita: L'Agnata, Tempio Pausania (SS) 07029, Italy*
*Tel: (079) 671384, Fax: (079) 634125*
*10 rooms, Double: €110–€130\**
*\*Includes breakfast & dinner*
*Minimum nights required: 3 Aug*
*Closed: Nov, Credit cards: all major*
*Other languages: some English*
*Region: Sardinia, Michelin Map: 566*
*karenbrown.com/italy/lagnata.html*

Country tourism has flourished in the last decade, especially in the highly popular region of Tuscany. However, most travelers still flock to the Chianti area, leaving many other parts of Tuscany wide open to discovery. Such is the gorgeous virgin territory of the Valdera Valley between stunning Volterra with its Etruscan origins and Pisa where everything has remained remarkably unspoiled. Affable host Sandro and his family bought a 100-acre farm property here and are restoring the ancient farmhouses piece by piece with guests' comfort foremost in mind. So far, eight neat apartments with one or two bedrooms and five guest bedrooms have been completed within three adjacent stone houses and are tastefully appointed with local antiques. Within one of the houses is the pleasant dining room with large arched windows where breakfast and dinners upon request are served, all prepared by Sandro's mother, who also conducts cooking lessons. Olive oil, wine, fruits, and vegetables all come directly from the farm. There is a beautiful borderless swimming pool and Sandro supplies guests with mountain bikes and a long list of interesting local itineraries. Easy day trips include Florence, Siena, San Gimignano, Lucca, Pisa and Volterra, famous for its alabaster artisans. *Directions:* Il Selvino is located off the main road 439 from Volterra (20 km) between Terricciola and La Sterza at Pieve a Pitti (marked on most maps).

*IL SELVINO*
*Host: Alessandro Sgherri family*
*Localita: La Sterza, Via Pieve a Pitti 1*
*Terricciola (PI) 56030, Italy*
*Tel & fax: (0587) 670132, Cellphone: (338) 6209229*
*5 rooms, Double: €90–€110*
*8 apartments: €150–€200 daily*
*Minimum nights required: 3, Open: all year*
*Credit cards: MC, VS, Other languages: some English*
*Region: Tuscany, Michelin Map: 563*
*karenbrown.com/italy/ilselvino.html*

Since 1830, the remote 12th-century castle and 4,000-acre farm of Titignano have belonged to the noble Corsini family who now offer travelers 15 guestrooms in the main house, a swimming pool, and three apartments in what was originally the farmer's quarters. They are pleasantly decorated with scattered country antiques. Management is in the hands of Monica and Francesca, delightful hostesses who take care of everything from looking after guests to cooking and serving. Meals are shared at a long table in one of the castle's graciously neglected rooms with an enormous gray-stone fireplace sporting the family coat of arms, and lofty ceilings made of the stamped terra-cotta blocks typical of Umbria. Off the dining hall are the spacious bedrooms, each with modernized pink travertine bathrooms and decorated eclectically with unrefined antiques and wrought-iron beds. They have a worn charm about them. Common areas include a living room with bright floral sofas around a fireplace, a game and TV room for children, and a large terrace with a breathtaking, sweeping view covering three regions. Bikes are available for touring the regional park of the River Tiber (part of the property). *Directions:* Leave the Roma-Florence A1 autostrada at Orvieto. Follow signs for Arezzo, turning on route 79 for Prodo. Follow the long winding road for 26 km past Prodo to Titignano. (30 km from Orvieto.)

*FATTORIA TITIGNANO*
*Hosts: Monica Gori & Francesca Marchetti*
*Localita: Titignano 7, Titignano (TR) 05010, Italy*
*Tel: (0763) 308000 or 308022, Fax: (0763) 308002*
*15 rooms, Double: €80–€136*
*3 apartments: €90–€136*
*Minimum nights required: 2*
*Open: all year, Credit cards: MC, VS*
*Other languages: some English, French*
*Region: Umbria, Michelin Map: 563*
*karenbrown.com/italy/titignano.html*

In the midst of the bucolic countryside surrounding Todi sits the pleasant bed and breakfast of Poggio d'Asproli. Bruno Pagliari, a sculptor with a long family history in the hotel business, transferred his family from Naples to this 16th-century stone farmhouse and ex-convent several years ago and has succeeded in his aim of creating elegant but comfortable surroundings to make guests feel at home. Each of the romantic guestrooms is unique in style and decor. Rich fabrics draped at bedheads give a canopy effect with matching bedspreads and nice big bathrooms have travertine marble sinks. The home is filled to the brim with antiques and lovely artwork (some by Bruno's sister, Lilli), which blend in well with the stone walls, worn brick floors, and beamed ceilings. Breakfast and candlelit dinners are served either on the outside terrace or in the elegant dining room. At one end is a cozy sitting area with white sofas around an enormous fireplace. A swimming pool among the trees is a cool spot for relaxing. Daughter Claudia has now taken over the general management of the bed and breakfast. *Directions:* From Todi, follow signs for Orvieto and take a left at the sign for Izzalini. Before Izzalini town, take the turning for Asproli and continue for several kms, following signs to the bed and breakfast on the left. Total 10 km from Todi.

❄ ☕ 💳 🚶 🐎 P 🍴 ≈ 🍷

*POGGIO D'ASPROLI*
*Host: Claudia Pagliari*
*Localita: Asproli*
*Todi (PG) 06059, Italy*
*Tel & fax: (075) 8853385*
*8 rooms, Double: €109*
*Open: Mar 15 to Jan 3, Credit cards: all major*
*Other languages: good English*
*Region: Umbria, Michelin Map: 563*
*karenbrown.com/italy/asproli.html*

Fortunate guests at the fascinating Tenuta di Canonica are assured of an unforgettable stay. Maria and Daniele, with son Michelangelo, have transformed a massive stone tower with foundation dating to the ancient Roman period and adjoining century-old house into a bed and breakfast of dreams. The spacious living room with stone fireplace and vaulted ceiling is reached down a few stairs from the entryway and looks out over the stunning valley down to Lake Corbara. Outstanding medieval architectural features such as stone walls, brick floors, and high, beamed ceilings have been enhanced by Provence-inspired colors. Stairs lead up to the library and bedrooms are divided between the three-story tower and house, respecting the epoch of each: bathrooms in the medieval quarters have gray stone tiles and travertine, while the others have white tile alternating with terra-cotta pieces. Each tastefully decorated, antique-filled room has some attractive feature, whether it be the more suite-like arrangements with sitting area or the smaller corner rooms with head-spinning views over hills and up to Todi. Common areas include a dining room and large swimming pool with 360-degree views. Cooking classes with a Cordon Bleu cook are also arranged. *Directions:* From Todi take the road for Orvieto, turning right at the sign for Prado/Titignano. After 2 km turn left for Cordigliano and follow the signpost for Tenuta di Canonica to the end of the road (1 km).

*TENUTA DI CANONICA*
*Hosts: Maria & Daniele Fano*
*Localita: Canonica, Todi (PG) 06059, Italy*
*Tel: (075) 8947545, Cellphone: (335) 369492*
*Fax: (075) 8947581*
*11 rooms, Double: €130–€220*
*2 apartments €800– €950 weekly*
*Closed: 15 Dec –16 Jan, Credit cards: MC, VS*
*Other languages: good English*
*Region: Umbria, Michelin Map: 563*
*karenbrown.com/italy/canonicatodi.html*

Just off the busy road that connects the major towns of Umbria—Perugia, Assisi, Spoleto, and Todi—is the elegant country house Giulia, which has been in the Petrucci family since its 14th-century origins. Later additions were built on to the main stone villa, one of which Signora Caterina has opened up to guests. Time seems to have stood still in the six bedrooms, all but one with en suite bathroom, and filled with lovely antique wrought-iron beds, armoires, and period paintings. They are divided among two floors, accessed by a steep stone staircase, the largest having a ceiling fresco depicting the local landscape. Another room with handicapped facilities has been added on the ground floor. Breakfast is served either in the chandeliered dining room upstairs, with Oriental carpets, lace curtains, and a large fireplace, or under the oak trees in the front garden during the warmer months. Part of the barn has been converted into two independent units for up to four persons, including a fully equipped kitchenette. Although the large swimming pool overlooks a rather barren field and the distant main road, it is a welcome respite after a full day of touring, which guests do a lot of from this strategically convenient location. *Directions:* Just off the Perugia-Spoleto route 75 between Trevi and Campello.

*CASA GIULIA*
*Host: Caterina Alessandrini Petrucci*
*Via Corciano, 1, Trevi (PG) 06039, Italy*
*Tel: (0742) 78257, Fax: (0742) 381632*
*7 rooms, Double: €78–€101*
*2 apartments: €52–€104 daily*
*Minimum nights required: 3 in Jul & Aug*
*Open: all year, Credit cards: all major*
*Other languages: some English, French*
*Region: Umbria, Michelin Map: 563*
*karenbrown.com/italy/casagiulia.html*

On the northern shores of Lake Bracciano, 45 kilometers from Rome, is the small town of Trevignano where ex-producer and music director Gianni's home is located a short drive up from town, taking advantage of the high viewpoint over the lake and surrounding countryside. The simpatico host's true passion is cooking and entertaining and guests are rewarded each day with a superbly prepared full meal based on traditional recipes whose ingredients come from his own organic vegetable garden and accompanied by select wines. Gianni also shares his vast knowledge of Italian cuisine by organizing lessons in his well-equipped kitchen. The six bedrooms on the upper three floors vary in size, from the smaller children's rooms to the master bedroom with hydrojet tub, air conditioning, TV, stereo, fireplace and terrace with lovely lake views. True coziness and comfort is dedicated to the common areas, which include living rooms with fireplace and grand piano, veranda dining room, garden, and swimming pool. There is one small apartment for weekly stays with double bedroom and living area with kitchenette for two to four persons. Enjoy the area's historical villages and Viterbo's thermal spas. *Directions:* From Rome's ring highway GRA, take exit 5 for S.S.2 Cassia bis to km 35,100. Leave at the Trevignano exit and drive 11.3 km to Trevignano. Continue through town to km 12.680 and turn right on Via Olivetello before the IP gas station.

*CASA PLAZZI*
*Host: Gianni Plazzi family*
*Via Olivetello 23, Trevignano, Romano (RM) 0069, Italy*
*Tel: (06) 9997597, Cellphone: (335) 6756290*
*Fax: (06) 99910196*
*6 rooms, Double: €80–€134*
*1 apartment: €500–€700 weekly*
*Open: all year*
*Other languages: some English*
*Region: Lazio, Michelin Map: 563*
*karenbrown.com/italy/plazzi.html*

The Veneto region has so much to offer travelers in art, history, and culture, yet remains terribly weak when it comes to charming bed and breakfasts. This is mainly due to the very strict regulations particular to this region. The Ca'Masieri is a pleasant combination of both hotel and bed-and-breakfast-like accommodation in a country setting. The countryside property has been in the Zarantonello family for three generations and was transformed into a restaurant and inn after Signor Giovanni looked for a creative way to maintain the farm. He and his partner, Angelo, opened the restaurant first, creating an intimate ambiance within three stenciled dining rooms in the main villa. The restaurant gained considerable recognition and the next logical step was to offer a place to stay in the stone farmhouse right next door. These two buildings and the attached barn form a quadrangle, with a gated-in terraced swimming pool. The seven bedrooms are very comfortable with many amenities, though their modern decor contrasts with the country setting. The five new suites in the adjoining wing (former stables) are more in keeping with the general ambiance of the place. Signor Giovanni is also on Vicenza's tourism board and can suggest many itineraries in the area (villas of Palladio etc.). *Directions:* Exit from autostrada A4 at Montecchio and go towards Valdagno. After exactly 10 km enter the town of Trissino and follow signs for Masieri up to the Ca'Masieri.

*CA'MASIERI*
*Hosts: Giovanni Zarantonello & Angelo Vassena*
*Localita: Masieri*
*Trissino (VI) 36070, Italy*
*Tel: (0445) 490122, Fax: (0445) 490455*
*12 rooms, Double: €120–€200*
*Open: all year, Credit cards: all major*
*Other languages: good English*
*Region: Veneto, Michelin Map: 562*
*karenbrown.com/italy/camasieri.html*

When the Marti family from Rome came across the abandoned castle of Montegualandro 18 years ago, it was love at first sight—only pure passion could have driven them to tackle such an overwhelming project as the entire restoration of the property following original plans. A winding dirt road (1.5 kilometers) leads up to the gates of the walled 9th-century castle. As you enter into the courtyard, the main building and family residence lies to the left and immediately to the right is a cluster of stone dwellings, originally farmers' quarters, with small tower, stable, pottery kiln, dove house, and private chapel. There are four rustic guest apartments, cleverly incorporating all original architectural features. All different, each has a living area with fireplace, very basic kitchen facilities, and bathroom, and is furnished with country-style antiques. A walk up in the turreted walls gives a glimpse of the spectacular view out over olive groves to the lake. An internet point has been set up in the newly restored library. The Martis take special interest in guests' needs, providing a breakfast basket upon arrival, and can also suggest easy day trips. Cortona is just 10 kilometers away. *Directions:* Montegualandro is marked on most maps. Leave the A1-Perugia highway at Tuoro. Take the road 75 bis towards Cortona and Arezzo. After 3 km, at km sign 44,700, follow the signs up to the castle or call from town.

*CASTELLO DI MONTEGUALANDRO*
*Hosts: Franca & Claudio Marti*
*Via di Montegualandro 1*
*Tuoro Sul Trasimeno (PG) 06069, Italy*
*Tel & fax: (075) 8230267, Cellphone: (347) 2372070*
*4 apartments: €550–€660 weekly*
*Minimum nights required: 3*
*Open: all year*
*Other languages: good English*
*Region: Umbria, Michelin Map: 563*
*karenbrown.com/italy/castellodimontegualandro.html*

The city of Turin, at one time the capital of Italy under the Savoia monarchy, is one of the country's leading industrial cities (home of Fiat), but is also home to a wealth of cultural events, museums (the Egyptian museum has the largest collection in Europe), and important monuments. Once you get past the rather dreary outskirts, the historic center is filled with monumental squares, baroque architecture, medieval quarters, the Royal Palace, theaters, and art galleries. Natural hostess and interior decorator Maddalena Vitale, with her children all grown, found herself with a large centrally located apartment just right for a bed and breakfast. She happily receives international guests in her tastefully appointed home within three bedrooms, each with private bathroom (only one en suite). The apartment lends itself well to the enterprise since the guest wing is separate from the hostess' private quarters. Double bedrooms named for their color scheme (blue, green, and white), two with twin beds, are very personalized and individual as in a private home with family photos, antique furnishings, and paintings. Breakfast with homemade breads and cakes is served in the rooms. Maddalena is an excellent source of information on the city's current events, best restaurants, or day trips into the nearby Langhe wine country. A true home in the city. *Directions:* In the center of Turin, four blocks from the train station. (30 minutes from Turin airport.)

*LA MADDALENA*
*Host: Maddalena Vitale Marrone*
*Via San Secondo 31*
*Turin 10128, Italy*
*Cellphone: (333) 2469532, Fax: (011) 591267*
*3 rooms, Double: €145–€185*
*Open: all year*
*Other languages: good English, French*
*Region: Piedmont, Michelin Map: 561*
*karenbrown.com/italy/maddalena.html*

The area of Lazio north of Rome known as "Tuscia" is rich in Etruscan history, small medieval villages, nature reserves, and three picturesque lakes. It is the homeland of the illustrious and powerful Farnese family whose palazzos and fortresses still stand as monuments of their glorious past. In the heart of this fascinating area not far from the coast is the ancient walled town of Tuscania, completely restored after the dramatic earthquake in 1978. Perla and her Argentine husband José brought back to life one of the buildings right in town, opening its doors as a cozy bed and breakfast and Michelin-star restaurant. A small reception area leads on one side to a lounge and wine bar (over 200 labels) and a courtyard. On the other side you find the cheerful, luminous restaurant with checked drapes and tablecloths, antique armoire, still-life paintings, large windows looking out over the tiled rooftops, and ubiquitous gallo (rooster) motif. Here José works his magic, serving innovative creations using seasonal local produce. (A 10% discount is given to our readers on meals.) Upstairs each very comfortable and appealing carpeted bedroom has its own color scheme in matching floral wallpaper, drapery, and bedspread. They have all amenities including air conditioning and are spacious, with high ceilings and marble bathrooms. Gracious hostess Perla guarantees guests' comfort and assists them in arranging local itineraries. *Directions:* In the center of Tuscania, well marked.

*HOTEL AL GALLO*
*Hosts: Perla Blanzieri & José Pettiti*
*Via del Gallo 22*
*Tuscania (VT) 01017, Italy*
*Tel: (0761) 443388, Fax: (0761) 443628*
*13 rooms, Double: €88–€128*
*Restaurant closed Mon*
*Open: all year, Credit cards: all major*
*Other languages: good English*
*Region: Lazio, Michelin Map: 563*
*karenbrown.com/italy/algallo.html*

The Aiola opened its doors to guests six years ago when the Campellis restored the farmers' houses on the wine estate's vast property in Chianti. The family's villa with its ancient origins sits across the street from the guest quarters, almost completely hidden by enormous oak and cypress trees, where the bedrooms, one of which sleeps four persons, all have separate outside entrances. Original architectural features have been preserved and rooms are decorated with wrought-iron beds and antique or reproduction armoires. The vineyards come right up to the house and a wide, open view of the hills is offered to the other side. The barn next door includes common areas such as the breakfast room, where Federica's fresh-baked coffee cakes are served, and a living room. With Federica's mother, Signora Malagodi, being the President of the Wine Tourism Association, visits to the cellar and the villa, and wine tasting begin right here at the Aiola. Federica and Enrico aim to make each guest feel special, dedicating much time to suggesting itineraries with maps and making reservations at restaurants, museums, and local concerts. At 12 kilometers from Siena and an easy distance from the highlights of the region, the Aiola serves as an excellent touring base. Total silence reigns here, with only the buzz of cicadas breaking it. *Directions:* From Siena follow route 102 just past Vagliagli—the Aiola property (well marked) is on this same road.

*CASALI DELLA AIOLA*
*Hosts: Federica & Enrico Campelli*
*Vagliagli (SI) 53010, Italy*
*Tel: (0577) 322797, Fax: (0577) 322509*
*8 rooms, Double: €95–€120*
*Open: all year, Credit cards: all major*
*Other languages: good English*
*Region: Tuscany, Michelin Map: 563*
*karenbrown.com/italy/laaiola.html*

Varenna is a quaint little village sitting halfway up Lake Como's eastern edge. It is situated at the point where the ferryboats for cars cross over to the other side of the lake to Menaggio. In the main piazza lakeside is the generations-old family-run Olivedo hotel with its pale-yellow façade where Signora Laura welcomes her guests. Time seems to have stood still within its old-fashioned interior. The reception area and side bar are dressed with faded floral wallpaper, scattered antiques, and a large grandfather clock chiming the hour. Off to the other side of the reception area is a dining room/restaurant with simple frescoes, serving all meals. A curved stairway takes guests up to the bedrooms, all of which have air conditioning and lake views. These are decorated simply with grandmother's furniture and old prints. A few steps away is a lovely 18th century home, La Torretta, which houses five additional bedrooms. There is no need to worry about noise except on Saturday nights since traffic is not allowed in the piazza. Olivedo serves as a good, economical base from which to explore beautiful Lake Como including its many gardens (Villa Serbelloni, Melzi, and Carlotta). *Directions:* From the Como branch of the lake, head north on either side of lake and take the ferry over from either Bellagio or Menaggio.

❄ ⚓ 🛏 🏊 ☎ 🎣 🚶 🐎 P ⏸ 🚭 ⚓

*OLIVEDO*
*Host: Colombo family*
*Piazza Martiri 4*
*Varenna (LC) 23829, Italy*
*Tel & fax: (0341) 830115*
*19 rooms, Double: €100–€130*
*Per person half board: €75–€95*
*Closed: mid-Nov to mid-Dec*
*Other languages: good English*
*Region: Lombardy, Michelin Map: 561*
*karenbrown.com/italy/olivedo.html*

It is a pleasure to be able to include such a perfectly efficient, family-run hotel as the Due Fanali, located in a lovely square next to the 12th-century San Simeon church with its original Tintoretto painting. The hotel is housed in a 12th-century palazzo, once part of the church complex. The Feron family had the building lovingly restored seven years ago to include the sixteen bedrooms (some with smaller "French" double) on the top three floors. A small elevator has been added for the convenience of guests. Extra care has been taken in the selection of appropriate antiques for the guestrooms, reception area, and breakfast room. The soft ambiance is that of an elegant yet warm home, accentuated by lovely Oriental carpets and rich-cream draperies. Breakfast is taken either out in the "garden" in front of the hotel or up in the delightful third-floor veranda, under the open terrace, with its superb view over the square to the Grand Canal. As an alternative to the hotel, there are four independent apartments near San Marco Square, divinely decorated and including bedroom, living room with view, kitchenette, and bathroom with hydro-massage tub. Take all these esthetic elements accompanied by the exceptional hospitality offered by Signora Marina and her daughter, Stefania, and you have a true winner of a hotel. *Directions:* The hotel is a five-minute walk from the train station or you can take the No. 1 waterbus to the Riva di Biasio stop.

*HOTEL AI DUE FANALI*
*Host: Marina Feron family*
*Santa Croce 946, Venice 30135, Italy*
*Tel: (041) 718490, Fax: (041) 718344*
*16 rooms, Double: €93–€210*
*4 apartments: €180–€388 daily*
*Minimum nights required: 2*
*Open: all year, Credit cards: all major*
*Other languages: good English*
*Region: Veneto, Michelin Map: 562*
*karenbrown.com/italy/fanali.html*

Your attractive young host, Giuliano Dall'Agnola, managed a hotel on the Lido in Venice for ten years before deciding to open his own in an historic 5th-century building. The building needed total renovation, but Giuliano was wise in his choice of location—it's perfect—tucked onto a tiny side street just steps from Piazza San Marco. Don't be put off by the exterior: it is an unimpressive gray building with a nondescript door. The entry hall too is quite simple, with a check-in counter and a staircase leading to the upper floors. But here the surprise awaits: the rooms, decorated by Marcella, are amazingly attractive and offer great quality for such a well-priced hotel in the heart of Venice. All the walls are covered in fabric and enhanced by color-coordinated draperies and bedspreads, while Venetian-style furnishings including painted headboards and Murano glass chandeliers complete the appealing ambiance. The amenities too far outshine what one would expect from a budget hotel. The soundproof rooms are air-conditioned, have direct-dial phones, mini-bars, televisions, and well-equipped, modern bathrooms. All of the rooms are sweet, some with views overlooking a small square. What makes this intimate hotel so special is the care of its owners who pamper guests like friends in their home. *Directions:* San Zaccaria vaporetto stop on all vaporetto boat lines, including the Alilaguna boats from the airport. The hotel is just 50 meters from the stop.

*LOCANDA AL LEON*
*Hosts: Marcella & Giuliano Dall'Agnola*
*Castello, Campo St Filippo e Giacomo*
*Venice 30122, Italy*
*Tel: (041) 2770393, Fax: (041) 5210348*
*9 rooms, Double: €90–€210*
*Open: all year, Credit cards: MC, VS*
*Other languages: good English*
*Region: Veneto, Michelin Map: 562*
*karenbrown.com/italy/alleon.html*

With admirable determination and family pride, Alessandro and Debora took on the task of renovating and running this hotel property, which has been part of the family for three generations. They deserve great credit since they are more concerned with providing warm hospitality and attention to guests' needs than with keeping up with Venice's inflated hotel rates. The spacious and luminous reception area with white travertine floors is a welcome oasis amid the city's more cramped hotels, bustling squares, and crowded narrow streets. Although only a three-minute walk from the Guggenheim collection and Accademia, it has the feeling of being away from the mainstream traffic. The front rooms have water views (higher rate) and all rooms maintain an original flavor with paintings and personal family objects, parquet floors and matching wood furniture, blue-colored armchairs, new bathrooms, and air conditioning. Four bedrooms have private terraces for a higher rate and other guests enjoy the delightful rooftop terrace. A full buffet breakfast and bar service and light meals at La Piscina are offered either in the breakfast room with country accents or out on the large front dock terrace where you can watch the boats going by. Reserve well in advance. Comfortable suites and apartments are available in a residential quarter just across the bridge. *Directions:* Take the No. 51 waterbus to Zattere, then follow the quay to the right to the hotel terrace.

PENSIONE LA CALCINA
*Hosts: Debora & Alessandro Szemere*
*Dorsoduro 780*
*Venice 30123, Italy*
*Tel: (041) 5206466, Fax: (041) 5227045*
*32 rooms, Double: €130–€189*
*4 apartments (or suite): €161–€239 daily*
*Open: all year, Credit cards: all major*
*Other languages: German*
*Region: Veneto, Michelin Map: 562*
*karenbrown.com/italy/pensionelacalcina.html*

The newly renovated Locanda San Barnaba stands out among the many choices of three-star establishments in Venice. The first outstanding feature is its location in a quiet neighborhood just a half-block walk from the vaporetto stop Ca'Rezzonico on the opposite side of the Grand Canal from St. Mark's (not something to be overlooked when lugging baggage through narrow streets and over bridges in Venice!). The intimate hotel in its 16th-century context has the feeling of the private home that it once was—it belonged to the grandfather of hostess Silvia—with each of its 13 guestrooms retaining its individual character. The first floor upstairs boasts a large frescoed former ballroom with stained-glass windows, very different in style from the air-conditioned bedrooms, which remain rather basic and are appointed in either pink, red, or blue hues with antique furnishings. The superior double rooms, at a slightly higher rate, have the added touch of a frescoed ceiling. A nice buffet breakfast is served in the beamed dining room or in the small walled-in courtyard garden just off the reception area, a rarity in Venice. Silvia and her amiable staff are always on hand to assist travelers with any needs. *Directions:* Take waterbus No. 1 to the Ca'Rezzonico stop. Directly in front is the Calle del Traghetto where the hotel is located on the left-hand side.

*LOCANDA SAN BARNABA*
*Host: Silvia Okolicsanyi*
*Calle del Traghetto 2785-2786, Dorsoduro*
*Venice 30124, Italy*
*Tel: (041) 2411233, Fax: (041) 2413812*
*13 rooms, Double: €170–€220*
*Open: all year, Credit cards: all major*
*Other languages: good English*
*Region: Veneto, Michelin Map: 562*
*karenbrown.com/italy/barnaba.html*

With just eleven rooms, including three junior suites, paired up throughout the six-floor building (luckily with an elevator), the intimate Santo Stefano was actually the watchtower to an ancient convent. The compact hotel, most recently a private home, is right in the middle of one of Venice's largest squares, leading to St. Mark's on one side and to the bridge for the Accademia on the other. Being close to the busy center, you can observe the Venetians going about their daily business. The hotel is owned by brothers Roberto and Marcello of the Hotel Celio in Rome, who have added fresh decorating touches to bedrooms and reception area. Just beyond is a miniature breakfast room, looking out to an ancient well, for days when the weather does not permit eating out in the front piazza. Touches of elegance in Venetian style follow through in rooms appointed with Barovier & Toso chandeliers, coordinated draperies and bedspreads, and painted antiques with a floral motif. Many amenities are offered including air conditioning. Renovation of all bathrooms included the installation of Jacuzzi and steam baths. Roberto is an experienced and amiable host with a definite aim to please guests. *Directions:* Take waterbus No. 82 to the San Samuele stop or No. 1 to the Accademia stop. Pass over the bridge and go straight into Campo Santo Stefano.

*HOTEL SANTO STEFANO*
*Host: Roberto Quatrini*
*San Marco 2957*
*Venice 30124, Italy*
*Tel: (041) 5200166, Fax: (041) 5224460*
*11 rooms, Double: €170–€350*
*Open: all year, Credit cards: all major*
*Other languages: good English*
*Region: Veneto, Michelin Map: 562*
*karenbrown.com/italy/hotelsantostefano.html*

Just 20 kilometers from the Swiss border, halfway along the shore of Lake Maggiore, at the point where the road curves back down to Verbania, is a farmhouse situated high above the lake (700 meters). It commands a 360-degree view that includes the Alps and Lakes Mergozzo, Monate, Varese, and Maggiore with its miniature Borromeo Islands (accessible by ferryboat). A 5-kilometer long road with many hairpin turns winds its way up to the turn-of-the-last-century house with tower. Energetic and friendly hostess Iside Minotti and her family run the inn and rustic restaurant, which is a busy spot and can get noisy in the summer when locals come up to dine or celebrate an event and take advantage of the cooler air and the spectacular view. Menu ingredients come directly from the vegetable garden and orchards to the kitchen, where sumptuous local specialties are prepared. The 25-acre farm includes riding stables, and the bed and breakfast can also arrange helicopter rides from the property for a breathtakingly scenic tour over the lake, boat excursions, and mountain bike rentals. Nine very basic no-frills bedrooms come in various combinations of twins, triples, and quads, each with a snug shower room. *Directions:* On the outskirts of Verbania, at a major road junction with traffic lights (Pallanza), take Via Azari (also signposted Trobaso) left for 1 km. Go sharp left at the signpost for Monterosso and up 5 km of winding road (I counted 43 hairpin bends).

*IL MONTEROSSO*
*Host: Iside Minotti*
*Cima Monterosso-C.P. 13, Verbania (NO) 28922, Italy*
*Tel: (0323) 556510, Cellphone: (335) 6442859*
*Fax: (0323) 519706*
*15 rooms, Double: €56–€65*
*apartments:€300–€500, minimum 3 nights*
*Open: all year, Credit cards: MC, VS*
*Other languages: some English, French*
*Region: Piedmont, Michelin Map: 561*
*karenbrown.com/italy/ilmonterosso.html*

Delightful Verona, with its Romeo and Juliet theme, is decidedly one of Italy's more romantic historic cities and the Domus Nova B&B well matches this magical aura. The distinguished 13th-century gray-white palazzo, renovated in the 16th century, fills one entire side of the ancient square where a statue honoring Dante stands. Guests pass through the enormous center archway, enter by a small side door, and take a little elevator to the top floor where three double bedrooms are found within two apartments. As with a private apartment, you use your own key to enter the attractive drawing room, off which two of the bedrooms are situated and where an elegant breakfast is served complete with silver service and porcelain china. The warm decor of these rooms, all looking out over the splendid square and distant hills through large windows, radiates charm and impeccable taste. Soft, muted tones and stenciled patterns on walls have been taken directly from themes found in the surrounding medieval and baroque buildings. The third room, a double twin, has a balcony looking onto the lively Piazza Erba and its daily market. The spacious rooms are appointed with antiques, Oriental carpets, and fine linens and have lovely marble bathrooms. All these exquisite touches combined with gracious hospitality offer guests an intimate and memorable stay. *Directions:* The Piazza dei Signori is next to Verona's main square, the Piazza Erba, in the heart of the city.

❄ ☕ ⛳ CREDIT ☎ ♨ 🚶 🏃 🐎 ♉ P 🎿 🚭 🖼 ⛵ 🍇

*DOMUS NOVA B&B*
*Host: Giovanni Roberti*
*Piazza dei Signori 18, Verona 37121, Italy*
*Tel: (045) 8015245, Fax: (045) 8043459*
*3 rooms, Double: €220–€250*
*apartment €350–€385*
*Minimum nights required: 2, 4 in apartment*
*Open: all year, Credit cards: all major*
*Other languages: good English*
*Region: Veneto, Michelin Map: 562*
*karenbrown.com/italy/domusnova.html*

For years Andrea and Silvia have literally opened their entire home to guests, welcoming and re-welcoming "friends of La Volpaia," their bed and breakfast. International guests gather together in the evenings out on the patio or in the converted barn for one of Silvia's delightful meals based on fresh vegetables and meats enhanced with their own extra-virgin olive oil. Conversation is never lacking with meals accompanied by La Volpaia's own Chianti (all beverages are included in the half-board rate). Andrea, a native Roman architect and sculptor, bought the wine estate with its 16th-century farmhouse 19 years ago and his pieces in olive wood are displayed in and about the property. The five cozy bedrooms are appointed with antiques, as is the large living room with fireplace. Beyond the patio where meals are served is the spectacular swimming pool with its heavenly views of what can only be described as a truly classic Tuscan landscape. Horses, personally trained by the hosts, are available for excursions into the surrounding countryside (experienced riders only). Guests are made to feel immediately right at home in this informal setting and so it is no wonder that many become "regulars" to this idyllic spot so close to the highlights of Tuscany. *Directions:* From the town of Vico d'Elsa follow Via della Villa (on the right) for 2 km, turning left at the wooden signpost for La Volpaia.

*LA VOLPAIA*
*Hosts: Silvia & Andrea Taliaco*
*Strada di Vico 5-9, Vico d'Elsa (FI) 50050, Italy*
*Tel: (055) 8073063, Cellphone: (368) 248287*
*Fax: (055) 8073170*
*5 rooms, Double: €220\**
*\*Includes breakfast & dinner*
*Minimum nights required: 3*
*Open: all year, Other languages: good English*
*Region: Tuscany, Michelin Map: 563*
*karenbrown.com/italy/lavolpaia.html*

Situated on Monte Faito between the Amalfi coast and Sorrento, Villa Giusso, a unique bed and breakfast, was a 15th-century monastery for cloistered monks. A long, very narrow road takes you up to the isolated, stone-walled property whose entrance is marked by an arched gateway with watchtower leading into a park. From there you have an enthralling view over Sorrento, the gulf, and Naples. The monastery itself is surrounded by a high stone wall within which is found a grass courtyard and ancient well still in use. The Giusso family has owned this beloved property for the past 200 years and siblings Onorina, Giovanna, Micaela, and Tullio's strong intention is to continue the restoration process while preserving its monastic features. A long corridor leads to a suite with two bedrooms and a bathroom and three double bedrooms, appointed with worn period furniture and huge paintings. Breakfast with local fresh ricotta, figs in season, and homemade cakes is served in the original kitchen completely tiled with 17th-century Vietri ceramics. Though not for everyone, Villa Giusso is fascinating and offers the visitor a unique slice of Italian history. Almost like staying in a museum. *Directions:* Exit at Castellammare from the A3, following signs for Sorrento. Drive to Seiano and just after Moon Valley Hotel take a left at the sign for Monte Faito. Drive to the Arola sign (4.6 km) and go first right up the narrow dirt road to the monastery.

*VILLA GIUSSO*
*Host: Giusso Rispoli family*
*Localita: Arola, Via Camaldoli 51*
*Vico Equense (NA) 80069, Italy*
*Tel: (081) 8024392 or 403797, Fax: (081) 403797*
*5 rooms, Double: €85–€105*
*Minimum nights required: 2*
*Open: Apr to Oct 30*
*Other languages: good English*
*Region: Campania, Michelin Map: 564*
*karenbrown.com/italy/giusso.html*

## Villa Verucchio     Tenuta Amalia/Agriturismo Le Case Rosse     Maps: 5, 6, 8

Villa Verucchio is a small commercial area just inland from the famous beaches of Rimini, the summer playground of young Italians attracted by its nightlife and budget rates. The Tenuta Amalia is a vast property owned by the Savazzi family, divided up into several different businesses, each run individually. Case Rosse is the red farmhouse transformed into a pleasant little bed and breakfast and there are also three different restaurants, vineyards, and a 27-hole golf course created around the family's 18th-century villa. Although it is a bit confusing at first, the bed and breakfast is right on the road leading to the golf club entrance. Lucia Gatei welcomes guests to the rustic farmhouse, which offers four double bedrooms upstairs and two on the ground floor. Each is appointed individually with country antiques and yellow bedspreads. A separate three-bedroom house nearby offers accommodation for six persons. Breakfast is served either out on the covered porch or in the beamed breakfast room overlooking a small garden and there is a cozy living room with large stone fireplace. From here you have easy access to the beautiful countryside bordering the Marches with such highlights as the independent state of San Marino, San Leo, Santarcangelo, and Urbino. *Directions:* From Rimini take the S.S.258 for 12 km to Villa Verucchio and watch for a sign on the right to the Amalia.

*TENUTA AMALIA/AGRITURISMO LE CASE ROSSE*
*Host: Lucia Gatei*
*Via Tenuta Amalia 141*
*Villa Verucchio (RN) 47040, Italy*
*Tel: (0541) 678123, Fax: (0541) 678876*
*6 rooms, Double: €65–€75*
*1 house: €500–€650 weekly*
*Open: all year, Credit cards: all major*
*Other languages: very little English*
*Region: Emilia-Romagna, Michelin Map: 562*
*karenbrown.com/italy/amalia.html*

Viterbo, along with the surrounding area called Tuscia, is rich in Etruscan history and offers a variety of attractions including ancient villages, thermal baths, and small lakes, all within easy reach of Rome. Cordial hostess Giovanna offers guest accommodation within three rooms in a private section of the family's large 14th-century home. This was originally a retreat for the monks of the nearby monastery, which lends its name to the street where this bed and breakfast is located: Santa Maria di Gradi. Once a countryside estate, Citerno is now surrounded by the city and neighboring properties, though it does maintain a large front garden. The well-decorated wallpapered rooms have antique furnishings, wood floors, and new bathrooms, with one room having an adjoining room for two extra persons. These rooms have an independent entrance, which leads directly into the sitting/breakfast room divided by a large brick arch. Giovanna also has a delightful restaurant, Il Richiastro, right in the medieval section of Viterbo, which features old recipes from other eras, serving homemade pastas and hearty soups in a casual setting. (Open from Friday to Sunday lunch only and closed in July and August.) *Directions:* On the west side of the ancient walls encircling the city of Viterbo is the Porta Romana. Via S. Maria di Gradi begins at this gate, leading to the city heading directly east. After .5 km turn into the driveway at number 70.

*CITERNO*
*Host: Giovanna Scappucci*
*Via S. Maria di Gradi 70*
*Viterbo 01100, Italy*
*Tel: (0761) 220500, Cellphone: (348) 4730458*
*Fax: (0761) 290149*
*3 rooms, Double: €62–€72*
*Restaurant closed Jul to Sep*
*Open: all year, Other languages: some English*
*Region: Lazio, Michelin Map: 563*
*karenbrown.com/italy/citerno.html*

Ninni Bacchi has done wonders in transforming her family's 300-acre tobacco and grain farm (just on the outskirts of the city) into a very comfortable bed and breakfast in an area that was once the heart of the Etruscan civilization. The Rinaldone is run more like a hotel than a bed and breakfast—arriving guests are warmly received in the luminous, open living room furnished with antiques surrounding a grand fireplace. On hand for guests at reception is cordial manager Sida. Downstairs is the large, arcaded restaurant dating back to the 15th century, where guests can enjoy the typical cuisine of the Lazio region or dine outdoors by the pool. The five bedrooms off the courtyard in the main house have the most character with architectural features intact, while the other five rooms and ten suites are lined up in two cottage-like wings, and are more spacious and modern in decor. A nice job has been done with the landscaping, pleasingly distracting the eye from the rather bland, flat countryside and encroaching commercial area hereabouts. Tennis, biking, and horse riding, plus the nearby thermal spa are some of the activities available as well as visits to ancient Viterbo and the gardens of Villa Lanti. Orvieto is 38 km away. *Directions:* From Rome (120 km away) follow signs for Viterbo. Take the Cassia road north of Viterbo for 3 km toward Montefiascone, turning right at the Rinaldone sign.

*COUNTRY HOTEL RINALDONE*
*Host: Ninni Bacchi*
*Strada Rinaldone, 9-S.S. Cassia km 86*
*Viterbo 01100, Italy*
*Tel: (0761) 352137, Fax: (0761) 353116*
*20 rooms, Double: €85–€115\**
*\*Breakfast not included*
*Minimum nights required: 2, Open: Apr to Dec*
*Credit cards: MC, VS, Other languages: some English*
*Region: Lazio, Michelin Map: 563*
*karenbrown.com/italy/residencerinaldone.html*

The northern part of the Lazio region holds many intriguing treasures to explore. Besides being less than an hour from Rome, it is the center of Etruscan history, with lakes, nearby seaside, thermal baths, and lovely gardens. Just down the street from the delightful Renaissance gardens of Villa Lante in Bagnaia is the gracious Villa Farinella, a very pleasant bed and breakfast within the 18th-century home of Maurizio and his family. Rita, his mother, lives in a restored farmhouse on the property and has passed her grandfather's ancient home down to her son. In order to revive the home to its original splendor, the bed and breakfast solution was a perfect one. The first floor is entirely dedicated to guests, with four cozy bedrooms entering into one of two spacious living/dining rooms appointed with original antiques and elegant chandeliers. Each quaint bedroom with new bathroom has its own floral theme, which is followed through in color scheme, wallpaper, bedspreads, and curtains. One particularly large room has frescoed vaulted ceilings. On the ground floor, for longer stays, a two-bedroom apartment with kitchen opens out to the garden. You will be delighted with the warm hospitality, historic surroundings, and very reasonable rate. *Directions:* From Viterbo drive towards Bagnaia (directly east) on Viale Trieste to the suburb of La Quercia. Just after the AGIP station turn left on Via Capodistria past houses to the end of the lane.

*VILLA FARINELLA*
*Hosts: Maurizio Makovec & family*
*Localita: La Quercia, Via Capodistria 14*
*Viterbo 01100, Italy*
*Tel & fax: (0761) 304784, Cellphone: (339) 3655617*
*4 rooms, Double: €70–€85*
*1 apartment: €500 weekly*
*Minimum nights required: 2, Open: all year*
*Other languages: French, good English*
*Region: Lazio, Michelin Map: 563*
*karenbrown.com/italy/farinella.html*

Since agritourism properties are practically nonexistent right along Lake Garda, it is nice to find a variety of alternatives in the scenic countryside a short distance away from its southern tip. Luigi and Emilia thoroughly enjoy opening up their home for guests and actively participate in creating local itineraries and even accompanying guests to the many artistic, cultural, and natural sights of the area. Luigi has a passion for outdoor sports such as cycling and canoeing down the Mincio river. The driveway leads to three colorful houses in a row overlooking the swimming pool and surrounding lawn to the front and the fields to the back. The farm produces excellent wine, cheese, honey, and salami. The 200-year-old farmhouse has been completely renovated and has six air-conditioned guestrooms (two are studio spaces with kitchenette) on the upper floors accessed by an iron staircase. They are very clean and new, with reproduction country furniture and some with beamed ceilings. Downstairs in the brick-vaulted dining room, a buffet breakfast is served as well as Emilia's homemade dinners. *Directions:* From the A22 autostrada exit at Mantova Nord and drive towards Brescia, turning off right on SS236 for Volta Mantovana. From the center of town there are signs leading to the Corte Onida just on the outskirts.

*CORTE ONIDA*
*Hosts: Luigi & Emilia Crotti family*
*Volta Mantovana (MN ) 46049, Italy*
*Tel & fax: (0376) 838137*
*6 rooms, Double: €60–€90*
*Minimum nights required: 2*
*Closed: Jan*
*Other languages: good English*
*Region: Lombardy, Michelin Map: 561*
*karenbrown.com/italy/onida.html*

# Index

A

Abano Terme
   Ciriani (Casa), 152
Abbazia di Monte Oliveto Maggiore, 86
Abbey of Monte Cassino, 130
Abbey Sant'Antimo, 85
Abri (L'), Saint Pierre, 345
Abruzzo, 30
Accommodation, 5
   Apartments, 6
   Rooms, 5
Acquaviva (Villa), Montemerano, 280
Agnata (L'), Tempio Pausania, 389
Agnolo (L'), Montepulciano, 282
Agrigento, 144, 145
Agrisalotto, Santa Caterina di Cortona, 361
Agritourism (Agriturismo), 1
Agritourism Associations, 3
Ai Due Fanali (Hotel), Venice, 402
Airfare, 18
Al Gallo (Hotel), Tuscania, 399
Al Leon (Locanda), Venice, 403
Alba
   Cascina Reine (Villa La Meridiana), 153
Albergo al Vecchio Convento, Portico di Romagna, 316
Albergo Sansevero Degas, Naples, 286
Alberobello, 136
Alcala, Misterbianco, 267
Alghero
   Porticciolo, 154
Alla Corte degli Angeli, Lucca, 256
Alpe di Siusi, 105
Alpina (Villa), Cortina d'Ampezzo, 210
Alzano Lombardo
   Cascina Grumello, 155
Amalfi, 132
Amalfi Coast, 134

Amalfi Drive, 132
   Emerald Grotto, 134
Antella–Florence
   Il Colle (Villa), 156
Antica Casa dei Rassicurati, Montecarlo–Lucca, 271
Antica Dimora, Florence, 226
Antica Fattoria del Colle, Deruta, 216
Antica Torre, Salsomaggiore Terme, 347
Anzio, 130
Aosta Valley, 30
Aprile (Hotel), Florence, 227
Apulia, 31, 135
Aquila Nera (Schwarzer Adler), 376
Arezzo, 91
Argenina (Borgo), Argenina–Gaiole in Chianti, 157
Argenina–Gaiole in Chianti
   Argenina (Borgo), 157
Asolo, 103
Assisi, 72, 90, 93, 94
   Malvarina, 158
   Rocca Medioevale, 95
   Santa Chiara, 94
   St. Francis's Basilica, 94
Assisi, Tordibetto di
   Podere La Fornace, 159
Aureli (Villa), Castel del Piano Umbro, 199
Axel Munthe, 69
Azienda Agricola Ricci Curbastro, Capriolo, 196

B

Bad Dreikirchen, Barbian, 168
Badia a Passignano Abbey, 74
Bagattino (Il), Ferrara, 224
Baglio Fontana, Buseto Palizzolo, 181
Baglio Fontanasalsa, Fontanasalsa, 238
Baglio Spano, Petrosino, 304
Bagno Vignoni, 85
Bagnone
   Mimosa (Villa), 160

Bagnorégio, 98
Baita Fraina, Cortina d'Ampezzo, 211
Bambin (Casa), La Morra, 249
Banks, 19
Barbarano Vicentino
  Castello (Il), 162
Barbaresco
  Cascina delle Rose, 163
Barberino Val d'Elsa, 79
  Casa Sola (Fattoria), 164
  Paretaio (Il), 165
  Relais Mulino dell'Argenna, 166
  Spinosa (La), 167
Barbian
  Bad Dreikirchen, 168
Barolo
  Gioco dell'Oca (Il), 169
Baschi
  Pomurlo Vecchio, 170
Basilicata, 31
Bassano del Grappa, 103
Belfiore, Ostellato, 297
Bellagio, 108
Bellaria (Villa), Campagnatico, 186
Belluno, 104
Benozzo Gozzoli, 96
Bergamo, 107
  Agnello d'Oro, 108
  Church of St. Mary Major, 107
  Cita Alta, 107
  Colleoni Chapel, 107
  Piazza Vecchia, 107
Besate
  Cascina Caremma, 171
Bettolle–Sinalunga
  La Bandita (Locanda), 172
Bettona
  Torre Burchio, 173
Bevagna, 95
Biancarda (La), Massignano, 262
Bibbona
  Podere Le Mezzelune, 174

Bologna
  Orologio (Hotel), 175
Bolsena
  Riserva Montebello (La), 176
Bolsinina (Casa), Monteroni d'Arbia, 284
Borgo San Lorenzo
  Monsignor della Casa, 177
Borromean Islands,, 111
Boscarecce (Le), Castelfiorentino, 200
Botticelli (Hotel), Florence, 228
Breuil Cervinia, 113
Brindisi, 138
Brisighella
  Palazzo (Il), 178
Brunello, 73, 82
Brunello di Montalcino, 86
Bucine
  Iesolana (Borgo), 179
Buonconvento
  Ripolina (La), 180
Buseto Palizzolo
  Baglio Fontana, 181

C
Ca'delle Rondini, Maerne, 259
Ca'La Somara, San Pantaleo, 359
Ca'Masieri, Trissino, 396
Cadenabbia
  Villa Carlotta, 109
Cala di Volpe
  Piccolo Golf (Il), 182
Calangianus
  Li Licci, 183
Caldana
  Montebelli, 184
Calvi dell'Umbria
  Casale San Martino, 185
Camin Hotel Colmegna, Luino, 257
Campagnatico
  Bellaria (Villa), 186
Campana (La), Montefiore dell'Aso, 274
Campania, 32

Camporeale
    Masseria Pernice, 187
Candelo
    Tenuta La Mandria, 188
Canelli
    Luna e i Falo' (La), 189
Canonica a Cerreto
    Canonica a Cerreto, 190
Capalbio
    Ghiaccio Bosco, 191
Capri, 67
    Krupp (Villa), 192
    Minerva (La), 193
    Sightseeing
        Anacapri, 69
        Blue Grotto, 67
        Cannone Belvedere, 69
        Marina Grande, 67
        Marina Piccola, 68
        Villa Jovis, 68
        Villa San Michel, 69
    Vuotto (Villa), 194
Caprino Bergamasco
    Ombria, 195
Capriolo
    Azienda Agricola Ricci Curbastro, 196
Car Rental, 19
Casa Sola (Fattoria), Barberino Val d'Elsa, 164
Casacce (Le), Seggiano, 371
Casagliana
    Monti Tundu, 197
Casale del Cotone (Il), San Gimignano, 351
Casale Il Caggio, Civitella in Val di Chiana, 209
Casale San Martino, Calvi dell'Umbria, 185
Casali della Aiola, Vagliagli, 400
Casalone (Il), Orbetello Scalo, 289
Casanova di Pescille, San Gimignano, 352
Cascina Caremma, Besate, 171
Cascina Cichetti, Murazzano, 285
Cascina delle Rose, Barbaresco, 163
Cascina Grumello, Alzano Lombardo, 155

Cascina Reine (Villa La Meridiana), Alba, 153
Casella (La), Ficulle, 225
Casolare di Libbiano, San Gimignano, 353
Casperia
    Torretta (La), 198
Cassino, 129
Castel del Monte, 137
Castel del Piano Umbro
    Aureli (Villa), 199
Castelfiorentino
    Boscarecce (Le), 200
Castelfranco Emilia
    Gaidello (Villa), 201
Castellabate
    Mola (La), 202
Castellina, 79
Castello (Il), Barbarano Vicentino, 162
Castello d'Albola, 80
Castello di Brolio, 79
Castello di Meleto, 81
Castello di Poreta (Il), Poreta–Spoleto, 315
Castello di Vezio
    Lake Como, 110
Castello di Volpaia, 81
Castelnuovo Berardenga, 79
Castelnuovo dell'Abate, 85
Castelraimondo
    Giardino degli Ulivi (Il), 203
Castelrotto–Osvaldo
    Tschotscherhof, 204
Castenaso
    Loghetto (Il), 205
Castiglione d'Orcia
    Ripa d'Orcia (Castello di), 206
Cefala (Villa), Santa Flavia, 362
Cefalù, 149
Champoluc
    Lo Miete Viei, 207
Chianti Classico, 73, 75, 78, 82
Chianti Wine, 79
Chiocciola (La), Orte, 291
Chiusa (La), Montefollonico, 87

Ciastel Colz, La Villa, 250
Ciconia (Villa), Orvieto, 294
Cinque Terre., 120
Ciriani (Casa), Abano Terme, 152
Citerno, Viterbo, 412
Citta della Pieve
    Madonna delle Grazie, 208
Civita di Bagnorégio, 98
Civitella in Val di Chiana
    Casale Il Caggio, 209
Clodia (Villa), Saturnia, 367
Cogne, 114
Collepino, 95
Colonnata, 120
Como, 110
Corniglia., 121
Corte Onida, Volta Mantovana, 415
Corte San Girolamo, Mantova, 260
Cortina d'Ampezzo, 105
    Alpina (Villa), 210
    Baita Fraina, 211
    Church of SS Filippo e Giacomo, 105
    Ice-Skating Stadium, 105
    Meublè Oasi, 212
    Museo Ciasa de Ra Regoles, 105
Cortona, 92
    Elena (Borgo), 213
    Il Melone (Borgo), 214
    Piazza della Repubblica, 92
    Stoppiacce, 215
Corvara, 105
Cosenza (Casa), Positano, 318
Country Hotel Rinaldone, Viterbo, 413
Covone (Il), Ponte Pattoli, 314
Credit Cards, 7
Crete, 87
Crocetta (La), San Casciano dei Bagni, 348
Currency, 19

D
dei Lecci (Villa), Siena, 373
delle Arti (Hotel), Florence, 229
Delros (Villa), Rome, 334
Deruta
    Antica Fattoria del Colle, 216
Desenzano, 45
di Petrognano (Fattoria), Pomino, 312
di Vibio (Fattoria), Montecastello di Vibio, 273
Diana (Hotel), Ravenna, 331
Dicomano
    Frascole-Il Cavaliere, 217
Digon (Hotel), Ortisei, 292
Doccia (La), Pelago, 303
Dogliani
    Foresteria dei Poderi, 218
Dolo
    Goetzen (Villa), 219
Dolomites, 104
Domenico di Bartolo, 77
Domus Nova B&B, Verona, 408
Driving
    Distances, 20
    Gasoline Prices, 20
    Maps, 21
    Road Signs, 21
    Roads, 21
    Tolls, 21
Due Torri (Hotel), Rome, 335

E
Eastern Umbria, 91
Ecureuils (Les), Saint Pierre, 346
Egadi Isles, 147
Elena (Borgo), Cortona, 213
Emilia Romagna, 33
English, 8
ENIT, 23
Entreves-Courmayeur
    Grange (La), 220

Erice, 146, 147
Euro, 19
Exploring the Wonders of Sicily, 140

**F**

Fagiolari, Panzano in Chianti, 302
Farinella (Villa), Viterbo, 414
Farm Names, Regional, 14
Fasano
    Masseria Marzalossa, 221
Fattoressa (La), Galluzzo-Florence, 244
Fattoria dei Barbi, 86
Felino-San Michele Tiorre
    Torre, 222
Feltre, 104
Fenice (La), Positano, 319
Ferdy, Scalvino–Lenna, 368
Feriolo–Borgo S. Lorenzo
    Palmira (Casa), 223
Ferrara
    Bagattino (Il), 224
Ficulle
    Casella (La), 225
Finding Your Bed and Breakfast, 8
    Directions, 8
    Transfers into Cities, 28
Fisherman's Island, 111
Florence, 51, 73, 78
    Antica Dimora, 226
    Aprile (Hotel), 227
    Botticelli (Hotel), 228
    delle Arti (Hotel), 229
    Hermitage (Hotel), 230
    In Piazza della Signoria, 231
    Orto de'Medici (Hotel), 232
    Palazzo Ruspoli, 233
    Poggio San Felice (Villa), 234
    Residenze Johlea (Le), 235
    Sightseeing
        Baptistry, 52
        Duomo, 52
        Galleria dell'Accademia, 51

Florence (continued)
    Sightseeing
        Michelangelo's David, 51
        Palazzo Vecchio, 52
        Piazza della Signoria, 52
        Pitti Palace, 53
        Ponte Vecchio, 52
        Uffizi Museum, 53
    Silla (Hotel), 236
    Torricella (La), 237
Fontana (Hotel), Rome, 336
Fontanasalsa
    Baglio Fontanasalsa, 238
Fontanella Borghese (Hotel), Rome, 337
Fontanelle (Le), Montemerano, 281
Fonte (La), San Gimignano, 354
Fonte de Medici, Montefiridolfi, 275
Food, 7
    Meals Offered, 7
Forcoli
    Torrino (Il), 239
Foresteria dei Poderi, Dogliani, 218
Franchini, Nicole, 12
Frascole-Il Cavaliere, Dicomano, 217
Friuli Venezia Giulia, 33

**G**

Gagliole
    San Rocco (Locanda), 240
Gaidello (Villa), Castelfranco Emilia, 201
Gaiole, 79, 80, 81
Gaiole in Chianti
    Meleto (Castello di), 241
    Tornano (Castello di), 242
Galatone
    Masseria Lo Prieno, 243
Galluzzo-Florence
    Fattoressa (La), 244
Gangi
    Raino (Villa), 245
Garda, Lazise, 107

Gardone Riviera–Lake Garda
   Vittoriale, 106
Gargan, Levada di Piombino Dese, 251
Gargnano, 106
Ghiaccio Bosco, Capalbio, 191
Giandriale, Tavarone di Maissana, 386
Giardino degli Ulivi (Il), Castelraimondo, 203
Gioco dell'Oca (Il), Barolo, 169
Giulia (Casa), Trevi, 394
Giusso (Villa), Vico Equense, 410
Gnocchi (Villa), Santa Margherita, 363
Godiolo, Modanella–Serre di Rapolano, 268
Goetzen (Villa), Dolo, 219
Grand Paradis National Park, 114
Grange (La), Entreves-Courmayeur, 220
Grazia, Orbetello Scalo, 290
Great Dolomite Road, 105
Greve, 79
Greve in Chianti
   Mezzuola (Casa), 246
Grotta di Addaura, 149
Grotte di Castellana, 137
Grotte di Castro
   S. Cristina (Castello di), 247
Gruppo Sella, 105
Gubbio, 93
Guido Monaco, 91
Gulf of Policastro, 134

H

Handicapped Facilities, 6
Herculaneum, 131
Hermitage (Hotel), Florence, 230
Hidden Treasures of Italy, 12
Highlights by Train & Boat–or Car, 42
Highlights of Southern Italy, 128
Holidays, 22

I

Icons, 10
Iesolana (Borgo), Bucine, 179
Il Burchiello, 50

Il Colle (Villa), Antella–Florence, 156
Il Melone (Borgo), Cortona, 214
In Piazza della Signoria, Florence, 231
Information on Italy, 23
Introd
   Lo Triolet, 248
Introduction
   About Bed & Breakfasts, 4
   About Italy, 18
   About Itineraries, 16
   General Information on Agritourism, 1
Isola Bella, 111
Isola dei Pescatori, 111
Isola Madre, 111
Italian Government Travel Offices, 23
Italy: Charming Bed & Breakfasts, 17
Itineraries
   Exploring the Wonders of Sicily, 140
   Highlights by Train & Boat–or Car, 42
   Highlights of Southern Italy, 128
   Mountain & Lake Adventures, 100
   Romantic Tuscany, 72
   Rome to Milan via the Italian Riviera, 116
   The Haunting Beauty of Umbria, 90
Itinerary Maps
   Exploring the Wonders of Sicily, 139
   Italian Highlights by Train & Boat–or Car, 41
   Mountain & Lake Adventures, 99
   Romantic Tuscany, 71
   Rome to Milan via the Italian Riviera, 115

K

Krupp (Villa), Capri, 192

L

La Bandita (Locanda), Bettolle–Sinalunga, 172
La Loggia (Fattoria), Montefiridolfi, 276
La Morra
   Bambin (Casa), 249
La Spezia, 120
La Tartana (Villa), Positano, 320

La Villa
    Ciastel Colz, 250
Lake Como, 108
Lake Garda, 45
Lake Lecco, 108
Lake Maggiore, 111
Lake Orta, 112
Lake Toblino, 106
Lake Trasimeno, 92
    Castiglione del Lago, 92
Languages Spoken, 8
Lazio, 34
Length of Stay, 10
Leno
    Villa del Balbianello, 109
Levada di Piombino Dese
    Gargan, 251
Levanzo, 147
Li Licci, Calangianus, 183
Liguria, 34
Limoneto, Syracuse, 382
Lisciano Niccone
    San Martino (Casa), 252
Lo Miete Viei, Champoluc, 207
Lo Triolet, Introd, 248
Locanda (La), Radda in Chianti, 324
Locanda del Castello, San Giovanni d'Asso, 357
Locanda del Loggiato, San Quirico d'Orcia, 161
Locanda delle Fontanelle, Montemelino, 279
Locarno (Hotel), Rome, 338
Loghetto (Il), Castenaso, 205
Lombardy, 35
Longare
    Vescovane (Le), 253
Loreto (Castello di), Loreto-Todi, 255
Loreto Aprutino
    Magnolie (Le), 254
Loreto-Todi
    Loreto (Castello di), 255

Lucca, 120
    Alla Corte degli Angeli, 256
Lucignanello Bandini, Lucignano d'Asso-S.
Giovanni d'Asso, 358
Lucignano d'Asso-S. Giovanni d'Asso
    Lucignanello Bandini, 358
Luino
    Camin Hotel Colmegna, 257
Luna e i Falo' (La), Canelli, 189

M
Macciangrosso, Macciano–Chiusi, 258
Macciano–Chiusi
    Macciangrosso, 258
Macinello, Montefiridolfi, 277
Maddalena (La), Turin, 398
Madonna delle Grazie, Citta della Pieve, 208
Maerne
    Ca'delle Rondini, 259
Magioca (La), Negrar, 288
Magnolie (Le), Loreto Aprutino, 254
Malvarina, Assisi, 158
Manarola, 120
Mantova
    Corte San Girolamo, 260
Maps
    Exploring the Wonders of Sicily, 139
    Italian Highlights by Train & Boat–or Car, 41
    Michelin Maps, 17
    Mountain & Lake Adventures, 99
    Romantic Tuscany, 71
    Rome to Milan via the Italian Riviera, 115
Maratea, 134
Marches, 35
Maréttimo, 147
Maria (Villa), Ravello, 330
Marostica, 103
Marsala, 146
Maser, 103
    Villa Bararo, 103
    Villa di Maser, 103

Massa Marittima
  Tenuta Il Cicalino, 261
Masseria Curatori, Monopoli, 269
Masseria Il Frantoio, Ostuni, 298
Masseria Lo Prieno, Galatone, 243
Masseria Marzalossa, Fasano, 221
Masseria Pernice, Camporeale, 187
Masseria Salamina, Pezze di Greco, 306
Massignano
  Biancarda (La), 262
Matera
  Sassi, 137
Matera, 137
Meleto (Castello di), Gaiole in Chianti, 241
Mengara–Scritto
  Oasi Verde Mengara, 263
Mercatale Val di Pesa
  Salvadonica, 264
Messina, 142
Meublè Oasi, Cortina d'Ampezzo, 212
Mezzuola (Casa), Greve in Chianti, 246
Michelin Tourist and Motoring Atlas of Italy, 9, 17
Migliaca (Casa), Pettineo, 305
Milan, 43, 124
  Regina (Hotel), 265
  Sightseeing
    Duomo, 43, 124
    Galleria Vittorio Emanuele, 43, 124
    La Scala, 44, 125
    Santa Maria delle Grazie, 44, 124
    The Last Supper, 44, 124
Mimosa (Villa), Bagnone, 160
Minerva (La), Capri, 193
Miranda (Locanda), Tellaro, 388
Mirano
  Mocenigo (Villa), 266
Misterbianco
  Alcala, 267
Mocenigo (Villa), Mirano, 266
Modanella–Serre di Rapolano
  Godiolo, 268
Modigliani (Hotel), Rome, 339

Mola (La), Castellabate, 202
Molise, 36
Monopoli, 137
  Masseria Curatori, 269
Monreale, 148
Monsignor della Casa, Borgo San Lorenzo, 177
Mont Etna, 142
Montalcino, 86
Montali, Tavernelle di Panicale, 387
Montasola
  Montepiano, 270
Monte Pellegrino, 140, 149
Montebelli, Caldana, 184
Montecarlo–Lucca
  Antica Casa dei Rassicurati, 271
  Satti (Casa), 272
Montecastello di Vibio
  di Vibio (Fattoria), 273
Montefalco, 95
Montefiore dell'Aso
  Campana (La), 274
Montefiridolfi
  Fonte de Medici, 275
  La Loggia (Fattoria), 276
  Macinello, 277
Montefollonico, 87
  Chiusa (La), 87
Montegualandro, Tuoro Sul Trasimeno, 397
Monteleone d'Orvieto
  Poggio Miravalle, 278
Montemelino-Magione
  Locanda delle Fontanelle (La), 279
Montemerano
  Acquaviva (Villa), 280
  Fontanelle (Le), 281
Montepiano, Montasola, 270
Montepulciano, 73, 82
  Agnolo (L'), 282
  Palazzo Comunale, 82
  Palazzo Contucci, 82
  Piazza Grande, 82
  Relais San Bruno, 283

Montepulciano (continued)
   Temple of San Biagio, 82
   Wineries, 83
Monteriggioni, 74
Monteroni d'Arbia
   Bolsinina (Casa), 284
Monterosso (Il), Verbania, 407
Monterosso al Mare–Cinque Terre, 121
Montestigliano, Rosia, 344
Monti Tundu, Casagliana, 197
Monticchiello, 83
Moulin des Aravis (Le), Pontboset, 313
Mountain & Lake Adventures, 100
Murano, 50
Murazzano
   Cascina Cichetti, 285

N

Naples, 133
   Albergo Sansevero Degas, 286
   Sightseeing
      Capodimonte Hill, 61
      Castel dell'Ovo, 64
      Castel Nuovo, 64
      Museo Archeologico Nazionale, 60, 134
      Palazzo Reale, 62
      Piazza Gesù Nuovo, 62
      Piazza Plebiscito, 62
      Spaccanapoli District, 62
      Theatre San Carlo, 63
      Uberto Gallery, 63
Narni
   Podere Costa Romana, 287
Negrar
   Magioca (La), 288
Nettuno, 130

O

Oasi Verde Mengara, Mengara–Scritto, 263
Olivedo, Varenna, 401
Ombria, Caprino Bergamasco, 195

Orbetello Scalo
   Casalone (Il), 289
   Grazia, 290
Orologio (Hotel), Bologna, 175
Orte
   Chiocciola (La), 291
Ortisei, 105
   Digon (Hotel), 292
   Uhrerhof (Hotel), 293
Orto de'Medici (Hotel), Florence, 232
Orvieto, 88, 97
   Ciconia (Villa), 294
   Rosati (Locanda), 295
   Sightseeing
      Chapel of San Brizio, 97
      Duomo, 97
      St. Patrick's Well, 97
Ospedaletto–San Venanzo
   Spante (Borgo), 296
Ostellato
   Belfiore, 297
Ostuni
   Masseria Il Frantoio, 298
Otricoli
   Spence (Casa), 299

P

Padru
   Tonino Corda, 300
Padua, 50
Paese delle Meraviglie, Poggio Nativo, 311
Paestum, 134
   Seliano, 301
Palazzina (La), Radicofani, 329
Palazzo (Il), Brisighella, 178
Palazzo Dragoni, Spoleto, 379
Palazzo Fanelli, Sarteano, 364
Palazzo Ruspoli, Florence, 233
Palermo, 148
Palmira (Casa), Feriolo–Borgo S. Lorenzo, 223

Panzano in Chianti
    Fagiolari, 302
Paretaio (Il), Barberino Val d'Elsa, 165
Passignano in Chianti, 74
Pavia Carthusian Monastery, 123
Pelago
    Doccia (La), 303
Pensione La Calcina, Venice, 404
Pensione Tranchina, Scopello, 370
Perugia, 93
    Fontana Maggiore, 93
    Piazza IV Novembre, 93
Pescatori, Isola dei, 111
Petrosino
    Baglio Spano, 304
Pettineo
    Migliaca (Casa), 305
Pezze di Greco
    Masseria Salamina, 306
Piazza Armerina, 143
Piccolo Golf (Il), Cala di Volpe, 182
Piedmont, 36
Pienza, 84
    Santo Pietro, 307
    Traverse (Le), 308
Pieve di Caminino, Roccatederighi, 333
Pisa, 119
    Sightseeing
        Baptistery, 119
        Duomo, 119
        Leaning Tower, 119
        Piazza del Duomo, 119
Pisticci
    San Teodoro Nuovo, 309
Planning Your Trip, 23
Plazzi (Casa), Trevignano, 395
Podere Costa Romana, Narni, 287
Podere La Fornace, Assisi, Tordibetto di, 159
Podere Le Mezzelune, Bibbona, 174
Podere Terreno, Radda in Chianti, 325
Podere Val delle Corti, Radda in Chianti, 326
Podere Villuzza, San Gimignano, 355

Poderuccio (Il), Sant'Angelo in Colle, 360
Poggi del Sasso
    Vicarello (Castello di), 310
Poggibonsi, 79
Poggio Antico, 86
Poggio d'Asproli, Todi, 392
Poggio Miravalle, Monteleone d'Orvieto, 278
Poggio Nativo
    Paese delle Meraviglie, 311
Poggio San Felice (Villa), Florence, 234
Polignano a Mare, 137
Pomino
    di Petrognano (Fattoria), 312
Pompeii, 130
    Sightseeing
        Casa del Fauna, 65
        Casa del Poeta Tragico, 65
        Lupanare, 66
        Terme Stabiane, 66
        Villa di Giulia Felice, 66
Pomurlo Vecchio, Baschi, 170
Pontboset
    Moulin des Aravis (Le), 313
Ponte Pattoli
    Covone (Il), 314
Pope Clement VII, 97
Pope Pius II, 85
Poreta–Spoleto
    Castello di Poreta (Il), 315
Pornanino, Radda in Chianti, 327
Porta del Tempo (La), Stroncone, 381
Porticciolo, Alghero, 154
Portico di Romagna
    Albergo al Vecchio Convento, 316
Porto Mantovano
    Schiarino Lena (Villa), 317
Portofino, 122
Portovenere, 120
Positano, 132, 133
    Cosenza (Casa), 318
    Fenice (La), 319
    La Tartana (Villa), 320

Positano (continued)
  Rosa (Villa), 321
Prato
  Rucellai di Canneto (Villa), 322
Proceno
  Proceno (Castello di), 323

R

Radda, 75, 79, 80, 81
Radda in Chianti
  Locanda (La), 324
  Podere Terreno, 325
  Podere Val delle Corti, 326
  Pornanino, 327
  Torre Canvalle, 328
Radici (Le), San Casciano dei Bagni, 349
Radicofani
  Palazzina (La), 329
Raino (Villa), Gangi, 245
Rates, 11
Ravello, 132
  Maria (Villa), 330
  Sightseeing
    Villa Rufolo, 133
  Villa Cimbrone, 133
Ravenna
  Diana (Hotel), 331
Recanati
  Telaio (Il), 332
Regina (Hotel), Milan, 265
Regions of Italy, 23
  Abruzzo, 30
  Aosta Valley, 30
  Apulia, 31
  Basilicata, 31
  Campania, 32
  Emilia Romagna, 33
  Friuli Venezia Giulia, 33
  Lazio, 34
  Liguria, 34
  Lombardy, 35
  Marches, 35

Regions of Italy (continued)
  Molise, 36
  Piedmont, 36
  Sardinia, 37
  Sicily, 37
  Trentino-Alto Adige, 38
  Tuscany, 38
  Umbria, 39
  Veneto, 39
Relais Mulino dell'Argenna, Barberino Val d'Elsa, 166
Relais San Bruno, Montepulciano, 283
Relais Valcastagno, Sirolo, 374
Reservation Request Letter in Italian, 13
Reservations, 11
  Email, 12
  Fax, 12
  Hidden Treasures of Italy, 12
  Telephone, 12
Residenze Johlea (Le), Florence, 235
Riomaggiore Monterosso, 120
Ripa d'Orcia (Castello di), Castiglione d'Orcia, 206
Ripolina (La), Buonconvento, 180
Riserva Montebello (La), Bolsena, 176
Riva, 47, 106
  Hotel Sole, 106
  Piazza III Novembre, 106
  Tower of Apponale, 106
Roads
  Autostrada, 21
  Raccordo, 21
  Strada Statale, 21
  Superstrada, 21
Robert Browning, 103
Roccatederighi
  Pieve di Caminino, 333
Rocco (Locanda), Sirolo, 375
Romantic Tuscany, 72
Rome, 54
  Delros (Villa), 334
  Due Torri (Hotel), 335
  Fontana (Hotel), 336

Rome (continued)
  Fontanella Borghese (Hotel), 337
  Fountain of Baraccia, 58
  Locarno (Hotel), 338
  Modigliani (Hotel), 339
  Old Rome, 59
  Santa Maria (Hotel), 340
  Sightseeing
    Baldaccchino, 56
    Colosseum, 57
    Festa de Noantri, 58
    Forum, 57
    Fountain of Baraccia, 58
    Michelangelo's Pietà, 56
    Museo di Villa Giulia, 59
    Pantheon, 57
    Piazza di Spagna, 58
    Piazza San Pietro, 55, 56
    Sistine Chapel, 57
    Spanish Steps, 58
    St. Peter's Basilica, 55
    Trastevere, 58
    Trevi Fountain, 58
    Vatican City, 55
    Vatican Museums, 56
    Via Condotti, 59
    Via Veneto, 57
    Villa Borghese, 59
  Stefazio (Casa), 341
  Venezia (Hotel), 342
  Villa del Parco (Hotel), 343
Rome to Milan via the Italian Riviera, 116
Romulus & Remus, 54
Rosa (Villa), Positano, 321
Rosati (Locanda), Orvieto, 295
Rosia
  Montestigliano, 344
Rosolaccio (Il), San Gimignano, 356
Rucellai di Canneto (Villa), Prato, 322

S
S. Cristina (Castello di), Grotte di Castro, 247
Safety, 24
Saint Pierre
  Abri (L'), 345
  Ecureuils (Les), 346
Salsomaggiore Terme
  Antica Torre, 347
Salvadonica, Mercatale Val di Pesa, 264
San Barnaba (Locanda), Venice, 405
San Casciano, 79
San Casciano dei Bagni
  Crocetta (La), 348
  Radici (Le), 349
San Fedele d'Intelvi
  Simplicitas (Villa), 350
San Gimignano, 75
  Casale del Cotone (Il), 351
  Casanova di Pescille, 352
  Casolare di Libbiano, 353
  Fonte (La), 354
  Podere Villuzza, 355
  Ristorante Dorando, 76
  Ristorante Il Pino, 76
  Rosolaccio (Il), 356
San Giovanni d'Asso
  Locanda del Castello (La), 357
San Margherita, 122
San Martino (Casa), Lisciano Niccone, 252
San Pantaleo
  Ca'La Somara, 359
San Quirico d'Orcia, 84
  Horti Leonini, 84
San Quirico d'Orcia–Bagno Vignoni
  Locanda del Loggiato (La), 161
San Rocco (Locanda), Gagliole, 240
San Teodoro Nuovo, Pisticci, 309
Sanctuary of Santa Rosalia, 149
Sant'Angelo in Colle
  Poderuccio (Il), 360
Santa Caterina di Cortona
  Agrisalotto, 361

Santa Flavia
    Cefala (Villa), 362
Santa Margherita
    Gnocchi (Villa), 363
Santa Maria (Hotel), Rome, 340
Santo Pietro, Pienza, 307
Santo Stefano (Hotel), Venice, 406
Sardinia, 37
Sarteano
    Palazzo Fanelli, 364
    Sovana (La), 365
Sassetta
    Tenuta La Bandita, 366
Satti (Casa), Montecarlo–Lucca, 272
Saturnia
    Clodia (Villa), 367
Scalvino–Lenna
    Ferdy, 368
Scapezzano di Senigallia
    Strada della Marina (Locanda), 369
Schiarino Lena (Villa), Porto Mantovano, 317
Schuler (Villa), Taormina, 384
Scopello
    Pensione Tranchina, 370
Segesta, 148
Seggiano
    Casacce (Le), 371
Selci Sabino
    Vallerosa (Villa), 372
Seliano, Paestum, 301
Selinunte, 146
Sella Pass, 105
Selvino (Il), Terricciola, 390
Sestri Levante, 122
Shopping, 24
    Duty-Free Goods, 25
    Tax-Free Cash Refund, 25
Sicily, 37
Siena, 76, 78, 81
    dei Lecci (Villa), 373
    Sightseeing
        Baptistry, 77

Siena (continued)
    Duomo, 77
    Museo Civico, 77
    Museo dell'Opera Metropolitana, 77
    Ospedale di Santa Maria della Scala, 77
    Palazzo Pubblico, 76
    Palio delle Contrade, 76
    Piazza del Campo, 76
    Piccolomini Library, 77
Sightseeing, 17
Silla (Hotel), Florence, 236
Simplicitas (Villa), San Fedele d'Intelvi, 350
Sirmione, 45, 106
    Sightseeing
        Piazza delle Erbe, 47
Sirolo
    Relais Valcastagno, 374
    Rocco (Locanda), 375
Siusi allo Sciliar
    Aquila Nera (Schwarzer Adler), 376
Solaio (Fattoria), Solaio–Radicondoli, 377
Solaio–Radicondoli
    Solaio (Fattoria), 377
Solferino
    Sorgive (Le), 378
Sorgive (Le), Solferino, 378
Sorrento, 66
Southern Tuscany, 81
Sovana (La), Sarteano, 365
Sovigliano, Tavarnelle Val di Pesa, 385
Spante (Borgo), Ospedaletto–San Venanzo, 296
Spence (Casa), Otricoli, 299
Spinosa (La), Barberino Val d'Elsa, 167
Spoleto, 96
    Cathedral, 96
    Palazzo Dragoni, 379
    Ponte delle Torri, 96
St. Francis, 93
Stazzano
    Traversina (La), 380
Stefazio (Casa), Rome, 341
Stoppiacce, Cortona, 215

Strada della Marina (Locanda), Scapezzano di Senigallia, 369
Stroncone
    Porta del Tempo (La), 381
Syracuse, 143
    Limoneto, 382
    Sightseeing
        Archaeological Park, 143
        Greek Theater, 143
        Ortygia, 143

T

Tabiano–Fidenza
    Tondino (Il), 383
Tangenziale, 21
Taormina, 142
    Schuler (Villa), 384
    Sightseeing
        Greek Theater, 142
        Roman Amphitheater, 143
        St. Giuseppe Church, 142
        Torre dell'Orologio, 143
Taranto, 135
Tarquinia, 118
    Etruscan tombs, 118
    Museo Nazionale Tarquiniese, 118
    Vitelleschi Palace, 118
Tavarnelle Val di Pesa, 79
    Sovigliano, 385
Tavarone di Maissana
    Giandriale, 386
Tavernelle di Panicale
    Montali, 387
Telaio (Il), Recanati, 332
Telephones, 26
Tellaro
    Miranda (Locanda), 388
Tempio Pausania
    Agnata (L'), 389
Tenuta Amalia/Agriturismo Le Case Rosse, Villa Verucchio, 411
Tenuta di Canonica, Todi, 393

Tenuta Il Cicalino, Massa Marittima, 261
Tenuta La Bandita, Sassetta, 366
Tenuta La Mandria, Candelo, 188
Terricciola
    Selvino (Il), 390
The Haunting Beauty of Umbria, 90
Tipping, 27
Titignano (Fattoria), Titignano—Orvieto, 391
Titignano—Orvieto
    Titignano (Fattoria), 391
Todi, 97
    Poggio d'Asproli, 392
    Sightseeing
        Cathedral, 97
        Roman/Etruscan Museum, 97
        San Ilario Church, 97
    Tenuta di Canonica, 393
Tondino (Il), Tabiano–Fidenza, 383
Tonino Corda, Padru, 300
Torcello, 50
Torgiano, 96
    Tre Vaselle (Le), 96
Tornano (Castello di), Gaiole in Chianti, 242
Torre Burchio, Bettona, 173
Torre Canvalle, Radda in Chianti, 328
Torre, Felino-San Michele Tiorre, 222
Torretta (La), Casperia, 198
Torri del Benaco, 107
Torricella (La), Florence, 237
Torrino (Il), Forcoli, 239
Train Travel, 27
Trani, 137
Travel Insurance, 11
Traverse (Le), Pienza, 308
Traversina (La), Stazzano, 380
Tre Vaselle (Le), Torgiano, 96
Trent, 105
Trentino-Alto Adige, 38
Trevi
    Giulia (Casa), 394
Trevignano
    Plazzi (Casa), 395

Treviso, 102
Trissino
    Ca'Masieri, 396
Trulli District, 136
Trulli houses, 136
Tschotscherhof, Castelrotto–Osvaldo, 204
Tuoro Sul Trasimeno
    Montegualandro (Castello di), 397
Turin
    Maddalena (La), 398
Tuscania
    Al Gallo (Hotel), 399
Tuscany, 38

U

Uhrerhof (Hotel), Ortisei, 293
Umbertide, 92
Umbria, 39

V

Vagliagli
    Casali della Aiola, 400
Val Gardena, 105
Valle dei Templi, 145
Vallerosa (Villa), Selci Sabino, 372
Valnontey, 114
Varenna, 110
    Olivedo, 401
Vence
    Sightseeing
        Basilica di San Marco, 49
Veneto, 39
Venezia (Hotel), Rome, 342
Venice, 48, 102
    Ai Due Fanali (Hotel), 402
    Al Leon (Locanda), 403
    Pensione La Calcina, 404
    San Barnaba (Locanda), 405
    Santo Stefano (Hotel), 406
    Sightseeing
        Bridge of Sighs, 51
        Campanile, 49

Venice (continued)
    Sightseeing
        Galleria dell'Accademia, 51
        Gondolas, 102
        Grand Canal, 48
        Motoscafi, 102
        Palazzo Ducale, 49
        Peggy Guggenheim Museum, 51
        Piazza San Marco, 49
        Piazzale Roma, 102
        Rialto Bridge, 50
        St. Mark's Cathedral, 49
        Vaporetti, 102
Verbania
    Monterosso (Il), 407
Vernazza, 121, 122
Verona, 47
    Domus Nova B&B, 408
    Sightseeing
        Capulets' Palace, 47
        Castelvecchio, 47
        Cathedral, 47
        Piazza dei Signori, 47
        Ponte Scaligero, 47
        Roman amphitheater, 47
        Roman theater, 47
Vescovane (Le), Longare, 253
Vicarello (Castello di), Poggi del Sasso, 310
Vico d'Elsa
    Volpaia (La), 409
Vico Equense
    Giusso (Villa), 410
Villa Carlotta, 109
Villa Cimbrone, Ravello, 133
Villa Cipressi,
    Lake Como, 110
Villa del Balbianello, Lake Como, 109
Villa del Parco (Hotel), Rome, 343
Villa di Gargnano, 106
Villa of Casale, 143
Villa San Giovanni, 142

Villa Taranto
    Lake Maggiore, 111
Villa Verucchio
    Tenuta Amalia/Agriturismo Le Case Rosse, 411
Vino Nobile, 73, 82
Viterbo
    Citerno, 412
    Country Hotel Rinaldone, 413
    Farinella (Villa), 414
Volpaia (La), Vico d'Elsa, 409
Volta Mantovana
    Corte Onida, 415
Volterra, 78
    Sightseeing
        Museo Etrusco Guaracci, 78
        Piazza dei Priori, 78
        Porta all'Arco, 78
Vuotto (Villa), Capri, 194

W

Website, Karen Brown's, 5
Western Umbria, 96
What to See and Do, 15
When to Visit, 15
Wineries, 78
    Cantina del Redi, 83
    Castello d'Albola, 80
    Castello di Brolio, 79
    Castello di Meleto, 81
    Castello di Volpaia, 81
    Dei, 83
    Fattoria dei Barbi, 85
    Poggio Antico, 86

# IMAGING IN ITALY

*Imaging in Italy* will transform the way you see and think about the world around you. You will learn practical visual and photographic skills that will allow you to capture the richness and romance of **Rome**, skills you will carry away for use in any future setting. Through on-site photography, informed teaching, group activities, engaging experiences and self-expression, you will learn to use the same tools and skills practiced and refined by innovative photographers, artists, writers and creative thinkers from the Renaissance to the present.

*Our program is for everyone who enjoys photography and wishes to deepen their ability to see more fully, to develop their imaginative powers, to expand their creative capacities while applying these skills to photography - indeed, any activity involving thinking, seeing and self-expression in work or daily life.*

We are pleased to announce that Imaging In Italy has partnered with KB Travel Service to offer you a complete travel package. If you would like more detailed information, have questions or would like to reserve your place in our 2004 program, visit our website at:

www.Imaging-In-Italy.com

or contact our travel specialist at:

KB Travel Service & Imaging In Italy
16 East Third Avenue
San Mateo, CA 94401
Phone (800) 782-2128
Fax (650) 342-2519

KAREN BROWN wrote her first travel guide in 1976. Her personalized travel series has grown to 17 titles, which Karen and her small staff work diligently to keep updated. Karen, lives in Moss Beach, a small town on the coast south of San Francisco. Karen, and her husband Rick, settled here in 1991 when they opened Seal Cove Inn.

NICOLE FRANCHINI was born in Chicago and raised in a bilingual family, her father being Italian. She received a B.A. degree in languages from William Smith College and the Sorbonne, Paris, and has been residing in Italy for many years. Currently living in the countryside of Sabina near Rome with husband, Carlo, and daughters, Livia and Sabina, she runs her own travel consulting business, Hidden Treasures of Italy, which organizes personalized group and individual itineraries. *www.htitaly.com*

CLARE BROWN was a travel consultant for many years, specializing in planning itineraries to Europe using charming small hotels in the countryside. The focus of her job remains unchanged, but now her expertise is available to a larger audience—the readers of her daughter Karen's travel guides. When Clare and her husband, Bill, are not traveling, they live either in Hillsborough, California, or at their home in Vail, Colorado, where family and friends frequently join them for skiing.

ELISABETTA FRANCHINI, the artist responsible for many of the illustrations in this guide lives in Chicago with her husband, Chris, and their two young children, where she paints predominantly European landscapes and architectural scenes. A Smith College graduate in Art History and French Literature, Elisabetta has exhibited extensively in the past 20 years. *www.elisabettafranchini.com.*

BARBARA MACLURCAN TAPP, the artist who produces most of the illustrations for Karen Brown Guides, was raised in Australia where she studied in Sydney at the School of Interior Design. Although Barbara continues with freelance projects, she devotes much of her time to illustrating the Karen Brown Guides. Barbara lives in Kensington, California, with her husband, Richard, and daughter, Georgia.

JANN POLLARD, the artist of the cover painting has studied art since childhood, and is well known for her outstanding impressionistic-style watercolors. Jann's original paintings are represented through The Gallery, Burlingame, CA, *www.thegalleryart.net* or 650-347-9392. Fine-art giclée prints her paintings are also available at *www.karenbrown.com.*

# Travel Your Dreams • Order Your Karen Brown Guides Today

Please ask in your local bookstore for Karen Brown's Guides. If the books you want are unavailable, you may order directly from the publisher. Books will be shipped immediately.

_____ *Austria: Charming Inns & Itineraries* $19.95

_____ *California: Charming Inns & Itineraries* $19.95

_____ *England: Charming Bed & Breakfasts* $18.95

_____ *England, Wales & Scotland: Charming Hotels & Itineraries* $19.95

_____ *France: Charming Bed & Breakfasts* $18.95

_____ *France: Charming Inns & Itineraries* $19.95

_____ *Germany: Charming Inns & Itineraries* $19.95

_____ *Ireland: Charming Inns & Itineraries* $19.95

_____ *Italy: Charming Bed & Breakfasts* $18.95

_____ *Italy: Charming Inns & Itineraries* $19.95

_____ *Mexico: Charming Inns & Itineraries* $19.95

_____ *Mid-Atlantic: Charming Inns & Itineraries* $19.95

_____ *New England: Charming Inns & Itineraries* $19.95

_____ *Pacific Northwest: Charming Inns & Itineraries* $19.95

_____ *Portugal: Charming Inns & Itineraries* $19.95

_____ *Spain: Charming Inns & Itineraries* $19.95

_____ *Switzerland: Charming Inns & Itineraries* $19.95

Name _____ Street _____

Town _____ State_____ Zip _____ Tel _____

Credit Card (MasterCard or Visa) _____ Expires: _____

For orders in the USA, add $5 for the first book and $2 for each additional book for shipment. Overseas shipping (airmail) is $10 for 1 to 2 books, $20 for 3 to 4 books etc. CA residents add 8.25% sales tax. Fax or mail form with check or credit card information to:

### KAREN BROWN'S GUIDES
Post Office Box 70 • San Mateo • California • 94401 • USA
tel: (650) 342-9117, fax: (650) 342-9153, email: karen@karenbrown.com, www.karenbrown.com

# Karen Brown Presents Her Own Special Hideaways

### Karen Brown's Seal Cove Inn

Spectacularly set amongst wildflowers and bordered by cypress trees, Seal Cove Inn (Karen's second home) looks out to the distant ocean. Each room has a fireplace, cozy sitting area, and a view of the sea. Located on the coast, 35 minutes south of San Francisco.

Seal Cove Inn, Moss Beach, California
toll free telephone: (800) 995-9987
www.sealcoveinn.com

### Karen Brown's Dolphin Cove Inn

Hugging a steep hillside overlooking the sparkling deep-blue bay of Manzanillo, Dolphin Cove Inn offers guests outstanding value. Each room has either a terrace or a balcony, and a breathtaking view of the sea. Located on the Pacific Coast of Mexico.

Dolphin Cove Inn, Manzanillo, Mexico
toll free telephone: (888) 497-4138
www.dolphincoveinn.com

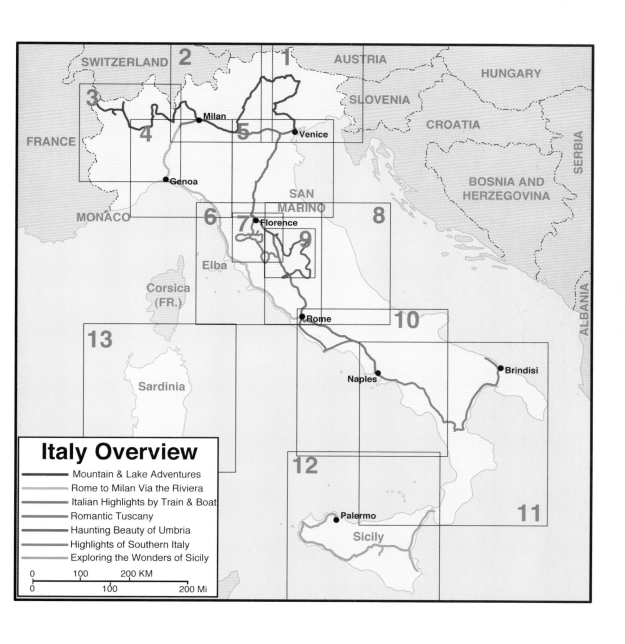

# Italy Overview

- Mountain & Lake Adventures
- Rome to Milan Via the Riviera
- Italian Highlights by Train & Boat
- Romantic Tuscany
- Haunting Beauty of Umbria
- Highlights of Southern Italy
- Exploring the Wonders of Sicily

| 0 | 100 | 200 KM |
| 0 | 100 | 200 Mi |

SWITZERLAND
AUSTRIA
HUNGARY
SLOVENIA
CROATIA
FRANCE
SERBIA
BOSNIA AND
HERZEGOVINA
MONACO
ALBANIA

Milan
Venice
Genoa
SAN
MARINO
Florence
Elba
Corsica
(FR.)
Rome
Sardinia
Naples
Brindisi
Palermo
Sicily

2
1
3
4
5
6
7
9
8
13
10
12
11

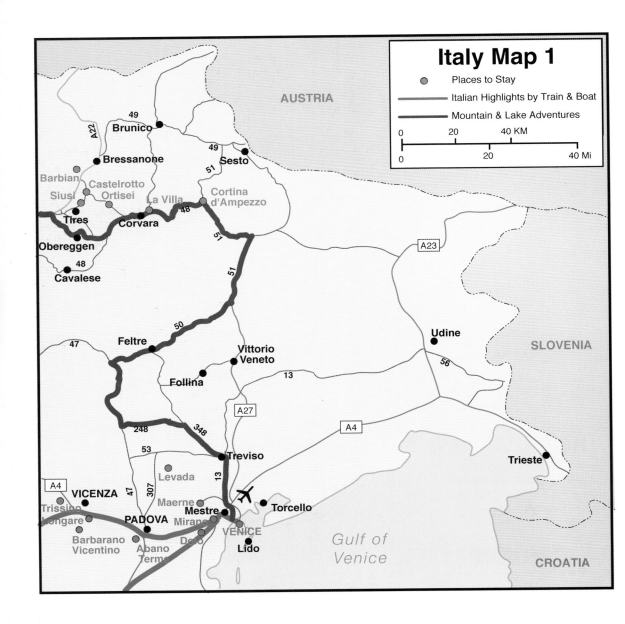

# Italy Map 1

- Places to Stay
- Italian Highlights by Train & Boat
- Mountain & Lake Adventures

0    20    40 KM

0        20        40 Mi

AUSTRIA

A22

49

Brunico

Bressanone

49

Sesto

51

Barbian

Castelrotto

Siusi   Ortisei

La Villa

48

Cortina
d'Ampezzo

A23

Tires

Corvara

51

Obereggen

51

48

Cavalese

50

47

Feltre

Udine

SLOVENIA

56

Vittorio
Veneto

Follina

13

A27

248

348

A4

53

Treviso

13

Levada

Trieste

A4

VICENZA

307

47

Maerne

Mestre

Torcello

Trissino
Longare

PADOVA

Mirano

VENICE

Barbarano
Vicentino

Abano
Terme

Dolo

Lido

Gulf of
Venice

CROATIA

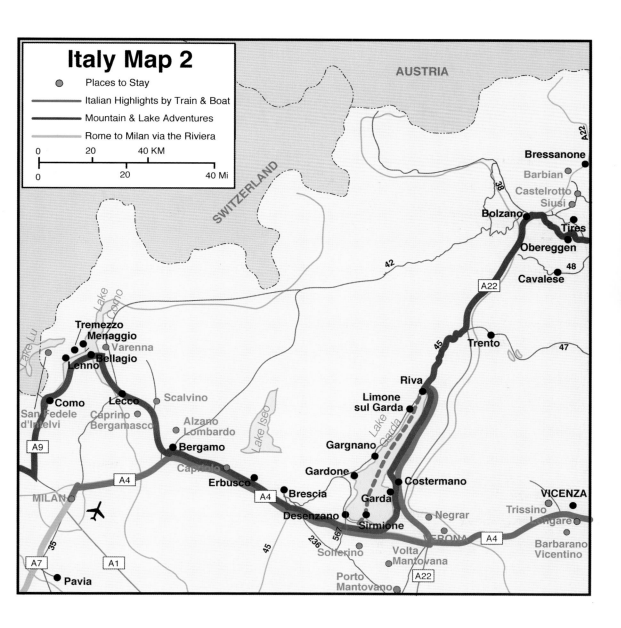

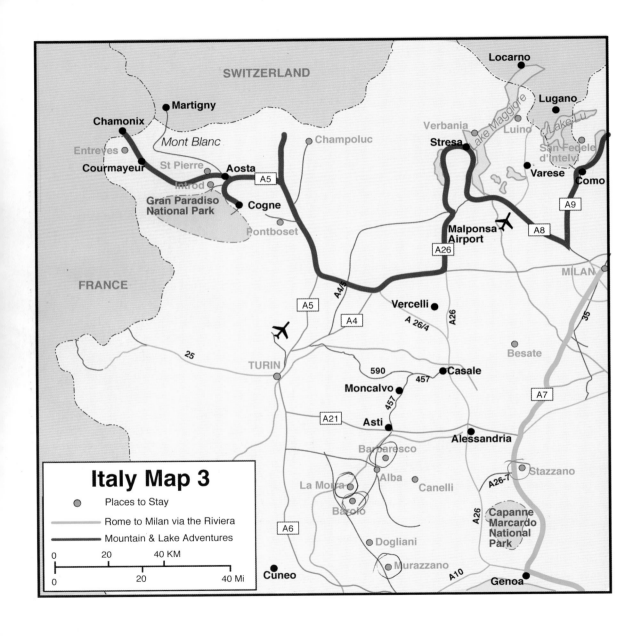

## Italy Map 3

- ○ Places to Stay
- ── Rome to Milan via the Riviera
- ── Mountain & Lake Adventures

0      20      40 KM

0      20      40 Mi

SWITZERLAND

FRANCE

Locarno

Lugano

Martigny

Chamonix

Mont Blanc

Champoluc

Verbania

Lake Maggiore

Luino

Lake Lu

San Fedele d'Intelvi

Varese

Como

Entreves

Courmayeur

St Pierre

Introd

Aosta

A5

Stresa

Gran Paradiso National Park

Cogne

Malponsa Airport

A9

A8

Pontboset

A26

MILAN

A5

A4/5

A4

Vercelli

A 26/4

A26

Besate

35

25

TURIN

590

457

Casale

A7

Moncalvo

457

Asti

A21

Alessandria

Barbaresco

Alba

Canelli

Stazzano

A26-7

La Morra

Capanne Marcardo National Park

Barolo

Dogliani

A26

A6

Murazzano

A10

Cuneo

Genoa

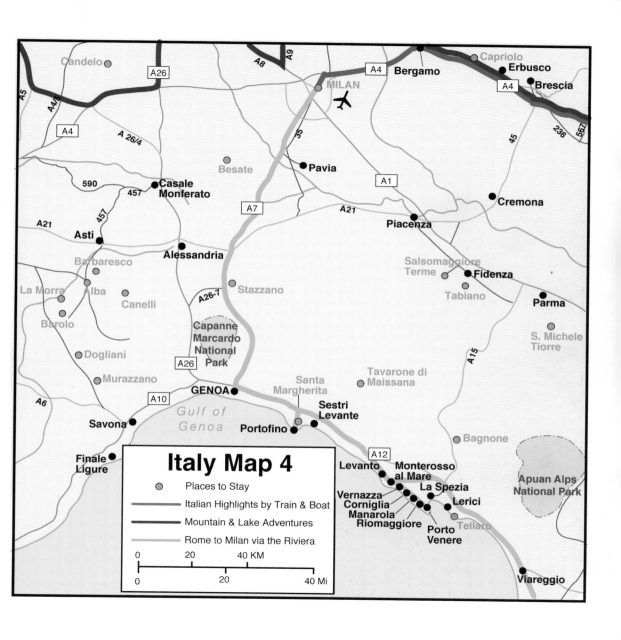

Candelo

A26

A8 A9

A4 Bergamo Capriolo
MILAN Erbusco
Brescia
A4 A4

A5
A4/5
35

A4
A 26/4
236
567

Besate Pavia 45
590
Casale Cremona
Monferato 457 A7 A21 A1
A21 A21 Piacenza
Asti 457
Alessandria Salsomaggiore
Barbaresco Stazzano Terme Fidenza
La Morra Alba A26-7 Tabiano Parma
Canelli
Barolo Capanne A15 S. Michele
Marcardo Tiorre
Dogliani National
Murazzano Park A26 Tavarone di
A6 Maissana
GENOA Bagnone
A10 Santa Sestri
Savona Margherita Levante Apuan Alps
Portofino National Park
Finale Gulf of A12
Ligure Genoa Levanto Monterosso
al Mare
Vernazza La Spezia
Corniglia Lerici
Manarola
Riomaggiore Porto Tellaro
Venere
Viareggio

## Italy Map 4

● Places to Stay

―――― Italian Highlights by Train & Boat

―――― Mountain & Lake Adventures

―――― Rome to Milan via the Riviera

0    20    40 KM

0    20    40 Mi

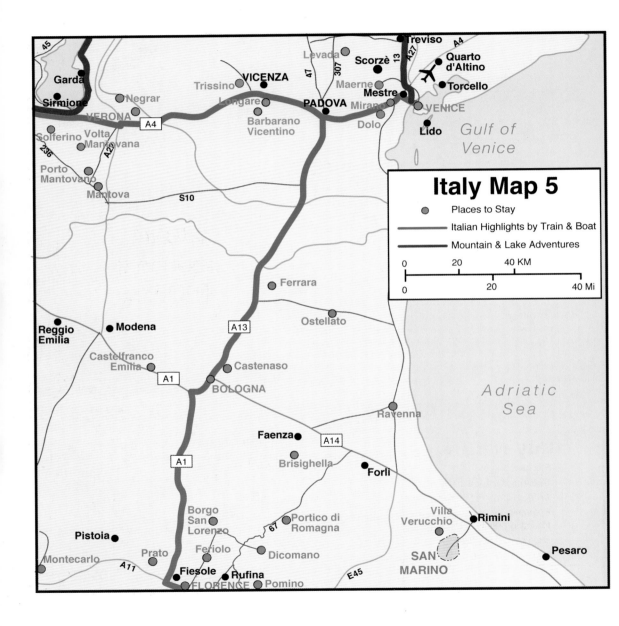

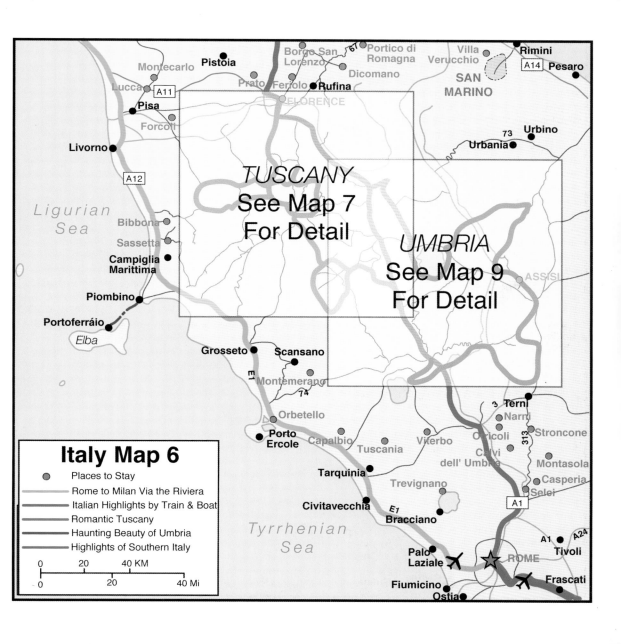

## Italy Map 6

- Places to Stay
- Rome to Milan Via the Riviera
- Italian Highlights by Train & Boat
- Romantic Tuscany
- Haunting Beauty of Umbria
- Highlights of Southern Italy

0    20    40 KM
0    20    40 Mi

*TUSCANY*
See Map 7
For Detail

*UMBRIA*
See Map 9
For Detail

*Ligurian
Sea*

*Tyrrhenian
Sea*

*Elba*

Montecarlo
Pistoia
Borgo San Lorenzo
Portico di Romagna
Villa Verucchio
Rimini
Pesaro
Lucca
A11
Prato
Ferfolo
Dicomano
SAN MARINO
Pisa
FLORENCE
Rufina
Forcoli
ASSISI
Livorno
Urbino
Urbania
73
A12
Bibbona
Sassetta
Campiglia Marittima
Piombino
Portoferráio
Grosseto
Scansano
E1
Montemerano
74
Orbetello
Terni
Narni
Stroncone
Oricoli
Calvi dell' Umbria
Montasola
Casperia
Selci
Capalbio
Viterbo
313
Porto Ercole
Tuscania
Tarquinia
Trevignano
Civitavecchia
A1
Bracciano
E1
Palo Laziale
ROME
Tivoli
A1
A24
Fiumicino
Frascati
Ostia

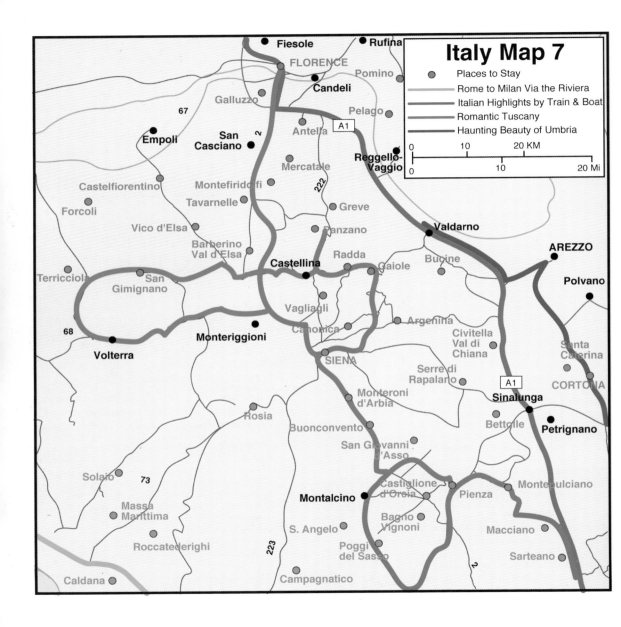

## Italy Map 7

**Legend:**
- Places to Stay
- Rome to Milan Via the Riviera
- Italian Highlights by Train & Boat
- Romantic Tuscany
- Haunting Beauty of Umbria

0   10   20 KM
0   10   20 Mi

Fiesole
Rufina
FLORENCE
Pomino
Candeli
Galluzzo
Pelago
San Casciano
Antella
A1
Empoli
Mercatale
Reggello-Vaggio
Castelfiorentino
Montefiridolfi
Greve
Forcoli
Tavarnelle
Vico d'Elsa
Panzano
Valdarno
Barberino Val d'Elsa
Radda
Bucine
AREZZO
Terricciola
Castellina
Gaiole
Polvano
San Gimignano
Vagliagli
Argenina
Civitella Val di Chiana
Santa Caterina
68
Canonica
Volterra
Monteriggioni
Serre di Rapalano
CORTONA
SIENA
A1
Sinalunga
Monteroni d'Arbia
Bettolle
Rosia
Petrignano
Buonconvento
San Giovanni d'Asso
73
Solaio
Castiglione d'Orcia
Montepulciano
Massa Marittima
Montalcino
Pienza
S. Angelo
Bagno Vignoni
Macciano
Roccatederighi
Poggi del Sasso
223
Sarteano
Caldana
Campagnatico
67
2
222
2

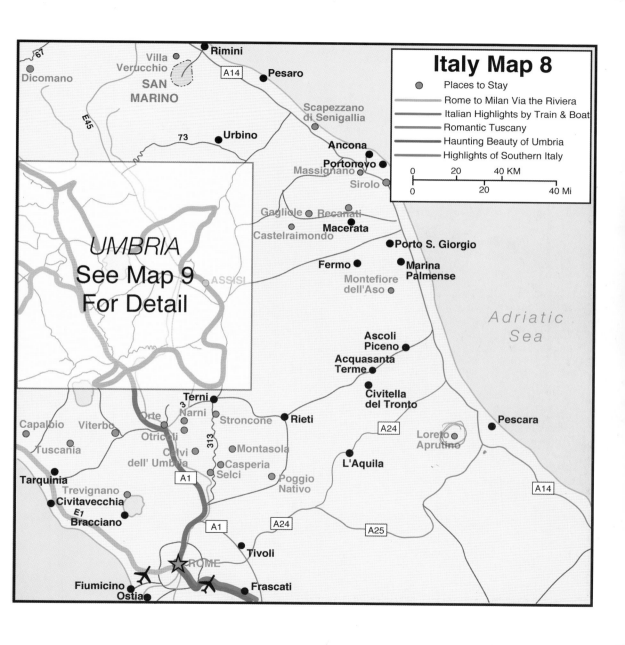

# Italy Map 8

● Places to Stay
— Rome to Milan Via the Riviera
— Italian Highlights by Train & Boat
— Romantic Tuscany
— Haunting Beauty of Umbria
— Highlights of Southern Italy

0    20    40 KM
0    20    40 Mi

Dicomano

Villa Verucchio

Rimini

A14

Pesaro

SAN MARINO

E45

73    Urbino

Scapezzano di Senigallia

Ancona

Portonovo

Massignano

Sirolo

Gagliole  Recanati

Castelraimondo

Macerata

UMBRIA
See Map 9
For Detail

ASSISI

Porto S. Giorgio

Fermo

Marina Palmense

Montefiore dell'Aso

Adriatic Sea

Ascoli Piceno

Acquasanta Terme

Civitella del Tronto

Terni

Narni

Stroncone

Rieti

A24

Loreto Aprutino

Pescara

Capalbio  Viterbo

Orte

Otricoli

313

Calvi dell' Umbria

Montasola

Casperia Selci

Poggio Nativo

L'Aquila

A14

Tuscania

Tarquinia

Trevignano

Civitavecchia

E1

Bracciano

A1

A1

A24

A25

ROME

Tivoli

Fiumicino

Ostia

Frascati

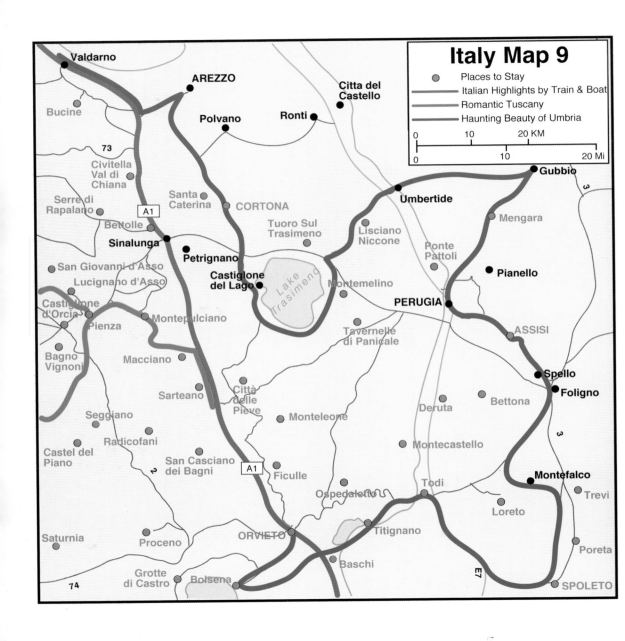

# Italy Map 10

- ● Places to Stay
- ⁂ Archaeological Site
- ━━ Highlights of Southern Italy
- ━━ Italian Highlights by Train & Boat

0 — 25 — 50 KM
0 — 25 — 50 Mi

A1
A24
Tivoli
★ ROME
Frascati
✈
148
Frosinone
A1
Latina
Formia
Anzio
Gaeta
Caserta
Cuma
A3
Ponza
Ventotene
A30
Herculaneum
NAPLES
Pompeii
Bay of Naples
Castellamare
Ischia
Vico Equense
Ravello
Salerno
Sorrento
Amalfi
Positano
Capri
Bay of Salerno
Paestum
Castellabate
A3
Acquafredda
Maratea
Tyrrhenian Sea
A14
Vieste
Gargano National Park
Monte S. Angelo
Foggia
A16
Potenza

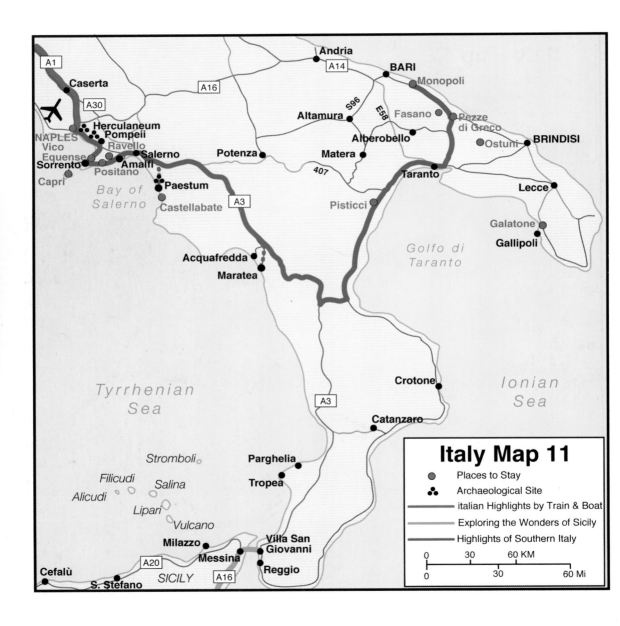

A1

Caserta

A30

Herculaneum
Pompeii
NAPLES
Vico
Equense Ravello
Positano Salerno
Sorrento Amalfi
Capri

Bay of
Salerno

Paestum

Castellabate

A3

Acquafredda

Maratea

Andria

A14

BARI
Monopoli

A16

Altamura S96

E58 Fasano

Pezze
di Greco

Alberobello Ostuni BRINDISI

Potenza Matera

407

Taranto Lecce

Pisticci

Galatone
Gallipoli

Golfo di
Taranto

Ionian
Sea

Tyrrhenian
Sea

Crotone

Catanzaro

Stromboli
Filicudi Salina
Alicudi
Lipari
Vulcano

Parghelia
Tropea

Milazzo
Messina
Cefalù
A20
S. Stefano SICILY A16

Villa San
Giovanni
Reggio

## Italy Map 11

Places to Stay
Archaeological Site
italian Highlights by Train & Boat
Exploring the Wonders of Sicily
Highlights of Southern Italy

0          30          60 KM
0          30          60 Mi

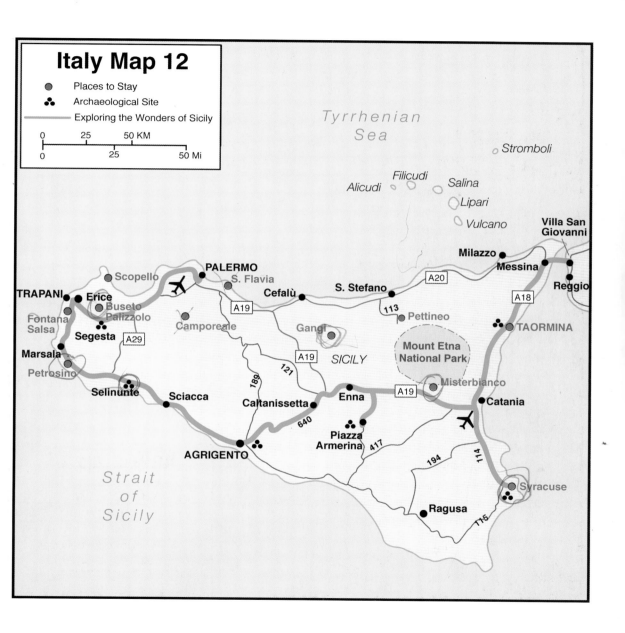

## Italy Map 12

- ● Places to Stay
- ⋮ Archaeological Site
- —— Exploring the Wonders of Sicily

0   25   50 KM
0   25   50 Mi

*Tyrrhenian Sea*

*Stromboli*

*Filicudi*
*Alicudi*          *Salina*
               *Lipari*
          *Vulcano*

**Villa San Giovanni**

**Milazzo**
Scopello              **Messina**
**PALERMO**
S. Flavia                    **Reggio**
TRAPANI                Cefalù    S. Stefano        A20
**Erice**      A19                           A18
Buseto                    113
Palizzolo          Camporeale      **Pettineo**      **TAORMINA**
Fontana                    Gangi
Salsa    **Segesta**        A19        Mount Etna
        A29            *SICILY*      National Park
**Marsala**
Petrosino              121
              A19
**Selinunte**    Sciacca              Misterbianco
                            A19    **Catania**
        Caltanissetta   **Enna**
        189
        640            **Piazza**
**AGRIGENTO**       **Armerina**   417
                        194   114
        *Strait*
        *of*              **Ragusa**   **Syracuse**
        *Sicily*              115

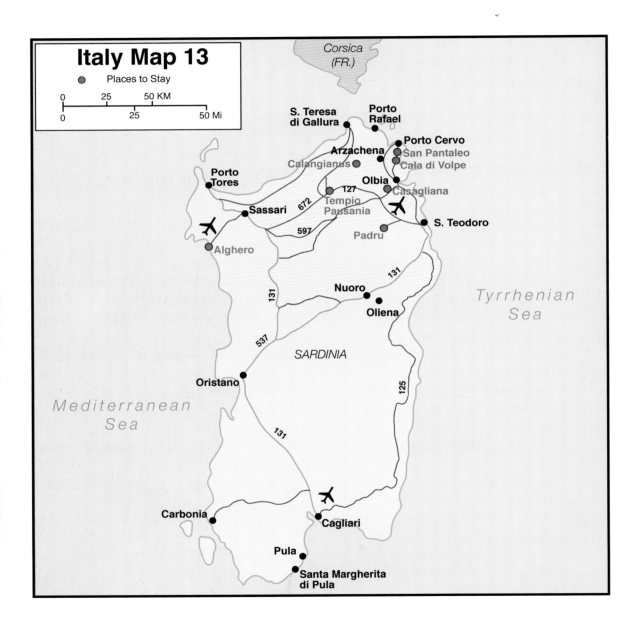

# Icons Key

We have introduced the icons listed below in our guidebooks and on our website (*www.karenbrown.com*). These allow us to provide additional information about our recommended properties. When using our website to supplement the guides, placing the cursor over an icon will in many cases give you further details.

| | | | |
|---|---|---|---|
| ❄ | Air conditioning in rooms | 🍴 | Restaurant |
| ⛱ | Beach | ❀ | Spa |
| ☕ | Breakfast included in room rate | 🏊 | Swimming pool |
| 🛒 | Children welcome | 🏃 | Tennis |
| 🍲 | Cooking classes offered | 📺 | Television w/ English channels |
| CREDIT | Credit cards accepted | 🔔 | Wedding facilities |
| 🛎 | Dinner served upon request | ♿ | Wheelchair friendly |
| ☎ | Direct-dial telephone in room | 🏛 | Archaeological site nearby |
| 🐕 | Dogs by special request | 🏌 | Golf course nearby |
| 🛗 | Elevator | 🚶 | Hiking trails nearby |
| 🏋 | Exercise room | 🏇 | Horseback riding nearby |
| 🔥 | Fireplaces in some rooms | ⛷ | Skiing nearby |
| 🍸 | Mini-refrigerator in room | 🏄 | Water sports nearby |
| 🚭 | Some non-smoking rooms | 🍇 | Wineries nearby |
| P | Parking available | | |